Letters from the Gover

T0118596

BERINGIANA is a series of publications relating broadly to the explorer
Vitus Bering. Its scope encompasses Danish-Russian relations, exploration
of the North Pacific, Russian eighteenth-century culture and history,
Sibirian studies, the history of Russian America.

Series Editor: Peter Ulf Møller at the Slavic Department, Aarhus University

The logo of the BERINGIANA series, designed by Lotte Bruun Rasmussen, is
a free variation of Vitus Bering's coat-of-arms. Its "bear" (German: Bär) and
"ring" components are drawn from the explorer's surname.

Letters from the Governor's Wife
A View of Russian Alaska 1859-1862

Edited by Annie Constance Christensen

With an Introduction and an Epilogue by
Annie Constance Christensen and Peter Ulf Møller

Aarhus University Press

Letters from the Governor's Wife. A View of Russian Alaska 1859-1862
© Annie Constance Christensen and Aarhus University Press 2005
Cover: Lotte Bruun Rasmussen
Cover illustration: Anna and Hampus Furuhjelm in St. Petersborg 1859,
cf. letter No. 11. By courtesy of Olivia Söderhjelm
Illustration on the back cover: Tlingit mask, carved of deciduous wood, representing a man
whose face is painted with family crest designs. The mouth is perforated.
Printed by Narayana Press, Gylling

ISBN 87 7934 159 4

This publication has been supported by grants from
The Danish Research Council for the Humanities and
The Aarhus University Research Foundation

Aarhus University Press
Langelandsgade 177
DK – 8200 Århus N

www.unipress.dk

Table of contents

Editor's preface

Anna Furuhjelm's letters to her mother Ann von Schoultz form a kind of diary of her first years in Alaska as the Russian Governor's wife. A few hours after their wedding on February 2nd 1859, she departs for Alaska on a sledge with her husband Hampus Furuhjelm from Helsinki, and writes the first letter to her mother on the evening of the same day. Her last letter – No. 52 – was left unfinished on October 17th 1862, as the news reached Alaska that her mother had died.

The letters were numbered by Anna herself. Except for Nos. 32 and 51, they have all been preserved and are now kept in the archive of the University Library of Åbo, Finland (Åbo Akademis Bibliotek, Handskriftsavdelningen, Furuhjelm, Annie 14). Besides Anna's letters, there are two short letters from her maid, Ida Höerle.

All editorial additions are in square brackets. Abbreviated words, for instance 'yr', are given in their full form: 'y[ou]r'. A question mark immediately after a word – discerned[?], for example – means that I am not completely sure I have read the word correctly; two full stops followed by a question mark – many [..?] lips, for example – means that I have omitted an unreadable word. The letters have been slightly abbreviated. Some passages that discuss or inquire about friends back home, and also some of Anna's much repeated religious reflections have been omitted. All omissions are marked by three full stops in square brackets [...]. The short letters Nos. 7 and 44 have been omitted all together for that same reason. All underlined words have been rendered in italics.

Anna's orthography and punctuation has not been corrected. The peculiarities in spelling that catch the modern eye are due to archaic spelling or haste. The orthographical norm was not yet fully established. She writes: 'desert' (for a sweet course), 'trowsers', 'tare' for 'tear'. Parallel forms existed, for instance 'honour/honor', 'expense/expence', 'English/english'. – Anna had no formal education in English. For spelling problems, she consulted "Grandmother's spelling book" (Letter 33, cf. the present edition, p. 128). Misspelling occurs since she writes quickly and rarely seems to find time to read what she has written: 'govenor', 'woud', 'exellent', 'probaply', 'discription', 'for' for 'four', 'bands' for 'banns'. Another peculiarity is her indifference to writing double or single consonants: 'arrive/arive', (to) 'finish/finnish', 'innocent/inocent', 'British/Brittish', 'occasion/occassion', 'droll/drol', 'summer/sumer'. Some slight errors have been corrected, such as 'to' for 'do', 'that' for 'than', 'in' for 'it'.

Anna often uses Swedish, German or French words and expressions. They probably come to mind because she has spoken these languages frequently, or because they seem to express her thoughts better. In the first case they are easy to translate, but in the second the translation might seem somewhat awkward.

The following abbreviations have been used in the editorial text: Swed./ish, Fr./ench, Ger./man, Rus./sian, RAC – Russian American Company.

The Russians still used the old Julian calendar at this time. Anna Furuhjelm often writes a date in both 'old' and 'new style'. In the 19th century, the difference between them was 12 days.

All information about persons mentioned in the letters, is given in the index of names.

I would like to thank The Danish Research Council for the Humanities and Aarhus University Research Foundation for making the publication of my great-grandmother's letters possible. Moreover I would like to express my gratitude to Leif Ludwig Albertsen, Doris Metzner, Hanna and Martin Ehrensvärd, Julian Lewis and my precious husband Jørgen Christensen for invaluable help in deciphering gothic German handwriting and illegible English words, and translating and editing all that had to be written in English.

Århus May 2005
Annie Constance Christensen

Introduction

An arranged marriage

After 1830, it seems to have been an unwritten rule that anyone appointed governor of Russian America had to bring a wife with him. The Board of Directors of the Russian American Company wanted no mistresses in the governor's house at Sitka. It was a matter of upholding the dignity and morals of the colonial administration – the representative of Russian empire and Christian civilisation in these remote parts of the world.

Governors of the colonies in Alaska were normally appointed for a period of five years, and the Board could very well imagine the privations and temptations connected with being a lonesome man at this northern outpost of civilisation, without a spouse of European upbringing and Christian belief to stand by his side. When the first Russian missionaries arrived in Alaska in 1794 to preach the gospel to the heathens, they were appalled to find their compatriots – fur hunters and merchants – living in unconjugal, or even polygamous relationships with native women.[1] One of the early governors left behind a native mistress and their three illegitimate children on returning home after his term in Alaska.[2]

Arriving at Sitka in 1830, Baron Ferdinand Wrangel was the first governor to bring his wife with him from Russia. "Her coming was an event of some import, for the young baroness transformed life in the rough frontier capital. The old 'castle' which was the Chief Manager's residence now featured formal dinners and balls. The casual relationships of company employees with the local women gave way to permanent wedlock, and the old roistering social life of the town acquired a higher tone".[3] All later Russian governors of Alaska were to follow the Wrangels' example. Married appointees brought their wives, and unmarried ones faced the task of finding a wife before their departure for Sitka.[4]

In early 1858 Johan Hampus Furuhjelm, an unmarried Russian naval officer of Finnish birth, received a proposal from the Russian American Company to become the next governor of Russian America for a term of five years, from 1859. He was then harbour master of the Port of Aian, a gloomy place on the eastern coast of Siberia. He had served there since October 1855 (from 1856 as Captain of first rank).

---

1 Bolkhovitinov 1997-1999, 1, p. 268.
2 Pierce 1986, p. 11.
3 Pierce 1986, p. 13.
4 Pierce 1986, p. 40.

Describing social life in Aian in a letter to one of his friends, Furuhjelm wrote: "Apart from three married book keepers, one ditto priest and one ditto junior commissioned officer, Aian is inhabited only by workers with their wives. Nevertheless, I have from time to time arranged a dance for the local fops. They dance vigorously with their own and each others' wives – the only ladies in Aian."[5]

In the autumn of 1857 Furuhjelm's two unmarried sisters arrived unexpectedly at Aian by ship from Finland. They had been sent around the world to their unmarried brother, who – in the opinion of their elder brother Otto – was most able to provide for them. The sisters' unexpected arrival seems to have upset any budding marriage plans the 36 year-old bachelor may have had. In February 1858, Furuhjelm wrote to his benefactor and friend Arvid Adolf Etholén, another Finlander who had been Governor of Alaska (from 1840 to 1845), informing him of his decision to accept the post of Governor. Later in the letter, Furuhjelm confides: "I had very seriously considered going to Finland for a period of time to get married, but now, after the arrival of my sisters, I have given up the idea, since sisters and wives will never agree, as they say". Moreover, he concluded with irony and resignation: "I must consequently end my days as an old, sulky bachelor. But even in this matter I console myself that everything happens for the best and that I can live as a monk, if I have to, which I have already proved".[6]

The way of the monk, however, was not really an option for a future governor of Alaska. But time was running out for Furuhjelm. Since Aian had nothing to offer by way of a suitable partner, it was quite clear that his one and only opportunity to get married before going to Sitka would occur when he came to St. Petersburg to receive his instructions. He arrived in time for his official appointment by the Board of Directors, which took place on December 1 (old style), 1858. As for finding a wife before his imminent departure, he had to rely on the advice and services of good society in Helsinki (Swed. Helsingfors), in spite of the fact that he had not set foot there for eight years. And good society did not let him down. By the time Hampus arrived in the Russian capital, a suitable candidate for the role of governor's wife in Alaska had already been singled out. Her name was Anna Elisabeth von Schoultz. Although she belonged to one of Helsinki's noble families, she was nevertheless a newcomer in Finland and more cosmopolitan than most of her Finnish relatives.[7]

Anna was born on March 4, 1836 in Karlskrona, an important naval harbour in southern Sweden. Her father, Nils Gustaf von Schoultz (1807-1838), was of Finnish stock, but his branch of the family had moved to Sweden when Finland became a part of the Russian Empire in 1809. Nils appears to have been a very charming young

---

5   Copy of an undated letter from Furuhjelm, probably from 1856 or early 1857, in the editor's possession.
6   Copy of a letter from Furuhjelm to Etholén, February 26, 1858 (old style), in the editor's possession.
7   Annie Furuhjelm 1932, p. 107.

man, but he was definitely also an adventurer. By the time he met Anna's future mother, he had already taken part in the Polish Rising against Russia in 1830-1831, and served in the newly formed French Foreign Legion in Algeria. Too restless to settle down to married life in a provincial bourgeois setting, he left his family a couple of months after the birth of Anna, his second daughter, to try his fortune in the United States. He became involved in a haphazard rebellion to liberate Canada from British colonial rule, was taken prisoner, sentenced to death and executed at Fort Henry on the St. Lawrence River in December 1838.[8]

Anna's mother, Ann Cordelia von Schoultz, née Campbell, was born in India in 1813, but had been sent back to Britain at the age of five by her Scottish parents, to go to school. Ann and Nils met in Florence. After they got married, Nils brought Ann, his mother-in-law and his sister-in-law with him to Sweden. In 1842, six years after Nils fled home, Ann moved with her two daughters to Germany, a country she knew from her youth. Although she was eventually informed about her husband's violent death, she never revealed any of this to her daughters, and Anna sincerely believed herself to have been raised in "a happy, innocent Home, where nothing impure or unclean ever entered".[9] After three years in Heidelberg, the small family settled in Darmstadt in 1845. Anna and her elder sister Florence received a German education, but spoke English with their mother. Through a friend, they made the acquaintance of the young princes Ludwig ("Louis") and Heinrich, with whom they played and later danced at the balls of the court of Darmstadt. Prince Louis eventually became Grand Duke of Hesse. In 1894 his daughter Alix was to marry Tsar Nikolai II and become Russia's last empress, under the name of Alexandra Feodorovna.

Anna and Florence spent many happy years in Germany. In 1856, the family visited their relatives in Finland for the first time. They were received with much cordiality and warmth. That is probably the reason why Anna's mother, having been seriously ill in 1856, decided to move to Finland in 1857. She may well have assumed that her daughters would not be left without support there in the event of her untimely death. They settled in a five-room flat at 27 Mikael's Street in central Helsinki.[10]

Because of her multinational background and upbringing, Anna spoke English, German, French and Swedish. Though only 22 years old in 1858 – and 15 years younger than Furuhjelm – she was thought of as a suitable first lady of the Russian American colonies. Her newly retrieved Finnish relatives played an active role in positioning her for what seemed a most advantageous marriage. In the summer of 1858 Anna spent some time at Tavastby, the estate of Adolf and Margaretha Etholén. Mrs. Etholén was a cousin of Anna's vanished father. "Uncle Adolf" and "Aunt Margeret" told her about Russian America and life in the colonies. We know already that the future governor Furuhjelm was Etholén's protégé. By early December Anna

---

8   Pipping 1967.
9   Letter No. 41, cf. the present edition, p. 191.
10   Annie Furuhjelm 1932, p. 115.

was, in her own words, "thinking of Hampus now already", and he too had heard of her.[11] It seems likely that Etholén played an active role in arranging the match.

The new governor of Russian America had to be installed in his office in Alaska before the end of June 1859, together with the wife he still lacked. So when Furuhjelm finally arrived in Helsinki shortly before Christmas, there was no time to lose. A ball was arranged in the house of Marie and Fabian Langenskiöld on December 24, 1858, the latter being another cousin of Anna's father. Here Anna and Hampus met for the first time. Hampus is reported to have been standing in the doorway of the salon, unceasingly watching Anna, while she danced with the other young people. As for Anna, she had ample opportunity to inspect the dignified slender figure of the governor who actually looked quite youthful. She may possibly have agreed with the opinion that his dark eyebrows and dark moustache, in combination with his grey hair, made him resemble "a French marquis from *l'ancien régime*".[12] She may even have found an opportunity to look into his dark eyes. In any case, they both seem to have liked what they saw. On January 10, 1859 they became engaged, and on February 2 they were married. Due to the tight time schedule, they had to have their banns read twice on one Sunday.

After the wedding lunch, for 60 invited guests, also at the Langenskiölds' home, the newly married couple set out from Helsinki on their long journey to Sitka in Alaska. The first leg was a sleigh ride to St. Petersburg. Anna's elder sister Florence had been invited to accompany them as far as to London. Anna's mother stayed behind in the Helsinki flat, together with her German servant Babette Fischer and her nephew Ormelie. Anna was never to see her again.

On the very first day of the journey, Anna wrote a letter to her beloved mother. It was the first in a long series, in which she was to share her thoughts and impressions from the New World or, more precisely, from *her* new world, which had two unknown continents to be explored: married life and Russian America. These letters make up the present book.

Russians in the New World

At the time Anna set out to discover Alaska for herself, little more than a century had elapsed since Europeans first learned of its existence. Its coast was sighted on July 17th, 1741, at 58°14' northern latitude, by a Russian navy expedition under the command of Vitus Bering, a Dane by birth. A small party of seamen went ashore on the island now called Kayak Island to get fresh water. The German naturalist Georg Wilhelm Steller went with them and nearly made the first contact with the local Americans, when he came across the remnants of a fire, which seemed to have been left in the middle of a meal.

---

11   Letter No. 30, cf. the present edition, p. 111.
12   Annie Furuhjelm 1932, p. 108.

Ann von Schoultz, the mother of Anna Furuhjelm.

Bering himself never made it back from the expedition, but died on an uninhabited island now known as Bering Island, where his ship the *St. Peter* was stranded on the return voyage along the Aleutian string of islands. Surviving crew members, however, brought home tales of the incredible wealth of furs in this part of the world, and soon Russian entrepreneurs set out to exploit it. Fur hunters, usually part owners or employees of small trading companies based in Northern Russia and Siberia, started coming to the Aleutian Islands in search of valuable pelts, especially those of sea otters. A merciless slaughter of these animals began. The native Aleuts, being highly skilled hunters, provided cheap labour, and a great many of them perished in the process.

Typically, company-owned ships would take parties of "promyshlenniki" (hunters, traders) to promising locations in the newly discovered territories, leave them there with a stock of supplies, and call again after a number of years to fetch the men and their harvest of pelts. The ships might also bring replacements for a following term. As hunting activities gradually reached further eastwards, larger trading companies emerged and became increasingly dominant.

A new era began with the arrival in the 1780s of the rich and energetic merchant Grigorii Ivanovich Shelikhov, who was destined to play an important role in the Russian colonisation of North Western America. Shelikhov saw very clearly that further growth of the fur trade required permanent Russian settlements in America. His company, founded in 1781 in partnership with another well-to-do merchant, Ivan Golikov, gambled by building three galiots in Okhotsk, on the east coast of Siberia. In August 1783 the small flotilla set out under Shelikhov's command, with

192 labourers and some livestock on board.[13] One year later Shelikhov arrived on the island Kodiak near the base of the Alaska Peninsula. Having ruthlessly subdued the native inhabitants, who were unfamiliar with the effects of gunfire, he founded the first Russian colony on American soil. Kodiak became the stepping-stone to further Russian expansion into the New World.

Shelikhov remained on the island together with his wife Natal'ia for two extremely active years (1784-1786). He organised fur hunting, built houses, fortresses and boats, taught the native Eskimos, whom Russians called "Koniagi", to keep goats and grow vegetables, converted some of them to the Orthodox faith and even founded a school, where 25 native boys, given in hostage to the colonists, started learning Russian.[14] In the summer of 1860, Anna, together with Governor Furuhjelm, paid a visit to the former centre of Russian America and left her vivid impressions of the island in two letters to her mother.[15]

After Shelikhov's return to Russia, he and his partner Golikov petitioned for government support, including a monopoly on trade in the North Pacific. They argued that one strong, united company was necessary in order to sustain Russian commercial interests and territorial claims in the region. In spite of protests from competing merchants, their proposal gained support from high-ranking officials in Irkutsk and St. Petersburg. In 1788, Shelikhov and Golikov presented their ideas – and their application for 200,000 roubles – directly to Catherine the Great. The Empress awarded them with silver medals for their achievements, but, rather unexpectedly, refused all their requests. Philosophically, she was in favour of free trade and against monopolies. Politically, she was too cautious to provoke England and Spain by openly laying claim to unexplored American territory.

Initially, the Russian expansion into the North Pacific had taken place without attracting too much attention from other European powers. But in the last three decades of the 18th century other nations had become increasingly interested in exploring and mapping this unknown region, and in establishing to what extent the Russians were already present there. In 1769 Spain began to push north from Mexico into Alta California, and by 1784 nine Catholic missions had been established, stretching from San Diego to San Francisco.[16] Several Spanish naval expeditions explored the coast further north, and in 1789 the Spanish ambassador in St. Petersburg warned Russian ships not to encroach on Spanish-American territory, which allegedly extended as far north as Prince William Sound, at 61° northern latitude.[17]

For a while it looked as if the Northwest Coast might become a colonial realm divided between Russia and Spain. However, the international rivalry for exploration

---

13 Bolkhovitinov 1997-1999, 1, p. 118.
14 Al'perovich 1993, pp. 89; Bolkhovitinov 1997-1999, 1, pp. 126-127.
15 Letters Nos. 36 & 37, cf. the present edition, pp. 144, 146, 157.
16 Haycox 1997, pp. 6-7.
17 Al'perovich 1993, p. 145.

and overseas possessions in the region was soon joined by England and France, and later also by the United States. Captain Cook, during his third voyage, mapped a long stretch of the Northwest Coast in 1778, and passed through Bering Strait into the Arctic Ocean. In 1786, the French expedition of Lapérouse also investigated the coast of Alaska and visited both the Spanish colonies in California and Petropavlovsk on Kamchatka. The Russian-Spanish rivalry slackened in 1790 when England forced Spain not to lay claim to American territory north of Nootka Sound, at 49°35'.[18]

There were also a couple of official Russian naval expeditions, by Krenitsyn and Levashov (1764-1771), and by Billings and Sarychev (1785-1794), following up on Bering's discoveries.[19] But the most important part of the Russian empire building in America was done by merchants.

The creation of a Russian monopolist trading company comparable to the British East India Company (EIC) or the Dutch Vereenigde Oost-Indische Compagnie (VOC) had to wait until after Catherine's death in 1796 and the accession to the throne of her son Pavel. By then Shelikhov had passed away, but his widow skillfully looked after the family business. Following the merger in 1798 of Shelikhov's and Golikov's company with that of the wealthy Irkutsk merchant Nikolai Myl'nikov, Emperor Pavel I graciously directed, in 1799, that the new company "be called the Russian American Company under the patronage of His Imperial Majesty" (RAC), and that it be granted exclusive rights and special privileges for a period of twenty years. [20] The founders' invested capital of 724,000 roubles was divided into 724 shares, and 1,000 additional shares were issued and offered for sale to the Russian public. The subsequent emperor, Alexander I, and several members of his family and his cabinet, were among the new shareholders.

An imperial decree signed by Pavel I on December 27, 1799, specified the privileges granted to the RAC. The decree was also an official statement of Russian territorial claims in the North Pacific. Based on her rights of first discovery, Russia claimed possession of the coast of America from 55° northern latitude to Bering Strait and beyond, and of the archipelagos extending from Kamchatka to America and to Japan. The Company received permission "to profit from all hunting and other ventures presently established along the coast of America [...] and likewise on the Aleutian, Kuril and other islands located in the North Pacific Ocean." In addition, the RAC could "undertake to make new discoveries, not only above 55° northern latitude, but to the south as well; they may occupy lands they discover and claim them as Russian possessions, [...] provided that these newly discovered territories have not previously been occupied by other nations or have come under their protection".[21]

---

18 Bolkhovitinov 1997-1999, 1, p. 300.
19 Bolkhovitinov 1997-1999, 1, pp. 197-250.
20 For an English translation of the charter and other foundation documents of the RAC, see Dmytryshyn 1989, pp. 3-23.
21 Dmytryshyn 1989, pp. 18-19.

However, the new company not only received special privileges, it also had to accept a number of obligations. One was "to support the Christian Greek Catholic mission in America which is working to teach the Holy Gospel and enable the illiterate people in America and on the islands [in the North Pacific Ocean] to gain knowledge of the True God".[22] The first Orthodox mission to be appointed and sent to America was a group of 11 priests, monks and lay brothers. They arrived on Kodiak in 1794. Soon after, the leader of the mission, Father Ioasaf, was appointed bishop-vicar of "Kodiak and the adjacent islands in America".[23] He was summoned to Irkutsk and consecrated in 1799, but drowned on his way back when his ship went down in a severe storm.[24]

In spite of this early set back, Russian clergymen were quite successful in converting the Aleuts and the Koniagi to the Orthodox faith. They organised schools and built chapels and churches. Their work had a lasting impact: almost all inhabitants of the Aleutian Islands and Kodiak, who were classified by the RAC as "dependent" natives, have remained Orthodox. The missionary efforts encountered more obstacles when it came to the "independent" Tlingit Indians (or the Kolosh, as the Russians called them), who lived on the mainland and on islands further down the Alaskan coast. The Tlingit outnumbered the Russian colonizers many times over. While the number of Russians rarely exceeded 500, there were between 15,000 and 20,000 Tlingit, according to an 1860 Russian estimate.[25] Only a small minority converted to Orthodoxy.

To lead RAC's activities on location in America, the Board of Directors appointed the Siberian merchant Aleksandr Andreevich Baranov who thus became the first chief manager or *governor* (in Russian: glavnyi pravitel') of Russian America. By the time of his appointment, he had already been the Kodiak-based manager of Shelikov's affairs for almost ten years. With tireless energy, in spite of numerous difficulties and setbacks, Baranov continued exploring the coast and developing the Russian network of permanent settlements, outposts and seasonal hunting bases. Under his direction, the Russian American Company increased its earnings and grew. Baranov's projects were often visionary and far-reaching. He tried to develop trade with China, the Sandwich (Hawaiian) Islands, and Chile. In 1812 he founded Fort Ross in California, not far from San Francisco. It was to supply Russian America with grain, since agriculture was almost impossible in Alaska. In the end, however, Fort Ross proved incapable of feeding the northern colonies and was sold off in 1841.

Baranov was also the founder, in 1804, of Novo-Arkhangel'sk (New Archangel, present-day Sitka), Russian America's new capital and the ultimate goal of Anna's long journey in 1859. The town was built on the island of Sitka (now Baranof Island),

---

22 Dmytryshyn 1989, p. 4.
23 Bolkhovitinov 1997-1999, 1, p. 271.
24 Black 2004, pp. 235-236.
25 Black 2004, p. xiii; Dmytryshyn 1989, p. xlix.

which had in previous years served as a summer base for parties of RAC fur hunters exploiting new grounds further down the American coast. The Tlingit had put up a stiff resistance against the emerging Russian settlement on Sitka. Never subdued, they remained independent of RAC's colonial rule. As late as in 1855, during the tenure of Furuhjelm's predecessor, Governor Stepan Voevodskii, the Tlingit attacked Novo-Arkhangel'sk, killing seven Russians and wounding fifteen. Voevodskii estimated Tlingit losses at about fifty.[26]

Novo-Arkhangel'sk had developed at a moderate pace. In 1860, one year after Anna arrived, its population – according to an official Company report – totalled 1,024.[27] This figure, which did not include a Tlingit settlement just outside the town's palisade, is not particularly impressive. Nevertheless, Novo-Arkhangel'sk was for several decades the most urban settlement on the entire North American west coast, until the Californian gold rush in 1849 gave momentum to the rise of San Francisco. It had a shipyard, a warehouse, workshops, grain and saw mills, and three churches: the Orthodox Cathedral of St. Michael the Archangel, the Lutheran church, erected on the initiative of Governor Etholén, and the Tlingit Orthodox Church of the Holy Life-Creating Trinity, built into the palisade as a precaution. The streets had board sidewalks. There was a club where gentlemen played billiards, a hospital, schools, an excellent library, a museum of natural history and ethnography, private residences and Company barracks, and last, but not least, the governors' magnificent manor house, often referred to as "the Baranoff Castle".[28] Built on the top of a steep hill overlooking the town and the harbour, it was to become Anna's next address after her mother's city flat in Helsinki, and the first home that Governor Furuhjelm and his wife had shared.

The penultimate governor

In 1818 the 71 year-old Governor Baranov was replaced by an officer of the Russian Imperial Navy. From then on, until the sale of Alaska to the United States in 1867, 13 governors, all high-ranking naval officers, handled the interests of the RAC in the colonies.[29] The advent of a new type of governor marked a substantial increase of government involvement in the Company. Under the new rules that were laid down in the second RAC charter of 1821 (and restated in the third charter of 1841), the Emperor appointed a governor from among naval officers. The governor was responsible not only to the RAC Board of Directors in St. Petersburg, but also to "Supreme Government Authority".[30] He had to play a double role: that of a mer-

---

26 Black 2004, p. 269.
27 Fedorova 1973, p. 205.
28 Black 2004, pp. 275-279.
29 The navy governors have all been portrayed in Pierce 1986.
30 Dmytryshyn 1989, pp. xxxviii-xl & 365.

chant, and that of an administrator with far-reaching rights and obligations. Baranov had been a cunning trader and a ruthless manager. Most of his naval successors in the office felt more at home with the role of an administrator. By the beginning of Furuhjelm's tenure (1859-1864), the Company had long been a normal part of the Imperial administrative machinery and closely supervised by the Ministry of Finance, although formally separated from the state finances.

The second charter came together with an Imperial decree prohibiting foreign merchant ships from trading in the Russian colonies of the North Pacific.[31] North American vessels, most of them from Boston, had during the past 25 years been hampering RAC activities on the Northwest Coast. The 'Bostonians' traded provisions, firearms and rum with the natives, in return for sea otter pelts, which were then sold to the Chinese at Canton where the Russians were not permitted. A practical Baranov had nevertheless made the best of the situation: Shiploads of supplies bought from the American traders had more than once saved the Russian colonies from starvation. The new decree sought to put an end to the foreign competition. By warning ships from other nations not to anchor along "the entire Northwest Coast of America [...] from Bering Strait to 51° northern latitude", it also suggested a southern limit to Russia's territorial claims in America.[32]

The Russian decree stirred up anger in the United States and in England, but the three nations eventually solved their problems peacefully. The Russians were more than willing to bargain, since they lacked the naval power to back their claims. The ensuing negotiations provided the proper occasion for US President James Monroe to assert the famous 'Monroe doctrine' in his annual message to the Congress (December 2, 1823): "that the American continents, by the free and independent condition they have assumed and maintain, are henceforth not to be considered as subjects for future colonization by any European powers". The Russo-American Convention of 1824 and the Russo-British Convention of 1825 defined a new southern border for Russian America at 54°40', but permitted a restricted continuation of American and British hunting and trade north of this border for another 10 years.

The new link between the Russian navy and the RAC, formalized in the second charter, shows that the Russian government intended to let the navy play a permanent role in sustaining the overseas colonies. It was to patrol the coasts of the Russian possessions on both sides of the North Pacific. Together with the Company's own ships, it was also to supply the American settlements with provisions and other goods from Russia, and to transport the colonial fur catch back to Russia or to other markets. The first step in that direction had already been taken in 1803, when two company-owned ships under the command of naval captains Krusenstern and Lisianskii departed from Cronstadt. In the course of their circumnavigation, they rendered a variety of

---

31   For an English translation of the decree of September 4, 1821, and the subsequent second charter, see Dmytryshyn 1989, pp. 339-366.
32   Dmytryshyn 1989, p. 339.

services to the RAC before returning to Cronstadt in 1806. A series of multi-purpose voyages between the metropolis and the North Pacific followed. By 1864 at least 65 such voyages had been launched, 33 of them by the Russian government and 19 by the Company, and the last 13 by "other Russian owners".[33]

The bonds between the Navy and the RAC were to play a decisive role in the career of Johan Hampus Furuhjelm (in Russian called Ivan Vasil'evich Furugel'm). He was born in Helsinki on March 11, 1821, the same year that the second RAC charter was issued. His family belonged to the Finnish nobility and included another three sons and three daughters. Young Hampus was educated at home until, at the age of 15, he joined the First Finnish Marine Unit. From then on, he received no financial support from his father, who was on the verge of ruin. In 1839, Furuhjelm was promoted to midshipman (the lowest rank of a Russian naval officer) and then to lieutenant in 1845. After five more years of naval chores in the Gulf of Finland and the Baltic and Black Seas, his career took a new turn.

On the recommendation of Etholén, Furuhjelm was assigned to the Russian American Company in the North Pacific. He arrived at Sitka at the beginning of May 1851 and served there as harbour master until the end of the year. In 1852-1853, he navigated in the Pacific, visiting Honolulu, San Francisco and Shanghai on business for the Company. Later in 1853 when his RAC transport "Prince Menshikov" was drafted as a supply vessel for the Russian navy expedition to Nagasaki, Furuhjelm became a participant in the 'opening of Japan', the series of events that marked the beginning of Japan's rapid modernization.

The opening of Japan first brings to mind the American Commodore Perry and his squadron of navy steamships. As they approached the Japanese capital Edo (now Tokyo) in early 1854, emitting columns of black smoke, they looked so ultra-modern and irresistible that the Shogun decided to abolish 200 years of isolationism and sign a peace and friendship treaty with the United States. The treaty opened two Japanese ports to American ships and promised help for any American ships wrecked on the Japanese coasts. It also allowed American ships to replenish their supplies in Japanese ports.

It is less known that at the same time a Russian navy expedition under Vice-Admiral Putiatin was also trying to 'open' Japan. In fact, Perry and Putiatin's squadrons were racing one another for the prize of being the first to establish official relations with Japan. Putiatin's secretary, the classic of Russian literature Ivan Goncharov, memorably told the story of the Russian expedition. His narrative was entitled *The Frigate Pallas* after the flagship. Furuhjelm is named on several pages of the book, which was first published in 1858 – the eve of Furuhjelm's departure for Alaska – and the author gave him a dedicated copy. Due to the expedition, Furuhjelm's name also appears on detailed maps of the Sea of Japan. He was the first to sight a small, unknown island in Peter the Great Bay. Putiatin named it Furugelm Island to honour the able commander of one of his four vessels.

---

33 Gibson 1976, pp. 76-82.

When England and France joined the Crimean War in March 1854, Putiatin's squadron became a target for their warships in the Pacific. The expedition was called off, and its ships were given separate wartime assignments. Putiatin was soon able to re-open his negotiations with Japan, which resulted in the signing of a Russo-Japanese treaty in late December 1855. Furuhjelm remained in the area along the Tatar Strait (between the island of Sakhalin and the Asian mainland) that had recently become a focal point for Russian expansion, conducted partly in the disguise of colonization by the RAC. He was promoted to lieutenant-captain at the end of 1853 and to captain of second rank a year later. In July 1854, he became chief manager of Sakhalin, but the presence of French and English men-of-war prevented him from beginning his new assignment. His next destination was Aian, further up the East Asian coast. Furuhjelm served as harbour master of the new Siberian port designed to replace Okhotsk as the central Russian port on the Sea of Okhotsk. As we already know, he remained in Aian until the Company once again had him in mind in 1858.

While the RAC Board was deciding on Furuhjelm's candidature as governor, Russian statesmen were at the same time secretly discussing the possibility of selling Russian America to the United States. Their arguments focused on security and economy.

The problem of how to defend Russian America gained true importance as the Crimean War approached. In 1854 for the first time, a contingent of Russian infantrymen was shipped to Alaska: 100 lower ranks and two officers from the Siberian line battalions. (Another 100 men and four officers followed in 1857, after the Tlingit Indians' attack on Novo-Arkhangel'sk mentioned above).[34] Still, the Russian government had no illusions about its prospects of protecting the American colonies from Britain's superior navy. However, as it turned out, Russian America was left in peace throughout the war, thanks to a neutrality agreement between the RAC and the British Hudson's Bay Company.[35]

With a letter from the new Tsar Alexander II's younger brother, Grand Duke Konstantin Nikolaevich, commander-in-chief of the Russian navy from 1853, to Foreign Minister Gorchakov, the discussion on selling Russian America re-opened in 1857. Konstantin argued that it would be better for Russia to sell Alaska to the Americans before they seized it, since the United States was clearly determined to rule North America "undividedly". Considering the deplorable situation of Russian state finances after the war, the income from the sale could also give the navy budget a much-needed boost.[36] Other proponents of the sale pointed out that it would further improve Russo-American relations, and that Russia's interests in the Pacific would be more secure if her possessions were concentrated on the East

34 Fedorova 1973, p. 157.
35 Bolkhovitinov 1997-1999, 3, pp. 375-379.
36 Bolkhovitinov 1997-1999, 3, pp. 380-381.

Asian coast.[37] All agreed that an American takeover would be better for Russia than British rule in Alaska.

Alexander II thought his brother's suggestion deserved some consideration, and called upon his Minister of Naval Affairs, the former governor of Alaska, Baron Wrangel, to give an estimate of the value of the colonies. Wrangel, who was at heart against selling, calculated the minimum value of Russian Alaska based on the yearly profit on RAC shares. He concluded that the government should ask at least 7,442,800 silver roubles for Russian America, but added that even 20 million would be a bargain price in view of the region's potential.[38]

Proponents of the sale found it hard to envisage the potential Wrangel saw. The maritime fur trade had remained an important business of the RAC. But gone were the days when pelts were the soft gold of Russian America. The fur catch had declined steadily for decades. "By the mid-1850s Russian America was producing only 1000-2000 sea otter pelts annually [...] and most of the fur catch consisted of fur seals and beavers."[39] Instead, RAC activities underwent considerable diversification. Fishing, preparation of salted and dried fish, whaling, flour milling, lumbering, shipbuilding, coal mining, brick production, tea trade with the Chinese at Shanghai, export of a variety of products to the booming new city of San Francisco (fish, timber, prefabricated houses and, especially, ice) – all of this generated new occupations and new income, and helped reduce import expenses.[40] Still, it did not necessarily amount to an argument against selling the colonies. Since Grand Duke Konstantin pressed for a quick decision, Furuhjelm could well have become the last Russian governor in Alaska. However, the Foreign Minister convinced Alexander II not to rush this matter but wait for the American government itself to express some real interest in purchasing Russian America.[41]

Furuhjelm became the second-last governor of Alaska and was well acquainted with the man who actually became the very last governor: Prince Dmitrii Petrovich Maksutov. They had both taken part in Putiatin's expedition to Japan and in the Crimean War in the Pacific theatre. Maksutov had been decorated for outstanding bravery in the defence of the port of Petropavlovsk on Kamchatka against the attack of an Anglo-French squadron. In December 1858, he was appointed assistant governor of the Russian-American colonies and second-in-command to Furuhjelm. Following his superior officer's example, he also married in great haste shortly before departing for Alaska.[42] Anna and Hampus attended the wedding in St. Petersburg, on February 16, only two weeks after their own marriage, and Anna gave a full report in a letter to

---

37   Bolkhovitinov 1997-1999, 3, pp. 370-1.
38   Bolkhovitinov 1997-1999, 3, pp. 381-83.
39   Gibson 1976, p. 35.
40   Gibson 1976, pp. 37-43.
41   Bolkhovitinov 1997-1999, 3, p. 386.
42   Pierce 1986, pp. 44-45.

her mother.[43] Maksutov's bride, Adelaide Bushman, was half English, half German, and became Anna's intimate friend in Novo-Arkhangel'sk. The Maksutovs took the 'all-Russian' and less expensive route to Alaska: by land through Siberia to Aian, and by the company barque *Nakhimov* from Aian to Sitka (Novo-Arkhangel'sk), where they arrived on September 14, 1859.[44]

Anna and Hampus were able to choose a different route for their particular five-month blend of an official journey and a honeymoon. "Instead of the arduous trip by sledge across Siberia, or the eight-month voyage around Cape Horn, the Furuhjelms travelled to Sitka by a new, easier, but more expensive route. It was by way of Germany, England, Panama, and San Francisco".[45] So far their arranged marriage was working well, and Anna's letters from the various legs of the journey are full of affection for "my darling Hampus". Furuhjelm took over as governor at Sitka on July 2, 1859.

---

43   Letter No. 8, cf. the present edition, p. 36.
44   Pierce 1986, p. 45.
45   Pierce 1986, p. 41.

Anna Furuhjelm's Letters

No. 1 Henriksdal – onsdag natt [Swed. Wednesday night] d[en] 2. Feb[ruari] 1859

My own precious, beloved Mother! –!
Here we are! Your three children – and as we have such an exellent opportunity to send you a sweet "Good night" I am inexpressibly happy, and hope to make you so too. O my own most precious Mother! May God in His great mercy be with you – give you strength & comfort you – do not grieve darling Mother! I am happy – have all I can wish for in this world, & far, far more than I ever have deserved – Pray only for your child, that she may always remember the vows she today has made before the Lord, & that she may make her husband happy – perfectly happy – and that we may both walk in the ways of the Lord for ever. –

I can never forget your look at me last Sunday in church – your whole heart and soul lay in your eyes – & tonight too, when we parted. O not for ever – only for a short time – O Mama! He, who has already been so wonderfully good & merciful towards us, He will permit us to meet again – Pray & hope & trust that it will be so my own precious, precious Mother. –

With my whole heart, I thank you for all all you have done for me, O may God bless you for it – & may He grant me strength to act in all things according to what you have tried to teach me – then you will be blessed through y[ou]r children.–

The others wish to write – I must stop – O my sweetest, ownest Mother Goodnight & God for ever bless you, is the most heartfelt prayer of y[ou]r own fondly loving & devoted Child

Annie

Min dyraste, saknade moder!
Wi hafva lyckligen ankommit till första station – och funno der öfverste [Constantin von] Schoultz med familj. Tänk vår förundran och jag må säga –. – Jag känner mig så lycklig och så nöjd att sitta bredvid Anna, att jag sannerligen tycker hela verlden hafva ändradt sig. – Men adjö, sötaste mor; [måt]te vår Herre nådeligen bevara er och en gång i denna verlden låta oss återse hvarandra. Ännu en gång adjö!
    HFuruhjelm
[Swed. My dearest, precious Mother! We have happily arrived at our first station – and found there colonel Schoultz with his family. Imagine our surprise. I must

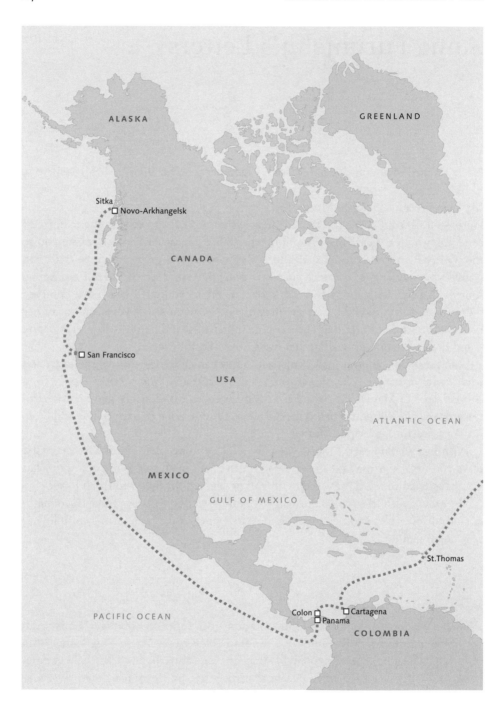

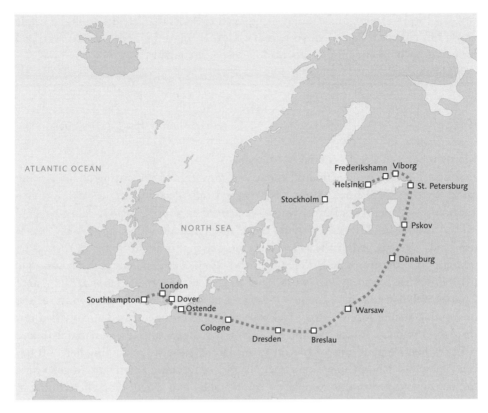

The journey from Helsinki to Sitka, Alaska

say –. – I feel so happy and content sitting next to Anna that I truly think the whole world has changed. But goodbye sweetest Mother, may the Lord preserve you and let us see each other again in this world. Once more goodbye.

  HFuruhjelm]

No. 2   Fredrichshamn d[en] 4. Feb[ruari] 1859

My own beloved, dearly cherished Mother!
In Uncle Eduards [von Schoultz] room you now behold me sitting at his writing table, writing these lines to you. We reached this place last night at 9.½ after a 12. hours sledging from Borgå, where we arrived at 3. on Thursday morning, […] – Fru [Swed. Mrs] E[lfving] brought me a large bouquet with 3. large calias, was it not kind? We stopped at the Hotel here on arriving, ordered rooms & then came straight on to the dear kind Uncle E[duard] who came out to meet, receive & welcome us. Indoors we found gentle sweet Tante [Swed. aunt] Xandia, Hanna, Ella, Tante Charlotte, Hilda and Ida Galindo – they were all so so bright, and happy to see the interesting young couple – they had expected us to dinner, & had already had tea, thinking it too late for us to come – We soon got supper and tea, & remained there till 12. when Hampus and I drove off to our Hotel, Florence remaining here – It has been snowing all night so we have every chance of reaching Petersburg in good time tomorrow – Our sledge is completely comfortable, you fancy yourself reclining in a cosy armchair, or even in bed. –

  My own darling Mother, you will receive a telegraphic despatch, please God the day before these lines reach you, but I could not leave you without a letter for Monday, knowing what happiness it will cause you to hear your child is well, "happy, pleased and contented" – O my own Mother! My heart and my thoughts have constantly been with you – I have been following you out and in of every room – I pray God earnestly to bless and preserve you my precious Mother – & to let you still have much joy & cause of thankfulness through your children.

  O my own Mother! thank you a thousand times for your fond, devoted love. I am so happy – and now Goodbye and God bless you – Be strong & happy – Hearty love to dear dear Marie [Langenskiöld] & her dear husband – tell them I can never forget their kindness & friendship – Now I must stop & with my own Hampus dear love, & a fondest kiss from me, I embrace you & fold you to my heart & send many loves and kisses to dearest Babette [Fischer] & my [..?] and am Y[ou]r own devoted & happy Child

Annie Furuhjelm

No. 3   *Petersburg.* Sunday Ev[enin]g February 6. 1859

My own beloved Mama,

Your Annie sends you a warm and loving greeting from her new home – thank God
– we reached it safe and well last night, or rather yesterday afternoon at four o'clock,
and found everything in perfect order, waiting for our arrival. Tante M[argeret
Etholén] had been here in the morning, and sent several little things she thought we
would require, and placed a lovely little flower table in the window of the so called
"cabinet" filled with the most fragrant hyacynths, tuples [i.e. tulips] and a myrtle in
the centre. You cannot think what a delightful feeling it was to come here, into your
own home. Hampus took me through all the rooms, asking me if I was pleased, and
looking so perfectly contented and pleased himself. O I hope he may be very happy
– and trust God will give me the strength, the will and the desire, ever gladly and
cheerfully to fulfill my duties towards him as his wife – Indeed Mama, he deserves
to be happy – his heart requires sympathy, affection and fond care – he has been too
long alone & uncherished – but now, with Gods help, he shall be so no longer – I
am so happy, so thankful, to be the one chosen by him, and have but one wish, one
desire, that he may never, never find himself disappointed in me. –

But now I will tell you all about our journey – taking up my narrative at Fredrichshamn from which place I last wrote to you. Uncle Eduards were all delighted to
see us & as kind and warmhearted as they have ever shown themselves towards us.
We had supper & tea there the first evening, slept at the inn, & returned to coffee
at 9. […] Our health and happiness was drunk in champagne, & after a last farewell,
we got into our sledges & continued our journey – There had fallen an immense
quantity of snow during the night, so that instead of having too little, as we had
feared, we had too much of a good thing, & were not able to drive fast, especially as
our sledge was of so enormous a size – We reached Wiborg that evening at 10. had
tea & beefsteaks at an hotel, which by the bye was a very good one, received a visit
of Col[onel] Bortram[?] & set off again at 12 – travelling all through the night, &
reaching this place at 4. the following day. But all this you have I trust heard, through
the telegraphic despatch, which we sent yesterday, after Hampus & my little sister
returned from their baths.

Tante M[argeret] sent 3. times to inquire if we had arrived, & waited dinner for
us till 6½, when we went up to her, & were received warmly and kindly & heartily.
It was indeed strange to meet all my dear Tavastby[46] friends under such completely
different circumstances – but darling Mother, the feeling was such a pleasant and
happy one. It does my heart good to see Hampus bright smile and look of content-
ment, and to hear him say he feels happy, and a different man. How I wish you
could see us, and our dear little home, where we are so comfortably established.
O how I wished it had been possible for you to come with Uncle Adolf [Etholén],
who arrived today – And no letter from home! I took for granted you would write
sweetest Mama – but no – no! – I must wait till tomorrow & trust I may then not

---

46   Tavastby, the estate of M. and A. Etholén in Finland.

Adolf Etholén by
J.E. Lindh, probably
1839. Oil on canvas.
Private collection.

be disappointed.– […]

   After having slept till 9½ this morning, we got up, dressed & had breakfast, Florence having come to visit us at 10. but found herrskapet [Swed. the young couple] in négligée – No sooner had we finished coffee, than *Dr Collan* & his brother an officer came to call upon us, & were both introduced to me. Then we drove off to the english church.[47] My heart swelled with delight when I entered with Hampus (O, he is *so* good) at my side & heard the well known familiar sound of an english hymn – We soon found places in a row & I was astonished to see so large a congregation, & so handsome a church with marble columns all the way down on both sides – The sermon was good & delivered in a fine, pleasant voice. How I thought of you my own Mother & wished you lived here, for the sake of the english church. –

   After the service was over, we went to the Isacs church[48] – the magnificence of

---

47   Built in 1814-15, rebuilt in 1876, situated in Angliiskaia naberezhnaia 56. Name unknown.
48   St. Isaac's Cathedral in St. Petersburg had been completed and sanctified as late as in

which far surpasses the power of my description – I have never seen any building which made so solemn an impression upon me, as this grey earnest, serious, imposing looking church, with its pollished granit pillars, & bronze foundations, its pollished flight of granit steps and its bronze doors with bas reliefs representing scenes out of our Saviours life –

The impression it made upon me was *awful*, though not in the way the word is generally used – you understand me, dont you my own Mother? – I cannot describe the exterior far less, the interior, with its paintings, marble walls & pillars, silver and gold figures and railings, malacite and lapis lazuly pillars & guilt foundations, ornaments of the most costly description, polished stone floor etc – etc – But it is a most splendid magnificent building, and the only one of its kind in the world I should suppose. – You would be delighted with it, and all the fine buildings & statues here. Certainly S[ain]t P[etersburg] is a splendid town – but I have seen too little of it yet, to be able to give you any idea of it –

My own beloved Mother! My hearts most warmest thanks for all all the fatigue & trouble of these few last weeks. I am constantly thinking of last Wednesday, & what a happy, beautiful day it was – and when I hear Hampus say "I thank God from the depth of my heart for it" – I cannot say how happy I feel. –

But darlingest Mama! Do not think me selfish! O no! pray do not – & do not for one moment suppose I am so taken up with my own happiness that I forget you – or do not miss you, long for you often, & pray & trust you are calm & happy – though my heart sinks when I remember how lonely you are. O Mama! I can *never never* be sufficiently thankful for Gods untold mercy in having given me such a Mother! – how undeserving I have been – & how much sorrow I have often given you – forgive me – forgive me, my own Mother –

I have just read my dearest's letter – how happy it will make you – Is he not as good & pure as gold? – May God ever bless him, & make me a deserving wife –

We are going to read morning and evening together. – [...]

Good night and God for ever bless you my most precious Mother – Dear love to Babette and Ormelie [Hannay] – does Amanda keep the rooms tidy? And what do you do all day? Where have you been, & who have you seen? Tomorrow we go to the french theatre, & next day & Wednesday to some other theatres. –

I have bought a very pretty white bonnet with feathers and white roses for 16. Rub[les] –

A fond kiss from Y[ou]r own loving Child

Annie

1858. It was named in honour of St. Isaac of Dalmatia, because Peter the Great was born on St. Isaac's day.

No. 4   *S[ain]t Petersburg*. Feb[ruary]. 9th 1859.
                                                              Wednesday

Good morning my own precious Mother! and dearest thanks for your sweet letter, which gladdened my heart on Monday night on returning from the french play, where we had all three been together, and been very pleased with the performance.

I cannot say how happy you made me my beloved Mother! especially as I had been disappointed at not hearing from you at the same time as Florence, and consequently shed my first tears since I have been married – No! not quite – the first, and the bitterest were at parting. – We thought as Florence's letter was addressed to the American company, ours would also have been so, and could not conceive how I should have been left without a line from you – We were at the Etholens, and went from there to the theatre. My heart told me you had written, but notwithstanding, I was a wee bit foolish. Well, you may fancy our delight was great, when we found the longed for post had arived & immediately sat down to read our shares – Hampus had a very kind letter from his father, of which I daresay he has already told you, – after having taken some supper, we read the Bible, and went to bed happy and grateful. –

Indeed, my own Mother! I wish you could see your child's perfect happiness – It would do your heart good – I can only say that each day finds me more deeply grateful towards Him, who has given me such a husband, and each day I pray more fervently, to be able to be all and all to him, who is, and ever will be, all and all to me. –

It is so delightful to see with what real pleasure he reads to me, and listens to me reading to him – In the morning it is I, who read english, and in the evening he reads out of the swedish Bible – and with Gods Blessing, I hope *nothing*, may ever make us forget Him.

Mary Cautleys letter was so very kind – I hope we may soon meet – what delight it will be to me, to present my own dearest Hampus to them all, of whom I know they will all grow very fond.

I am so thankful to think you are so resigned, so perfectly contented and happy – though of course you must feel sorrow too – But precious Mother! He will give you strength – and O! I so fervently trust He will permit us to meet again in Joy and health. And we shall write very, very often to eachother – Thank you my darling Mama, for the nice warm dressing gown, which I shall be so glad to wear, and think of my own Mother, to whom it once belonged. […] – You cannot think what a splendid *ermine talma* quilted with white satin, and trimmed with broad quilted white satin ribbon inside, Hampus has given me, and has now ordered a muff of the same description. – He is *so very* good – O! how happy I am to be his wife. –

I will send you more hair, I was afraid, the locks would be lost. –

I have begun keeping accounts, & find that money flies – My blue dress is to come home today – tomorrow we hope to call on the Driesens – Last night we saw an *inferior ballet*, beautifully danced – tonight we go to the opera "Il Giovani" [W.A.Mozart]. Forgive me pray that I write so unconnectedly – Hampus secretary,

Mr Goschkin is waiting to go out with us – time flies here like in London – We go to bed late, & have breakfast at 10. or 10½ – […]

Do you remember this day week? O Mother! One week has gone over my happiness! And it is all *so* wonderful – My own Hampus has written to you – I am so glad, he is so fond of you. […]

And now I must finnish, though I could write more. The meeting at Henriksdal was more than painful. they had tea & champagne, and seemed to compassionate Fl[orence] & looked upon it as broken – Tante D[oris][49] proposed Hampus to take Fl[orence] to Sitka! –

He was disgusted with her – May God ever bless you & preserve you from all trouble & annoyance there – O my precious, precious Mother – May His mercy be near us –

Love to dearest Ormelie and Babette – and fond kisses to you from
Y[ou]r own devoted Child

Annie

No. 5   S[ain]t Petersburg. February 11th 1859
                                                              friday ev[eni]ng -

My own beloved, darling Mother!
Last night, on returning from the russian baths, I found your dear letter waiting for me, for which I now wish to send you my warmest and fondest thanks. I cannot conceive how our telegraphic despatch, which we sent off on Saturday evening, only reached you on Monday m[o]r[nin]g and am distressed to think you should have waited so long. Thank God, you are well and strong, my beloved Mother! how happy would I be could I take you by the hand, press a kiss upon your mouth, then on your eyes, and feel y[ou]r arms fondly laid around me! – O that I had a good likeness of you! but you will promise me, darling Mama, to send me one in a letter, the very first time you are in any town, where good portraits can be made. Promise me sweetest Mother! You cannot refuse so natural a request! –

I have been waiting to get home my dress to have ours taken for you – it came home today & looks perfectly splendid – I wish you could see it – I have been obliged to buy more stuff to make a new body to the black silk, Hampus sent me – it fitted so badly, looked such a figure[?] and was the greatest trouble to fasten – I would have been perfectly unhappy to see this handsome blue dress thus spoilt. – […]

Who in earth wrote that article[50] in the newspaper? – did it not greatly astonish

---

49   The parents of Carl von Schoultz were against the marriage of their son to Florence von Schoultz.

50   A short article about the wedding and their impending journey around the world in *Helsingfors Tidningar* 5.2.1859.

you? I assure you, it is exceedingly flattering for Hampus & myself and shows the general good will people entertain for us. I was much pleased, though at the same time perfectly stupefied but then, it is not every day that an Hampus Furuhjelm, a man of such good reputation, loved and esteemed by all, comes to H[elsing]f[or]s to be married in the forenoon, and in the evening of the same day, commence a journey half round the world! – it was an événement for Helsingfors –

I daresay many of our friends have kept the article in memory of us, and that great day! – Who showed it to you first, and what did you say when you read it? –

Many thanks my own dearest Mother, for having sent my things – I hope they will soon reach me safely – as yet I have not heard anything about them. –

Just now the bell rung – I hope & suppose it is Hampus. –

Saturday morning. It was so – and Adalbert [von Schoultz] was with him, we were all delighted to see him. Hampus bought me a cap, and I was for the first time dressed in one and looked a perfect little "Fru" [Swed. wife]. Otto Nyberg and his wife came too, and several others, friday being Etholens day of reception. We came home at 12. – Darling Mama! You cannot think how happy I am in possession of my dearest Hampus – we have Wikström in every morning, which is so pleasant – may it please God to be with us – and may we be able to do him good, and to teach him his duty as a christian. –

Hampus and I paid several visits yesterday – the Driesens were the first – as we both thought, it w[ou]ld be wrong of us not to go to them because their brother & sister have behaved unworthily – that is not their fault – We were warmly received, and Hampus was obliged to promise to let me spend next Monday with them; they will come for me & Florence, and Hampus will come in the evening. Ida was as usual – they seemed astonished to hear Florence was going to England, though at the same time very glad. From there we drove to some Generals where H[ampus] wished to introduce his little Wife, but were only received by one, his chef, who told me he intended calling on us today; so here I am sitting in my green gown, ready to receive him – I was interrupted by Dr Collan, who came to look at Wikström, poor creature he has had a dreadful cough, & looks pale and thin.

[…] Now I must write to Aunt Mathilda. Just now my muff came home, [the rest of this letter is missing.]

No. 6   S[ain]t Petersburg. Feb[ruary] 13th 1859
                                          Sunday night 11. o'clock

Good evening, my own beloved Mother! I have only just returned from the Etholen's, where I spent the day, Hampus having dined out with Uncle Adolf, and spent the evening also with him at Dr Collans, and as I wish to sit up for him, I take to my pen, and fancy myself sitting beside you, telling you all about everything. I was very glad to be able to speak with Tante M[argeret] about Sitka, and many things of importance, and feel more and more what great *responsibility* will lie upon me, and how I ought in every thing to set a good example, seeing that all I do, say or have done, will be remarked and most likely followed. My most earnest wish and desire is, with Gods help, to be able to do good to those with whom I come in contact, and in all things to act according to my words – But I feel so weak and full of faults, and am afraid of not doing what I ought to do – Should Hampus ever be disappointed in me, and find me different to what he had expected, I would be perfectly miserable. But then, I pray God so earnestly, this may never be the case – but that I may in all things show myself worthy of him, and be a Joy, a Blessing and a comfort to him.

Another thing which frightens me, is that he has heard *too* much good of me – has heard me praised & lauded to a perfectly unmerited degree; – how painful for him, to find out the mistake – which sooner or later, he must, knowing full well, how many, many ugly faults I have, and how they will and must make themselves perceived ere long. Of course he never expected to find perfection in me, more than in anybody else – but still, I see he thinks too highly of me – O! how happy I would be, *to be* such a one he now thinks me.

The door was just opened – I suppose, he has come home – though I don't hear his voice yet – No! it cannot have been him. –

We went again to the english church this morning – I cannot say how nice it was and *how* happy I was to hear that beautiful Te Deum again, which I have not heard for ever so many years – But the service is really too long – I became perfectly tired today – I am sure Hampus thought the same thing, not being accustomed to the english service. […]

We have to buy an evening dress tomorrow, which must be ready by Wednesday at 4. when we are first invited to a dinner given by the "Amerikanska companiet" [Swed. (Russian-)American Company] – and then to Mr. Makzotoffs wedding, which takes place first in the greek & then in the english church, after which the whole company drives home to supper I suppose. I would have wished not to go at all, seeing the expence my toilette for that one evening will be, but as Hampus is his chief, he says it would not do not to be present, and without me he will not go. –

Florence is also invited to the dinner, which is very attentive of the charming Company. A nice little bill it will be, by time my dress is bought and made up – My blue body costs no less than 28. R[oubles] S[ilver][51] – the things are very handsome to be sure, and the whole fits very well. What do you say to that? –

Monday morning. We have just had coffee, and Hampus has gone out on business – it is snowing hard, & the atmosphere is so thick, I see no chance of any photographs being taken today, and still I should so much like them to be sent in time for us to receive an answer from you here my own precious Mother! […] but why did you not write by Thursday's post? Vainly I waited, and vainly I hoped for a letter – surely I will not be disappointed today – remember how soon we shall not be able to hear

---

51   Roubles silver were more valuable than roubles banco ('paper roubles').

often, and must content ourselves with one letter every 2. months – therefore pray write very very often, & don't pay your letters – so that *that* may not be the cause of silence – thank God, we can pay them both ways, & are only too happy to be able to do so. Florence has written to Carl, I trust he will be happier after he has heard from her again. Darling Mama! What do you think you will do next summer – will you go to England and if you do, will you return to Finland – [...]

I am writing this, dressed in your most comfortable dressing gown, which looks so nice, & feels so warm and cosy – Eugenie Lilles cap is on my head, and I am only waiting for my room to be ready to dress – and as it is ready, I must go – else Hampus will still find me undressed when he returns. I have this moment received a note from dear Florence enclosing this for you – also 2. tickets for a matinée musicale next Thursday at 2 – I hope we shall go – but as Hampus is not at home, I could give no answer. –

I have reread all your dear dear letters – and thank you from the depth of my heart for all the love they contain. I am afraid my letters are full of myself – O – do not think me selfish – the longer I am separated from you, the more I feel how much I love you, and how much I owe you, and how little I have been to you – but as long as there is any breath in my soul I am Y[ou]r own fondly loving grateful child

Annie

Hampus is too lazy to write himself, indeed you cannot conceive how lazy he is, but sends his dear love. –

No. 7   *S[ain]t Petersburgh.* Feb[ruary] 16 –
                                                        Wednesday 1859 –

[...]

No. 8   *S[ain]t Petersburgh. Feb[ruary] 19 1859*
                                                                    Saturday

Good morning my own most dearest Mother. This is a lovely bright day – there has been a little frost and consequently the air is far purer and clearer. We have this minute finnished breakfast; your picture stood before us on the table – it has become so very dear to me, now that I am away from you, and have no better likeness. Hampus went out before I was dressed, and came home with a huge parcel under his arm, containing writing paper, enveloppes, sealing wax, mended pens etc – etc – yesterday morning he went out in the same way, and brought home a quantity of magnificent oranges. But now my precious Mother, I must first send you fond love, thanks and kisses for y[our] last dear letter, and then tell you all about the dinner & wedding of last Wednesday. I wrote to you by the last post, and told you we were invited, and that we were going out to buy a dress. It is an exceedingly pretty one – rose de chine, à double jupes [Fr. with double skirts], with stripes and small fringes – lovely colour – To dinner I was told I could not have a low body, nor at the wedding a high one – so I told my splendid Madame Boivin to make the dress with a high cape & long sleeves, which without any trouble could be taken out, and berthe and short sleeves put on – I wish you could have seen me when I was dressed – it looked so handsome. The little cape, which was trimmed with deep rose fringe lined with white fringe, fell just over the shoulders, the sleeves open up the back of the arm, were trimmed in the same way. I had a brusselles lace collar on, and a headdress of roses with black velvet and festoons of beads, which cost 18 R[oubles] S[ilver] and was very pretty. My dress cost 60. and nearly 40. to make up – We arrived at Uncle Adolfs rather late, but fortunately Mr Stökel, the russian minister or ambassador in America, had not arrived yet. The dinner was given for him and Hampus. Baron Wrangel, General Korsakoff, General Lüppfeld and Admiral something else, and General Polimkoffsky, were introduced to me, the latter I knew already and was most kindly spoken to by all – As soon as Mr Stökel came, he was introduced too, dinner was announced, and Mr Stökel gave me his arm, Gen[eral] Korsakoff gave his to Florence and a third gave his to Aunt M[argeret] – and forthwith we proceeded to the dining room, which was beautifully lighted, and the table decorated with splendid flowers. We sat down 12. to dinner, which consisted of the most dainty recherchér things you can imagine and tasted exceedingly well. 15. R[oubles] S[ilver] a cover, without wines! Champagne was not wanting, Gen[eral] Polimkoffsky proposed my health, and said "restez plus que cinq ans, Madame, c'est pour notre avantage" [Fr. Stay more than five years, that would be to our advantage]. – Mr S[tökel] and all the other gentlemen drank our health, Gen[eral] P[olimkoffsky] came all round the table, & touched glasses with all. We had most delicious *sterlette, venison, asparagus, pheasant,* puré made of hjerpar [Swed. hazel hens], fruit pudding served with fine liquor as sauce, ices, desert consisting of the most exquisite pears I have ever tasted, costing 1.50. a piece, grapes, apples, confects – in one word, everything was perfect. At 7. we got up from table, adjoined to the drawingroom, where coffee was served, and Baron Wrangel a very little, but manly and knightly looking man, with snow white hair, and mustashous, told me his wife had been the first European lady at Sitka, when he was Gouvenor there, some years before Uncle Adolf. He was very friendly and said: "Wir müssen nähere Bekanntschaft mit einander machen" [Ger. We must get to know each other better]. When they were all gone, I took off my pelerine and pulled off the long sleeves under which were long white tulle illusion "engageants" as they are called, & put on the berthe, made of net blonde, rose narrow ribbon and lovely bows of broad ribbon – Every one declared the dress to be lovely. We had a long, long drive to the russian church, where Fürst [Ger. Prince] Makzotoff and Miss Bushman were to be married first, & then in the english church. Our carriage stopped outside the church, where a quantity of carriages were standing. We got out, went up a broad staircase, came into a crowded tambour and then walked into a filled drawingroom, where all the guests seemed to be waiting for the bridal pair, but no one meeting us. Hampus asked his neighbour if this was not Makzotoffs wedding, to which the answer was "no"! – fancy our consternation. We walked out again, put on our things & came downstairs, all the servants staring at us in great astonishment. Hampus had left his palto in the carriage, went out to call the coachman, but no one answered. Half an hour were we there waiting – In the mean time the bride arrived, Hampus rushed backwards and forwards but no carriage was to be found. It was now nearly 9. At last we succeeded in getting another carriage, drove back over the long bridge to the english church, & found the whole company getting into their carriages. So we came home after another cloak for H[ampus] and then for the 3rd time back through Wassiljeostroff to the Makzotoffs, where we arrived after 10. We related our tale of misfortunes, and congratulated the happy pair. But one thing I can tell you, Hampus and I said over and over again how much, much nicer our wedding had been than this one, which appeared to me to be fasligt tråkigt [Swed. terribly boring]. The bride was not at all pretty but had a nice expression. She sat beside me nearly all the evening speaking english, & comparing dates, we found she had been engaged on Monday 10th Dec[ember] after having seen him twice, & having seen him for the first time in Nov[ember]. Was it not strange. Tea, fruit, ices and bonbons were handed about, and then the bride suddenly disappeared & soon afterwards came out in a white morninggown with pink ribbons, and a cap with rose ribbons on her head. I thought this an extraordinary custom & supposed it to be a russian one. All her friends & relatives embraced her tenderly, we said goodbye and came home. I forgot to tell you of Tante Natalies kindness in sending her Therese with Ida to dress me, & a great comfort she was, I don't know what I should have done without her.

On Thursday we were at a musical morning, & enjoyed it very much indeed. I wished so much you could have been with us. Yesterday we went to the Ermitage & were delighted with all we saw. Dr Collan met us there, & accompanied me through several rooms, showing me the best pictures – two Murillos took my fancy exceedingly. On my saying to him, I wished you could see it all, he said I would be delighted to show it to y[ou]r Mother, should she ever come here – when you write tell her so – which I promised to do and now have done. He is such a very kind, nice man, & so fond of my Hampus, & friendly towards me. It appears he had spoken much about us to him. Now my own beloved Mother what else shall I tell you – We go please God, next Thursday. Gen[eral] P[olimkoffsky] has procured us a diligence, wholly and entirely for our own disposal. We get 6. horses conducteur & coachman, may stop where we like and as long as we like – I thanked him exceedingly for all the trouble he had taken – […]

We were photographed yesterday, & the artist promised to have it finnished by Wednesday – Our own Mother is the only one who gets a picture from here. […]

And now my ownest darling Mother Goodbye – May Gods best blessing ever surround you and His strong arm support you is the earnest prayer of
Y[ou]r fondly loving happy Child

Annie

No. 9   Petersburg Feb[ruary] 21st 1859 –

Many thanks my own precious Mother, for your dear letter of last Thursday, which we found on the table on Saturday night – returning from the french theatre, where we saw a very pretty piece exceedingly well acted. Hampus and I laughed so at your disposal of all our old dresses and flowers – You must be glad to be rid of them.

Yesterday evening the whole Etholen family drank tea with us – Hampus and I stopped at a bakers shop on our way home from dinner, and chose some nice things there, then we came home, and rested ourselves – for you cannot think how little we sleep here, and how tired I get. A little before 7. Hampus awoke me; I put on my black dress and rose cap, in order to look like a "värdinna" [Swed. hostess], arranged the rooms, placed candlesticks, put the cakes, oranges and apples out for tea, and went into the drawingroom to receive my dear guests. How I wished for you! – Dr Collan is a frequent visitor of ours, he came last night too, and is a very kind, agreeable man. Uncle Adolf had been at a dinnerparty, and came later than all the others – We talked, played domino with the children, and had I thought a very nice evening. You can't think how nice it was to be hostess – and how strange it sounded in my ears to be thanked for the pleasant evening, and to have my hands kissed by the children. […]

We are sending you today 3. vol[umes] of Bulwers last novel, the fourth is not here yet – a packet of curry powder – a book for Ormelie and view of Sitka – the picture of ourselves will come home on Wednesday, and shall be sent by the next post. Hampus sought up Capt[ain] Alftan yesterday, and brought home all my things – many thanks for them my own Mother. […]

Has not my Hampus shown himself a prime correspondent. He sends you his dear love but cannot write this time, he is out on business. –

Goodbye my own darling Mother – dear love to all – I wrote to Marie and Mina G[ripenberg] by last post.

May God ever bless & preserve you is the fond prayer of Y[ou]r own loving Child

Annie

No. 10   Wednesday 23rd Feb[ruary] 1859
                                                                     S[ain]t Petersburg.

My own beloved Mother!
Your last letter, though addressed to Florence, was brought here yesterday morning, and I took the liberty to open it, knowing I should find something for me inside
– many, many thanks my own Mama, for writing by each post day, as we asked you
to do – soon, soon it will be impossible. You say my last letter contained nothing or
little – I know it was so – but forgive me my Mother – Hampus was talking to me
all the time, and Florence was there too, and we were joking together, but since then
you have had a terribly long letter, with which I trust you were well pleased.
[…] This day three weeks was our wedding day! I have just taken out my wedding
dress, and put it on my bed to look at – I am so glad to have it with me, it is a remembrance of that happy day;
    We have most wonderful weather, after two clear days, and frosty nights, it has
now again changed to rain and snow, and the streets are one deluge of puddles. I
drove with Adalbert to the Nybergs yesterday – Hampus could not come – It took us
half an hour to get there – fortunately they were at home, and glad to see us – Little
Anna has grown such a fine, handsome child – they are nice people; tomorrow they
promised to call upon us and Fru Makzotoff too – her husband was here yesterday,
& excused his Wife, who caught cold in church. She must be a well educated person,
judging by the list of books she has given us to purchase for them at New York – how
I long to buy books and music, & many other things. […]
    I will tell you, why our letters generally are double postage, though single weight,
because we can scarcely ever get them finnished by 1. o'clock, having so many in-
terruptions, and after 1 – they are double. My last letter was also stamped with 2.
stamps & the post sent the servant back to say there must be extra 11. kop[eks] why
I cannot conceive.
    Dear Aunt Mathilda's letter to you was so kind – I rejoice so much to see her, and
hope they will be fond of us both. I have already assisted Hampus in correcting &
translating an english letter to the Company at S[ain]t Francisko. It was so pleasant
to be of some use, though Hampus knows english so well, he scarcely requires much
help. – I think we shall be some time in California, as Hampus has business to settle
there – and as we must be at Sitka by the 1st June, we have not much time to spare
– Everything takes such time here – it was not before the day before yesterday, that
all was settled, and today the Secretary brought 240. half imperials in gold, which
were handed over to me to count, and are now sealed, & locked up in my drawer
– the rest of the money we get in bills on England & Germany I believe. Hampus has
been out a long time already, but I know he begun a letter to you last night, and has
been studying your last, I know not how many times. I have written to my father
in law – Hampus wished me to do so – is it not strange his not coming to take leave
of us? […]

And now I must bid you Goodbye – this is the last letter from S[ain]t Petersburg – May our gracious Father be with you my beloved Mother! May His Blessing also accompany us on our journey – [...]

From Warsovie I write again –

God ever bless you is the prayer of Y[ou]r own attached, & loving Child

Annie

No. 11   S[ain]t Petersburg Feb[ruary] 25.
friday morn[in]g 1859

My own most precious darling Mother! The last letter from this town, which has grown dear to my heart – I have been so happy here. My own Darling! Goodbye – Farewell! and God in His mercy ever bless and keep you, and accompany us with His Blessing on this our long, long journey! – Thank you for your dear letter just received! O I would have been so disappointed not to hear from you. Pray God to bless us my own Mother! and that I may never forget to thank Him for His wonderful goodness and mercy!

O Mama! these have been happy days! I could have embraced our dear rooms, I quite love them –.

Our photographs are by all called beautiful – My Hampus is admirable, so am I, except that having no fitting black dress, the blue is light and makes one look rather thick. Hampus is delighted with mine! May you be so too – Think I kiss and love you, when you look at it – I was thinking of you my own Mother! – Here are my cards – one for you – one for Marie, one for Uncle Charles, and one for Eugenie – Hampus forgot to leave out his, but I will send you one from Dresden – And now once more Adieu my precious Mother – from Warshau more –

We have a lovely day – Dearest love to you and much to all friends, & thank dear Uncle C[harles] and Tante Albertina for their letters –

I fold you to my heart, and think you lay your dear hands on my head and give me y[ou]r Blessing – Your own loving Child

Annie

Adjö, älskade mor. – Photografien af Anna och mig är öfverlemnad åt T[ant]e Margareta. – Jag är aftagen i full skrud och borde derföre vara i styl med Anna. – Ännu en gång Adjö, älskade saknade mor. Måtte vi en gång råkas ännu. Helsa vor älskvärda Marie Langenskjöld ifrån Mammas

tillgifnaste son

J. H. Furuhjelm

[Swed. Goodbye beloved Mother. The photograph of Anna and me has been given to Aunt Margareta. I am in gala and am therefore in the same style as Anna. – Once again goodbye, beloved precious Mother. May we once meet again. Give our love to our amiable Marie Langenskjöld from Your most loving son J. H. Furuhjelm.]

No. 12   *Dunaburg.* Sunday Feb[ruary] 27.
                                                                   6½ ev[enin]g 1859

My own Darling Mother!

Having to wait here for horses, we immediately avail ourselves of the opportunity of sending you a few lines, to tell you, so far, so well. We left S[ain]t P[eters]b[ur]g at 2. on friday and went all through the night, finding our coach ready, waiting for us at Pskoff. I cannot say we were comfortable, Florence and I packed up into a small, narrow space, but at least we were not cold. –

We went on all day, and stopped last night at an Inn, where we got in Emperors rooms, had beds made up, and slept very well indeed till 6. this morning, when we got up had coffee and proceeded on our journey, my dear Hampus sitting beside me. Now we are dining, and go through the night. – I have been telling Hampus about the Schaeffers kindness to you at Darmstadt, and hope I have prepared him to like them. There is an old piano in the room, which I played my old tunes on.

How is my own Mother? How I look forward to getting a letter at Dresden – It is snowing hard, we have difficulty to get on –

Goodbye and God bless you my own Mother. Florence and Hampus wish to write. I am always thinking of you, and am so happy – My dear love to all –Y[ou]r own loving Child

                                                                              Annie

My own dearest Mother,

As far as this, we now are on our way to Warshaw having had a pleasant journey nothing particular occuring since we left S[ain]t Petersburg. The country is flat, desolate and now covered with snow; the wolf I saw this morning skulking close to the wood looked not at all out of its place – a good deal more comfortable than any at the Zoological Gardens. My own Mother this is all I have to say you do not know and have not heard everyday.

  Your own loving
  Florence
  Give my love to everybody.

Sist af alla går jag att lemna vår älskade, saknade moder underrättelse om min egen dyra Anna och Florence: båda äro de friska och glada samt den förra vid lika gladt lynne som förrut. Hvad mig åter beträffar, så känner jag mig så lycklig att sitta bredvid Annas varma sida. –

Vår resa går långsamt dels tillfölje deraf att vi få vänta på hästar dels [..?] deraf att snön ligger djup; – men bara vi hinna till Warschawa så blifva vi ju oberoende af alla dessa olägenheter. Adjö, älskade Moder. – Nästa gång hoppas vi kunna skrifva ifrån Warshawa.

Mammas tillgifne

J. H. Furuhjelm

[Swed. Now it is my turn to let you know about my own precious Anna and Florence: both are healthy and happy and the former in as cheerful a mood as before. As far as I am concerned I feel so happy to sit at Anna's warm side. We travel slowly, partly because we must wait for horses, partly because the snow is so deep; but if only we get to Warsaw we shall no longer depend on such matters. Goodbye dear Mother. We hope to be able to write to you from Warsaw next time. Your loving J. H. Furuhjelm]

No. 13   Warschawa den 4. Mars 1859 –

Good morning my own most darling Mother! This is your Childs twenty third Birthday! in spirit I have felt your warm kisses on my cheeks, and heard all your dear wishes for my wellbeing, and received your Blessing; I have also been with you my beloved Mother and gone over in my mind all the happy birthdays, I have spent with you, surrounded by your love: O how I thank you from the depth of my heart for all you have been to me, for y[ou]r tender love, and for all you have ever taken such care and trouble to teach me. O Mama! now I feel so deeply, how much I owe you – now that I am away from you, and married to one, whom it is my greatest wish and desire to make as happy as it is possible for human beings to be. I feel so thankful to you, for having taught me what Life is – what its real meaning is – and what our aim and object is as inhabitants of this world. A whole new world is now opening itself before my soul – Life's earnest seems to have begun and I can only day by day pray God more fervently, that He would graciously teach me to do my duty assiduously and give me a pure & a clean heart, and an increasing desire to love and serve Him who has ever been so merciful towards me. – I thank you my own Mother, for having led my mind on the right way, and for having taught me, that "to Love and fear God, and serve Him, is the first & greatest commandment" and that with true and living Faith, even dark and painful days when they come, can become light, and peaceful. – And now my own Mother, what shall I tell you about our journey? I leave all descriptions to Florence, who is such a good hand at such like – and especially as I know she has already written all and everything about our awfully tiresome journey. No words of mine can describe how glad I was when we finally reached this town, and found ourselves lodged in a clean, large, handsome & well arranged Hotel. O I was, & am so tired and tonight at 9½ we start by the Express for Breslau, where we hope to arrive at 12 tomorrow forenoon; On Sunday we will be at Dresden, and I shall see my own dearest Mrs Hawthorne. There too,

I trust, we will be met by a sweet letter from you, to which you will immediately receive an answer –

The Warshau Ballet is, as you perhaps know, the best in Europe, and we had hoped to be able to get tickets for last nights representation, but unfortunately it so happened, that yesterday was the Emperor's birthday,[52] or some such day, and it was a free night, for which no tickets were sold, but cast about on the streets for anyone to pick up, and no respectable people go on such nights. We drove out in the afternoon, bought a p[ai]r of boots & gloves for 60 kop[eks] – very good indeed – a wide-awake for Hampus, and brown veil for myself. –

This minute Hampus has given me such a very pretty gold bracelet, in gold links with a locket hanging to it; Florence is drawing the pattern. It is so very pretty and at Dresden I will get his hair to put in it – Was it not sweet of him, my own darling husband – We are going to drink champagne today, in honor of the day, and your health too sweetest Mother dear – Now I must go and pack up our things – therefore Goodbye and God bless you my beloved Mother. Give my love to Marie and her husband & many thanks to Faster [Swed. aunt, father's sister] for her kind letter and love to all dear friends. A fond kiss to you, Ormelie & love to dear Babette from Y[ou]r own Child

Annie

No. 14   *Dresden*. March 7th 1859

My own most precious Mother!
From this dear old familiar place, I send you my hearts fondest greeting and many, many thanks for your dear and most welcome letter, which Mrs Hawthorne sent me this morning by faithful old Jacob. I was very disappointed yesterday on arriving here, to find no letter from you sweetest Mama, but hoped and was not again disappointed, it would come today – O how happy I am to hear you are well and getting on well my most dearest Mother! Our letters to you, can surely not be more welcome or longed for, than yours are to us, and I only grieve to think the time has come, when distance forbids us to hear as often as the heart would wish. I hope you received our short letters from Dunaburg and long ones from Warshau we have tried as much as possible to write when ever we were at any post station, knowing how you would long to hear from your children. Our journey from Warshau went fast and well – We left it by the nighttrain on friday 5½ aftern[oon] and reached Dresden, yesterday morning at 4 – On getting out, our first discovery was, that the secretary having our passports and baggage [..?], was not there; he had gone on when we changed trains at Görlitz – The

---

52   Actually not the Emperor's birthday (Alexander II was born on 17th April 1818), but the 4th anniversary of his accession to the throne. (This information was kindly provided by Mr. Jerzy Timoszewicz, Warsaw, chief editor of *Pamiętnik Teatralny*.)

people were however civil enough to let us get our luggage out, trusting to our honesty in not claiming other than our own property. We drove to the Hotel Bellevue.

Wednesday 9th I was disturbed sweetest Mama, and have not been able to continue my letter – But today it must go, for you may not be kept waiting any longer – Thank you so much for your dear letter, which made me so happy; it is so comfortable for me to see you are in good spirits and ever rejoicing at your childrens happiness – Indeed my precious Mother I understand your feeling and as far as it is possible for human creatures to foreout see, you have every reason to believe your childs constant happiness is secured – I am very thankful we will be so entirely dependant upon each other, as we have of course to make acquaintance with each others faults, none of us being so blind as to suppose the other to be without any. –

He deserves to be so happy! O dear Mother! Gods mercies towards me have been wonderful! how good, how gracious has He not shown Himself towards me this year! O that I may rightly understand, and fully appreciate the extent of His loving kindness and that I may send up my hearts warmest thanks day by day. – O! that I may ever be a dear, loving Wife to him – a comfort and a Joy, as long as our lives are spared to one another.

We were so glad to hear about Papas visit and attention to you – It was a great pity we did not meet again – I hope he will answer my letters – and trust there will ever be a good Verhältniss [Ger. relationship] between us – Poor Esperance [Furuhjelm]! but staying with you, darling Mama, must do her good. –

And now, what do you say to Carl being here? You cannot think how I fell from the clouds with astonishment, and how happy I was to see him – O! how wonderfully kind Mrs H[awthorne] is – truly she is an angel of Peace – no one has such lovely thoughts of kindness as she has – I cannot describe how delightful it is to see the two together, and to see how happy they are to meet after all the trouble and anxiety they have gone through – I fully hope they may be married this year – and that dear Carl will get a good place and be able to live comfortably on his income –

Dearest Hampus bought such a sweet silk dress for her yesterday which we have given Oehlshlägel[?] to make up for her, with high and low body. She was so pleased – I cannot say what a delightful feeling it is to give to others – Hampus is such a good dear brother to her – Dearest Mama how have I deserved such a husband? but I am so very happy – and hope to make him so too. [...] We have ordered our photographs, and hope they will be good ones – Mrs Duffin, Miss Macleans, Miss Jones & Mrs H[awthorne] get a copy, then 4. to H[elsing]f[o]rs, one to Pauline S., 1. for Florence and Carl and 1 for Lambs & Cautleys. Have you received ours yet? I do trust you liked it – I have never seen so beautiful a one – it is like an engraving – [...] We are not going to Paris, and I believe not to Darmstadt either. We telegraphed to London to ask when the american C[ompany] ship Garitza would be ready to start, and the answer was by the 15th April – else Hampus would have been obliged to go alone to England tomorrow, and leave me here with Florence and Wickström to follow next Monday – as he could not bear the thought that Carl and Florence should be separated

*Anna and Ham-
pus Furuhjelm in
Dresden 1859.*

one day when he has time to remain till 15 March – You may fancy how unhappy I was – I could not bear the thought of being left behind, & coming on alone, & my Hampus introducing himself alone in England; at first I put myself against it, but then, better feelings, & above all the good angel Mrs H[awthorne]'s influence got the better of me, & I saw how selfish I was, & how beautiful of Hampus to make such a proposal – and then my reward was, that at 11½ at night the answer came from London, & put all right again, and made me so happy. He sends his dear love – I am to say: "Hampus is so busy, he is changing money, and Hampus is sure Mama will forgive him if he does not write this time". –

The damask cloth and napkins are beautiful, and not a bit spoilt. And now my own beloved Mama I must again finnish, but hope to write soon again – Hampus is waiting for me to go out – [...]

Ever and ever Y[ou]r own fondly loving Child

Annie

No. 15   Sunday. March 13th 1859.
                                                         Dresden –

My own dearest, darling Mama!

Whilst my sposo [Italian 'husband'] is reclining on the sofa opposite me, and Mrs Duffins Mina is on her knees packing up our linnen, which we bought and had made up here, I take to my pen to send you one more letter from this dear town, where I have always spent such happy days. Darling Mama you cannot conceive how little time I have had to write or do anything – I don't know how it is – but certainly the days have been too short, and we have generally kept dear Mrs H[awthorne] waiting for dinner, or any other meal, we happened to be at – I wish my darling Mother, you could see the things we have purchased here – they are so good, and so well made, you would be so pleased if you could look at our stores which are now being packed up. I will tell you what we have bought. –

    3. doz[en] dayshifts. ½ doz[en] trowsers. 4. doz[en] pockethankerchiefs. 2. doz[en] trowsers. 2. peignoirs. 6 doz[en] towels. 2 doz[en] p[ai]rs of sheets, 1 doz[en] of which are double and fine, the other doz[en] single & coarser, 6 doz[en] pillow-shifts. 1 doz[en] small tablecloths. 6 doz[en] tablenapkins – 2 large tablecloths for 24. persons and 4. doz[en] tablenapkins – 2 tablecloths for 12. and 2. doz[en] tablenapkins. 6 doz[en] teanapkins all these things are worked I mean hemmed, and embroidered in red *A.F.* and the coronet, was finnished in 3. days and cost 834 Th[alers] 12 gr[oschen] 5 pf[ennig]. In England we buy all cotton things – sheeting and toweling for the servants, nightgowns, nightcaps and trowsers and dressing-gowns for myself – pieces of cloth; stockings, dresspieces etc – etc – then I have ordered here a travelling bonnet, which is very pretty – dark brown straw, trimmed in and out with brown, costing 5 Th[a]l[ers] 15 gr[oschen] – two woolen dresses, one grey merino, and one [..?] brown reps, it looks quite like poplin, very handsome – Oehlschlägel[?] has made them to fit exceedingly well – also a black silk, heavy ripped silk cloak, lined with black and slightly wadded very handsome, costing 50 Th[alers] & from Hampus as Vielliebchen [Ger. philippine] a long black cloth trav-elling jacket – 11 Th[aler]s. Florence's silk dress is sweetly pretty. I am so happy for her – she will look so nice in it – I hope she will take great care of it – Now I think I have mentioned all the things we have bought except – 30 Th[aler]s worth of music. What do you think of it darling Mama. Wickström is quite equipped, we have hired a cook & a maid for me, who understands housekeeping and everything about a lady – she looks a very respectable person about 40. years of age, and I trust she will answer well.

    So this week has also come to an end, & tomorrow we must go – [...]

    Night 11¼. We have this minute come home from dearest Mrs Hawthornes, where we spent our last evening, and knelt down and prayed all together, before starting on our long and many distant journeys. May the blessing of God go and remain with us! O! that His Holy Spirit may abide with us, and cleanse our hearts from all unrighteousness. I cannot tell you how nice it was this evening – I thought of you my beloved Mother, and the last time we all knelt together in that house – Please God, it may not have been the last time. Everybody has been so kind and so fond of my Hampus, I cannot say how happy it makes me. […]

Hampus and I have just had prayers and now he is gone to bed, where I must soon follow him – but though it is 12. I would not sleep before I had written to you my precious Mother, knowing how much I shall have to do still tomorrow, and we must be at the train at a little before two. We are writing to Darmstadt to ask for your letter, and please God we shall find one in England. I long to hear how you liked our picture – I wonder how you will like these we send with Costi [von Schoultz] – I don't like them much.

O darling Mama! how are you! O that I could see you once more! May God Almighty be with you forever, and may I soon see y[ou]r precious handwriting again. Have you got our samovar, which we used at P[eters]b[ur]g & send as a re-membrance to you – kiss dearest little O[rmelie] – dear love to Babette, and I send her an almanach for this year – Love to Marie and Uncles and Aunts. I hope you like the beautiful head of Christ my Hampus chose for you – O! he never forgets you – and thinks of so many little nice things – My own precious! God bless him – I feel wonderfully tired always in my limbs – Mina was a great help to me – she packed very well indeed, and took home some work to do for me. Good night my own darling Mother. What are you doing now? God for ever bless you and us all – O such fond dear warm kisses from Your own own Child Annie

Good morning, darling Mama!
We are all packed and ready – Will you kindly distribute these little pictures of the Dresden gallery to our 4. Marshalks, we wished them to have a little memento of that day as well as our bridesmaids, & I sincerely hope and believe, none of them will think us "egenkär" [Swed. selfish], for wishing them to remember us and that day – Write to me about it to England sweetest Mother – Dearest love and many kisses I send you – God bless you my own beloved Mother is the ever constant prayer of
Y[ou]r own loving Child

Annie
14th March

No. 16   London. March 19th
                                              Edwards private Hotel No. 12
                                              Georg St[reet] Hann[over] Sq[uare]

Good morning my own precious Mother! You see by the above, that we are in old, well known quarters and I cannot tell you how well and how comfortably lodged we are. My first thought on arriving is always: "I wish darling Mama, could look in upon us, and see how happy we are, and how nice everything looks around us" –

O my Mother! God has been merciful beyond measure, in giving me such a husband! if you knew him as I do – and if you could see him now, you would indeed rejoice more than ever, and would feel even happier at your childs happy lot, than you did when we left you, six weeks ago yesterday.

To see the one you love happy – O! what can be more beautiful – and truly, I think I may humbly say "Hampus is happy" – his eyes and his smile are so bright, so sweet, it fills my whole heart with inward Joy and gratitude. His principles, his views and thoughts are the most upright and honest & noble – his wish is to do his duty strictly and unshrinkingly – indeed the russian american C[ompany] know not, what a jewel they have in him – he thinks of their interest as if it were his own and can't bear to squander their liberal supplies wantingly – I tell him, he is too good towards them – and ask him not to scruple about their money! Surely, when they send him to the end of the world, they must allow him to have the best of everything – besides which, they have to do their justice given unlimited means – why should he then not spend it? –

But now to tell you about our journey –

We left dearest Mrs H[awthorne] on Monday afternoon at ¼ to 3 – parting from many dear friends at once. Carl and Costi too. God bless them both, the dear creatures. By Costi we sent several photographs, also some collars, our hair and a long letter, all of which things I hope will reach you safely [..? ..?] very long – My german maid came at 2 – and is here with us – I like her very much –

We travelled all through the night and came to Cologne at 8½ – an hour afterwards we started for Ostend, arrived at 6 – drove down to the Dover steamer, and got under weigh an hour afterwards. It blew a perfect storm, we were 9. hours crossing and O! so tremendously sick – even my dearest husband was sick! Sailor though he is – he does not remember when he was so last – At 5. we reached Dover and slept at the Dover Castle Hotel – very comfortable, clean and respectable – had breakfast at 11 and left at 12 reaching London at 3½ – We had a very nice english *gentleman* with us in the carriage, who spoke with us and was in every way very kind – for our two servants were put into a firstclass carriage at Dover, though they showed their 2nd class tickets, so Hampus was charged [..?] for it, by one of the conductors at the last station before London – when the man came to our door with the charge, this gentleman said it was wrong of them to charge anything, seeing foreign servants could not be expected to know where to go, and that it was their fault for not attending better. He said he would ask to speak to the inspector in London, & was sure the money would be returned – He did so immediately on arriving, and we had to sign a paper but as yet nothing has been returned. He asked if he could do anything more for us, recommended us to this delightful Hotel, and after thanking him sincerely, we parted. –

Was not this the *real* englishman? We drove here first, chose our rooms, had our things brought up and then went with Florence to Henry [Phillips] – Edward opened the door, and was very glad to see us – Henry was in the painting room, where we immediately went, and saw dear kind Henry – who received us warmly and affectionately. He seemed very pleased with my Hampus, and he liked him, and was delighted with his pictures. He paints beautifully – I was mostly struck by one of the light large pictures for Lady Walgrave "Memory". You may perhaps remember the sketch many years ago. He has now been painting it full length, and I cannot tell you, how exquisite I think it. Hampus was quite charmed with it. – [...]

We are going to the Opera tonight, if Henry can procure a box for us – we are to see Balfs new opera *Satanella*, which is making great furore here –

Last night we made a long list of all the things we require – Henry has kindly promised to help us in giving good addresses – he liked Costi very much, and I know will be very fond of my husband when he knows him better.

We have 3. nice rooms – one drawingroom with lovly carpet and all that is nice and comfortable and 2. bedrooms, one off the drawingroom, serving Hampus as dressingroom – our bedroom is very large – We pay one guinea a day for them, and are in the 2nd story. Now my own beloved Mama I must conclude – [...] Tell Marie as we did not go to Paris I could not buy her dresses – Love to Esperance – how is she, and how do you like her – Dearest Florence is well – I must send and ask if she is writing too. Kiss sweet Ormelie and much love to Babette, I am sorry Jacob did not succeed in finding a better almanach – Florence has just come – she will write a few lines here – God bless you my own beloved Mother Y[ou]r own loving Child

Annie

My own dearest Mother, As writing still is not easy for me, forgive my not writing a letter yet. I am well and happy, very happy. It is so pleasant to be here. About the last week Costi will tell you all. About the present I shall write as soon as possible. I do not know how long I shall be in London – Anna is writing to Nettleden now.

To Uncles and Aunts I shall write when I can. Do not judge of my love by these lines – Before all thoughts are in order I can not write.

Ever Your own loving and most grateful Florence

No. 17   *Cheltenham* March 21st 1859

My own beloved Mother,
You will be glad to see the head of my letter – here Florence and I are staying with our dearest friends since Saturday night, when we arrived from town, [...] Only think my own Mama, we are most likely leaving England by the steamer next Saturday the 26th and in that case start from London next friday for Liverpool. The only alternative is next Saturday or Saturday week the 2nd April. Hampus was in great distress what to do – his duty is pressing sorely upon him, for he fears the Company

might think him neglectful, and tell him he has been amusing himself, instead of doing his business – Now you know, we only arrived in England last Wednesday, and immediately went about our work – so we have certainly not been idle – but those 9. days at Dresden have put us out – though we would never breathe such a thing to dear happy Florence. I have told my dearest husband, never for one moment to put me into consideration, but to do exactly what he thinks right and best to do – If he finds we can not stay on to the 2nd April, then I am perfectly ready to go on friday, though I shall only have seen my friends a very short time, and some not at all – and they will not have seen him – If, on the other hand he cannot get ready this week, I am most delighted to stay, and hope he will in that case come here on a short visit. I wrote to him yesterday and will do so again today, and hope to receive a letter from him by this evenings post. – […]

Thank God Mrs Savary is much better, in fact she looks better than ever, and goes to church. They had so much to ask us and were perfectly excited with Joy. The two dear ladies gave me a beautiful brooch as a wedding present – it belonged to Mrs Savary. It is amathists and topaces with a splendid topace in the centre and embossed silver setting round it, and then a row of alternate amathists & topaces round the edge. It makes great effect – Was it not kind of them. When I came home and showed it to Aunt Mathilda, she run upstairs after her "wedding present" which was a most handsome gold bracelet. You draw it over your hand, and then tighten it to fit your arm. A large carbuncle, with a diamond in its centre forms the clasp, and a peice of gold hangs loose like a ribbon. It is beautifully worked, soft links you know. I wonder if you at all understand my discription. Also a large family Bible for Hampus and me, but I have not seen it yet. Was it not so very kind. – O! how much love and kindness God has thrown in my way. –

I must tell you about what we ordered in London. Hampus has had a regular plate chest made by Pickett, and ordered such handsome things to be put in it. 1. doz[en] of every kind in real silver, tea and coffeepot, 2. sugar basins, cream jug, sugar spoons, salt cellars & spoons, fishknifves & breadbasket and mustard pot all silver, and 2. doz[en] plated things, with my initials and coronet. He would receive no refusal – I beseeched him to have H.A.F. but he would not hear of it, and said it should be done as he chose. I understand quite well why he wishes it, but I should so much much better have liked his initials. All the linen we purchased at Dresden is worked the same way. Then he bought a beautiful dressing case with engraved silver tops. O! he is *so* kind and only thinks of how he can give me pleasure. How did I ever deserve such a husband – He is so noble minded, so very sweet and gentle. O Mama! I love him with all my heart, and hope I may make him very very happy. You cannot think how I miss him, and how I long to see him again. I have his picture with me; the Lambs liked it very much. […]

It is perfectly wonderful to see with what love and affection all think of Florence & sympathize with her. Every one is ready to receive Carl were he to come to England. If they are not to be married in Finland, and not at Gothenbourg, why this is the only place remaining, though how could you come over darling Mama. And what will you do sweet Mother? if I could only know where you would live supposing Ormelie leaves you. Surely you would remain in Finland – seeing you have all y[ou]r things there, and please God we live so long, Finland is always our country, seeing our husbands are born and bred there. –

Afternoon. […] I had a letter from dear Fanny Bayley with much love to you – but none from Hampus. I cannot hear from him before tomorrow morning, and hope not to be disappointed then. Every body hopes to see him, they will take no refusals – unfortunately he dislikes parties and is shy of strangers.

Behold what it is to have a Wife with friends! –

And now my own precious Mother, I must bid you goodbye, & write to Hampus.

Dear love to Ormelie and Babette and all friends – O darling Mama, when shall I hear from you next? I hope you will write to Sitka, or have done so already – It is perfectly uncertain which route we take, over New York or Barbados. God bless you my own darling Mother – many fond kisses from Y[ou]r own most loving child

Annie.

No. 18   Sunday London March 27th
                                                   10 night. Edwards Hotel

My own beloved Mother,
What are you about? And why do you not write? I cannot say how unhappy I am at your long silence, for I fear I shall leave England and all dear to me, without another line from you. It is 3. weeks tomorrow since your last letter – O Mama! what is the matter with you? Are you ill or what has happened? I wrote to Ellen Bechtold asking her to forward your letter to me and received the answer some days ago, saying there was no letter for us. All this makes me very sad – for *when* shall I see your precious handwriting again? Months and months may pass ere I get a letter from you – before I can get answers to all the many letters I have written. Can you suppose us as sailing already? but no – you knew we were coming to England – then why have you not written. –

But I will not distress you my own precious Mother, but try to remember all I have done and seen since I sent my last letter from Cheltenham. If I remember right we sent our last on Tuesday just after hearing from Hampus, that I might expect him that evening. Great was my Joy to see him again, and to introduce him to the dear kind Lambs, who received him most warmly and kindly. As Hampus could only stay one night Aunt Mathilda had asked our friends, Mrs Savary and her sweet Mother, and the Bradshows to tea, who wished very much to make his acquaintance. They seemed all very much charmed with him, especially the nice Captain B. who, though suffering from gout for some time, came out that evening, on purpose to meet Hampus. He would call me "Mrs Sitka or Madame von Clop Sticks" finding my name an outrageously difficult one to pronounce. He wished to give us a dinner party, so did Mrs Dalgell, and they were both very much disappointed when they heard Hampus proposed returning the next morning. I cannot say how very glad I am the Lambs saw him, even though it was such a very short acquaintance, and I know they are glad themselves. On Wednesday we paid our farewell visits to all friends, and packed our things in the forenoon, so as to have the rest of the day before us. Aunt Mathilda was out shopping for me, and bought patterns of different kinds in case I should ever require them. The evening passed quietly and merrily – we laughed a great deal. We each got a very nice photograph of Dr and Mrs Lamb, which gave us endless pleasure. On Thursday morning Aunt M[athilda] prayed for us before starting, imploring Gods Blessing & Guidance. O! it was so beautiful – I felt so thankful, and so calm and happy, though the tears ran down my cheeks, and it felt like parting from dear, dear friends. […]

On friday Mary [Cautley] and I went out shopping and chose one of Collard's semi grand pianos for 100 £. I tried several and was particularly charmed with Erards Flügel [Ger. grand pianos] – but they were too expensive – 160 guineas. However the one we have bought is a very nice and good one, & is to be packed in a tin case, and sent on board Garitza at Plymouth. Mary, Henry and Florence dined with us that evening, and very pleasant it was. We had a charming dinner and plenty of champagne, and never ceased wishing you could have been with us. O Mama! this is always my first thought, when I am in any way enjoying myself – Could darling Mama but be with us – Is it not a fairytale to think of your daughter living comfortably at an hotel in London, and being able to see her friends, and rejoice with them? O! it is more than wonderful.

My maid began packing yesterday – It is perfectly awful the quantity of things we have and the fatigue of packing them is not small –

Mr Saturn called upon us this morning – I wrote to ask him to call upon me, as I wished to see him before going on so long a journey, and to so distant a land. I have been often having pain in my left side, and feeling so languid and uneasy, I wanted to know if my heart was affected – He told me no – and that it was all nervousness and of no consequence at all. He was very kind and recognized Florence immediately, and remembered you. We went to the Crystal Palace in the afternoon with Henry, & spent some very nice hours there. Henry got a wheelchair for me, that I should not tire myself too much, and wheeled me along everywhere. Mr Groves, a very nice young man indeed and secretary of the Palace, Mr Ferglenson the manager, and Mr Scott Russell, all were with us. Mr Groves wheeled me a long way, and made me the present of an exquisite bouquet he had cut for me there. Florence got one too. Was it not kind and nice? Henry says we may be very proud of that – he never remembers any lady having got a bouquet in the Crystal Palace. Hampus was delighted, though of course overpowered at first, as everyone is at the first sight. I thought so much of you my darling Mother, and the afternoon we spent there. Henry came home to dinner with us. We found a beautiful silver cup on the table, when we came home, which he and Susan presented to us – It is a very handsome one, and we immediately filled it with champagne and ice, and drank their healths, & all friends, and our beloved Mothers health quite alone. O! how we wished for you. –

Henry has taken Hampus to the Cosmopolitan Club, so I must read alone and go to bed, seeing it is 11. o'clock past. God bless you my own darling!

Monday 28. Again no letter? darling Mama what am I to think of your silence – I had a letter from my Father in law, but he did not mention you, nor Esperance, which is wonderful indeed. We are now in great confusion, packing such heaps of things. I cannot tell you how I long for Sitka – our stay here and everywhere else has been exceedingly pleasant, but still we both wish for our own home, & long for the day when we have no more packing and unpacking to do – Fancy your Annie going to the West Indies? I have had some cool dresses made, as everyone tells me I shall be roasted.

Monday Night. Now I must finnish this my own Mother, and write to you from my new writing case, which my darling Hampus gave me today, and which is most beautiful made of dark green morocco and nice fittings. He spoils me with all he does for me. He would like to give me what ever he reads in my eyes I wish for – Well sweet Mother we are going down to Nettleden tomorrow, and return the following day, leaving Florence with dear Mary. It will be painful to part from her, and sometimes I can hardly believe it to be true – my heart feels quite heavy when I look at her and think of you, and my old home and all the happy days of my childhood and the earnest Life opening itself to me now – though I am O! thank God so *perfectly, perfectly happy*, I cannot help feeling sad at parting from Europe and all the beloved ones I believe [i.e. leave] behind. I always go to my Hampus when I feel sad and depressed, and cry on his shoulders, and he kisses away my tears and comforts me. O! how good, how sweet and warm hearted and precious he is – And how great Gods goodness towards me has been, in giving me such a husband, whom I never can love and esteem sufficiently.

We have spent a great deal of money but have also got such delightful things. I wish darling Mama you could see our plate chest, which is so beautifully & amply filled. Elizabeth gave us a very pretty silver cruet stand, and Henry a silver cup.

[Florence:] My own darling Mother, while Hampus is reclining on the soffa and Anna is seated beside him – both romanticising – I take at one of the pens which are [..?] to write a few words to you – they shall only consist in an earnest entreaty – that you would not leave us without letters. This long silence is perfectly dreadful – O Mother, darling, dearest, surely you are quite well? O when shall your letter come. From Carl no letter either. Tomorrow we go to Nettleden – then I shall write you much [end of Florence's lines].

We may indeed say that we are completely well fitted out for five years at least and even more. Hampus bought the swedish bible for Wickström, and I wrote his

name in it, and said it was from you. He asked me to thank you most respectfully.
I hope he will read and love that precious book, and profit by it – [...]

My own Mother, did Costi give you the lock of our hair, which I sent by him
– Tell dear kind Eugénie, there is a photograph of us, ordered for her at Dresden.
Fancy, we have not yet heard from you, if our first picture made in Russia, arrived
safely – I could, and have cried when I think of how long it is since your last sweet
letter. Now my own precious Mother Good night, sleep well! What are you doing
now? O! if I could but know – could but see you once more.

Dearest love to all kind friends & relatives. "Ingen nämd och ingen glömd" [Swed.
Nobody mentioned and nobody forgotten]. God for ever bless you – May His Holy
Spirit be with you and give you Peace – A fond kiss to dearest little Ormelie and
love to Babette and a warm warm kiss to yourself from

Y[ou]r fondly, fondly fond Child

Annie

Tuesday 29th Ten thousand warm thanks my beloved mother for your sweet letter
which I at last received this morning to my infinite Joy and happiness – My darling
Hampus was just going to send a telegraphic dispatch today to console and beruhigen
[Ger. set my mind at rest] me. I will send another letter from Southampton my precious Mother. Thank God you are well, and nothing has happened, as I pictured to
myself – This must go now and the dentist is waiting for me, therefore farewell so
long – I will answer you from Nettleden, I hope to begin there at least – We opened
Aunt Mary's letter at Hampus wish to see what was in it, but only read [..?] letter.
The enveloppe is too heavy to send now – God bless you my own darling.

A fond kiss from Y[ou]r own Child

Annie

No. 19   *Woodside. April 1st 1859.*
                                                                           12. Night

My own darling Mama,
[...] Well darling Mama, we went down to Nettleden on Tuesday stopped there one
night, had a cold though charming drive in a snowstorm through Ashridge Park up
to the house, saw the hall, green house, chapel and some of the rooms, came home
again, & got ready to depart – Dear kind Mary! it was so very delightful to see her
and her sweet husband in their lovely little home, and O such a comfort to know
our darling Florence would be in such good hands. –

It was a hard, hard parting! – but O! it might have been so very much worse. Thank
God she is there! and may she soon be married to Carl, is my most sincere prayer

– O sweet Mother! May we all meet again in some years! O that it may be the Will of our Heavenly Father! Well sweetest Mother, we came to Southampton in the very nick of time – for our steamer left the docks this morning at 9. and all our luggage was obliged to be put on board before – after that we had the whole day to ourselves, and went into the town to look about, order some soda powders, pills and dry lemonade, and some cool clothes & dressinggown for Hampus, for which things we had no time left us in London. It was very cold, indeed these last few days have been quite sharp.

How are you my ownest darling? You cannot think how anxious I was not to hear from you, & O! how thankful, when y[ou]r letter finally came. […]

Give dear Marie a fond kiss & many thanks for her sweet letter, which I will answer some day, & send your letters darling Mama to Uncle Etholén, he will give them, and you the proper direction. –

Good night my precious Mother. It is nearly 1. & I am very tired and must still write a few lines to Aunt Mathilda – God ever bless and keep you & your whole house. Amen

Saturday afternoon 2nd
Outside Southampton

Here we are my own precious Mama, and I am seated in our little cabin writing these lines to you, after having first dressed and washed myself and made myself comfortable for dinner. This "Magdalena" is a very large handsome steamer, many passengers of all nations and conditions, a great [..?] and confusion prevails every-where, but we hope to be soon in order, and please God we have a good passage, I daresay we shall be very comfortable. The bells are ringing and the pilot is on board I believe, so we shall soon move, and these last fare well words will be conveyed to you my own darling Mother. We have both prayed most earnestly for Gods Blessing, and that He would guide us, & protect us during this voyage – O! how safe we feel confided to His never failing care, how thankfully we can go on our way rejoicing, knowing that not a hair on our heads can fall without His pleasure –

I have been thinking so much of you my own beloved Mother, and the day I went over one of the large East Indian steamers with you, and admired it so much. Who would then have thought I should so soon be on a similar one, not only as a gazer on but a passenger to S[ain]t Thomas – Changes! Strange changes!

O my own beloved Mother, when shall I again behold your handwriting. O! how I shall kiss your dear, precious letter. I earnestly pray for our Fathers most gracious care and protection over you. Be happy! Be cheerful my Mother. Your children are so and pray for you, & think of you continually with the most tender love; and commit you lovingly and confidingly to our Lords precious keeping.

[…] Fare well Europe! Fare well thou dear country where my precious Mother is – O God! protect it and her, for ever & ever Amen. God protect this country and my Florence & all dear friends over the world. –

Hampus wishes to add a few lines – therefore my own most precious Mother Goodbye –

I shall soon begin a journal for you – O may Gods blessed angels watch over you, and y[ou]r whole house prays your own most fondly loving & grateful Child

Annie

Saknade dyra Mamma!
Med ankare uppe och under full fart sänder jag Mamma vor sista helsning ifrån gamla verldens stränder. Måtte den nådige Guden bevara Mamma och låta oss en gång återse hvarandra. Måtte han ock vid detta tillfälle låta mig kunna säga: Jag har varit en ömm man för älskade, dyra Anna! Ja måtte Han nådeligen höra min bön. Mammas

tilgifnaste son J. H. Furuhjelm

[Swed. My precious dear Mother! With the anchor aweigh and at full speed I send you our last greeting from the shores of the old world. May God in his mercy preserve you and let us see each other again. I wish to God that on that occasion I shall be able to say: I have been a good, loving husband for my beloved, dear Anna. May God in His infinite mercy hear my prayer. Your most loving son J. H. Furuhjelm.]

No. 20   On board "Magdalena". Atlantic
                                                            April 13th 1859

My own most precious Mother!
After more than one weeks voyage over the Atlantic, I at last am able to take up my pen and write to you my beloved Mother, a thing which I would have wished to do long ago, but unfortunately have been hitherto prevented by sickness. Even now my hand shakes, and it is difficult to keep yourself steady on your chair, the swell is so great. We have most lovely weather, and the West Indian heat is gradually beginning to make itself felt. I trust, you have this day Wednesday received my last letter from Europe, which I sent on shore by the pilot, and you are consequently thinking of us as sailing over the deep blue Ocean. I need not tell you I was sick for you know I am no good sailor – though considering all things I think I have been wonderfully "rask" [Swed. well]. Now, we have got into smooth water, it is rather disappointing to be sick still, though I generally feel better every other day. –

O! my precious Mother! I have had wonderful thoughts of late – a feeling of intense solemnity comes over me sometimes, combined with deep, deep gratitude. O Mother! I think I have every reason to believe a great, great Blessing is in prospect for us! And O! my Mother! how much I have thought of you – how much I have longed to have you to speak to about it. I have prayed God to be with me, and if He should so have blessed me, to help me to prepare now for the right understanding of the great responsibility He puts into my hands. O Mama! I cannot say *how* happy I am! and how earnestly I thank God for all His wonderful mercies! I write to you so soon about it my Mother, because I hope you will send me all manner of instructions, and advices, such as only a loving Mother can give, from whom it is so beautiful for me to receive them. Thank God I am quite well excepting sickness, headache & sometimes momentary depression of spirits. But it has grown dark quite suddenly – so Good night sweetest Mother. I must go to join my darling Hampus on deck. –

Thursday Night 14. April. Still more wind, and an increase of swell, which will I fear make these lines very illegible – But I so wish to write a little bit every day if possible. It is nearly 9. the four men are dinging all manner of Waltzes and Polkas into my ears, which I would heartily wish to *be able* to escape hearing, seeing false notes are of no rare occurrence. Just now they have struck up that glorious ever welcome old "God save the Queen" and to it I gladly lend my ear. And so the Concert ends for tonight. This has been a lovely day, spent on deck all forenoon; but I am obliged to lie down before dinner, feeling so tired after some hours sitting on those hard benches upstairs. I have not been able to go down to any of the meals, having vainly attempted to do so several times, but always with bad success. I am reading a most interesting book just now, the 3rd since we are on board, called "The life of Charlotte Brontë" by Gaskell [published in 1857], being the collection of letters written and received by "Currer Bell" [pen name of C. Brontë] the wonderful author of "Jane Eyre" and "Shirley" and would recommend it to your prompt perusal, if it is possible to procure at H[elsing]f[o]rs. In S[ain]t P[eters]b[ur]g you would certainly find it. I am only sorry not to have her works at hand, as there often occur quotations from them, and it is most interesting to see, how her own life and experience, is generally speaking depicted some where. You remember that wonderfully exciting description of the mad dog biting "Shirley" and her heroic courage in [..?..?] the son without saying a word to anyone? Well! that is a true picture of what her favourite sister Emily did, & she wrote it with "streaming eyes" as Gaskell says. Do try for the book sweet Mother. –

There is no small excitement on board, owing to some theatricals the officers have got up, and are making great preparations for. It is said to come off tomorrow evening, but I am afraid the weather will prove an impediment. And now my darling Mother I must again say Good night! And Gods Blessing be ever with you. What lovely clear nights you have now. and I hope spring is coming! I am sitting on a campstool, with my desk on my trunk but it shakes too much to continue. My Hampus is taking a cold bath downstairs, & when he comes up we will read and then I go to bed – or even I shall be there before he comes. Good night my own, own darling Mother. –

April 16th. My words were verified. It blew hard all day, and I was obliged to remain in bed, and be very sick and uncomfortable. My darling Hampus, has I see given you a minute and most correct description of how our days pass – has he not written a sweet letter, consequently there remains nothing for me but to speak in general about ourselves and everybody else. A set of more vulgar, ungentlemanly people, with only one or two exceptions, I never saw – the Spaniards especially so – and I would have thought them chevalresque, but then we must consider the specimen on board are not "first rate" – however there is one spanish family, to whom I am very partial, consisting of father (a german & from Berlin), mother, sister & two little boys of 4. and 2. The mother is a very sweet pretty lady of 22. married since the age of 14. She speaks very broken pretty german, as her husband speaks spanish perfectly well. The sister is the poor girl described in Hampus' letter, and the little boys are the prettiest and best behaved children on board. The eldest is dark & like his Mother very pretty – the youngest my pet, is a fair haired blue eyed little urchin, who only speaks a little german, and calls me "Viel liebe Frau" [Ger. Dear Madame]. I can never take my eyes off him, when he is near me – not that he is at all a beauty, but that there always is to me something intensely fascinating in childhood at that period. The only gentleman who speaks to me, is a Scotchman, Captain Montgomerie and a very nice, agreeable man. I asked him the other day, if he was aware part of his family had established themselves a few hundred years ago in Sweden,[53] which he did. […]

Darling Mama! do tell us what your plans are & where you intend settling in the event of sweet Ormelie being claimed by his parents. You know letters are so long in route, you may have left Finland ages before we can hear of it, therefore do write about your plans before, and keep in good spirits my precious Mother. […] – Tell all my friends how often I think of them, and how much I love them – but to none of them can I write before we are in our own distant Home. No words can express how I long for that moment! The farther we come and the shorter the distance becomes, the greater grows my desire. […]

Sunday 17th. We have got into the tradewinds, and are enjoying most lovely weather, though somewhat hot. I was well enough to attend prayers on deck this morning, and was very thankful. It is such a nice sight to see all the sailors in their white trowsers and blue shirts with their caps in their hands ready to hear the words of God; they looked so solemn and the whole scene was so I thought. I was only sorry the Captain left out so much, we had only the 2nd Lesson, no Litany and no Communion Service. How exquisitely blue the Atlantic is! last night when I came down into my Cabin, the moon was shining right in, and the sea looked like a vast [..?] of liquid silver; I looked out of the port, up at the stars, & sent you greetings – I wondered what you were doing my own darling Mother.

On Thursday morning I hope we shall see land again. I cannot say how I look forward to eating those delicious tropical fruits though Hampus says it is dangerous to eat much of them. We leave S[ain]t Thomas for Panama, the same day we arrive; now I pray we may have fine weather, and a speedy passage. I am growing so impatient to reach Sitka, and long to settle down into all my Hausfrau [Ger. housewife]

---

53   One branch of the noble family Montgomery moved from Scotland to Sweden in the 1720s and was enrolled in the Swedish House of Nobles in 1756.

duties, to unpack our linnen chests, and have everything arranged nicely in its proper place – to open our platechest etc – etc. But all this seems to be centuries off still. Do you know, we make and cause great excitement on board – we are as it appears the topic of conversation for all the spaniards and frenchmen, who shower question upon question upon Mr. Koschkin. Who are we? what are we? We must be tremendously rich, but very proud seeing we make no acquaintances, have the best cabin and two servants. Who was and what was my Father, am I of a very good family – what is Hampus' pay? Mr Koschkin replied 70.000 francs a year. And I was quite glad of the answer. What does it concern them how much we have. Then they think H[ampus] must be very jealous of me. He is afraid of leaving me alone, in the evenings he is seen to persuade me to walk with him, when I evidently don't wish for it, and so on. All this the secretary reported to Hampus, who told him, when he was again beginning to relate what people have told him. That he is not to come with this gossip to him, he does not care to hear it – One night they proposed the Emperors, then my and Hampus healths! – Is it not good fun? –

*Monday 18*th. Good morning my own darling Mother! How are you today? We are now fairly in the tropics, and the heat is overpowering at times though it is not yet half as warm as it will be further on. I am seated in the saloon, finding much nicer and cooler than on deck, where the sun is roasting.

A young lady of the name of Miss Coghill is busily employed turning a brown wide-awake into a three corned hat, for one of the performers of "Bombastes Furiosa" tonight – After some mutual conversation last night I found out, that she is a cousin of Madelaine and Helen Bruce, and the Miss Halls, of which Cousins she is very fond. She also knows the Darbengs[?] at Jamaica very well, and is returning there to join her father. A little flirtation is carried on between her and a young American, greatly to the amusement of all around. There are only 2. other young ladies besides – but hosts of young men. We seem to be near the end of our journey, for all the luggage is being taken up to be sorted. All together the scene is gayer today than usual and thank God, I feel more than usually well and able to enjoy the beauty and the novelty of the tropics. How exquisite the nights are! No sooner has the sun set on one side, and so rapidly that you have scarcely time to admire it, before it is drowned in the blue waves, than the glowing golden moon rises as rapidly on the other side and rides gloriously, high up in the sky. Then the reflection on the sea is most magnificent. I could hardly keep my eyes off it, and could not help wishing I was a poet or a painter. And how I thought of you my own Mother, and spoke of you with Hampus and told him you were a worshipper of Nature. You would enjoy it all so much. To me, it seems all like a wonderful dream! In the tropics! Why I never thought I should see them! But wonderful things will and do happen in this world of ours. Another gentleman has been added to my list of acquaintances, a dutchman, Capt[ain] Uhlenbeck. Born in East India, and educated in England – he is now going to join his Vessel, & returns to Holland next year, where he has a Wife and two children 19. and 16. He is an agreeable man. My german maid was very ill and good for nothing the first week, but has mended now, and promises to do very well. I hope she will prove a comfort to me and that she won't by degrees show any bad sides – Wickström is most flourishing, his cough is quite gone, and he has literally grown fat on this voyage. I am glad to see he is a good man. I don't remember now if I mentioned having bought the Bible for him, with which he was very much pleased, and sends his respectful thanks. Now I must begin a letter to sweet Florence.

Tuesday 19th. Now I can tell you about last nights performance, which was very amusing, and is consequently going to be repeated this evening. I enclose you the program, which Capt[ain] Montgomerie wrote out for me. It will doubtless amuse you to see it. The first piece was nothing – the second very good and well played, especially by "Jacob" one of the mates. The scene was very nicely got up, you could never suppose you were on board ship in the middle of the Atlantic. At 10. it was all over and there came supper to which every one was invited by the Captain. The prompter Capt[ain] Read[?], then got up and proposed the health & begged to return thanks to the Captain and all performers for the pleasant evening they had procured us. Of course the Capt[ain] thanked and drank the "kind prompters" health – then some body else stood up and proposed the ladies health, all these speeches were received with loud cheers, and Hip! hip! hurrah! – this health was answered by the purser, then a Captain in the R[oyal] Navy was glad the evening had given satisfaction, and only wished any trouble of his might have persuaded the company to contribute pounds instead of shillings – then the young medical man belonging to the ship proposed the health of the Army and Navy, which was first answered by Capt[ain] Montgomerie, & then a maiden speech by [..?] Johnstone. After this, all the foreigners health was proposed, which I wished my Hampus to return thanks for, and which the company seemed to expect, he being the first foreigner on board, & "Colonel! Colonel"! was heard in some quarters, but he did not wish to do so – so after waiting a little Capt[ain] Uhlenbeck spoke. Thus the supper ended and we went to bed at 11.½. – The moon was again exquisite.

Today it is very warm and I do not feel well.

Wednesday 20th. It is the last day. The Captain says we shall be in S[ain]t Thomas tonight, or at least outside it. I cannot say how glad I am. But oh dear! this heat is dreadful! especially to one so unaccustomed to it as I am. The nights are the most trying. We cannot with impunity sleep with the port open though we did so one night, but sneezed all day afterwards. I bought no muslin dresses in England, thinking they would get so troubled & crumpled in my box, I should not be able to wear them, but now I repent not having done so. I have only thin barèges and some prints, and some lose morninggowns. Tomorrow, or the day after, we expect to leave S[ain]t Thomas for Panama, where it will be hotter still. Last night we were suddenly deluged in a terrific shower of rain, which came on during the theatrical performance. The poor actors were the worst off I think, for some of them literally swam in water – It was pitch dark too, so we had to grope our way downstairs, amidst peels of laughter, best we could. It was a pity it came on so soon – as we lost the last and best piece in consequence. – The young artist on the Concertina, played many pieces to us afterwards & we got some iced punch after our shower bath.

There was a lottery too yesterday 32. tickets and 7. prizes which the stewardess had brought from England on purpose. We had 4. tickets but won nothing. The Secretary had 1. and gained the first prize, a large workbox, which he begged leave to present to me. He was not present when the lots were drawn, so Hampus asked a young lady to draw for him, which procured him this good fortune. Some of the passengers thought he ought to give her the prize – but as he did not know her, nor even exchanged a word with her, he thought it would not be necessary – We have been married eleven weeks today! – It seems to me we must have *always* been married – so soon you get accustomed to one another, and cannot imagine how you ever lived without eachother before. O Mama darling! I do so earnestly pray, that God will always be our Guide and Leader through Life – and that we may daily grow in Love towards Him, who has done so great things for us. Not only now – but who has lovingly and mercifully led us all the days of our lives. O! that I may never, never forget Him! forget to give Him thanks, deep deep thanks, for all he does for me. And O! that He may teach me to see my own faults, and give me the strength to correct them; that I may have a lowly and pe nitent heart, and humble & meek spirit. And that I may be all and all to my own precious husband, and make him happy. How delightful it will b[e to come][54] home – to Sitka I mean! I cannot s[ay how] I long for that day. I long to set to work busy[ly and p]lay on my beautiful new piano and stu[dy [..?]] the new music I bought at Dresden. I hope [I shall] be able to take cold baths, though Hampus says, the sea is always very cold at Sitka. I bathed yesterday – and enjoyed it most amazingly – I had no idea there were such nice baths to be had on board – This afternoon I will bathe again.

Dearest Mama, I think I must have some mistake about the numbers of my letters, for on entering them all into my letterbook today, I find this must be the 20th instead of 18th. I am very anxious about one thing, and that is that it appears we cannot prepay our letters, which is a great grief seeing this letter is so dreadfully heavy, it will I am afraid cost several Roubles Silver, when delivered at H[elsing]f[o]rs. What am I to do. But instead of putting it into the letterbox on board, we intend going to the Post office at S[ain]t Thomas and asking about it ourselves. Well, now it is all changed – we have been discussing the best way of sending our letters, and have decided upon sending them all under one large cover to the Board of Directors of the R[ussian] A[merican] Company at S[ain]t Petersburg, who will forward the letters to you. Now that's decidedly the cleverest thing we could do. –

How monotonously days pass on board a ship. This is the Holy Easter week! – Next friday is Good friday! – We shall be on another steamer and I am afraid see no outward sign of the great day it is to all Christians! […]

---

54 The interpolations here and in the next couple of lines are due to a hole in the letter.

O, do write immediately my own precious Mother. May God our Fathers richest Blessing rest upon you – & be with you for ever. Goodbye my own, own Mother! A thousand fond kisses I send you. Once more Adieu! Ever & ever Yours own most fondly loving Child

Annie Furuhjelm.

No. 21   Easter Monday. April 25th 1859
                                              On board H[er] M[ajesty's] Ship "Trent"

My own precious Mother!
Though this cannot be a long letter, I begin notwithstanding on a large sheet of paper, wishing all my letters to be of the same size. I would have had this on stocks ere this, if it had been possible for me to write. But I have been so very unwell especially on Good friday and half of Saturday, that I was perfectly good for nothing. Today I am better again, and immediately sit down to send you my own precious Mother a few lines. I am told this letter, and the one posted at S[ain]t Thomas will arrive by the same post – but it will always be nice for you to hear from every place we are able to write to you from. –
    I was delighted with S[ain]t Thomas, as we saw it from our ship – and it was with a heart beaming with Joy I accompanied my own husband on shore on Thursday morning at 7. o'clock – The sun was already very powerful, but the novelty of the whole scene made me forget it. I could scarcely realize to myself that it really was I, who was landing in an West Indian Island, where Negroes and Negresses swarmed around us, and the large leaf of the Cocoa nut tree waved over our heads. I walked up the alley planted on either side with these trees, leaning on Hampus' arm as in a trance, admiring everything I saw and wishing you could have seen it too. The "Commercial Hotel" was the one we had been recommended to, and thither we bent our steps – It is a large straggling house (if you can use that expression) with stone floor – open gates, pillars and staircases in no mathematical order – After passing a sort of shop on the ground floor, we found our way upstairs, where a Negro showed us into a large, lofty & tolerably cool room, a sort of table d'hôte; to the right hand you entered a large sort of balcony open on three sides with painted pillars supporting the roof – here we found plenty of "gungstolar" [Swed. rocking chairs], and some gentlemen reclining in some of them. The view was very pretty, – below us a small garden, filled with all sorts of tropical flowers, and beyond that, the sea. We ordered tea & bread & butter and banana's – after which repast we strolled out in the heat, and entered a Roman Catholic church, where I was glad to say my prayers and thank God for His mercies towards us, and His protection so far on our long voyage. I am sure God is ready to hear our prayers, be it in a Roman Catholic chapel or any other church to which we do not belong, provided we offer them up in a humble spirit

and in the name of our blessed Saviour – Surely then, all places must be equally holy. –

How the rest of the day was spent, Hampus has already told you in his letter. S[ain]t Thomas is built upon three hills, which are only projections of higher hills behind the town, on the middle one stands Government House, very small and insignificant looking – Our's at Sitka is much larger and handsomer, though the place itself is smaller. S[ain]t Thomas is as you know a danish possession[55] – Had we been staying there any time, it would have been fun to visit the Governor. Capt[ain] Uhlenbeck was obliged to wait there 10. days, his ship had already left. He walked down to the boat with us, so that even there we had some one to bid us a friendly Fare well – We invited him to visit us, if he should ever pass Sitka, which he promised to do with the greatest pleasure. Hampus gave me a beautiful nosegay, which we brought on board with us. I wished to send you one of the flowers, but it appears they had taken the whole bouquet away, as we cannot find it today.

Our cabin is very comfortable, the best one on board. The Captain is very civil indeed, and we may in all things consider ourselves very fortunate. I had a great fright last night. Thank God there was no danger, though there might have been.

I was laying awake at about 3½ when I suddenly heard a tremendous row upstairs, and screaming of voices and running backwards & forwards. The wind was blowing rather hard – I immediately thought of fire and woke Hampus. He jumped out of bed, put on dressinggown and boots and rushed out to ascertain what was the matter. I lay trembling all the time he was gone, and prayed most fervently, that He who had graciously permitted us to proceed so far safely on our journey would be with us now in the hour of danger. –

The engine stopped and we were rolling backwards and forwards. – When Hampus returned, I asked him to tell me the truth, which he did. One of the ropes of the rudder had broken, and the engine had become hot, so that they were obliged to stop it and pour cold water over it; you may think all this was not pleasant; but thank God it was discovered in time and we saved from Fire. In an hour and a half we began to go slowly, and now all is right long ago – We had just passed S[ain]t [..?], where we stopped a couple of hours, and the Captain told us this morning his first step was to rush on deck and see if we were near the shore, on which place we should have been driven up against it, and great might have been the danger. Thank God for His mercy! – We had only a tolerable good fright & no further consequences. –

O! I must tell you about Miss Coghill. You know I mentioned a flirtation was going on between her and a young American – well! *she did* carry it on with a vengeance and regularly "bet her cap at him" – He seemed to have been kind and polite to her from the beginning – so my young lady began to be very intimate with him. They were always together. She worked "kissing" slippers, & he read novels to her – she never walked with any but him to whose arm she seemed to cling closer day

---

55   St. Thomas was a part of the Danish West Indian colonies until 1917.

by day. At night they would separate themselves from the rest of the company and walk in the forepart of the ship alone. She would be reclining in a graceful attitude on one of the benches on deck in the moonlight, with her faithful American at her side – Everybody began to speak and make remarks about it – and all the young men laughed with him about it. She even spoke in a very foolish way about him to the young spanish girl – and said she would be so lonely and unhappy without "Johan"! – However the last night we were on board the Magdalena, was the climax of all that's shocking. Miss Coghill & Mr. Cay never separated from 6 – 11. at night – they first walked up and down – then they stood arm in arm looking at the moon or water, and then without the slightest shame, she seated herself behind the rudder, where she was seen half laying, half leaning on him, and remained there several hours without moving. She seemed to be crying – At 9 we dropped anchor off S[ain]t Thomas, though we could have gone in perfectly well and it appears the Capt[ain] did it to please Miss Coghill, who was anything but anxious to part with her new friend. Well at 10. all the ladies disappeared. Miss C[oghill] still remained. – Hampus and I really wished to watch her and see how long she intended to stay. However Hampus soon was going to give it up as a bad job, & I urged him to remain – there were only gentlemen on deck now – and it was quite dark. – At last just near 11. I even became impatient & got up and left her to herself – She seems to have seen the last lady had left, and presently after came down too. The next day at 9. they parted! We have heard several accounts of the tragical scene. They went into the Captains cabin, the door was open, & opposite it was a glass, which reflected all to a host of young men who had placed themselves on purpose to witness the scene. She cryed most bitterly, flung herself into his arms & in fact sobbing and kissing took no end. He left her, looking rather serious, as tradition says – & presently afterwards the Capt[ain] took her on deck, where the poor girl burst into an hysterical flood of tears. – Now considering she neither knew who or what he was, had never seen him before, was alone on board, without any one to look after her, this was very bad behaviour. He of course promised to come to Jamaica after 8. months – but I don't suppose he ever dreamt of doing such a thing. So here you have a regular gossiping letter. –

And now I must bring this letter to a close – for the mailbag will be made up immediately.

Darlingest Mama! You know it is impossible to write the same thing to everyone, & as everyone expects to hear everything, please read or translate as much of my letters as you think proper to Marie, Uncle Charles, Moster [Swed. aunt, mother's sister] Lisette and Mina. I know they must all be interested in us, and all concerning us. Perhaps darling Mrs Hawthtorne to whom I would so willingly write, would like to see this – but do as you like. Only I hope no one will think me "naughty". I would write if I could. – [...]

With a Childs fondest love & affection Ever Your own fondly attached

Annie

No. 22   Panama! Aspinwall House.
                                                    April 29th 1859 – friday.
                                                    Lattitude 10.

My own beloved Mother!
From this far renowned old place, I again take up my pen to continue my narration.
I cannot say how glad I am once more, and if only for a few days, to be on shore,
away from all the discomforts & smells of the best and most comfortable steamer.
We arived here yesterday afternoon at 2 – after five hours railwaying, across the
Isthmus. How am I to describe the wonderful beauty of the tropical woods we passed
yesterday? – It was truly like driving through a most choice greenhouse, where all
the most exquisite and rare tropical plants had been collected. Nowhere can nature
be richer, more profuse, and more generous than here. Everything grows in wild
confusion. Palm trees of manifold description, Banana's, fig trees, lovely creepers
encircling each tree, and hanging down in most beautiful flowers, lilac, white and
red – trees innumerable of which I know not the name – in fact all manner of most
beautiful plants, flowers, trees, creepers, leaves and grasses. And then the hot sun
shining down smilingly upon it all, and thousands of grasshoppers and humming
insects flying & jumping about.
    We left Colon at 8 ¼ in the morning, after a very fair passage from S[ain]t Thomas,
and especially good from Cartagena, where I closed my last letter. We slept Wednesday night on shore. The railway across the Isthmus, is I think, one of the most
wonderful in the world. We were told that every 10 feet of ground cost one man's
life, & of the 300. workmen, that used to be transported there, each time scarcely, 25.
returned. So we were literally going over thousands of graves. The thick impenetrable
forest had to be cleared away sufficient to allow a narrow road to be made for the
railway to pass over, here and there bridges to be made, of which one is a very large
iron one, "á jour" [Fr. open] – you look through it into an immense depth. Some
years ago it was made of wood & had a roof, but the river swollen after the heavy
rains carried it off, and now they have built this one. The train goes very slowly,
the whole way is zig-zag – everynow and then you pass, or stop at a pretty, clean
looking little station with a garden in front of it, filled with Bananas & figtrees; now
and then native villages – their huts either open on all sides, with only a roof, or
closed and covered with dry palm leaves – almost black, men women and completely
naked children were lazyly hanging about everywhere. At one of these villages we
bought pineapples, custard apples, cakes, loveapples, oranges – which the natives held
up to the windows, offering them for sale. The heat was dreadful – the carriages are
very inconvenient – like the Wurtemburg ones, only made of wicker work and very
narrow.
    Here I was interrupted by my Hampus, who had been out in this terrific heat to
procure our berths. We have the stateroom – which is very large, I daresay larger
than the cabins we had on our previous voyages, though they were always the first.

We have paid 100 £ for our places to San Francisco, and 181 £ we paid from South-ampton to Colon, so you see this is no small expence to the Company. Crossing the Isthmus, which is only 25 miles, cost 81 £! Each pound of luggage being charged 10. sous. I believe there are 100 in a dollar, & four shillings in a dollar – consequently 4 d[ollar]s a pound! Now! if this is not ruinous, I wonder what is?! – –

Friday Night 9. o'clock. I could hardly go on this morning, sweetest mother, the heat was too overpowering, I had to fly to my Bananaleaf fan, which is scarcely ever out of my hand, and reclining in a rocking chair, or standing behind Hampus' chair, looking over his shoulder into the *most interesting* book he was studying – gave myself over into the open stretched arms of idleness. – O! I could not live in the tropics! or at least were I doomed to do so I think I should do nothing all day, which would be a completely wasted Life. You must know our family is increased by one parrot and two little Lovebirds – which Hampus bought for me at Cartagena. The parrot (Lorito) in spanish, speaks that language very fluently, but we are going to teach it english. It amuses me very much. The three birds lived in complete harmony up to this day, when the big one fell to tormenting and flying at the little ones. I was in terror of their life and asked Hampus to buy me a separate cage for them, which he did, & now they are all happy and contented I hope.

I ought to speak first about Cartagena, one of the spanish mightiest and richest towns in olden times, but now a most dilapidated, wretched and miserable looking place. The narrow, dirty suffocatingly hot streets look at night, or rather when dark, the time we were there perfectly "hemsk" [Swed. awful]. I expected to see a robber at every turning – the black figures gliding silently along in the dark, some of the women with sigars in their mouths, did not look very pleasant and the large vampire bats flying about our heads, made a most mysterious noise. We went into the old Cathedral, well worth seeing, though it was too dark to recognize any of the pictures, and the air was stifling – from there, we found our way to an Hotel recommended to us, as "very good" – after mounting a broad, *dark* stone staircase we came into a veranda, where a negroe was lying asleep in the corner, woke him and asked for the master or the mistress of the Hotel. A very fine lady, speaking english with a german accent, presently made her appearance – We asked for a carriage "not such a thing to be had in the whole town!" "Is there anything worth seeing?" –

"No! – Nothing at all – the view from the walls & the Cathedral is all there is" –

"Is there anything particularly belonging to this place to be bought as a curios-ity?"

"No – nothing what ever" –

"Can we have ices – cream ices?" –

"Ah no! not in the whole town" –

"Goodnight" – "Goodnight" – – –

We went on the walls and saw the sea, that was all. After rambling about some time, we met the Admiralty Agent of our ship, going to spend the evening at the english Consuls, who had invited us too, but we declined feeling too untidy & tired – & returned to the above mentioned Hotel asking for tea. –

"O yes – you can have some tea – do you like it strong?"

"Yes" –

We went into the drawing room, and then on the Verandah, where our hostess followed us, and was amiability itself – She was a German by birth, her husband a Pole, they had come from the United States 5. years ago, and were now settled in Cartagena. She was an educated & well informed person – I conclude she had been a gouverness – her husband read too, & conversed freely on many things – Judging by the time we had to wait, we might have expected a splendid repast, but when we were invited to partake of it, it turned out to be almost undrinkable tea, rancid butter, dry and sour rolls, hard venison! – by which you may conclude of the quantity we eat. – We paid 2. dollars and returned to the shore, where a boat was waiting to row us to the "Trent" – this was the best part of all – the phosphor essence was lovely. On mounting the steps, I knocked my watch against it, the balustrade broke the glass, bent the gold lid and stopped it altogether! – So much for a pleasure trip to Cartagena, which looked [..?] beautiful from our ship. –

And now Good night, my sweetest Mother! – It is too hot to write more – I must go & cool myself before going to bed – I am very tired – my back especially. –

By the bye – My own Darling, who is going to sleep at my elbow over a letter to Esperance – says: "Next to Annies kisses *ice* is the best thing in the world."

Saturday 30th. Good morning my own Mother! I have been sick all the morning, and unable to do anything. –

Later – 5 o'clock. As I had finished writing these words I was again obliged to jump up in a great hurry & frightened my Darling so much by spitting a wee bit of blood, that he immediately sent for a Doctor. When he came, he assured me it was of no earthly consequence in this climate, & that it frequently occurs, though in England or Paris it would be thought a dangerous thing. He is a Frenchman – a very nice gentleman, and told me I seemed to be in excellent Health and of a very good constitution, and need not be alarmed about anything – but that all was, as it ought to be, & that most likely the distressing sickness would soon cease altogether – though I am not so sanguine, I am relieved to know that the strange feeling in my left side, which disables me to sleep on it at night is nothing unnatural. O! sweetest Mother! Is not all this a great Blessing? and are you not happy too? – Do you know darling Mama, judging to the calculation table and mode of using it, given in "Bulls hints to Mothers" an excellent book, given me by Mrs Savary, I may with Gods help expect that supreme happiness on or about the 12th or 13th December. – O Mother! what wonderful exquisite changes. Hampus is *so* happy! and we daily pray God to give us his Blessing and to teach us to understand our duties as parents. I am so glad to have that Book and the 2nd Vol[ume] "Management of children", which I bought at Southampton.

Sunday afternoon 1st *May.* All *your world* has been at the "Kaisaniemi"[56] this morning, drinking coffee in the open air and listening to the students singing "Ser hur solen ler" [Swed. Look how the sun smiles] under Pacius direction. I thought of it last night and early this morning, though at six with us, you were sitting down to dinner, or getting up from it. – I wonder much what sort of weather you have – if this 1st May is like the last – cold & miserable, or, as I flatter myself it is warm and spring like. Now the streets are beginning to look dry and clean, after they have for some weeks been in a most dreadful state of mind and mire. The view from the dear Lilles' windows, is with every day becoming prettier, as the time approaches when my little Godchild becomes 1 year old. O precious Mother, *when ah when* shall I hear from you? –? –

But time is precious, and we are every moment expecting to hear of the ships arrival, so I must finish this today. And to return to Panama.

We are lodged very comfortably at "Aspinwall House", a large Hotel, kept by a frenchman. Our bedroom forms a corner, so that we have the Verandah on both sides, & are able to make a delicious draft with all doors open – Next to it is a very large [..?] sittingroom, according to American fashion.

Panama is an old, ruined looking town – with narrow streets & high houses all built in the same spanish style. You never see any of the ladies out during the day – but later they appear in *tremendous* crinolines in black silk dresses (considered the most elegant) or very light silks with low bodies & lace capes silk mantilla and no bonnets – or in Ball costume. How they can exist in silks, is more than I can tell. –

Anxious to see the fine view, and involuntary thinking of Henrik Borgström, we sauntered forth the first evening, and walked on the walls. –

There lay the Pacific, blue, smooth and tranquill before us, with beautiful islands, and wooded ranges of hills – But we had come too late, it was too dark to see anything distinctly. The next evening friday, we were rewarded by going out earlier, and saw the fine view to advantage. I thought so much of you – how delighted you would have been – there was something so calm & passive, so solemn about the whole scenery – I thought I was in another century. But how describe it? I can't – it was not imposing at all – not out of the common splendid – but there was something most enjoyable and delicious – I picked some wild flowers for you my darling Mother, and one for my dear Mina. Tell her so. – I will send it with this – Yesterday afternoon at five, we were driven by the Omnibus to the public gardens, where we mounted a steep hill, planted on either sides with pineapples and Banana's and many other fruits. At the top of the hill, was a pavillion from where we had a beautiful view – Right before us, a richly grown valley with the most variagated verdure from quite light, to deep yellow green, a rich red sand road winding through it and at a distance the tower of old Panama, and the battlefield, where Morgan[57] beat the spaniards, who fled to

---

56   Kaisaniemi, a restaurant then outside Helsinki, but now in the city itself.
57   Henry Morgan, a buccaneer, beat the Spaniards in January 1671.

the islands, and left the whole town with all its riches to the enemies. To the right the blue Pacific & its islands – lower down on a flat projection the present Panama, surrounded by fortified walls, which cost 50. millions dollars, and are now not worth the half, or even less. – On the other two sides fine woods and pretty villas – and at a distance the hills. It was very fine and we enjoyed it amazingly. Here I also picked a pretty little wild flower for you. –

The conductor told us, about 480[?] different kinds of fruit grew wild here – there is not a tree a bush that does not at some time of the year bear fruit. But the natives are the laziest people in the world and consequently the Country is poor, and nothing is exported from it – they could have three crops of corn in the year – but they wont work and pay 4. dollars a tun. The only thing they trade with is cattle, which they sell to the steamers and American men of war, and other vessels entering the port. –

There are buried riches in the town now – I mean millions of dollars in ready money – sometimes new pieces of 1812 – and 1790 – come out, which have never been in circulation before – The natives, and not only they, but many others pass their days in their hammocks, which makes "the Country poor" as the Conductor said. When we came home, we sat in our rockingchairs at the open Verandah and ordered tea. Some of the other passengers played the piano, and presently about 8 or 10 gentlemen arrived and soon after them a bowl of [..?]. When all the glasses were filled, two of the gentlemen came up to us, speaking french, inviting "Monsieur et Madame" to do them the honour of taking a glass – they introduced themselves as the Peruvian and french Consuls. – We thanked, and accepted where upon they drank our health, and one of the gentlemen took a seat, and conversed a long time with us. Every one knows who we are – to our surprise we found this in the Panama paper,[58] which we cut out and send you. –

I can't bear the Americans – they are such coarse vulgar people. I quite dread the crowd on board the steamer to San Francisco – […]

Monday. We have this minute come back from a drive in the Country, where we took a fresh water bath, and were met with the news that the steamer is come and we must be off – therefore sweetest Mother Goodbye – there is no time to loose – Dearest of love to all friends, and fond fond kisses to y[ou]rself from Hampus and myself –

God bless you my precious Mother – from San Francisco more – Your own fondly loving Child

Annie Furuhjelm

The Panama newspaper paragraph, & all the flowers were forgotten.[59]

---

58   *Panama Star & Herald*, Saturday Morning. April 30, 1859: "Colonel J.H. Turuhjelm [sic], Governor of the Russian possessions in America, accompanied by his lady, Secretary and servants, is at present in town *en route* by way of San Francisco to Sitka".

59   This sentence was added by someone else, probably Anna's mother.

No. 23   *San Fransisco. California.*
                                            Wednesday. May 18th 1859. –

My own Beloved Mother!
Two days ago we reached this wonderful town! And are since then most comfortably
lodged and kindly accommodated in the house of the russian Consul, Mr Kostromitienoff, an old acquaintance of my husbands. His wife speaks english, I am happy
to say, and his six children do so fluently, as if english were their native tongue.
They are a very kind, agreeable family – we feel ourselves already quite at home.
Mrs Kostromitienoff has a most soft, pleasant voice, and puts me much in mind of
Ida Driesen. I can just fancy Ida looking like her at the age of 36, and as Mother of
five sons and one daughter.

My last letter darling Mama, left Panama I hope on the 8th; we left it on the 2nd.
After four days waiting for the passengers from New York, they at last arived on
Monday morning 2nd. So we hired a boat, and in it, had a full hours row to the
"Golden Age". The 1100. passengers from America, came in the afternoon, by a
steamer and early on Tuesday morning we sailed. –

I have never seen a more splendid ship than the "Golden Age" – and though it
appeared to be smaller than the "Magdalena" the vessel we sailed from England
in, it was in truth much larger, at least built in a perfectly different way, so as to
accommodate nearly 1300. people including the crew. It had four stories, of which
the 4th was the only one without beds. Our stateroom was in the coolest part of the
ship, though very small. We were perfectly roasted, boiled, stewed the first 8. days.
I never felt anything like it – and 1100. fans were all day long in constant use. You
seemed to be oozing away – if you lifted your little finger, you were covered with
perspiration. The only part of the day when I felt comfortable, and able to live, was
during dinner – Having the best place, seated beside the Captain at the head of the
table, I got all the breeze coming down the windsail at my elbow. My wardrobe was
ill suited for the climate. I shall know better another time, for you certainly have to
make the voyage once, in order to know what is best. –

From 5 o'clock in the morning till 8. at night you heard the rattling of plates &
cups & saucers. There [were] five breakfasts, five dinners and five teas each day,
for the Cabin passengers, without counting the stewards, stewardess and waiters
meals, and the steerage passengers. It was amusing to hear what part of the daily
consummation was. Three bullocks killed daily – 3. doz[en] fowls – 1600. pounds
of potatoes, three sheep – and then the salt provisions. What quantities of sugar,
tea, coffee, bread, butter and drinkables I know not – but they were in proportion.
There were 10 cooks and two kitchens, and the table was well served, and had the
best of everything. The poor waiters must have been sufficiently tired – the day after
tomorrow their labour begins again. The Captain was a very gentlemanly, nice man,
and especially civil towards us – We were to have what ever we wanted. –

I cannot say much in praise of the Americans. I can't bear them – they are the most ungentlemanly, vulgar & it appeared to me uneducated people I know as for chewing & spitting! – I never saw anything like it – they beat the Swedes, Finlanders & Germans hollow. – There was one lady with whom we became acquainted, she was Hampus neighbour at dinner, who seemed to be a nice person, and was very kind – but she, like many of the others, spoke dreadful english. *Was* instead of *were; is* instead of *are*, most uneducated english – and almost all had a nasal twang. They had splendid diamonds on their fingers, & wore them constantly but put their knifves into their mouths – took up chicken and cutlet bones with their fingers, and put their elbows on the table at dinner! – Now what I was puzzled to know, and would wish to ascertain is this: Were they *ladies* in America? or were they not – do all speak such *bad* english – I don't mean the accent – but the positively bad grammar. That gentlemen spit and they *all* use their knifves instead of forks, I know – Mary Jones told me so – but I expected to meet educated people; et voilà ce que j'ai trouver [Fr. and look what I found]. When you write to Dresden, please tell Mary Jones, what my impression about the Americans has been. She asked me to write and tell her – but now it is perfectly impossible, as I am behind hand with all my letters, not having been well enough, or had opportunity to begin them before, and they must be posted tomorrow – I trust my own Mother, this will reach you the middle of July and find you at *Palsi* [the small estate of H. Furuhjelm's father] I suppose. –

Afternoon. I have this minute got up from a delightful nap, in which I indulged myself, not having slept more than a few hours these last 3. nights, and feel all the better for it. –

Oh Mother Darling! No words of mine can tell how thankful I am to be here. We have such great great reason to thank God from the depths of our hearts for His wonderful mercy towards us, in having permitted us to reach this far distant land safely. We have been six weeks at sea, and not had one storm! have had the most beautiful passage imaginable. O! how good He is towards His children! [...]

I cannot give you any amusing description of our voyage from Panama. One day passed like the other – and on the whole the 13. went very fast. – I was often very sick and wretched, some days I felt better, and was all but one day, able to come to dinner at five. The last 5. days were quite cold – the change was so sudden and so acute I caught a heavy cold, which still hangs upon me. [...]

On Sunday night 15th May we were all kept in great excitement – some expecting to reach San Fransisco at 7 – some at 9 – but to frustrate our hopes, a dense fog set in at about 5, and threatened to keep us out all night, or perhaps still longer.

Thursday noon. I have just returned from a drive into the country, where I have seen such exquisite flowers, I could not help wishing you had been there to see them too. The Consul presented me a most lovely bouquet, which I shall take with me to the Opera tonight. We are going to see "Ernani" [G. Verdi]. But to return to the fog – it cleared a little at 7 – so we went on slowly, stopping every now & then to fathom. I went to bed at 12 – thinking it useless to remain up any longer, as it would be too late to go on shore. – At 2. o'clock I awoke, and heard a tremendous noise outside – thousands of voices speaking & screaming – "International Hotel carriage here" – "private coach here" "Rail way omnibus here" "luggage wagon here" etc – etc – and at once it dawned upon my sleepy, confused brains that we must be at San Fransisco. A few minutes afterwards there was a knock at our door, and a russian question screamed out of which I only understood "Ivan Wasilitsch"[60] and immediately conjectured it to be a message from the R[ussian] Consul, which it also was. Mr Klinkowström congratulated us, on our safe arrival and told us there were rooms ready waiting for us at Mr Kostromitienoff's. But it was too late to go on shore, so we remained over night & came here at 8. the following morning.

Well! here we really are! and have been three days in this new town. It is perfectly wonderful to think it is the work of ten years. There are buildings as large as any in London – shops like S[ain]t Petersburg plenty of any and everything, and the finest climate in the world. Another 10. years will, I suppose, make a still greater change, and people will settle here from all quarters of the globe. There is now such constant communication with Sitka (everyone here knows where and what Sitka is) it no longer appears to me to be out of the world. Every one says it is very changed and every one seems to like it. Mrs K[ostromitienoff] has a sister married there, and she often sends her whatever she requires, and has promised to send me whatever I may be in want of – So you see darling Mama, I feel actually much nearer you know [i.e. now], than when we were at Panama or in S[ain]t Thomas.

It is never very warm, never cold here. At about 12. in the forenoon it generally begins to blow, and the evenings are quite chilly. You never walk in muslin dresses here, always silk – the former would be too cold. There are excellent preachers, and this town is one of the most churchgoing people in the world. There are prayermeetings every day – and drunkenness has decreased to a wonderful extent. They have a temperance society, to which only six belonged last January – now already 300.

Just nu tog Annie min arm och förde mig till bordet hvarpå detta bref ligger. Jag förstår hon vill att jag skall fortsätta. Thyvärr är mitt sinne så upptaget af andra af- färer att jag endast kan se på Mammas porträtt som ligger bredvid mig. – Derföre, adjö älskade Mor. Mamas most affectionate Hampus.

Älskade Esperance! – Emottag en hjertlig helsning ifrån din bror, som nu icke hinner skrifva. [Swed. Just now Annie took my arm and led me to the table where this letter lies. I understand she wants me to continue. Unfortunately my mind is set on other affairs and I can only look at Mama's portrait which is lying on the table – Therefore goodbye precious Mother. Your most affectionate Hampus. Dear Esperance! – Your brother who has no time to write now, sends you his warmest regards.]

You cannot think sweetest Mother how busy my own Darling is. I feel now what it is to be the Wife of a man of importance – a man of business – I scarcely see him to speak to all day long. From the hour we arived there were visitors for him, and

---

60   Johan Hampus Furuhjelm was called Ivan Vasil'evich Furugel'm in Russian.

men who came to make their "Aufwartung" [Ger. respect, i.e. to pay their respect]
– Some of their wiwes have called upon me, but I have not been anywhere yet,
being so tired & having such a distressing cold in my nose. I have also had to wait
for a bonnet to be made. My white terry velvet became black after one weeks wear
in London, & it looked most unladylike when brought out to daylight in San Fransisco. I took off the feathers & roses and gave it to Ida [Höerle], who will, I doubt
not, look very sweet in it, for she dresses very well, and has two or three silk dresses
– but she is never what is called "smart", always decently and quietly attired. The
maidservants in this town always go in silks & velvet mantillas, long ribbons and
even feathers in their bonnets. They get tremendous wages from 200 to 500 dollars
per annum. Ida gets 100 Th[a]l[er]s and has the promise of 120. if I am satisfied with
her. I trust no one will entice her away from me. I think you would like my summer
bonnet, it is made by the 1st french milliner here. A very fine white straw, with 2.
long black feathers on 1. side and rose ribbons with roses & black velvet in the rûge.
The newest fashion, & certainly very elegant. I have also ordered a winter bonnet,
rich dark blue velvet with blue feathers and black lace. I tell you even these small
things Mama darling, because I think it will please you to hear about everything.
We have been buying a bed chest of drawers & wash handstand with white marble
slabs. Also bed, matrasses & blankets. My Hampus is now out ordering books – he
bought me a californian gold thimble yesterday, & today a most comfortable easy
chair. He always thinks of something for me – O Mama! he is such a precious, precious husband! I can never thank God sufficiently for the Blessing He has bestowed
upon me. He has already been the means of bringing this family nearer their and
our God. He told Mr K[ostromitienoff] he ought to read the Bible with his wife &
children and told him how we read together. The immediate result of which was that
the Consul reads one psalm & one chapter and then a prayer morning and evening
with his family and ourselves, and thanks Hampus so sincerely for having asked him
to do so. May the Blessing of our Father rest upon them all, and may they all soon
find the comfort & Joy in communion with God, which all must surely feel, who
draw nigh unto Him. This touched me so – I felt quite overpowered with Joy. O, my
darling husband. He is in great agitation and distress about the ice affair,[61] which he
has been sent here to arrange. He never goes out, before kneeling down to ask for
enlightenment from above, and for strength to be able to do his duty. The other day
he went with a heavy heart – & after many hours absence came back much brighter,
& immediately thanked God that the days business had past so well. O Mama! must

---

61   In 1854 a contract had been made in St. Petersburg with a firm from San Francisco,
     which had been given the exclusive rights for 20 years to buy all ice, fish, coal and
     timber that was exported from the Russian-American Company. – 9.1.1860 Hampus
     Furuhjelm succeeded in making a new, much more favourable 'ice contract' with the
     American firm for a 3 year period. Furthermore the RAC got the right to sell its coal,
     fish and timber at its will (Bolkhovitinov 1997-1999, 3, pp. 358-359).

not this make me supremely happy? O, so deeply grateful? I only wish you could see us and judge for yourself of our happiness. – […]

I have felt so unwell and mal á mon aise [Fr. uneasy] these last three days, I have not had spirits to write. But I will begin in time and have letters ready for the next mail a fortnight hence. […] I certainly think it would be best for you to send your letters over New York to the care of the Russian Consul Mr Kostromitienoff San Fransisco – there are often opportunities to Sitka. I am thirsting for letters from home – from you my beloved Mother.

Our ship, by which we are to sail to Sitka, has been lying waiting for us this last month. The Captain Roslund, is a native of Åbo, and has been 12. years in the Russian American Company's service. He has put his ship in prime order for us and only waits Hampus' orders to set the sails. We ought to reach Sitka in 15. days. I fancy the old governor Woiwotsky is in great impatience, & thinks we are never coming. I don't think we shall leave this before the beginning of June, so that one month hence, I think we shall be in Sitka. And won't I be glad. How I wish I could make myself equally beloved as Aunt Margeret. Every body remembers her with the greatest love & affection. She did so much good, and was so kind towards everybody. I pray God I may do all I can to make myself loved by those with whom I will come in contact and that I may be able to set them a good example. It will be so pleasant to visit the school[62] and look to the progress the children make – to distribute bibles and good books amongst them. If I only once knew the russian language; but that will be a hard task I fear, though I understand a great many words already and often guess at meanings. […]

Soon all the world will "flytta på landet" [Swed. leave town] – Mama, Esperance & Ormelie amongst the rest – Babette too – and Amanda will go home is not that the way?

Mrs Kostromitienoff came just now for my letter. My precious Mother Farewell – In a fortnight you will hear again from me.

Dearest and fondest love from us both sweetest Mother – God bless you my own Precious – Love and Kisses in profusion from

Your fondly devoted loving Child

Annie

---

62   In 1839 a school for girls of mixed blood, the so-called Creoles, and female orphans was opened in Novo-Arkhangelsk (Fedorova 1973, p. 244).

No. 24   *San Fransisco. May 29th 1859.*
                                          Sunday afternoon

My own beloved Mother,

On this lovely day I must begin writing to you. We have been to the prespyterian church, where we heard a most excellent and most instructive sermon preached by the Rev[eren]d Mr Scott. I cannot say how truly edified Hampus and I were by his discourse, and by his beautiful extemporary prayer. Though I prefer *no other form* of worship, to the one of the church of England, and do not like a service without those beautiful old prayers in the Common prayerbook, I must say you cannot go to hear Mr Scott or any other earnest, zealous preacher like him, without feeling infinite comfort, and deriving real instruction, and enlightment on the subject preached upon. I thought of you all, my beloved, precious Darlings! – and tears started to my eyes when I remembered the strange, distant country we are in – but O! I felt so sublimely happy at the assurance we were all united in *one Faith one Hope* – *one Love!* I seemed to be nearer you. We were all together! – Then I glanced at *my own precious, precious* husband by my side, and thanked Him for *that mercy!* Hampus was as pleased with the sermon as I was, it treated of "the personality of the Holy Spirit" – I had never heard anyone before speak so exactly according to my own views of the Holy Trinity, as Dr Scott did. He said, it was a Holy mystery, not to be explained nor properly comprehended, by any human being; we were to receive it with childlike and implicite faith, believing all the Holy Scripture says about it, even though it passes our comprehension. I think *no* explanation, can ever give us a clearer view on the subject, but very probably would easily confuse and mystify us – Therefore as all things are possible with God I firmly *believe* all the Bible tells us, & am truly thankful to Him who has granted me such faith. Dr Scott wishes to impress on the minds of his hearers, that the Holy Spirit, though perhaps less spoken of, than the other two heads of the Holy Trinity, is equal in all things to them, is as equally personified, as God the Father, and God the Son – and, that we can make no difference between the three, or believe more in the one, than in the other, seeing we have never seen God the Father, nor God the Son, though we may some times find it easier for our comprehension that the Father and the Son *are one* and yet two than that the Father, the Son and the Holy Ghost *are one*, and yet three! –

Now, I find, I cannot give back what I heard, I cannot put what I mean into words, and will therefore stop – But I was deeply impressed, and am thankful to have been at Dr Scotts church today. – My own sweet Mother! in which church were you? if at H[elsing]f[or]s I suppose in the german one – Now you are sound asleep – It is 6½ with us, we have just come from dinner, with you it must be 3½ in the morning and soon the sun will rise – […]

I have again had to consult a doctor here about my side – he ordered mustard poultice, or half a dozen leeches – the latter remedy I did not use – finding the pain or uneasiness or what name I am to give it, often changing place. Generally in the region of the heart, under the breast, some times in the waist & shoulder – I think it is rheumatism, caught in the tropics. I was certainly very imprudent sitting all day long in a draft, and sleeping so all night without any flannels on. Mrs K[ostromitienoff] gave me an excellent mixture to rub the side with morning and evening, and then apply warm flannel, and I am happy to say it helped me. I am wearing tricot jacket and shall in future be more prudent and careful! I am thanks be to God perfectly well, and always thinking of the coming event – indeed the *crowning Blessing*. Darling Mother! I wish you could be with your child then! – Wonderful enough, I have not been sick since I am on shore, at least only occasionally, though I never feel comfortable in the forenoon. –

Last Thursday, I had a three hours and a half sitting at the dentists – I suffered some exquisitely acute pain – but it could not be helped. My Darling was with me and I held and clenched his hand all the time. I was never in the hands of a more conscientious dentist – the Americans, do their work quite differently to english ones. Fancy Mr Saunders, (Queen Victorias & Londons best dentist) looking at my mouth, stopping *one* tooth & saying, when I return there would probaply be some work to be done, and his stopping falling out after *six weeks*. Mr Crane examined my mouth, pronounced the tooth in question to be a very bad case, as he could not help me, without causing me suffering – but, if left alone, I would soon suffer more. The cavity was on the outside, the worst place, but too small to hold anything – he would have to cut deeper, and also make a whole in the middle. – The first time, I was without Hampus, & had another one done, not being able to muster up courage enough to go through the operation. – On Thursday I had 3. done – and most thoroughly. Please God I am safe now a few years – if during our stay at Sitka, I ever come here again, I shall not fail to visit Mr Crane. We paid 23. dollars. – Mr Koschkin has to pay 75 [..?] – his teeth are so neglected –

Do you remember, how I formerly suffered from moist hands, staining and spoiling my gloves? It has perfectly disappeared now – and is a great relief to me. I have grown a little thinner in my face, hands and arms lately, though I am not thinner than I was the week before we were married, so you need not be frightened. Hampus has grown much stouter there is no fear of his ring falling off now – he looks much younger, and is thank God in better health and spirits. But he has had much care and anxious business here, which keeps him often from sleeping and takes away his appetite. I am afraid it will force him to return here after a few months, and then I shall be left alone. O! I cannot bear to think of it – and hope it may not be so. –

Now I think I must go down, and walk a little in the Verandah – So goodnight darling Mama.

Monday Ev[enin]g 30th May. My own precious, darlingest of Mothers! I am alone in my room – Hampus is at an Committee and will not be home for ever so long – So I cannot occupy myself better, or more agreeably than in writing & chatting with you. But there goes the teabell and I must go. –

And now it is nearly 10. I have had a warm bath and am in my bed, waiting for my Darling, whose voice I thought I heard down stairs. The mailsteamer must have come, I hear just a noice coming up from the wharf. O! tomorrow I shall know if I am to have a very happy day! – I trust it may be so. – I bought six such pretty little embroidered caps today, and many other articles necessary for a small being. Don't you think a blue glacé silk quilt, with a white glacé silk lining, quilted in the sewing machine on both sides, will be sweet? I am making such a one – the same rich blue like the beautiful dress you gave me; it will be 1. y[a]rd and half a quarter long – O! it is such happiness getting all the articles for those small things. I would not grudge any money on them – & like ten times better to spend it on such things, than on anything expensive for myself. I wish you my precious Mother, could work something for me, and send it me, but I am afraid it is perfectly impossible. – This is a ruinous country to live in – fancy our washing Bill for 7. weeks washing, being, O Mother! 54. dollars – or 11. £! –

Tuesday Ev[enin]g 31st. My own Mama! I have this moment finished writing a letter of business for my darling! It is the third I have written here. I cannot say how happy I am to be of use to him; the gentlemen of the Committee have remarked it too – and said something about it to Hampus – I daresay they are all anxious to see what kind of creature I am – and tomorrow their curiosity will be satisfied, as we are going to a large Ball given in the American theatre, to which we have been especially *invited,* by the chief manager. – As I have my whole toilette complete, and had only gloves and a lace pockethankerchief to buy, it will rather amuse me, to see the Californian society, shining in all their diamonds. – I had to alter the waist of my dress a little – but Ida is a clever workwoman and did it all in no time – We are going at 9. or 9½ & remain there a couple of hours – It is wonderful how being married, changes many of your former tastes. I no more care for Balls and parties now, than if they never existed – though as a young girl I liked them often too much. I am only longing for Sitka! for our own, own home. *Thursday. June 2nd.* This is quite a lost day! I find Balls late hours and such like dissipation are no longer the things for me. I do not wish to go to another, while I am not so strong as usual. In fact, that kind of Life has I am glad to say, lost all its charm – I found the evening last night so long & tedious; I was longing to get home and into bed. I have kept such early hours these last 2. months, always being in bed before ten, often retiring at 9. that to come home at 2. in the morning, having gone out at 10½ was more than enough and I consequently got up at 10. today and have felt ill & sick all the time. – The Ball was very well arranged for *this place,* it was the first of the kind they had had, and was therefore generally admired, & spoken of as "the finest thing we have ever seen" in this days paper. To my ideas it afforded no such splendour – it was as mixed & queerly dressed an assembly as the "Societäts Baler" [Swed. society balls] in H[elsing]f[o]rs. Of course there were some exceptions – the music was exellent. In honest truth my toilette was the finest, the most tasteful in the room – the Americans have no taste – they overladen themselves from top to toe, and think that splendid.

The mail steamer came in, whilst we were at the Ball, and I went to bed, with the flattering hope, of waking next morning to receive letters from you. But alas! I was bitterly disappointed, not even a line from Florence. There were only businessletters form S[ain]t P[eters]b[ur]g and from Sturm in Hamburgh. The illustrated London News was of 9th and 16th April – It looks war[63] like they say. I cannot yet believe in the truth of Russia & France having formed an alliance against Austria. Hampus is not inclined to believe it. He says Russia had such immense losses in the last war,[64] she has not sufficient men to produce in so short a time. Germany would be in great confusion if the news is true – and poor Phillip [..?] will have to join his regiment. Well! I wonder what effect War would have upon us at Sitka?

We have been married four blessed months today! This morning I asked Hampus if I had made him happy during that time? He said "I thank God for it; you truly have done so" –

June 3rd. I am continually disturbed, and am afraid you will find this letter very unconnected and full of dates my own Mother. I don't feel very strong now – and am not so well this week as I have been all the previous ones. But that will soon pass over. Mrs K[ostromitienoff] tells me just at this time, (3. months) you must be most careful, and never are so well, as you are after the 4th month is past. Therefore sweetest Mother forgive and excuse if this letter is dull and stupid. If we were but at Sitka, or on the way at least. I have so much work to do, so much cutting out, and making ready for the school children to work, that I begin to feel restless and fidgetty to be off – Mrs K[ostromitienoff] is working away busily at my quilt, which will be very pretty I think, and strong and lasting too. Mr Davidoff, a russian officer who is here for a short time, told me today his letters received by the last mail from S[ain]t P[eters]b[ur]g were of *31st March, 1st April.* So I wonder why you did not write. Perhaps you sent your letters over Siberia? in which case they will not be in Sitka before the end of the year – but we surely gave you the Russian Consuls address, asking you to send your letters this way? […]

This time last year we were making preparations for going to Tavastby! Was it not like a preparation for going to Sitka? You heard constantly from Aunt Margeret about her 5. years life there, till you seemed to be at home there! O! how wonderfully wonderful! Who could have supposed, that the anniversary of *that time*, would find me there? I really think it was a merciful interference of Providence, to make you better acquainted with the place, which was soon to become y[ou]r childs Home. I like to think so – don't you Mama Darling? And just look, how fast time flies! Four months have already passed since we parted – how soon will not five, even six years pass, if we are all spared so long? How much we shall have to say to each other, I

---

63 The war between France and Austria started at the end of April 1859. It ended two
    months later, after the battle of Solferino.
64 The Crimean War 1853-1856 between Russia on one side and Turkey, France and Eng-
    land on the other.

like to think of that time, even now – What changes will have taken place! and where will you be? – Hampus and I are continually speaking about you – neither of us think you will remain in Finland. Nor do I think you will live in England – Hampus always think you will choose Dresden, having that darling Mrs Hawthorne there, and I too think, this is not an impropable event. You have always loved Germany – and there dear Babette would be happy again. – […]

I hope Olga Ammondt is well. I shall never forget the imploring look she gave me on taking leave of me, with her beautiful large eyes full of tears, praying me to promise her, if ever I could be of any use or help to her little girl, should she be no more, when I return, that I would not fail to be a friend to her. Dear Olga! May God preserve her and her husband still many and many a year, and may they live to see their little Constance the Joy & delight of their heart. Why does this thought of death persecute her – I mean why does she believe she will die soon? "Du vet, Anna!" she said, "du kunde vara henne en gång af stor nytta!" [Swed. You know, Anna, you could be of great use to her then!] – Emilie Berg Hadi[?] made me promise the same thing. I earnestly pray that both children may never be deprived of a fond Mothers care – who can make up for it? But I seem to understand Olga's feeling *better now*, than I did then – for I some times think of myself in the same way, and when my heart is overfull of joy and thankfulness at the hope which fills my breast, the thought comes over me, "O! if it were not to be Gods will, that I should live to enjoy that happiness" – Don't think I indulge myself in such thoughts – they only come over me at times – and I suppose, are natural to my state. For God forbid! that I should ever mistrust Gods goodness – He, who has given me *all things*! To whom alone, I owe my present entire happiness!

We had such a nice hour before luncheon. I was working at a pair of slippers for Hampus, and he read Washington Irvings "Alhambra" aloud to me. How beautifully it is written. My Darling has bought all his works for me. I have not seen him since luncheon; he came in when I was done – I saw a cloud was over his brow – some disagreeable news from the Advocate I suppose. O! that this business were finished – and we on board the "Codiac" under full sail for Sitka. This you see is my daily wish.

*June 5*th *Sunday*. […] I wished to write to Babette herself, telling her, how I have made 16 lbs[?] of preserved strawberries and 9. lbs[?] gooseberries, thinking of her all the time, and inwardly thanking her for the good instruction she gave me in that way. Tell her it turned out very good, and is going to Sitka with us. The fruit here is splendid – grapes will soon be ripe – Mrs Kost[romitienoff] will send some to Sitka. Peaches, apricots, plums, cherries, apples – everything of the best kind. But the climate is extraordinary. The forenoons are very fine indeed; but every day regularly at 12. it begins to blow and the sand, on which the whole town is built, flies about in volumes, almost blinding you – the evenings are cold. You always go out in the forenoon with an overcoat on y[ou]r arm, and up to this day, the ladies wear fur tippets and muffetees. Is not that queer. […] How does my little pupil play? has he made great progress, and what have you settled about the piano? Tell me everything, you possibly can think of darling Mama – and write often; *once a month*. Don't pay your letters, but pray, pray write. Perhaps one letter more from this country and then I cannot say when you will hear again. I promise never to miss an opportunity either by Siberia or this way. Anyhow precious Mother, you know beforehand, that I expect the great event, the great Blessing about 12th or 13th December – I pray God, I may hear from you before that. And now Goodbye and God ever bless and preserve you, my own dearly loved Mother. I address this to Uncle Adolf, supposing he will surely know your address – I hope you are somewhere in the Country, if not in England, enjoying, fresh air, lakes, berries and long, warm nights.

My Hampus speaks for himself – Give kind love to Esperance – a fond Kiss to Ormelie and herzliche Grüsse an die liebe Babette [Ger. kindest regards to dear Babette] – A fond, warm embrace darling Mama from Your own devoted Child

Annie

Love to all friends. I hope I have not forgotten to mention any. *farewell*!

No. 26[65]   Sitka! Sunday July 3rd 1859 –

My own precious Mother!
We have not yet been 24. hours in this our new Home! But thanks be to God that we are here at last! After five months incessant travelling, and many shorter and longer stoppages on the way, we landed here finally yesterday forenoon at 12. o'cl[ock] July 2nd being the day five months we were married, and the day we parted from you my own Mother. To express my feelings of Joy, gratitude and delight, would be impossible. For althou' this journey, has in every way been one of great and manifold interests, and one which will ever remain in my memory as beautiful, still my *"Sehnsucht"* [Ger. longing] to reach Sitka, *our home*, was, especially since our landing at San Francisco, growing intenser and greater day by day, and hour by hour. I was longing to be doing something – longing to make a home for my Hampus – and to say the truth, was even tired of travelling so much. You can therefore easily understand the feelings, which filled my whole heart and soul yesterday morning at 6. when Hampus, who had not gone to bed all night, came in to my cabin saying "We see land! – we are long since in our own territories – in a few hours we shall be in Sitka" – I wished to get up immediately, but Hampus told me to lie still, as it was very foggy and cold, and not worth my while going on deck yet. So, having had many disturbed nights rest, owing to a heavy storm which commenced at 12. on Tuesday night and continued the whole of Wednesday 29th June, then a violent

---

65   Anna wrote and sent No. 25 a couple of days after she started to write No. 26.

Novo-Arkhangel'sk 1851. With the governor's residence at the right and at the left the Tlingit Orthodox Church, built into the palisade. The Royal Library of Copenhagen.

squal on friday evening, & one or two more during the night, I soon fell asleep with a happy and tranquil mind. At 7. Hampus woke me, and told me to make haste up, else the snow piked mountains and many islands, would soon again be shrowded in dense mist and lost to my view. Up I got, and dressed, washed and combed my hair in no time, anxious to get the first glance of our future home. When we came on deck, I was indeed delighted. Such beautiful lofty mountains, their summits covered with snow, resembling the views I have seen of the Alpes, and numerous islands dotted here and there, met my eye. Unfortunately I could not see much, nor very distinctly, for they were all more or less obscured by fog – and I am told you have not many days in the year, when they are to be seen free from fog. But still it was splendid – far surpassing any of my expectations, which was a most delightful surprise. The sea was like one large sheet of glass, and for the first time, I saw the back of a whale – a small one however. How I wished for you my precious Mother! wished, that so ardent a lover and appreciator of Nature in all its variegated beauty, could have seen, what my pen can but so poorly describe. And how I longed to be able to draw, so as to give you some idea of the scenery, which neither of the views of Sitka you have, give. Notwithstanding the conviction and perfect assurance of a complete failure I am going to make a bold attempt at a sketch, the very first fine day we have. We were called down to breakfast soon after eight – the deck was being scrubbed, the "parade" staircase being arranged and all its brass ornaments cleaned, the Imperial flag as sign that the Governour was on board was hoisted, another one, or rather a streamer was fluttering from the topmast, all the sailors were dressing and cleaning, and everyone looked supremely happy at the thought of being at their journeys end. I felt quite well when I got downstairs, and had finnished eating a boiled egg, and was half through a second, when I suddenly felt sick and got a fainting fit, without loosing consciousness, so that a little Eau de Cologne and bathing the temples, & lying down for a few minutes soon restored me, and I drank a cup of tea with great pleasure. It was the 2nd I had on board the "Codiac". After breakfast I came up again, but Hampus told me I had better dress so as to be in readiness to go on shore, as soon as the boat came off for us. We had been three weeks minus one day on board, all of which time I lived in your blue and grey dressinggown my own darling Mother, and blessed you many and many a time for it, such a comfort it was to me. However as we were to be received in state I dressed in my black silk, ditto cloak and pink bonnet, and looked like a lady walking the boulevards of Paris, instead of being at the end of the World. Two cannons were now fired to call the steamer which was to carry us in. Hampus dressed himself too, wearing the gold embroidered coat he had on at our wedding, cocked hat sword and orders and looked very fine. As the steamer approached us, it fired nine cannons, to which we answered in return. What was our pleasure to see my Brother in law Hjalmar on board – he came off in a boat, & on to our ship, and his astonishment was great when my Hampus introduced his Wife. The brothers had not met for 8. years. Hampus found Hjalmar very much altered, being bald, though 3. years his junior, looking ill and old, whereas Hjalmar found Hampus looking "fetare, gladare och yngre, att det är en fröyd att se på honom" [Swed. fatter, happier, younger, so that it is a pleasure to look at him] – which you may suppose, made me not a little happy to hear. We ordered in wine immediately, and drank each others healths. It was so nice to meet him in this strange world.

Thursday Eve[nin]g July 7th 8 o'clock. We have just finnished tea, the sun is still shining brightly, and as Hampus & Hjalmar, are walking up and down in the next room, enjoying their pipes and cigars, I take up my pen and my story where I left off on Sunday. –

My own precious Mother! I have written to you since then, though you will receive the letter much later – I have sent you a small parcel by Admiral Woewodsky, the contents of which, will, I trust give you much pleasure. Well to continue with our arrival. My whole mind was of coarse [i.e. course] occupied with what I would see, and I was not a little anxious to see our house, which I soon discovered by the flag. Hampus looked pale and seemed to be in a nervous agitation – My heart beat too. As we neared the fortress the Captain gave the word of command, and nine cannons were fired – no sooner had we finnished, than the fortress answered. We were quite near shore by this time – I cannot express my astonishment at the Beauty of the scenery, which nobody had described to me as being so great as it really is. There were crowds of people assembled on the bridge; we stopped and a fine large "slupe" [Swed. slup: pinnace] rowed by 10. men immediately came off, bringing the Governors 2.

principal officers, with his congratulations & salutations. – Hampus bowed, spoke a few words, and then we two descended and were landed one minute afterwards. The old Governor, also "en gala" met us on the steps, and as we came up, all the assembly pulled off their caps, Hampus gave his palto to one of the servants, & we 3. passed on bowing to right and left. The regiment was drawn up in a straight line, officers & men presenting arms as we passed. Such was our entry and reception, the day was fine and the air warm, and my heart was happy and thankful. We passed our house, and went on to that where the Woewodsky's have been living since they left this one. Madame W[oewodsky] ran down to meet us, and although a perfect stranger to me, received me in the most affectionate manner, kissing and embracing me, and talking so fast, she was perfectly out of breath. And this I must say, and shall always be grateful for it, though I found her to be perfectly overpowering in conversation, affection, expressions of Love and regard during the three or four days we were together, I shall never forget the warm greeting she & her husband gave us in this foreign land. She gave us excellent coffee, and after an hours conversation took me into the garden, where she introduced me as future mistress. It began to rain and as dinner was ready we came home again. Our healths were drunk in Champagne. As soon after coffee as politeness allowed, we took leave, being, as you may easily conceive not a little anxious to see our own quarters. The Adjutant accompanied us, carrying the keys. You remember, you have a large, high flight of steps to ascend, which is divided into 3. parts, – two guards stand on the 2nd division, and the barracks are at y[ou]r right hand going up. At the top of the 3rd division there is a small square with benches, you open a huge door and find yourself in a porte cochère, turning to the left you mount some steps, open one glass door then another, and you are in the tambour [Fr. hall], with a door to the left opening into the Governors writingroom with four windows, then my room with four windows, long, narrow diningroom with 2. windows, after which comes another passage room with Ida's room & window, bath room 1. window, long passage & then large kitchen & menservants room – opposite Ida's door, a large room, generally nursery, but now garde robe. Upstairs you have four large reception rooms. First to the left, over Hampus' room, the billiard room with four windows and scarlet merino furniture – then the card room with four windows, large green plants, tables, chairs & musical clocks round the walls – Then the Ballroom with puce furniture, five large windows, 2. musical clocks & a huge Barrel organ, chandelier, branches all round the wall, glasses in every room between the windows, and a full length portrait of the present emperor [Alexander II], which hangs between two folding doors, leading into my reception room, with french blue furniture many flowers, musical clock, sofa and divans, lookingglass tables and four windows. Beside this room, are two shut ones – the *Kanzlei* [Ger. office], where the secretary and his clerks write all day long – they have a separate entrance – Opening off the long side of the Ballroom, you have Bufette 1. window and serving room 1. window. Then you have the garret with closets and ward robes and lock ups innumerable – But above all, you have a fine view everywhere. I have asked Hjalmar to make me a plan of the rooms, which he has promised to do. We have cannons on 3. sides and towers on four, and a nice walk with trees on two sides. Outhouses in number, though dilapidated. A famous bath house & washing and mangling rooms – Pigeon, fowl and pighouses and ice cellar and everything you can think of. The same afternoon I immediately set to work with the help of Ida and the servants, and we slept that night on our own nice bed and sheets. The room had already undergone wonderful change. The next day Sunday, was very unlike the holy Sabbath, as Hampus had to receive visits and give orders, we dined with the Woewodskys, returning home after coffee, when Ida and I again arranged the house. On Monday we dined at home, Hjalmar and the swedish Pastor Winter, being our guests. On Tuesday Hampus received in form the Government of Sitka – The whole town, gentlemen only, assembled upstairs at 10 – and then the 2. gentlemen mounted, Hampus looking as pale as death, & being very agitated. MadameW[oewodsky] called upon me, my room was then exactly as it is now, & I received no ends of compliments from the Admiral and his lady, over my good taste in the arrangement of the same. They remained about an hour – At 1. Hampus went to the farewell dinner given at the Club, whilst I dined par invitation with Madame and her little girl 7. years old. We heard them hurrahing – At 3. I came home, & found Hampus there too. He told me, his health had been drunk, and mine had been proposed by Mr Koskell the chief officer, now gone back with the Admiral, and was received with loud Hurrahs. On Wednesday, we gave a farewell dinner – my first – You may suppose, I was anxious it should succeed well – We had our own silver and linnen, and the table looked very nice indeed – We were only 8. and dined upstairs in the Ballroom, where we shall dine every day from next Sunday, when Hampus' officers, secretary and doctor dine for the first time with us and will do so every day afterwards.[66] I have fixed next Monday for receiving the ladys. I feel quite anxious and shy about it – But O! how I pray God for strength and His divine guidance, that I may do all the good I can, whilst I am among them and that I may be liked by them.

*Friday Eve[nin]g 8*th. Hampus and I have just returned from our afternoons walk and while tea is getting ready I sit down to chat with you, having a great deal to say, and only little time for it – the "Codiac" returns with Ice to San Francisco next Monday, or Tuesday at the latest, and I want to send a budget of letters by her. The Admiral and his family, left Sitka yesterday morning, accompanied by our lutherane clergyman, whom Hampus has sent to marry Ludmila [at Aian]. I cannot say how much I like him, and how fortunate I count our selves in having him – Everyone praises him – he is an old friend of Hampus & Hjalmar, who esteem him highly, not only as clergyman, but as a true christian and honest man in general. It was a real pleasure for me, to be able to make up a small parcel for my sister in law, to send by him – We also sent some preserves and wine for the wedding, and I wrote to her too.

---

66 "One of the benefits of the salary of an unmarried civil servant [and obviously also of unmarried officers] was a daily meal at the governor's table" (Varjola 1990, p. 39).

I suppose, Pastor Winter will be here again in September, and with him I sincerely hope to receive letters from you. His return will soon be followed by my first trial since I have been married – I cannot think of it without being unhappy – You will easily comprehend the real trial it is, when I tell you my Hampus has to return to San Francisco at the end of October, or beginning of November, and will not be back again before January –! During the hours of danger and pain – an hour which may at the same time be my last, he, my hearts Beloved, will be absent from me, and I shall be alone, in a strange and distant Country, amongst a people, whose language is not my own! O Mama! I cannot think of it, without my heart being ready to burst. Hundreds of miles of sea will roll in stormy tempestuous waves between me and him. At the time when I would most require his Love, his affectionate caresses, his encouraging words and looks – he will be gone! – Gone! – I can neither hear his voice, nor see his bright eyes – And then to think of him exposed to the wild elements in the worst part of the year – O! my whole heart is heavy and anxious at the mere thought – and it is my thought by day and night. – What should become of me, if I had not the Lord in whom to put my trust –? I know He is ever, ever near those that call upon him faithfully, and He will surely give me strength to bear that dreadful hour of parting and that vast, vast feeling of loneliness afterwards. – And O! He will surely, of His great & infinite mercy permit us to meet again after a few months. I pray daily for divine aid and assistance – for I am so weak and miserable. Another cause of anxiety is, that Hampus is so very careless of his health – when I am not near him, he will do all manner of imprudent things – especially swallow smoke, which Willebrand told him was like poison, and I cannot break him of. – But I must be strong for his sake, and strive to make the parting easier for him – my own Hampus! It is an equally hard trial for him, as it is for me, he often tells me, and says if I had any compassion with him, I would not let him see my tears. I try to do so – but often my heart is too full and I cannot help crying bitterly. O that I might accompany him! But Hampus will not hear of it, he says it is wrong and sinful of me to wish to do so, seeing I have no right to endanger anothers Life, which I certainly would do in venturing on a sea voyage so late as November, seeing I am always sick – and what would the consequences be? I tell him the consequences of parting and taking leave of him, may be as bad. But there is nothing to be done, and nothing to be said on the subject – turn it as I may it is equal on all sides. Saying, it were possible for me to accompany him, I should have to remain behind again, and would be perhaps 6. months without him in San Francisco – So there is no gain there. Please God, we all live so long, and health is granted us, I trust I shall be able to accompany him next summer on his tour through the Colonies – Hampus would wish me to spend the summer in "Codiac" an island 300. miles west of this, where there is rich, splendid milk, a nice house, and pleasant climate – During that time we would have some reparations and painting done at home, where it is much required. Unfortunately we cannot begin now, as the smell of oilpaint indoors would make us ill – It ought to have been done when the former Governor left the house. –

Though my Hampus did all he could to congéing Admiral W[oewodsky] with and in all honor, he has received the Government in anything but good order, everything is going to ruin – And our neighbours the Galosches, have showed themselves rebellious, and made an attack some time ago[67] – Hampus takes everything *very conscientiously* as you know; he is anxious and annoyed. I feel an inner conviction that all will be ten times better now than it was and that he will be loved by his "Unterthan" [Ger. subjects], I know – Morning and evening we pray God to give us enlightment and an earnest and willing heart, to fulfill our several duties righteously, that we may be a blessing unto the people – and may help those that stand in need of it – That we may be kind & charitable and that if it be His Will, their hearts may also be turned to do right, and not willingly to give him trouble and anxiety – that these poor wild Indians may still be taught, and brought to the knowledge of Christ and His Kingdom. They burn their dead only fancy! – and though missionaries have been sent out, none have been able to learn the Indian language! Thirty of these wild creatures will be here tomorrow – when there will be a dinner laid out for them upstairs in the Ballroom.[68] I hear the men placing tables & chairs already tonight – Hampus does not intend to have the guard about the house, as Woewodsky had – and I think that is already a good thing – for you must not let them think you are afraid of them. I intend placing myself at the window to see them arive, dressed out in their fine red & yellow blankets, and their faces hideously painted & tatooed. They will not show any homage to the Governor – they will not acknowledge him as their Superior – and while every man & child stands up & pulls off his cap as you pass, and the women courtsey, the Galosches remained crouched on the ground, looking perfectly frightful, & laugh & make remarks as you pass – I would not walk alone where they are for anything in the world – nor would Hampus allow me to do so. – I have visited the school, and hope to do so often, as it is sure to go much better when someone superintends it. There are 18. girls, mostly small ones – the youngest is 7 – and there are several of that age. We get up at 7 – have breakfast a little after 8. as soon as Hampus' officers who come with rapports are gone – After that I go about my household business, visit my little roebuck, which I am trying to rear, as the Emperor wants two – they are very difficult to bring up – & are obstinate & wont eat the first few days after they are brought from the wood. When I come in I order dinner, and it is enough to make all the cats laugh to see and hear me expostulating and consulting with the russian cook, who gives me some times such

---

67 This last violent confrontation in Novo-Arkhangel'sk between the Tlingits (or Koloshes, as the Russians called these Indians) and the Russians took place in 1855 (cf. the present edition, p. 17).

68 In 1841 A. Etholén had established "igrushkas", i.e. feasts, for the Tlingit Indians or 'Koloshes' to promote peace and good will. H. Furuhjelm revived these "igrushkas", although on a smaller scale, by inviting all the local headmen to the governor's house for a feast twice a year (Kan 1999, p. 115 and 149).

A Tlingit Indian.

long answers I am quite lost – Wickström in such extreme cases, acts as interpreter. However we manage to get a good dinner anyway. Ida keeps the keys of the pantry & storerooms, and gives out according to my orders. I have now a creole girl – she came today – I do hope I shall soon be able to speak a little. Then we have an excellent man called "Karavieff[?]" who cryed very much at loosing his former master and mistress. About 9½ Hampus goes out and returns at 12. when we read together – Sometimes I go into the garden in the forenoon – We dine at 1. & drink tea at 7 – go to bed at 10 – Hjalmar takes his meals with us, and is a very nice young man. Tomorrow he will measure the rooms, so as to make an exact plan. Now Good night my own precious Mother. –

Saturday 9th Good morning my own precious Mother!

After dinner. Hampus declares the dinners I give him are very good – I lament that we engaged a Cook in Germany, for I am afraid he will be discontented here, and I cannot wish for any better Cook, than the russian one now in our service – he understands everything, and is accustomed to the want of many articles, which the german may perhaps deem indispensable – However what cant be helped, must be endured – and I hope when he comes, he will make the best of everything. The Galosches were here this morning and held long speeches, which were translated by the interpreter. They did not seem to be very pleased with what Hampus told them – they have been dreadfully spoilt, having had more liberty than they ought to have had –! you cannot be at peace for them. Hjalmar & everyone says, this would be a most peaceful enviable place, were it not for these savage Indians, who are excellent warriors, and shoot perfectly well. Every step you take you have to think of them – the only pretty walk Sitka has, is now made a pest by them – they used not formerly to be allowed to be there, but the former Governor was as it seems afraid of them & did not drive them away. Hampus wishes to do so but how – and if he will succeed, is another question. We have a battery, and cannons and a watchman outside the wall which divides their village and wood from Sitka – but still they are so to say our next door neighbours. Some of them have most fierce physiognomies – they look so cunning and as if brooding some evil – others look very tame. Please God, all will go well and they will not give Hampus much trouble – at least I hope so. –

We have been here one week today. I like Sitka better each day – and though you are lonely here, and have to make a sacrifice in many respects in coming here, you can be perfectly happy – Your wishes are in every way attended to as if you were a king or queen. You can have what ever you like, provided it is at all to be had in Sitka. The best of everything is brought and reserved for the Governor. Most exellent fish in any quantity, paying nothing for the same. Milk, and it is very good at present, as many servants as you choose to have, paying them only so and so much per month, for coffee, sugar and tea. Two washerwomen, wood, *80 lbs*[?] *stearine candles* per month, a garden, gardener and all that will grow in it, black bread for the servants & many other things. Still, with all this, Aunt M[argeret] and others have told us, you cannot live on less than 4000 Rubl[es] S[ilver] a year. *Sunday 10th.* Hampus went to the russian church this morning, but I was afraid of standing so long, and therefore read the english service to myself. This is an exquisite day – one of the few we have the year round – We walked up down outside the library windows this morning – the sun was quite hot – the sky blue, and the hills perfectly free from mist, looking most lovely. It is a day made for a sketch – but alas! I know I cannot do anything worth looking at. I am told there is a painter here, who has taken many views of Sitka and the hills from different parts – I asked one of the officers today at dinner, to be kind enough to procure me some of them to look at – if they are at all good, I will send you some dearest Mama.

I wonder where you are, and what you are doing today? At this present moment you are asleep I hope, but I wish I knew in what part of Europe. I thought I had brought all my old letters with me – but I can neither find my Finnish ones, nor any of the english – will you please take care of them, as I should not like to have them lost – Hjalmar gave me 8. stuffed Colibri's the other day. I wish I could send them to you, they are so beautiful. It would be impossible to believe they live so far North as Sitka is, had you not seen them flying about the garden, fluttering about the flowers like a butterfly – I believe the Galoshes catch them and often amuse themselves by tormenting them. They are sweet little creatures, so small, so small, and still they can fly high up in the sky.

Monday 11th. Another such lovely day! Hampus and I took a walk in our garden before dinner, where I found it so warm, I was obliged to take off my cloak – the Colibries were flying about, sucking honey from every flower; they are the most graceful little birds I have ever seen. We sat a long time watching them, whispering rather than speaking loud, so as not to frighten them away. The garden is really a great pleasure; everything that grows there has the brightest freshest green colour, reminding you of tropical plants. We are going to take tea there this evening at 7 – I thought it would be so pleasant. There are benches and tables everywhere, and 2. very pretty pavilions, on the balcony of one of them I have told the servants to lay out the teatable – Don't you think it will be nice. My own darling is writing to you just now – I see him at his writing table – We always keep the doors open now, having had a division made for the bed and wash stand – The room is so large & airy, it is neither close, nor shut up. You see by the plan, though there are many rooms, *those* intended for private use are but few, and no well arranged, so that I am restricted to *one* room, & that bed- & sittingroom in one. Upstairs there are only reception rooms. I wanted to have the blue drawingroom for my sitting room, but it was not possible. The office is next door, & the secretary has constantly to pass through – I would also have been far away from Hampus, so that I should never have known when he went out, nor seen him during the moments he is not at work – in fact, I should have always been alone. Now I can see him, and know he is near me, even when he is too occupied to speak with me. But I am delighted with my room now – I think it looks so comfortable and "treflig" [Swed. nice]. There were no carpets anywhere, when we came, but Hampus has given me 3. handsome velvet ones, which makes a wonderful difference. The double windows are out now – and there is fresh air everywhere. The four first ladies of Sitka, came today by appointment, & even they immediately remarked the difference – and were delighted to feel the fresh air. They seemed to be quite nice people – It was so queer for me, younger than any of them, to receive their low courteseys and homages – I hope I made a good impression on them. The russian priests Wife, 26. years old, is a sweet, fresh looking person, & pleased me much. Everyone remembers Tante M[argeret] with love & friendship – She was so good towards the poor – & did everything she could to make the people comfortable. One of these days, we are going by our steamer to the redoute, a fortified settlement about three hours from here. We take the Cook and the servants with us, and provisions for dinner etc. – etc. –

I wish you could see a little Dresden china cup on 3. feet, which Mary Jones gave me, filled with flowers now standing on my writingtable. I picked them upstairs all except the geranium, which I have in my room, & brought from San Francisco – The rose and the fuxias are from M[ad]am[e] Woewodsky's day.

The writing table looks very pretty. We have the handsome family Bible the dear Lambs gave us, with the prayer book on the top on one side, and a carved folding book holder on the other. A handsome inkstand from Mary C[autley] in the middle, with candlesticks on either side – my writingdesk in front.

*Tuesday morning 12*th. Good morning own darling Mother!

Hampus and I filled up the rooms we mostly inhabit, yesterday afternoon, and so minutely did we do it, that we were several hours about it. I think you have now as complete an idea of our home, as it is possible to give. The Library and Maproom have a separate entrance, the door communicating with them, which is at the bottom of the stairs going up into the Bufette, is now walled in – but when Constance comes to live with us next year, Hampus intends to take them & fit them up for her & her nurse. The Library will then be removed into a handsome new building at the foot of our long staircase. My own Mama, where and how are you? and how is everything going on with you all? how intensely I long for letters – I cannot say! My little darling Ormelie, how is he, and what can he play now – how is dear Babette – does she speak of me often, and is she happy & contented? does she like our house. How is Uncle Charles and Faster Albertina? My fond love to them and dearest Moster. I wish precious Mother you could translate this for them – I cannot write so minutely to anybody else, and still I know they long to hear everything about us & our Home. Some how, when I have described everything to you, I cannot sit down & write it all over again – this has taken so much time too, that I have not written to anybody else. My dearest & fondest love & kisses to my own Florence – I hope she is married – & that she will write. […] God bless you, my own most precious & beloved Mother! The fondest kisses & embraces – Think that Annie gives them to you on 21st Sept[ember] though this will not reach you so soon. Goodbye then my own darling Mama. Ever & ever Y[ou]r own fondly loving Child

Annie

P.S. How do you like our seal sweet Mother? Picket made it – I think it is very well done. Love to Mathilda Furuhjelm and all her family, from us both.

No. 25   Sitka. July 5th 1859
                                                    Tuesday forenoon.

My own Mother!

By this opportunity I write but a few lines, seeing the post over California and Panama goes next week, by which you will get my first letter from Sitka, long ere this reaches you. Therefore I do not send my first letter by the old Govenor, Admiral Woewodsky, as I had at first intended, not knowing then of the ship going to San Francisco; You may most probably receive two or 3. letters before this little parcel arrives, which will not be before December – I hope my own precious Mother, you will like the little brooch, and wear it often. It is a very good likeness, though I look very serious, having felt very tired at the time it was taken I hope it will come in time for Christmas. Not knowing any of your plans, nor where you are likely to be spending next winter, I address it to Admiral Etholén, taking it for granted Aunt Margeret will know where you are – Should you be in England the Etholens will inform you of its arrival, and await your decision about where you wish to have it sent – In every way I take it best, not to send it to Helsingfors, where it might be lost. O Mother Darling! how inexpressibly happy am I not to be here – and after one or two weeks I trust & hope the house will be in perfect order. The former Govenors lady seems to have been a *real* russian, neither loving nor appreciating cleanliness, nor what essentially contributes to its maintenance, *fresh air*! Though we are in the month of July, we found every window hermetically sealed, and in some rooms only a few loopholes to let in the air, as if we were living in the Artic regions, instead of in a place, where everyone tells me, there is scarcely any winter, or at best, only three weeks of it! – I would suffocate were I to live blocked up like that – and most assuredly all health would fly out of even those miniature windows. The glasses are dirty, and nothing painted – As soon as "det gamla herrskapet" [Swed. the old master and mistress] have left, we are going to turn the house topsyturvy, and have the washerwomen in to clean. Notwithstanding all these drawbacks, my room par excellence looks even now most comfortable and I received no end of compliments from Monsieur & Madame Woewodsky yesterday, as to "votre parfaitement bon gout, Madame. Nous ne pouvons reconnaitre cette chambre" [Fr. your very good taste, Madame. We cannot recognize this room]. It is my greatest delight to put the house in order and make everything as comfortable as possible.

Later. I have been going about household affairs all the afternoon – We are going to have our first dinnerparty tomorrow – consisting of 8 persons, including ourselves – It is in honor of Admiral Woewodsky, for whom the public of this place gave a farewell dinner today, and presented him with a silver cup (pocal). My Hampus was also there, so Madame W[oewodsky] asked me to dine with her and her little Annika[?]. I cannot say how I hope all will go off well tomorrow – I have put the desert out, given out silver, and given various orders to the man & maidservant, who are both exellent people thank God. Our teatable is spread: it looks so lovely – how I wish you could see it my own Mother; or even that you could from where you are, see Hampus and Annie sitting at it together. O! how happy I am! how good, how merciful has not my Father been in His dispensations towards me. Lord I beseech Thee make me truly thankful. –

But in all my Joy, one heavy thought weighs at my heart – My own precious husband must return to San Francisco next November, and will be absent for two months! he will not be here, not near me in the hour of danger and Joy! O Mama! I cannot think of it without tears. The whole wide, vast, tempestuous ocean will separate me from him – He will be exposed to wind and storms! – and I not there! I wish to go with him – but he will not hear it mentioned – and says it would be a down right sin, that I have no right to put my life, and that of another being in danger, that it is my duty to stay. I know it is, and that it would be folly to go so late – But what shall I do without him? how often have I not cried bitterly on board the "Codiac", when the wind was howling, & the waves beating against our bark, at the thought of my Hampus soon again being exposed to worse storms – in the worst part of the year! – O Mama! do not think I have forgotten where to find and pray for strength. Indeed, indeed I should fall and sink, did I not trust in the mercy of a loving Father, who has of His infinite goodness brought us safely across half the globe. Truly I look to Him for aid and help, and confide my treasure in His hands, into His merciful care, knowing that He will permit us to meet again, if it be His Almighty will. But still I tremble to think of it, and know not, what will become of me – I cannot but think of the month of December, without the most serious feelings – Who can tell what God has decided over me? It is an hour of danger I have to go through – And alone, alone, amongst strangers, in a strange land. – But I must be strong! for his sake – and not make, what is absolute duty for him, more painful & difficult than it already is – When my feelings overpower me, he says I must help him to bear his trial – O my precious husband! – It will be a hard hour for him too – May God help us both – I pray daily for strength and support – Now I am getting weak again – so, no more about this. –

Wednesday Morning 9½. July 6th.

Good morning my own precious Mother. We have long since had prayers & breakfast, and I have been over the yard into the washing – wood and fowl houses, have fed my pigeons and chickens and must now finnish this letter, as I must superintend the laying of the table & look about several more things. Hampus is out – I am often alone, and get but a short peep at him during the day. It was such a delightful feeling when he came home last night, and I went to meet him at his door – he said "Ack, hvad det är skönt att komma hem till sin hustru" [Swed. Oh, it is so wonderful to come back to one's wife] – We were alone and undisturbed at tea, & afterwards sat half an hour outside, looking at the fire works, which were very fine. I have thought much of Babette – she would be charmed with my cupboards, presses, wardrobes, garrets. With the thousand conveniences this large house affords – I will give you a minute description in my letter going next week. This is a lovely day, the air is dry and warm, but it rains generally. Our garden is a great Joy to me – We can plant all manner of things in it, besides the pleasurable walks and shady seats & two summerhouses it contains.

How I wish our piano were here. I have an old crazy square one in my room – but it cannot give anyone satisfaction to hear it –

I was reading Milton last night – Some passages struck me as particularly beautiful, and beautifully expressed others again were so complicated, I often found difficulty in understanding the meaning. It is no easy thing to read Milton rightly, so as to convey the sense – and I longed for you my Mother, to read it to me. Hampus and I were busy reading Washington Irvings works – We read *Alhambra, Mahomed & Columbus* on board the "Codiac" – I am quite charmed with him as an author – We hope to have many pleasant evenings together – reading aloud & working. But I must finnish. Where and how is my Florence? dearest love and kisses to her. –

May this coming Christmas be a blessed one to you & all I love my Mother. May this find you well & happy – It will make you happy I know – Thank God I am perfectly well & active, & have got over my fatigues now –

God of His infinite mercy bless and keep you now and for ever – Love to all dear friends in Finland.

With a childs fondest embrace ever Y[ou]r own loving, loving

Annie

No. 27   *Sitka Saturday morning 6th Aug[ust]/25. July 1859*

My own precious Mother and Sister!

You may fancy my great disappointment and sorrow last Thursday, when after having watched the Bark "Sophie Adelaide" from 7½ in the morning, till 1. forenoon, the post was brought up to Hampus, containing only official letters and dispatches, and no end of Newspaper, a letter for Wickström adressed by your hand, but no single line for ourselves from anyone. Neither Mama, nor Florence had written to us. I could not believe my eyes – and vainly searched through all the papers & enveloppes, but found nothing. I assure, it was with a choking sensation in the throat I went upstairs to dinner. Almost all Hampus' officers had received letters. The secretary had one from S[ain]t P[eters]b[ur]g of *31st May* or *12th June* – our style. Not a line from you my ownest Mother, since *19th March*, and still I have written incessantly. In vain I think backwards and forwards, why this silence? But I cannot make it out. That you should not have sent off any letters since last March is a thing nothing will make me believe – but which way have you sent them? – I now beg you dearest Mother, and dearest Sister, where ever you may be, *always* to send your letters *Via New York and Panama* to the Care of the Russian Consul at *San Francisco*. I am sure we gave you this address long ago – – – –

Well, nothing can be done – and I must even have patience till the next ship comes – "Sophie Adelaide" returns to San Francisco tomorrow, with Ice, and will please God, be here again next October – The steamer which took the former Governor to Ajan,[69] returns in September – O! that I might receive some letters then. In November "Codiac" returns also from California, so that you see there is more communication than you thought, and if you will but send a letter every month, we might be kept

---

69   The port of Aian on the East Siberian coast had replaced the inconvenient port of
     Okhotsk. A new trading station was established in Aian and in 1845 the RAC moved its
     Okhotsk office to Aian, which became the principal port of transhipment (Bolkhovitinov
     1997-1999, 3, p. 76).

en courant of what you and the world are about – and should I be disappointed by 1.
post, the next might bring me two or three. Darling Mama! You have ever been the
best of correspondents – don't forget that your far absent child expects to be most
remembered. –

Where are you my Beloved Ones? – this question Hampus & I are constantly
putting to each other, and many are the conjectures we make as to what you can
be doing. It is indeed dreadful to know nothing, especially considering the painful,
recent occurrences and circumstances[70] in our family, at the time I left my maternal
Home. I often feel sad, and think something is wrong – troubles have not ceased
yet; – then I pray fervently to our heavenly Father, imploring Him to protect you
all, from Evil and more sorrows and trials, if so should be His Holy Will. O! that
my Florence were married! and Carl well employed – but Hampus thinks he was too
sanguine, and expected too much at once – seeing he was only a beginner, and no
practised Engeneer. However, I hope and trust, that they have been married, if even
only on 800. Rub[les] the first year – They could, with clever management, live on
that, which would be better we think, that again waiting an indefinite period. [...]

If you have left H[elsing]f[o]rs you have certainly also left your furniture, books
and pictures – Remember my precious Mother, that you keep something for me. I
could never be happy to see everything belonging to you, go into other hands – I hope
always to have for myself and my children, something from *my Home*. Something
of yours – I am afraid, you will be for immediately leaving yourself without any
silver, giving it to Florence – but some family silver I must have too. What has come
down from generation to generation is of infinite value, and I love our old things.

We are sorry, not to have ordered all our things of silver – instead of having two
doz[en] forks, large & small ditto spoons plated – But I tell Hampus, please God, we
return, and are in good circumstances, and are able to buy an estate in some lovely
part of Finland, we can always use our plated things in the country, and leave our
silver in town. These speculations are all supposing Hampus gets Uncle Adolf's place[71]
– as the Etholéns themselves think and wish. We are often Castlebuilding – at least I
am – my Hampus listens, with his eyes brightening (& you have no idea *how* bright
and lovely they are! – I call them my jewels) and the sweetest smile playing round his
lips – but suddenly he sighs, and looks sad, and tells me not to entertain such hopes
– that more wonderful things have happened, than a well to do man in the world,
becoming poor, & Vice-Versa – He prays God, that it may be His holy Will, that
he may always have the means to support his Wife and family comfortable – that
to see me in want, would make him utterly miserable. I always answer him, that I
never can thank God sufficiently, for all the Comforts He has mercifully bestowed
upon us, but, that I trust, should He think fit to deprive us of them, we should be

---

70   See commentary in letter No. 4.
71   A. Etholén was a member of the Board of Directors of the RAC in St. Petersburg 1847-
      1859.

equally contented and happy – and never murmur at our Fathers dispensations. When I build Castles, and think of the Future, thank God, I never have the feeling *"it will certainly be so* – and without riches I cannot live – or there is no possible chance of becoming poor else I would be unhappy" – No! thank God! I build my Castles quite innocently, finding great pleasure therein, and always know, that what God dispenses over us is for our Good! for our Best – therefor I am happy, and look cheerfully into Futurity. –

Our days pass as clockwork – At 8 breakfast. 1. dinner. 7. tea – We walk, read and I work a great deal. Thank God I am very well, and take a tepid bath twice a week – otherwise I always use cold water. But I feel anxious about one thing. I count five months now – and have as yet not felt any movement – My Book and everyone else has told me, the usual time is from 4. months, to 4½ – then why have not I felt any thing yet? You may suppose how anxiously I am watching – as it would be an undeniable proof of the fact, and also of the Life of the child. I feel strong and well, never, or next to never sleep or lie down in the daytime, and am always busy. O! I hope all may go well. If I could but have you to nurse me my own Mother! But now, I shall be in the hands of the friendly, fat nurse, and Ida, and my own Hampus will not even know the day or the hour, or if I am alive or dead! But Gods Will be done! – It will indeed be infinite Joy to meet after all is over – and then please God, to have a sweet little Babe to show him, and put into his arms – he will then first feel and know what Happiness it is to be a Father. Children must be the greatest possible Blessing – My heart beats with Joy at the thought of being called "Mama" – and when I pass the windows of the room named "Garderobe" in the plan, but which will be eventually the nursery, I seem to see some bright, round little face looking from it, and smiling and crowing at the sight of Papa or Mama. We have decided that you darling Mama, are to be Godmother, and my Father in law Godfather. I should also like to ask our dearest friend Mrs Hawthorne to be Godmother, seeing she has always been fond of me since I was quite a child, and has ever been like a Mother to me. My brother in law Hjalmar will be another Godfather. […]

You know Constance is to live with us – but Hampus wrote to his Brother in law Schneider, or requested Pastor Winter to tell him, that as I am expecting my confine-ment this year, and am totally unaccustomed to see anyone with that dreadful illness [i.e. epilepsy], it is his wish that she should remain at Ajan with her sister, under Dr Schneiders care, at least till next year. I would sincerely wish, she could remain altogether, for Ludmila is older than I by 10. years, and is accustomed to her sister, and would consequently not be nervous, which I on the contrary would always be – On the other hand, I would wish to do all I can for my Hampus' poor sick sister – Of course it will be as Hampus wishes. –

I wonder if you have another such lovely summer as the last. We have had unusu-ally fine, warm and lovely days – But today earth and heaven is grey – grey – grey – and it is raining incessantly. Regular Sitka weather. […] We have [been] here 1. month, or 5. weeks, and this is the 3rd letter to you my Mother. My own Mother! I hope you are not living too economizingly now – for Henry's debt is almost paid off, and y[ou]r household much diminished – then why, should you not live comfortably – I am always afraid, that even when you can, you will not buy for yourself what you require, but will always think that you must employ y[ou]r money otherwise. If Ormelie goes to England – and we think it is now high time, he should, so Henry thought, what are Uncle Hannays[72] arrangements for you, tell me candidly precious Mother. I trust Babette will remember her promise to me on my weddingday, to remain with you, I cannot think of you without her. My dear love to her – also to Ormelie, when is he going to send me a letter?

2 o'clock after dinner. This is the most tedious meal, though I have Hampus adjutant on one side and doctor on the other, both Germans, and quiet, gentlemen, the greater part of the conversation is carried on in Russian, of which I can as yet make no sense, occasionally only understanding a few words. I therefore generally retire immediately after coffee, so does Hampus – the gentlemen remain only a short time after us, sometimes they play the great "Positive" Mr. Koschkin having asked me if I would allow it. We have now an additional guest at our table, in a young russian Ingeneer L[ieutenan]t Sitoff, who has received orders to return home over Siberia, and will therefore have to remain over the winter, until Hampus again sends a ship to Ajan. He arrived on Thursday with the "Adelaide". Mr Kohlman the Captain of the same, is an old acquaintance of my husbands, and seems a very agreeable man. He dined with us yesterday and – today – this morning he sent me a large dish of fine oranges, hoping I would accept them. *Sunday forenoon.* The rain and contrary wind prevents Capt[ain] K[ohlman] sailing today – In November Hampus will most likely send him to Russia, round the world, when he will probably touch England; I wish to send home some of the basketwork the Indian plate here, which are really very pretty – The only thing against them is, that when you get them from their hands, they smell very bad, and must be thoroughly aired, before they can be used! You can also have very pretty things made of the ivory of the Morse, and I hope we shall be able to send you some specimens.

Now my own precious, beloved Mother and sweet Sister, goodbye – tell me always the date of the day you receive my letters. May Gods blessing abide with you and us all for ever and may I *soon* hear from you – With fondest, fondest love, ever Your own truly, devotedly loving Child

Annie

---

72   Ormelie, the son of S. Frazer Hannay and M. Campbell, lived in Europe with his aunt Ann, née Campbell (Anna's mother), while his parents were in India.

No. 28   *Sitka. Government House.*
                                                    September 9/21/59.

My own precious Mother, good morning!
And God bless you on this your birthday! May it be the will of our Almighty Father, that this day has found you *well, happy and free from care*, with no clouds
over your brow, no sorrow at your heart; but all peace and Joy, within and around
you. So, I pray God, of His infinite mercy, may be the case – Though one child is
far, far from you – I trust, your eldest and Firstborn is with you, and that you are
there, where you would most like to be, England, Germany or Finland! – Would I
know which. –

[H. Furuhjelm:] Älskade mor, – Jag instämmer af allt mitt hjerta i dessa Annies
välgångsönskningar på en dag, som redan i sig sjelf är oss kär och vigtig utan det
att den är en ibland de vackraste vi haft här, till och med Egecombs molnomhöjda
panna är klar i dag – ett tecken, tror jag, att frid och lung måste råda i Mammas hus
och att Sonuschka[?], den kära, redan längesedan hunnit målet för sina och Carls
önskningar. – I dag öfverraskades jag vid caffé bordet af en gigantisk kringla jemte
andra läckerheter dagen till ära, hvilka lifligt påminde mig hemlandet och förgångna
år. – Snart hoppas [jag] att vi får fira äfven inom vårt hus en födelsedag; åtminstone
dömmer jag dertill af den brådska hvarmed Annie håller på att sy mössor, som knapt
gå på min näfve. –
[Swed. Beloved Mother! Of all my heart I make all Annie's wishes my own – on a
day which already in itself is dear and important to us, and besides that it is one of
the most beautiful we have had here, even Mount Egecomb [i.e. Edgecumbe], usually in clouds, is clearly visible today – a sign I think that peace and quiet must rule
in Mama's house and that our dear Sonuschka[?] already long ago has seen her and
Carl's wishes come through. – Today I was surprised at the coffee table by a gigantic
cake and other delicacies in honour of the day, which was a nice reminder of home
and old times. I hope we shall soon celebrate another birthday in our house, at least
judging by Annie's haste sewing caps so small that they hardly fit my fist.]

After dinner. Now I must tell you my own darling Mama, how we have celebrated
this day. We got up earlier than usual, and Hampus went out before 8, to look at
the work. We had asked Hjalmar to come to breakfast at 9. instead of 8. which is
otherwise our hour. Whilst my husband was out, I made an Omlette, "aux herbes
fines", was my intention, but unfortunately Ida, who was to bake it, thought it was
sweet, and strewed sugar over it, which spoilt it. Then we had coffee, chocolate, and
a large "Bretzel" which turned out very good. The sun shone brightly down upon
us 3. as we sat round the table thinking & speaking of you my beloved Mother, and
I for one, wishing you amongst us. After we had finished, I called in the servants
one by one, and gave them chocolate and cake which reminded me of Tavastby, and

the loveable hostess there, whom I wish I was like. I dressed myself in my brown poplin dress in honour of the day, and Hampus put on a better coat. We read your favourite chapter 55 of Isaiah and prayed earnestly & devoutly for you – Last night after prayers, my own precious Hampus, prayed a short extemporary prayer for you my dearest Mother, and this morning I read his and Hjalmars congratulations for you. So you see, we have in all things born you in mind. Oh my own Mother! when shall I hear from you? when, when shall I know where you are? Hampus is lying on the sofa reading "The queens of England" with which lives, we are both exceedingly interested. I have the 1st Vol[ume] as my own private reading, and Hampus is reading Queen Elizabeth aloud to me. We have in that way gone through the lives of that wretched Henry 8th many queens, and have also read Mary of Modena King James II wife, Mary II. his daughter and Anne. I cannot say how interesting I find this work, and how well written. As you may suppose, my needle flies in such hours, and though I have a great deal ready, a vast deal still remains, and I am often afraid I shall not get all done; especially as the ship, by which we expect our flannel and different lawns & calicos, is so long of coming, and the magazines here, are empty, sighing for fresh supplies, of almost all things.

I must now bid you goodbye my own Mother, and return to my nightcaps, which are however not quite so diminutive, as Hampus has it! –

Thursday 22nd Sep[tember]. This day 2 years we landed at H[elsing]f[o]rs, and this day last year, I returned from the wedding at Terra Nova.

When I began my letter yesterday, I knew of no chance of its going for ever so long, though I told Hampus, some opportunities w[ou]ld surely soon occur, as it had been so the last time I began a letter; this day my words have been verified. A little boat with an *english* flag, was reported to have come in, & especially my curiosity, was as you may suppose immediately engrossed, wondering what it could mean. After a few minutes expectation, the "Portokaz" or 1st Adjutant came in, with a parcel under his arm, saying the Governor at Victoria,[73] had sent a steamer on trade along the coast. The Captain of the steamer sent a letter to some friend he had here, requesting him to purchase two p[ai]rs of boots for his little boy, who is with him. We got despatches from the english Governor "James Douglas" and no ends of newspapers – Illustrated news of the 4th June, which is pleasant and agreeable; we have learnt several new things by the papers. I saw Count and Countesse Perponcher, who were in England with their royal mistress Princesse Frederick William, who had on one occassion dined with the queen. It is queer to think we knew her once; I dreamt last night I had received 3. letters from you my precious Mother – but "Träume sind Schäume" [Ger. literally 'Dreams are foam'] – however I avail myself of this opportunity, and will address the letter to Henry, not knowing whether you may not be somewhere in England.

---

73   Victoria on Vancouver Island, founded in 1843 by the Hudson's Bay Company, was made capital of British Columbia in 1868.

Friday 23rd. As the post only goes tomorrow, I have still another date to give you my own Mother. This is a most tempestuous, terrible day – I pity the poor workmen – for the rain has been pelting all day, and "the wind is never weary" – I felt such a draft over my head in bed last night – This morning I put up my red shawl round the corner near the window, and round the top of the bed where Hampus lies, & hope we shall be more protected now – As soon as the weather improves I must have the double windows put in.

I am going to bake a loaf of Babettes bread this afternoon, to teach Ida how to make it. I cannot say what a treasure I have got in her. She is one of those good germans, who can put their hand to any & every thing – the quantity she goes through in one day, would meet with even our Babettes approbation. You know we hired her, as my particular maid. She works well, changes dresses and makes plain ones, very well indeed. She washes & irons all my fine things perfectly, keeps my room in order, has all the keys of "skafferi, källare, vind" m.m.m.m. [Swed. pantry, cellar, attic etc. etc.]. But now, you must know, she even officiates as Cook, and does her work above mentioned besides. On the Emperors nameday [30.8.], we had our first official dinner party of 36. gentlemen, I was not quite well & did not go upstairs. On this occassion our russian Cook not only forgot part of the dinner I had ordered, but made too little soup, so that 7. were left without any, for what he, in his terror at the miscalculation he had made, sent up these 7. unfortunates, was merely coloured water, stole half the wine for the jellies and made himself tipsy in consequence the day before. He was a terrible thief, and the personification of dirt and disorder; I could not enter the kitchen for fear of seeing something that ought not to be. He had been reprimanded and punnished several times by Hampus, but all to no effect – he thought himself unexceptionable and indispensable, knowing full well, he was the only Cook in Sitka, and did not alter his behaviour. However there had been too many complaints, and daily annoyance, we could bear it no longer – so Hampus sent him marching, as soon as dinner was concluded – to his utter astonishment no doubt – The house is cleaner, the atmosphere clearer since he is gone – Now he is in the wood cutting timber, deprived of all the marvellous quantity of things he stole from us, living upon salt fish. I shudder to think of his sins, & the awful, sinful waste. We have better and cleaner dinners ever since and no quarrels in the kitchen, as there used to be in his day. Ida is cook in the forenoons, and works, irons, washes, pickles or preserves in the afternoons, just as it may happen. She is an educated person, her Uncle was "Professor von Theologie" [Ger. professor of theology] at the Heidelberg university – her family is highly respectable – her father was an "Beamter" [Ger. official] at Berlin, and at his death, his children gained their own bread, though he did not leave them in perfect poverty. She has been 12. years with a Kaufman Familie [Ger. merchant's family] in Dresden, whose relation she is, and educated the children. Then she was with one of the richest Prussian Counts family, but left it having more to do, than she could manage. However she knows all about german highlife, & is neither vulgar nor forward, but a great help & a great comfort – Ever cheerful &

good tempered – well principled, & reads her Bible thank God – loves little children, & understands all about them from their birth. So I consider it a wonderful mercy of God, to have put her in our way. Her wages are 120. Thalers a year. She has never complained once of loneliness or any thing else here, which I consider a great deal, seeing she is quite alone. Wickström is in every possible way equally excellent – & as honest as daylight – Indeed we are fortunate in having these two servants, else I assure you, we would be the loser in many things. I only trust, the german Cook will be honest & clean too. – So much for private household matters. –

Thank God I am very well indeed, and as happy as the day is long – In my last, I told you about my fears at not having "quickened" – We soon after called in "Madame Terintieff" *the medical woman* or female accoucheuse of this place, & by her description, I immediately recognized what I had for some time considered *wind,* as being the proofs I wanted. Since then I have felt them daily and increasing in strength. I wonder if you would find me much changed. I am often astonished at myself. I could conceal it still very well even though 6. and a half month. I dream often very badly – & cannot make myself very comfortable in bed – turning from one side to another is very tiresome – I walk every day, weather permitting – indoors exercise is not wanting, and I never have a capricious nor a spoilt appetite, but lead as regular a life as well can be. We both do so – and pray God our child may feel the good effects of it.

Now I will tell you what I have made or rather give you a list of the Baby linen preparing. –

1. doz[en] small french cambric shifts trimmed with Valencienne. 1. doz[en] larger fine linen trimmed. 1. doz[en] still larger ditto. ½ small french cambric caps with lace insertion that are of different sizes for the 1st week day & night, & are made without tucks, so as not to hurt –

½ doz[en] Scotch cambric night caps, tucks and frills. ½ doz[en] batist ditto, ditto.

1. doz[en] batist finer day caps – 6. embroidered ones with Valencienns [..?]. – 1. christening (very fine, bought at Cheltenham). 3. doz[en] linen napkins – 2. doz[en] fine flannel ditto. 1. doz[en] fine fl[annel] "belly bands". 2. doz[en] fine linen sheets, and 2. ditto fine flannel to wrap the child in & and carry it in. 1. doz[en] linen sheets with broad hem & "hålsöm" [Swed. hemstitch] I think it is called in swedish, 1. doz[en] very fine ditto pillow slips. Mahogany cradle & blue silk quilt.

½ doz[en] jackets. 1. doz[en] long night gowns. 1. doz[en] long flanel petticoats, 1. doz[en] ditto cambric. 1. doz[en] ditto of different shapes & materials robes. 1. white cashemere shawl. 1. pink ditto. 1. blue, 1. rose [..?] jacket to put over low neck. 1. white embroidered cashemere hood. 1. fine done coloured cashemere cloak, trimmed with blue plush. These latter things were bought, ready made at Cheltenham. 1. doz[en] bibs. This is all I think – but half of it is not even begun yet. I am without materials, & anxiously awaiting the ships arrival. Batting sheets & flannel wrappers must also be made – Indeed there is no end to the wants of a little creature. But my excellent book "Bull" says too, "quantity must be more regarded than quality" where funds are small. Thank God for all His mercies – I have been able to have both – Do you like & approve of my things sweet Mother? –

O! how inexpressibly beautiful it will be, when with Gods mercy, and His divine Will, all anguish & pain is over, the little new born Babe is laid safe & well into its Mothers arms! – I cannot conceive what feeling must or can be more heavenly than that. – Ones whole heart must be full of deepest, deepest gratitude! –

I hope it will be a Boy, and have my Hampus golden heart and bright eyes. – Hampus hopes it will be a daughter. –

By the bye, I must not forget to tell you of a fine trick he played Esperance, and one we have often laughed at here. I was asking him one day, what he had told Esperance about me after we were engaged & what she had said to him about me, if she was pleased with his choice. Once E[sperance] asked him "Well, Hampus, how do you feel, are you very happy?" to which he answered "O yes kära Esperance! nog är jag lycklig, men olyckan är, att nu är jag kär uti Florence också!" [Swed. dear Esperance, I am happy, but the thing is that I am in love with Florence too now!] to which E[sperance] exclaimed: "O, älskade Hampus, är det sant? hur skall det gå?" [Swed. O, dear Hampus, is it true? How will it go?] –

I laughed very much at this & asked him if he had left her in that belief, or showed her he was joking. But unfortunately he does not remember having done so. So for ought I know, poor Esperance may be troubling herself silently & endlessly upon the subject. Mathilda F[uruhjelm] was quite right, when she asked me if I did not think Hampus "en skälm" [Swed. a rogue] – for indeed he is so fond of joking and can do so, so cleverly, I have several times believed him to be earnest, when he was all the time only making fun of me. He came home just now, perfectly drenched, and was in truth a dripping Neptune. My darling! he is conscientiousness itself – fair weather or foul, he goes out twice a day, to inspect all the workshops, and see if his men are lazy or industrious. He could not rest this afternoon till he had given orders for those men who were working in the open air without shelter from the rain, should go home. I am sure they like to work for him, he is so considerate and kind. Every day almost, something new comes home for the kitchen, which I have asked Hampus to have made. We wish to have all in order for the new Cook, when he comes, that he may not think, he has entered a dirty, neglected family – Everything bears token of no lady, no Hausfrau having looked after her house before us – and you know, even our experience of russian servants in Finland was, that they were no lovers of cleanliness. [...]

I wish I knew how these people here could be brought to hate sin, and to fear offending the Almighty – For truly, the immorality of this little place is not to be described – no age, neither extreme youth, nor being married, seems to be safeguard against it – I keep, and tell Ida to keep a strict watch over my little Creolian maid, for I should be unhappy, should she be lost, like many, like almost all of her age here. As yet, I have not seen anything wrong – and she has the reputation of being the best girl – her former master & mistress kept a strict look after her – and I hope she understands her own good better than to do anything degrading to her honour & self respect. She works very neatly – but the Creoles are all frightfully lazy. I have been several time to the school, and spoken seriously with the superintendent about the girls – She has so many complaints to make – all praise the time when Tante M[argeret] was here – the school then, they say, contained 50. girls, whereas there are only 17. now & all of them such little things, you cannot expect them to be able to understand much. I should like it to be put again on the best possible footing – but how? I am young, ignorant & unexperienced – But I pray God will help me, for it is my most ardent desire to be of use – to do some good – and to learn the art of being loved by them. – [...]

Hampus wishes to send off letters, so I must conclude – praying God to be with you all and to grant me the Joy of soon hearing you are all well and happy. –

Love to all dear friends – and many kisses to Y[ou]rself, Florence and Ormelie –
Fond love to dear Babette from
Precious Mother
Your fondly loving Child

Annie F[uruhjelm]

No. 29   *Government House.* October 20/4 1859

My own beloved Mother!
It is not pleasant to begin a letter with complaints and grumbling – though I am sorely tempted to do so, seeing I get no letters from you. So many vessels have already disappointed me, I am inclined to think you have forgotten me. Thank God, I heard that you were well, and intending to spend the summer at Palsi, through a letter from Esperance to Constance, of the 27th May, which she received here, a few days after her arival. I was more happy than I can express, to know you were well up to that date. Esperance did not mention Florence's name, so I take it for granted she is still in England, and not married, or going to be this year. I cannot say how I long to hear all about you, and what has happened since we left – My hopes, my ardent expectations are now fixed upon the "Sophie Adelaide" who is expected from San Francisco ere long; surely I must receive letters by her? We gave you 2. addresses I know, one to the Board of Directors, and the other to California. We received the H[elsing]f[o]rs newspaper up to June, and in vain did I search them all through, for the anouncement of our marriage – Surely sweetest Mother you must have forgotten to have it put in – and still it is such an important thing; the english papers too, up to that date, had not either our marriage inserted, and yet, aunt Mathilda promised me to have it done. I should have so much liked to read it in some paper.

About myself my own Mother, I am happy and thankful to be able to give you the best accounts. I have never felt in more perfect health, than I now do – and everyone says it is wonderful, how well I look, and how unchanged I am in appearance, which I know, will make your heart glad to hear. My future attendance, midwife and nurse, said it was always a good sign, when one looked so calm and well, as I did, and that she had seldom seen anyone look so. You remember, how fond I used to be at home, of lying on the sofa, and sleeping long in the morning? Well, now, I scarcely ever lie down during the day, in fact, I ought to do so more, and am never later than 7½ – though I generally speaking am up at 7. and busy all day long. Since yesterday, I have been in a perfect panic, for fear I should not have all my things done. I have but 2. months remaining, and in one month, all must be done, in case of a surprize – besides which, everything must be washed first; and the last month, I ought to be tranquil and have my mind at rest. My thumb is perfectly painful, from holding the scissors so long. I have given out work to right and left, but it is so difficult to get anything well done. Nothing fatigues me so much as sitting up at night; if anything forces me to remain up, beyond our usual hour of retiring to rest, I feel it 2. days after. When we first arived, I read so much, now the days pass often, without my reading anything but the Bible, and sometimes a few lines in the Cookery Book! – strange contrast! but never the less true. O sweetest Mother! would you not like to be here now? and would not I be glad? – The time for my precious Hampus' departure draws nearer and nearer. – I dare not think of what the parting will be! – But pray our Almighty Father, from the depth of my heart, that He will mercifully protect us both, and grant us the inexpressible Joy, of meeting soon again in health. We have already had one or two of the dreadful storms, which blow here in autumn – whilst I lay awake at night, I could not help trembling at the mere thought of my Hampus being exposed to them – and of the bitter loneliness I shall feel here without him! – But when once I am up and well again, I shall have the company, and constant thought and care, of and for my little child – O Mama! how inexpressibly sweet will not the moment be, when with Gods Will, I shall be permitted to lay his firstborn in his arms, and se him fondly press it to his heart. We speak of it so often – His eyes sparkle and shine doubly bright at the thought of being "Papa".

Monday Ev[enin]g 24th. I must write a few lines my own Mother, before going to bed, though I am already tired and yawning – but I have no time to write during the day. It is now 9. We have had tea long ago and after that, we all assembled in Hampus room, where Hjalmar, Constance and my own darling, talked over all manner of Home scenes and events. Some of them laughable, and enjoyable, others again sorrowful & painful. We often speak of my Father in law and earnestly hope the day may yet come, when "Förhållandena" far och barn emellan [Swed. the relationships between the father and the children], will mend. They have indeed all suffered and have heard many a hard word from their own father, and experienced many an unkindness. Such exemplary Brothers, are not often found. How have they not helped and provided for their 3. sisters – how many of their poor Fathers debts have they not paid. Gods mercy towards them all, has indeed been wonderful – all the 4. sons are well off – and have entirely provided for their sisters, these many years, already. Hampus' Grandfather was a rich "Egendom'sägare" [Swed. landowner] and had a splendid estate "Nodsjö"which "Pappa"inherited afterwards, but could not keep it up, and was obliged to sell it, being head over ears in debt – his family were thrown into real poverty and misery, and all union and household peace fled. Many & many are the painful scenes, Hampus has told me of – of his own poverty too, when a mere lieutenant in the finnish Navy – and his poor Mothers want of courage and strength to baffle against hardships – Ludmila, the eldest girl, is now married at Ajan, Constance is entirely dependant upon us, Esperance is with you – and Otto provides for her. I trust she is a comfort to you – and that she is happy and contented with you my darling Mama. I am afraid you keep y[ou]r rooms cold, as she says in her letter to Constance "Jag är ofta hos den goda Marie L[angenskiöld], der är så varmt och så skönt"[Swed. I am often at the good Marie L's, it is so warm and so nice there] – Precious Mother! do not spare wood – do not put yourself to any inconvenience – do not economize to y[ou]r own discomfort, *pray do not*. It makes me perfectly miserable to think you should do so. Surely there is no need for it *now*? Have you made yourself a warm cloak? – tell me if you will remain in Finland these coming years, or not – Oh! when shall I hear from you, and know all these outs and in's. We are glad that Papa was intent upon paying the 100. a y[ea]r even though you were so much against it, seeing E[sperance] is the only child he at all pays anything for, having entirely given over the others. And he can do so – his pension is high – I hope you have had a warm and pleasant summer at Palsi – little Ormelie will have enjoyed himself – I am sure – Where is my Florence? and how are her prospects – and what will she have to live upon?

You cannot think how dear, living is here – We have large expences – Meine tägliche Haushaltung [Ger. my daily household] consists of 17. mouths to be fed each day besides additional ones on Sundays and fête days – Our outlays in England were so great, that what with the large sum Hampus' sisters have cost him this year, we think we can lay by nothing. However I was quite proud of my Books last month – my accounts were much smaller – my Hampus was so pleased. If we had not to keep open table all the year round, we could live on the fat of the land. But you will scold me, and say Fy! fie Annie. But Mother darling, don't you know, that what brings everybody to the Colonies, is to save as much money as possible, & then with Gods Will, to live upon it at home.

But I have not yet told you about Constance['s] arival. So set your mind at rest dès le commencement [Fr. from the beginning], let me tell you she has thank God, been well since the 16th March – consequently 7. whole months, which makes us sanguine and prone to believe, she has mercifully been restored to health. Many changes have taken place in her system, and she is growing fatter with every day. May our hopes not be disappointed. It would be an infinite cause of Joy and gratitude, should she be quite, quite well. Poor Child! she has suffered dreadfully. Her mind is

Prince D.P. Maksutov and Princess A.I. Maksutova.

quite undisturbed – her face and features smooth & natural, her temper easy – and spirits good – Her memory is improving too. She often repeats herself, and is fidgetty and childlike – but perfectly docile, willing and takes nothing amiss. She arived with the Makzutoffs 3. weeks ago – And will be with us forever I suppose.

15/27. Wednesday Night. Thank God! I have at last had the inexpressible Joy and happiness of hearing from you, my most precious Mother. I cannot express how happy I am. Only last night I was lying almost one hour in bed shedding bitter tears, at having again been so mercilessly disappointed, in not receiving letters from you by the Vessel which came in from San Francisco. But my disappointment was soon turned into Joy – for at 9. this morning, another ship was announced, which came in safely at 5 – and the secretary soon after arrived with an enormous post. He was dripping wet, and brought me a small box of grapes and apples. Now it is late, and I am tired; especially after my disturbed and anxious night. But I cannot go to bed, before having sent you my warmest thanks and a thousand kisses. After having been disappointed so many times, and not having heard from you since March – you can imagine we were delighted – and thank God from the depth of our hearts for the good accounts we have this day received. But why you do not send a letter regularly each month, I cannot conceive! I could then have a connected and progressive account of you – whereas now – I have heard everything at such great intervals. For instance, through a letter from Aunt M[argeret] dated *20th July* in answer to mine from *San Francisco in June*, I heard you were all at Palsi – and enjoying yourself – this I could have heard from you – Otto's letter is of 24th July! – and yours only

11th June. But nevertheless I am so thankful for what I have heard, that I will not complain – But only beseech you darling Mama to send a letter each month – they accumulate at San Fran[cisco] and I can get several at once – instead of being 2. or 3. mails without any news. I must go to bed now – May our heavenly Father watch over you and us for ever and ever Amen. I cannot say how happy I am my darling Sister is at home again – Precious Mother is now no longer *so lonely.*

Sunday Night 25th Oct[ober]/6th Nov[ember]. […] Beloved Mother! my warmest and most affectionate thanks, for all you say about my more than happy prospects. But I thought, this coming event, would have filled you with more happiness, than it seems to have done! I expected you would have said more about it – Would have been overflowing with Joy and thankfulness. O my Mother! in the depth of my soul, I feel the truth of what you say concerning my Duty as Mother! *our* duty as parents! – Believe me – from the very beginning I have prayed for my Child! and have earnestly, O so earnestly prayed God to show and teach me my duties – that I might *never* forget children are a gift from above, are precious charges, committed to our care and training in all that is good and acceptable before God – and at our door, will the blame, and the shame lie, if we neglect to train them from their earliest infancy in the Way and nurture and knowledge of the Lord. Their souls are immortal. For them the Saviour died, and shed his precious Blood! should it not be our most heartfelt prayer & desire, to bring them early to Him, who said "Suffer little children to come unto me, and forbid them not, for of such is the Kingdom of Heaven"[St. Luke 18.16] – Daily, hourly I feel more and more "Life is real! Life is earnest" – what deep responsibility, what holy duties will soon be mine?! – And may our heavenly Father teach me and lead me the right way – may I never forget, that our precious Child is *first His!* – it is a loan from Him! – O Mama! how full to overflowing my whole whole heart is! So much true Happiness have I received from Him! First my husband – the best of husbands – to whom my whole heart belongeth – and now this Child? Mama! Do you know? do you understand how happy I am? and O! how deeply grateful for all all these undeserved, unmerited, but infinite Mercies? – – – Four weeks more – and I shall know what it is to pass through *that hour*! But I put my whole Trust and confidence in God – and pray Him to give me strength and patience – and if so be His Holy Will – to turn anguish into Joy unspeakable! Like a black shadow, over my otherwise bright heaven of Joy – lies my Hampus speedy departure. Perhaps I have him not more than one fortnight longer! – and then he will be gone! – and I shall be alone! alone!

This thought is overpowering at times! O my God! Give me strength! Abide with us – with him there! and me here! [..?]

Sunday Nov[ember] 1st/13th. This is a holy and solemn day for us. We have been together to the Holy Communion Table for the first time as husband and Wife. What inexpressibly great, and numerous mercies have we not to thank God for? O! how wonderfully good He has ever been, and still is towards us. I had so much wished for the Holy Sacrament, before my precious husband leaves me, and I fall ill – I needed strength and submission for the coming trial – and forgiveness for all my manifold sins. How wonderfully comforted I felt, I cannot say – and how full of holy peace, Joy and deepest thankfulness, as I knelt beside my husband at the altar, and heard those precious words of our Saviour spoken to us. I thought too of you my own Mother – of my Florence dear – and of the last time I partook of the Holy Sacrament, then kneeling between you and my espoused husband. We have crossed half the world since then – and how changed am I. Soon, perhaps sooner than we think – I shall be a Mother! – What holy duties will then be mine! – Oh, that the divine Spirit of God may teach me, to perform them with all diligence – without His guidance and assistance I can do nothing. When I feel my Child, moving within me, and look at all the preparations making for its reception into the world, I feel, as if no feelings could be holier and more beautiful, than those of a Mother's must be. Sometimes, it is true, my heart fails me, at the thought of suffering I cannot escape – and especially as I shall be quite alone – but then I pray for patience and support from Above, and feel sure, that my Father will help me, and let me live to welcome my Hampus back to his Home, Wife and Child, if so be His Almighty Will. –

I was obliged to stop writing the other night being too excited to write more – as I *must* try to keep in a calm frame of mind, and refrain from all causes of nervous and mental excitement. –

The other day I put the cradle in order – Hampus was out, & I wanted to surprise him when he came home. He returned rather too soon – I had not finished yet – but he was quite enchanted with the view. The snow white fine sheets & pillow, the white counterpane and dark green curtain, did, and do indeed look most inviting, especially so, by their diminutive size – The nursery is papered and painted – all is in order now, and my mind at rest, thank God.

Later. I have been reading D'Aubigné's History of the reformation, aloud to Hampus – have you read it? It is admirably translated, and an interesting work! – I hope by [con]tinual reading and speaking english with Hampus, which I do more[?] frequently since my Sister in law is with us, not to forget it – or rather, not to get out of practice – Please God I hope always to speak english with my children – and I flatter myself, that they will learn several languages at once, seeing Russian, English, German and Swedish are daily spoken in our family – With Mr Koschkin, I always speak french, and will continue doing so, even when I have attained knowledge of his own mother tongue, for fear of forgetting it altogether. I am happy to be able to tell you, I am making progress in russian – the servants all understand me – and my pronunciation is said to be good. I also write it a little, as my Books must be kept in russian; I mean the shopkeepers Books – and now I get on without Hampus, using the dictionary, when I do not know how the words are written – At the end of the month, I make up all my accounts, pay the Bills, and enter all the items, into my own Household Book – Last month the *extra's* mounted to an enormous sum – as we were obliged to buy cambric, shirting, linen & flanel *here* – and bought them also in England, but unfortunately sent them by the "Garitza" which seems to be never coming. Hampus desires me to say, that in April, you must always send one letter over *Ajan*, which will reach us in autumn, when the ships always come from there – all the other letters send direct to San Francisco – and do not miss a mail I beseech you, Mother darling. – [...]

Helsingfors is attired in its winter garments I suppose – It must be a year just now, since we first heard of Hampus, and since all my friends and acquaintances settled, that we would certainly become a pair – How time flies! –

Tuesday Ev[enin]g 3rd/15th Nov[ember]. I must write a [letter] every day now, so as to have all my letters ready by next [mail], when my Hampus goes, and will take them with him.

On the 1st October, the gentlemen of the Club were so civil as to give a Ball for "Anna Nikolaivna"[74] where I was obliged to dance 5 francaise, and stay till nearly two – You can easily imagine how tired and sleepy I was, and how I longed to get away from all the honor paid me, and creep into my comfortable bed. The Ball commenced, or rather, the guests were invited at 7. It was nearly 8. before we were there, Hampus having had a chair arranged for me, in which I was carried by 4. men, and they then returned for Constance, whilst I waited in Mr Koschkins room's which he had offered me as room of retirement. Hampus waited in another room, and as soon as Constance arrived, and we were in order, we entered the Ball room, going first through an anty-room, crowded with gentlemen, who all bowed most reverentially as we passed – I first, then C[onstance] and then Madame Makzutoff, who however ought not to have waited for me, but have been there as 1st hostess to receive me. In the Ballroom, the walls were lined with ladies; all rose and bowed and immediately the music struck up. I was not a little "förlägen" [Swed. awkward, i.e. I felt quite awkward] you may suppose, having to pass up the whole room, bowing to right and left, and was glad when I reached my seat, and dancing commenced, or at least the Polonaise. My 1st cavalier was a young officer, master of the Ceremonies that night, Hampus led Princess Makzutoff. Of course I did not dance anything else – There were preserved pineapples and new confîtûres and Bonbons – very good ices, Wine, lemonade and almond milk and supper at 12. It was so strange to me, to see with what distinction one is treated – everyone makes room, and in fact, you are le roi et la reigne des Colonies [Fr. the king and the queen of the colonies] – I asked myself over and over again "Is it I? is it Anna v[on] Schoultz"? who but the other day was a little obscure 'Fröken' [Swed. young lady], and is now such a grand Lady in all eyes? – My Hampus is a perfect Governor in every respect – his look and appearance inspire[?] love and respect; he looked so handsome, and has such an affable, agreeable and noble way with everyone. I was tired enough the following day, but nevertheless got up in time to have coffee ready for Hampus at 9. I was dressed in a low black silk dress, made in London, black silk mantilla, and headdress of pink roses with black velvet and beads, bought in P[eters]b[ur]g. We have this year neither given Ball or

---

74   Anna Furuhjelm was called Anna Nikolaevna Furugel'm in Russian.

parties, owing to the circumstances I am in, and also being without a proper Cook, it would give no end of trouble. When Hampus is gone, we shall live like mice, and economize as much as possible. Now darling Mama, do send me your likeness – it is my most earnest wish and desire. You can always send a small parcel over Ajan, also by the Company's ship, which generally leaves S[ain]t P[eters]b[ur]g in Oct[ober] or even over Panama; for Mr Koschkin got several that way. I have ordered six p[ai]rs of boots from P[eters]b[ur]g; they are really the best and strongest – here they are dear and worse than bad; From Hamburg, we have ordered many things – not for present use – but to take with us, when we return home, please God we live so long, as everything is ten times dearer in Russia. Don't you think I am fortunate in my maids? My own german one, can make dresses and is useful in every way, and has today made me a very pretty cap – the other one, Wendla, from Finland, makes shoes, dresses and is in every way clever with her needle. She came with Constance and Ludmila 3. years ago, and is accustomed to the former's attacks, should they return again, which God forbid! She has now been 9. months without any attack, and is getting rounder and fatter day by day. It is indeed a wonderful mercy – we cannot be sufficiently grateful to God for it – I am becoming more sanguine every day. She has a nice little room at the other end of the house, where Wendla also sleeps. She is a good girl, and a great help to me just now, as she teaches the unexperienced rus-sian Cook how to make many good things, which her Mother taught them at Palsi. I daresay you have already found out how proficient Esperance is in that way – for Hampus and C[onstance] say, that in their greatest poverty they always had good food. I hope you have sent me a long description of how you spent your summer. I quite long for one of your delightful long descriptive letters sweet Mother. My Hampus will have the first perusal of them at San F[rancisco] and I hope they will be some comfort to him in his loneliness. I wish you could see my Baby linen – it is so pretty and complete – O Mother! what Joy! what a Blessing is in store for us. May Florence also know the same, some day.

Sunday 8th/20th. As the time for my Hampus departure draws nearer, I feel more and more sad, and sorely depressed – and how fervently and incessantly do I pray God to help me, and give me strength and Faith – for "all things work together for good, to those who love God" [Romans 8:28] – This has been a day of trials – and I feel very very sad and nervous. Our poor sister, whom we had all hoped was quite well again, had a fit this morning before leaving her bed, and has been weak and uncomfortable all day. I cannot say how deeply this has grieved me; one can so feel for her poor, poor girl – With every day, her faith in her complete restoration has been growing stronger – and now by one blow it is all chattered again. I would give anything not to be nervous. But it is my bounded duty now to keep myself from being exposed to seeing one of her fits – I cannot be alone with her – and she knows it too, and even asked me not to come in, when I went to her room twice this morn-ing – but still, the feeling is inexpressibly painful – I do pity her from the depth of my heart, and would wish to do all in my power to comfort her, and to make her feel happy. She is my Hampus' sister – and though he never would exact from me, the nursing and attending of her, it cuts me to the heart to be obliged to leave her alone, and thereby make her feel more. Truly, she is the one most tried. But she has been *so gentle* – and said she must still thank God, who has permitted her to be well 9. months. Then, this being a great festival, a church, or rather the Sitka church holiday,[75] we were obliged to have a dinner for 36. persons, & this evening Hampus was obliged to go to the Club, and I am alone, and it is the last Sunday he is at home! – So Mama darling! You will understand my heart has been full to overflowing, and I felt miserable when H[ampus] had left me. Thank God I sought and found Comfort in the Holy Scriptures, and feel far, far happier and calmer than I did. I went to see Constance just now – She was sitting on her bed reading, and seemed easier and more comfortable. Please God, this night will pass without any fit. She may be a long, long time free from any – but still we must be careful of her, & never let her go out, or about the staircase alone.

A fortnight ago, I again had a touch of the nervous toothache, in one of my front-teeth, which to my utter astonishment and vexation has decayed in the space of a few months, having been perfectly sound in June, when I was at San Francisco. So it comes true with me, that you lose a tooth with a Child – I account that for its rapidity. I was perfectly knocked up with fright that day; but thank God, thanks to Mr Koschkins kindness, who had some Gutta percha, Hampus has stuffed it splendidly, and it feels all right now. Today another stopping has fallen out of one of my wisdom teeth. O thou poor humanity! as long as we have teeth we must suffer from them.[…]

I am sending you round the world a few pencil views of Sitka, and a few curiosities made by the natives – I am sorry they are not better, but as yet we have not found anything else. –

Wednesday Ev[enin]g 11th/23. My own precious Mother and sister. I must finish this evening; tomorrow by this time my own beloved husband will be at sea! We have been packing, all is ready – provisions in quantity – so I hope my Darling wont suffer hunger or thirst. I can't believe he is going! God give me strength – and O! that He of His infinite mercy will protect my own husband and let us meet soon, soon again. I am so stupid, I cannot write more – I have no thought but one. –

Everything is ready for your little Godchild sweet Mother – I believe Hampus wrote long ago to tell you of our earnest wish that you should be our Firstborns Godmother. My Hampus will finish this sheet – He will most likely be "Papa" there, tho' he will know nothing about it. And so Goodbye and God for ever bless you my dearest Mother and sister. O! that I may have happy news to communicate next time I write. God's will be done! He will be with me. Amen. And God bless you, my own

---

75   The 8th November (old style) is St. Michael's day. The ortodox cathedral at Sitka was consecrated to the archangel St. Michael, the patron of Novo-Arkhangelsk (New Archangel). The cathedral burnt down in the 1960s, but has been rebuilt.

own most precious Hampus! my beloved Hampus – think of your Annie when you write these lines. –

Much love to all dear friends none forgotten.

For ever Y[ou]r fondly loving Child

Annie F[uruhjelm]

No. 30   Sitka. Dec[ember] 4th/Nov[ember] 22. 1859

Again I take up my pen my own beloved Mother, to send you a few lines, not wishing any opportunity which offers itself, to be lost, knowing, that the greatest Joy I can give you, is to let you hear from me, as often as possible. I am alone! My own precious husband left me last Thursday week, the 12/25[76] Nov[ember] in the afternoon at 2 o'clock – O! I cannot say what it was to part from him – and how all life & Joy seems to have left me with him – the days are long and sad – and though I really try to keep calm and quiet, as I faithfully promised my Hampus, I would, the emptiness and loneliness I feel in & at my heart is often more than I can bear – But, thank God except the day he went, when it was utterly impossible for me to control my feelings, I have been resigned & quiet. I have had such cause for gratitude in the lovely weather we have had all along – My Hampus left me under propicious auspices – for the sun was bright, not a cloud to be seen, nor a breath of wind – & I had just feared storms & gales so much. It has been an infinite relief to my mind, & solace to my heart, & I cannot sufficiently thank God for His mercy in granting me this comfort. As Hampus went by the steamer I take it for granted, at least I fondly hope, that he is reaching, or has reached California today – & Oh! that he may find all affairs satisfactorily settled there, and consequently return much sooner than I dared hope. But everybody tells me, he will come home sooner than I think. May he then find all well at home – his Wife, his Child, his sister – O! that blessed, happy day. – it often keeps me awake at night, only picturing it to myself. –
When I saw him put on his cloak, the truth seemed to rush like a springtide to my heart, and it fairly overwhelmed & overcame me. I shall never forget it – it seemed like despair for one moment – Hampus came in with me again, gave me water and Eau de Cologne, brought me into our bedroom, and there we again prayed together, & with his dear hands on my head, he called down Gods Blessing upon us. –

O Mama! if you knew what a husband Hampus is! what a Jewel, a gem his heart – That big, pure, noble heart – that loving, gentle, affectionate heart –! Truly & gratefully I say it, I am blessed in being his Wife – I am proud of my husband – any Wife would be obliged to be so, for all that is true, high and good, you will find in

---

76   It should be 12/24. There was a difference of 12 days between the old and the new style in the 19th century.

him. My only prayer is, that I may be able to make his home after his heart, so happy and bright as he deserves. –

Where ever I turn my eyes, they meet with some sign of his love and care for me. This very writing book, lying on my knees, is from him, & before me are these words written in it: "Åt min älskliga hustru Annie, af Hampus [Swed. To my beloved wife Annie, from Hampus]. – Thou art all fair my love, there is no spot in thee" [Song of Salomon 4.7] – a verse he is passionately fond of quoting.

The longer I live with my Hampus, the stronger grows the conviction, and the more I feel, how impossible it would be to be so happy, did not the same faith, the same blessed Hope, the same Love, unite our souls, and bring our prayers together at the everlasting throne of Peace. Though we are separated in body, we *meet there*. Is it not so? –

I have, thank God, been perfectly well, since Hampus went, except the 1st few days, when my whole body felt as if crushed, and I could hardly crawl, so that I was obliged to keep very quiet. I have not put foot outside the gates since I am alone, but walk up & down outside the house when it is fine. It is so slippery too downstairs, and the staircase more than fatiguing, besides it would be so dull & lonely without him – so I keep up here, where no one can see me, nor anyone disturb me. The only persons I have seen, are the good Pastor, Princess M[akzutoff] and my nurse who comes 3. times a week – And so I am quietly abiding my time, praying God for patience & strength, & wondering and even hoping, each night when I lie down on my lonely bed, that it may be the last one before the great Crisis! I have written a long letter to Aunt Mary, the first since my marriage, I hope it will please her, & make up for my long silence. This letter will I trust reach you at the end of March, or in April. It will go over China to Calcutta, & so by the overland mail home. Hampus is sending a ship to Shanghai for tea, & by it I am writing this letter & one to Aunt Mary. The vessel leaves most likely next Wednesday – this is Sunday. How I wish it could at the same time be the bearer of the joyful news to you. I am going to address the cover, & tell my maid Ida, in case I should be taken ill before, to write to you about it, & put the letter in the same enclosure. How glad I should be! I am lying on the sofa & cannot, as you see write well – but sitting upright for a length of time, is too trying now, and not advisable either. What strange feelings my present situation give rise to – how wonderful a thing is before me! & so perfectly novel, it is impossible to understand how great the suffering will be – & though I fancy it dreadful – I suppose my imagination can never *come up to* what the reality will be! – O my Mother! that you were here! Little could I believe this time last year, what great changes time would have made for me by the time the date came round again. I was thinking of Hampus now already – he too had heard of me – Gods ways are wonderful! – & how has he not strewn my path with roses! – We were in the midst of sadness and sore trials for our darling Florence last year. And God helped her too – Perhaps she is married now? when shall I know? and when will she write? her picture hangs above my head – the light of the lamp falling full upon her face, gives a life expression to her eyes – it is an excellent likeness – I am so happy to have it. Precious Mother! Send me yours – I am so longing for it – let us have a good likeness of "Grand mama" to teach y[ou]r little Godchild to love. The one of Esperance was not bad. […]

Tell Professor Lille, I have spoken a great deal about him, with Pastor Winter, who is an excellent man – educated & refined, and a good, zealous clergyman. His brother is the Platz Mayor [Ger. approximately 'commandant'], married to that fine russian lady. It is such a comfort having *such* a man as y[ou]r clergyman – you can speak to him, and be comforted by him –

Constance, has thank God not had another fit since – though we must expect it again, for I firmly believe her illness is incurable – though to be much improved, as is the case with her – for the doctor has at least been able to bring it so far that she has been 8. months well, & I have heard of a man who had the same complaint being cured so far, that he [had] but one fit in the year – God grant it may be so with her. You cannot think how considerate & thoughtful she is just now – she spends nearly all the day in her own room – & when she is here, always calls in Wendla to sit in the adjoining room, so that I may not be frightened – She promised Hampus to be very careful – darling Hampus, he was more anxious than he wished to show. She is exceedingly anxious y[ou]r 1st letter from Palsi should come, and hopes to hear a great deal about your summer there, & how you liked it – she entertains great love for Palsi, & often speaks about the happy days there with her "älskade Mama" [Swed. beloved mother] – poor girl! she sighed so deeply today when I was telling her about you – & said "huru lycklig är icke den som ännu har en Mama" [Swed. you must be so happy to have your mother still] –

Monday Ev[enin]g. As you see my own beloved Mother, I am still up and well though I have a presentiment, and a strong one, that I shall be taken ill soon, very soon, perhaps tonight – I feel for some hours a strange feeling in my back, which they say, is the beginning – I should be so happy, could this letter be the conveyor of the happy news to you, and my own sister – though it is a most strange coincidence, that it should not first be told you by my own Hampus. –

Has Augusta Munck been confined? do tell me about all I know – everything is of interest – Constance is so impatient for her little niece or nephew to be born, she is always fancying she hears a bustle, and thinks it has begun – she dreamt too, I had sent for the woman. –

O my husband! my Beloved! why are you not here – I feel my spirits sinking, why are you not at my side to comfort & encourage your *Annie*? – *Why? Why?* But "the Lord is my shepherd, I shall not want" – and "Yea, though I walk through the valley of the shadow of death, I will fear no evil: *for Thou art with me*; thy rod and thy staff shall comfort me" [Psalm of David 23] – *Amen!* –

O that I had my husband to pray with and for me now! –

Mother! precious Mother – thy prayers are with me, thou art thinking of thy child – God bless you ten thousand times my own Mother, for *all, all* you have ever done for me – O! how infinitely much your children owe you! May God reward you for all you have been to us, my Mother – & may you still live to see the reward of y[ou]r trouble & care –

But – Mama! if I am not to live – if it is the Lords Will! – Mother dear! I may not repine! – write to my most precious Hampus! to my hearts dearest treasure, comfort him – comfort him – you can do so my Mother – and our little angel! Be a Mother to it – and teach it to love & fear God – and to think of its Mother, who will incessantly pray for her precious Child in heaven.

Goodbye beloved Mother! you have been the very best & fondest of Mothers – forgive me all the sorrow I have caused you unwillingly it is true. –

Is it wrong of me to write so? – then it is best I stop – my heart is so heavy, so lonely. –

My own precious Sister God bless you! O! may you be as truly happy as I have been – My fond love to Carl – a kiss, hundreds, to you all my dearest ones –

Ever & ever Y[ou]r fondly truly loving Child

Annie F[uruhjelm]

Saturday Dec[ember] 10th

As I am still up and well, and feel more cheerful today, I again take up my pen, most beloved Mother – fearing the last pages may distress your mind, which is the last thing I wish.

Well, now my Hampus must be at San Francisco – head over ears in affairs I fancy – God grant that troublesome ice business may at length be satisfactorily settled, and all parties contented. We had such lovely weather the first 10 or 11. days after Hampus went; I was so happy for the long frost – the ice on the lake was 10. inches thick, the men had commenced cleaning it, & were just to cut it, when suddenly the weather changed into snow, thaw & rain, and all labour is lost, and the ice too – Since Tuesday it has not stopped snowing first, but these last days raining in torrents. Hampus would have been so happy – & hoped to be able to send a ship with Ice at the beginning of January – but I fear it will not now freeze again for long. –

I have worked a penwiper and a bell rope for Hampus since he went, and hope to have time to arrange his room before he returns – But I shall scarcely be well yet, if the longed for event does not take place soon. I should be so happy to be up & perfectly strong by his return, that he may enter a house of Joy. If I had but my piano! I begin to fear "Garitza" will never come – it would be so delightful to have it now – I have nothing else to do – & am unable to sit long at anything just at present – the blood rushes into my head – & I am so "uncomfy" – the days are long & dreary – I read a little, walk about the rooms, sit down again, work a few stitches & think a great deal. How wonderful a year, has not this one been for me!? What changes in one twelvemonth! O! it is beautiful in truth, but more than strange. Yesterday was "Anna-dagen" [Swed. St. Anna's day] – how well I remember it last year – & the many cakes sent to us, & the friends in the forenoon. Mina G[ripenberg] drank tea with us, & the rest of the world was at the Veteranen Ball. I am sure you had many visitors and "kringles" [kringla: Swedish cake] yesterday – & you all thought of me. Constance had a splendid one made for me yesterday – I was surprised by it, when I came out to the breakfast room – she had baked some small cakes too, and my maid had decorated the table with green leaves, & brought me a bouquet of green to my bedside when she came in to wake me. All your pictures were decorated yesterday, & my heart & thoughts were much with you. [...] I wonder if Ormelie still thinks of me, and when he will write. My dear love & many kisses – As for Florence, she seems to have given up the idea of writing? still I long for a long letter from her – Tell me all about her outfit – how much was made at home, & what she got in England, how she was dressed as bride, in fact *everything*. [...] – By the bye, I am afraid I have taken the key of the indian chest of drawers with me – at least I see a key on my ring, which is of no use, & does not belong to any of our things. Take care of my letters & other things I left at home, darling Mother. And now I must again stop. This is a dull & stupid letter, written under painful and joyful impressions – But still I send it – thinking it will give you Joy only to see my handwriting, & I would wish to give you as much Joy as lies in my power – Did Florence tell you all, all about us? & all about my precious Hampus – how dearly, how fondly you would love him, yes, dote upon him, if you knew him even as Florence now knows him. I know she loves, & ever will love him as the dearest of brothers. What a beautiful, exquisite thing, an unspoilt temper is – a bright, cheerful disposition, a quiet roguish jokeful spirit, as he has – His eyes sparkle – & twinkle so at times, & he says the funniest things in the drolest way – I think his children will idolize him – & truly he will be wrapped up in them – But God forbid! he should spoil them – the thought of having spoilt indulged children, is a perfect nightmare to me – O God grant, us strength & wisdom, to fulfil our duties as parents better. –

Once more adieu, precious Mother and Sister; fond love to dear old Babette, & *write once a month* to Your own loving Child

Annie

Sunday *29 Nov[ember]/11. Dec[ember]* 12½ o'clock f[ore]n[oon].

My own beloved Mother your child is well and in happy, happy expectation – It has begun! the woman is here & seems to think all will go well – Oh! thank God thank God – I know not if she counts these 3. hours as labour – but the pain is increasing. God bless my precious darling husband – oh! that he were here

Sitka d 13 Dezember[77]
1859 Nachts 2 Uhr

Gnädige Frau!
Heut Nacht mit dem Schlage 12 Uhr, wurde Frau Gouverneur von einer kleinen Tochter glücklich entbunden. Mutter und Kind sind ganz munter. Den 12ten Morgens 9 Uhr fühlten sich Gnädige Frau unwohl, die Hebeamme wurde sogleich geholt, Mittags 12 Uhr fingen die kleinen Wehen an, und dauerten bis 4 Uhr, dann wurde es schlimmer, gnädige Frau gingen geführt, immer im Zimmer auf und ab, von 7 Uhr wurde es sehr schlimm, und gnädige Frau waren dann im Bett, als die grossen Wehen kamen, hatten die gnädige Frau furchtbare Schmerzen, und riefen beständig den lieben Gott um Beistand an, Gott half dann auch. Bei den grössten Schmerzen und Qualen war gnädige Frau aber immer geduldig und standhaft. Wie es 12 Uhr schlug, war das kleine Mädchen da, es schrie gleich lustig in die Welt hinnein. Ein wunderschönes Kind, gross und stark, daher kein Wunder das gnädige Frau so viel leiden mussten. Das kleine Mädchen ist ganz das Ebenbild vom Herrn Oberst. Das Köpfchen des Kindes ist voll schöner blonder Haare. Jetzt schlafen Mutter und Kind ganz ruhig. Bei der Entbindung waren zugegen, die Hebeamme, eine Madame Klinkowströhm, und meine Wenigkeit.

Den 13te Dezember
Mittag 11 Uhr.

Alles geht Gott sei Dank gut! Mutter und Kind sind den Umständen nach wohl. Gnädige Frau schlafen jetzt, nachdem Sie zuvor etwas Hafergrütze getrunken hatten. Gnädige Frau ist so glücklich über das Kind, und gnädige Frau danken immerwährend den lieben Gott daführ, das alles so gut gegangen ist. Kurze Zeit darauf wie das Kind gebohren war, kam die Nachgeburt, und auch so schnell und gut. Um keine Verantwortung zu haben, liess ich heut den Arzt holen, der meinte auch, dass alles ganz gut sei. Heut Nachmittag soll das Kind an die Brust gelegt werden, und vieleicht kann ich Ihnen gnädige Frau noch melden, wie das gegangen ist, ehe das Schiff abgeht. ich wache über gnädige Frau, und lasse mein Herzblut für meine gute gnädige Frau ich hoffe mit Gottes Hülfe, wird gnädige Frau, Herrn Oberst, welchen wir in 4 Wochen zurück erwarten, bis an die Stubenthüre entgegen gehen. Das Kind ist reizend, gesund und wohlgebildet, gross und dick, und bis jetzt sehr gut und ruhig. Gnädige Frau und Kind schicken der lieben Grossmama und Tante tausend Grüsse und Küsse. Das Bild von Ihnen gnädige Frau, kommt nicht vom Bette der jungen Mutter weg.

---

77   It should be 12th December.

Mit Ergebenheit der gnädigen Frau
unterthänige
Ida Höerle
1000 Grüsse von gnädige Frau. Alles geht gut.

[Ger. Sitka, December 13,
1859, 2 a.m.

Your Ladyship!
Tonight, at exactly 12 o'clock, her Ladyship gave birth to a daughter. Mother and child are quite well. At nine o'clock on December the 12th, her Ladyship felt unwell, and the midwife was sent for at once. At noon the pains set in. Then at 4 p.m. it got worse, her Ladyship walked with help up and down the floor, at 7 p.m. it got very bad, and her Ladyship was in bed all the time. As the second stage pains set in, her Ladyship was in terrible agony and prayed to God for help, and God helped. In the greatest pain and agony her Ladyship was always patient and brave. When the clock struck 12, the little girl was there and cried merrily. A beautiful child, big and strong – no wonder her Ladyship had to suffer so much. The little girl looks very much like the colonel. Her little head is covered with pretty fair hair. Now mother and child are sleeping soundly. Present at the childbirth were the midwife, madame Klinkowströhm and my humble self.

December 13,
11 a.m.

Everything is well, thank God. Mother and child are in good shape, considering the circumstances. Her Ladyship is asleep, after having taken some gruel. Her Ladyship is so happy with the child, thanking God all the time that everything went so well. The afterbirth came quickly and easily shortly after the child was born. In order not to be solely responsible I sent for the doctor who also found everything well. This afternoon the baby shall be put to the breast, and perhaps I will be able to let you know, my Lady, how everything went, before the ship leaves. I watch over her Ladyship and I give my life's blood for my good lady, and I hope – God willing – that my lady will walk to the door to welcome the colonel, whom we expect back in four weeks' time. The child is lovely and healthy, and big and fat, and so far good and quiet. Her Ladyship and the child send a thousand greetings and kisses to dear grandmother and dear aunt. Your picture, my Lady, never leaves the young mother's bed.

Your most humble servant
Ida Höerle
Her Ladyship sends her love. Everything is well.]

No. 31   *Government House.* Sitka *Feb[rua]ry* 2nd!1860

My own beloved Mother! On this happy, happy day, I must at least begin a letter to you, even though I shall not be able to write much. This is a day of double importance to us, not only in being the 1st anniversary of our weddingday, but as being the christening day of our little precious Child, our Firstborn! our little darling daughter, who has today at 12. been baptized and received the name *"Annie Fredrique"* after her two Grandmama's. Oh Mama! how happy I am! I cannot express it in words! One year today we have been married, and what a husband God has given me! Oh! what happiness has become mine in becoming his Wife! what Blessings the Almighty has showered upon me this one year!? A husband! a Home! a Child! truly, nothing what my heart can wish for, is wanting – it is complete, perfect happiness, and my whole soul is full of gratitude, of love and infinite thankfulness to Him, who is the Giver of all good gifts, and from whom I have received all these wonderful mercies; so undeservedly – so unmerited. His Goodness & loving kindness is beyond measure – "what am I, that the Lord should be mindful of me?" – And He alone it is, who helped me through all my troubles, who upheld my spirits & comforted my sorrowful heart, when my precious husband left me this day 10. weeks, and I thought my life had gone with him too. He it was who strengthened & comforted me in the hour of pain & anguish when I thought it was more than I could bear, & He graciously permitted me to bring a well formed, strong and healthy child into the world. Oh, and finally, He permitted me once more to clasp my beloved husband to my breast, & put his Firstborn into his arms – should I not praise & thank him for ever? – And now I am well again and can write and tell you all things, my own Mama. And therefore let me begin, where I stopped. –

My Hampus left me on 12/22nd[78] Nov[ember]. How I bore that dreadful parting you know – Hampus has told you already – thank God *that* is passed, and now that I have him again, I will not dwell on the past. –

We can never be thankful enough, that notwithstanding the great mental excitement I had gone through I was permitted to go my full time. Ida, that good and trustworthy Ida, has written all about my confinement, which went so well. – I think I had a tedious & very long labour – For although the pains I had from 10 – to 3 – were spurious, and not violent, the real labour pains lasted from 4. to 12. when the child was born. I fancy the nurse made me walk too much, for I was on my feet from 10 -7½ ev[enin]g & consequently the labour was protracted; at least so it seems to me. Oh! it was hard to be without my Hampus at such a time, when I required every word of encouragement. – At 7½ I lay down for good – I could not keep on my feet longer – Mrs Klinkowström stood on one side, Ida on the other, the nurse sat at my feet – I pulled & squeezed them mercilessly – & they must have been not a little tired, I fancy – however they were a great comfort to me, & I can never say how

---

78 It should be 12/24.

good and kind Mrs K[linkowström] was – she acted a Mothers part towards me. Well at last the child was born "as the clock struck midnight" – I heard all hours but that one strike; never, never can I express the feeling which I had then – I folded my hands in mute & humble prayer – & thanked, thanked from the depth of my heart. I could not have spoken – not for anything in the world at that moment. I heard and felt the little Being at my feet – it was a surpassingly beautiful feeling. They carried it away to wash & when it was dressed brought it for Mama to kiss. After some time the nurse made me all comfortable, & I thought I would sleep – but I did not close my eyes till 4½, and felt quite well almost. The next day too I was so excited & felt as if nothing had been – so free from pain – it is indeed wonderful how all, all pain is gone as soon as the Child is born. Towards evening however I felt weak & wished to sleep but could not – and this is a wonderful thing – though I lay so quiet, & tried all I could to find rest, I could never fall asleep before 12, 1 or 2 and then I would sleep only a few hours. Once I was awake all the night through & all the following day. Was it not strange? – Well, the 3rd day came, & I rejoiced to put my little one to the breast, a thing I had long before been looking forward to with such pleasure – the breasts became slightly hard but neither painful nor extended – no milk – the 4th the 5th day, still no milk, only 1. or 2. drops. Baby was put to the breast, but of course cried at finding nothing. We now sent for an older Baby to pull out the nipple – but it cried too when it found out there was nothing – & the nipple was perfect they all said – Now I began to fear I should have no nourishment for the child and was very unhappy – the doctor still encouraged me, and said the milk will still come – but no milk came – 9. days past and I was to get up the next day; but lo & behold in the night I got violent fever & great pain in the lower bowels & the womb – the fever continued 24. hours, & on the 11th day I was wheeled into Hampus' room, having fainted as soon as I put feet to ground – I felt excessively weak & fainted twice again. Now I put the child regularly to the breast, hoping the sucking would bring the milk, & prayed God so ardently to give me nourishment for the child I had brought into the world; but it was not to be my lot – and so I went on hoping, praying and trying, but all of no avail – and to this day I cannot understand, *what* made *me*, who am so strong & healthy, & who was so wonderfully well during the whole time of my pregnancy, be without milk – What became of it? no one here, has ever seen such a case before. At the end of the 3rd week, I had again violent fever & pain as before, then one day's interval, and fever again – All this must have been caused by the nonappearance of milk – or what do you think? Mrs Maksutoff, who was confined 6 weeks after me, also of a little girl, & who had previously been suffering, and always looked delicate, has a quantity of milk, and has had no fever, neither did she faint on getting up – this is the 12th day, and she walks quite well, and feels no pain anywhere. I remember that you did not nurse us – at least me only 3. months – why? was it through insufficiency of milk? pray tell me darling Mama – perhaps I have inherited some cause which makes it impossible for me to nurse any children God sees fit to give us. I would give much to know what is the reason

– O Mama! such a disappointment as it is to me, you cannot imagine – & how I have cried! & how I have prayed. But it was not the Lord's will, & I may & dare not repine. However Hampus will write to Dr Willebrand about – I have heard of ladies for some reason or other, not being able to nurse their children, but I have never heard of no milk coming. – Well, we were obliged to feed the little darling with cow's milk, as they told me a nurse was not to be had here – the women being so bad, and so full of disease – the cow's milk was very, very poor – the poor creatures are so badly fed – I could not get unmixed milk – of course Baby could not get fat on such poor nourishment; how I longed for Hampus to come home, that he might contrive some way to get pure milk – To all my anxiety & trouble, this was still added, that after 6. weeks, a catarrhal epidemic, which carried away many children, broke out here, & Baby got a cough too. I was sometimes perfectly miserable, & thought perhaps Hampus might return, and find his little daughter had been a bright dream – a momentary vision – But here again, God comforted me, and oh how earnestly I prayed to Him for help and strength, patience and humble submission to His Will. I rubbed Baby's chest with warm tallow & oil, kept her bowels open, saw that her stomach was not overloaded, and hoped she would be better before her papa came home. Thank God it was so. – Hampus arrived on 24th January. I had gone to the window as usual, as I did 20. times a day, but there was a thick fog at sea, such as we have now had for 6. weeks or more, combined with rain & even snow, and went away sighing "no ship! no ship" – ten minutes afterwards I went again, and what was my rapture, in seeing a steamer in full steam, rapidly approaching – I screamed out for Joy, & rushed upstairs to look through the telescope. Soon all Sitka was astir, everyone longed for H[ampus'] return, our flag was hoisted, and canons loaded. Baby was sleeping so sweetly after her bath. however she soon awoke, and I dressed her prettily. I cannot describe how happy I was – at last I saw my beloved Hampus coming as fast as possible up the long staircase – the gate opened – then the glass door in the passage, and I rushed into his arms. – What inexpressible Joy! – All sorrow, all loneliness and emptiness of heart was forgotten, happiness and thankfulness reigned in their stead – And Mama! what Joy, to see his Joy at coming home & seeing me again – oh so fond and loving – it fills me with unbounded feelings of happiness, to be so loved by him. He was soaking wet, we waited a little, and then I brought his precious child to him, & laid her in his arms – He looked so pleased – so happy – But his first question was: "do you nurse her yourself? She is so thin" – & when he knew all, he said, nolence volence, a wetnurse must be found & immediately. So we sent for my nurse & consulted with her, but there seemed to be no prospect of succeeding. An Aleutian woman, whose Baby had died 7. days before, was sent for – O! she looked so dirty, so poor & thin – We sent her to the "Badstuga" [Swed. sauna] dressed her cleanly and then tried if the milk would increase by sucking. But no – that would not do – so I bethought me of a young woman I had heard was clean & respectable, whom I had sent food to last August when she was confined, & whose Baby had tried to suckle me – a tremendously fat & healthy looking child – We sent for her, &

though her milk is now 6. months old soon, & our child not 2. months yet, and she was willing to become wetnurse & had plenty of milk, we thanked God, and took her, and 2. days afterwards Baby's cough was gone, & she is thriving wonderfully. How happy I am you can well imagine – And now, that you know all my griefs, I must also tell you what a good, sweet, lovely child she is. For to you, I may speak about her, without tiring you, or being called vain and partial. She has never been an ugly Baby – though red like all Babies, she looked sweet from the beginning. She has dark hair like mine, a high forehead like her Papa, very large dark blue eyes, which shine like diamonds, so bright they are – they too are like Hampus – long eyelashes & pretty eyebrows, you can see the lines over her eyes quite distinctly, though they are not so dark yet – then she will have Mama's nose – a pretty little mouth & short upper lip – her head and her brows very well developped, and all her limbs so prettily shaped – Mama's hands too, long fingers & a high chest – so I think she will sing and play and be a clever child. She has certainly inherited her fathers sweet, gentle disposition – she cries very little, only when she is hungry & has always slept well. She is very fond of being bathed – & never cries then – but lies so quietly, enjoying herself all the time. It is such a pleasure to me, bathing & dressing her – and especially now, when I am often rewarded by such a sweet smile. She is making her first attempts at crowing – & is quite her fathers delight – Indeed it is inexpressible delight to be a Mother – & to have such a precious little being to care for and think of. May we bring her up with all care & tenderness, and may the Lords Blessing ever accompany & surround her through life – We chose the 2nd v[erse] of 18th Psalm for her, and have written it under her name in the large Bible. She cried almost the greater part of the christening, having been woken out of her sleep to dress her. She wore a long, white embroidered robe, bought in England, and embroidered cap with 3. rows of quilled valencienne & rosette on one side; the robe was trimmed all over with little pink bows; she looked so sweet. Our german cook made a splendid repast, all the dishes stood on round stands which he had made, decorated with sugar roses & green leaves. In the middle stood a sort of Krokan [Swed. ornamented pastry-cake], only not so "grann" [Swed. splendid] as the one we had at our wedding – the guests were very silent & stiff – We had ices & champagne & I drank your health my Mother. After dinner I turned the organ & we had a turn or two round the room. After all the guests had taken leave, I went to church accompanied by my husband, and kneeling before the altar, I was churched, and offered up my deepest thanks, for God's infinite mercies towards me. We then returned home, and asked Pastor Winter to tea. I played in the evening on our beautiful piano, which arrived during my confinement. I cannot say what a pleasure it is to me to have, but especially because it gives Hampus such great pleasure – he is so fond of music, and likes to hear me play. My music I bought in Dresden, is very good – I have all Beethoven's symphonies and 3. of Mozarts for four hands – all Mendelsohns "Lieder" a great deal by "Schuman", & "Stephan Heller" company pieces too, & several things by "Chopin". The piano was quite in tune when it came, but now it is already out of tune, caused

Florence and Carl von Schoultz.

I think, by the room it first stood in being too warm, and the atmosphere being damp. What do you think Hampus & I have been doing this week? I have taught him to play an air out of "Il Trovatore" [G. Verdi] with one finger, & I accompany him. It is quite wonderful how soon he learnt it, & understood it – I am quite proud of him. We have no end of laughing over our lesson, & Hampus is quite [de]lighted. Constance is fond of hearing me play, & always thanks me for the pleasant evening she has had. Poor girl! she has again been so ill – once she had 5. attacks in 12. hours. This was whilst I was still "en quarantaine" so thank God, I have never yet been so unfortunate as to see her ill – We were all so careful – Hampus had given her strict orders, not to be alone with me, before he left – & afterwards, when she had attacks every day, I never saw her – She has now become more accustomed to her own little room, & likes it, so she is there mostly, only in the evenings with us. She has been well 10. days again now –

But now I must first thank you and then answer your precious letters my darling Mama, No *14. 15. 17!* which Hampus brought me. But where is No. *16*? or did you only make a mistake? No. *13* too, I have never received. Surely they cannot be lost. I see mine have all reached you safely, & right happy am I to hear, they have given you Joy my sweetest Mother.

I was so glad to hear you "trifvats" [Swed. were happy] at Palsi, & though your desolate description of its utter loneliness & comfortlessness did not exactly surprise me, I can understand, that after the first few days with all their sad impressions about those that formerly had inhabited that little Palsi, had passed away, you could be happy and cheerful there, amidst wild stones and berries, bubbling streams & green islands, & happy am I to think you were able to escape from town during summer. Esperance too, I see you are quite fond of – I cannot say how it pleased & surprised me to hear that Harald [Furuhjelm] had written of his own accord to thank you; I think it was so pretty of him, and I am consequently going to write to him – They have warm, warm hearts, all those brothers, but my Hampus is the prize amongst them. It was untold delight to hear that Florence was at last to be married, that Carl had good prospects, & that their bands might be published. Judge then of my Joy, when Hampus met me with the news "Florence är gift" [Swed. Florence is married] – I wished you had told us a little more about it all – Hampus & I, were expecting to hear an account of all the pretty things she got in England & what she had bought herself, but not a word of it did you say – Did she buy "Bulls hints to Mothers" as I recommended her? What about her stay in England? not a word have we heard – I can never forgive her, not having written a line since or before her marriage – naughty girl! God bless her, dear sweet sister. The Lord has at last rewarded her for all her troubles & sorrows – May they be spared to each other for many, many years, if so be God's will, & may they too soon have a sweet Baby to gladden their hearts, like our little Annie. You have not told me, what Carl's place is, I mean what he is engaged as, nor what his yearly income will be. It is strange your two daughters should be married in the same year. That was quite a delightful "Lysningsdag" [Swed. the day when the banns are published] at Palsi – I could so rejoice for Florence – but only fancy I feel quite jealous that no Champagne was drunk on our "Lysningsdag" – Now Marie must make up to you for the loss of both your girls. How is she? I wish she would write to me, I wish to write to her by this opportunity.

So you intend turning Finland a cold back sweet Mama, and migrating once more to England. What will you do with all your books & furniture? Had Carl bought anything in that way, or would they find a house ready furnished? We much marvel at Florence's 7. trunks, I had only 1. when I left you. I think she must have looked quite lovely as a bride; & how beautiful & solemn it was, you had the organ to play. The wedding breakfast too, seems to have been in your own rooms, not downstairs. –

Monday. [...] My bedroom, being a large one, & connected with another on each side, I was able to have it well ventilated & aired during my confinement, there was never any unpleasant smell, nor was I stuffed up in bed – I had only the half of the blanket, I could not bear more. But something must still have been wrong with me, else why did I get no milk, & why did I get fever 3. times? as for medical attendance we have none. Dr Berent, whom Gustaf knows, as they were on the same ship, *knows nothing!* – it is quite painful to ask him anything, for he never knows what to say – we never get a good, a real doctor to the Colonies, where he would be so necessary, but always young men straight from College, who have never had the slightest practise. We must pray God, mercifully to preserve us from real sickness, for neither doctor, nor good medicines have we. –

The midwife, & nurse at the same time, was excellent, she was 4. weeks with me, & bathed the Baby, but from that time I did it myself; but anything out of the common, happening to the lying patient, puts the poor woman out of all counting – & she knows no help. [...]

You want to know the fate of Florence['s] blanket and your 3. pillows? – all safely with y[ou]r daughter Annie at Sitka, and no small pleasure is it to me, to see "von Schoultz" in large letters written & worked by Florence on them. The blanket was nailed over one of the windows when I was ill, & y[ou]r precious little Grandchild, has often lain on the pillows. I have just been in the nursery to have a peep at Baby – she was sweetly asleep in her little cradle. She is 8. weeks old today – wonderful it is that she sleeps so much, the greater part of the day & all night; last night she slept from 9 – ev[enin]g to 5. mo[rnin]g without waking. You would love her so – she is so good, & has such a sweet, darling little face. I send you a little piece of her hair in this letter.

We have never been able to have family prayers with the servants here, as they are all of different confessions, or rather speak different language, & do not understand one in common. This is a great pity. Ida is, as you will see by her letter, not an uneducated person. She is the daughter of rich "Bürgerleute" [Ger. middle class people] & was at an institut in Berlin. Her father was "Amtman"[79] & died suddenly leaving them unprovided for – their mother too died a short time before, & the children were entrusted to their guardian. Two sisters are very well married; one in Dresden to a rich merchant, another to a clergyman in Switzerland. Ida's Uncle was very rich, *Professor Hörle* [..?] Theologie at Heidelberg, Babette perhaps remembers his name, & left to each of them some money. She need not be in service to gain her bread – but she has a firm character, & wishes to be independent, & active as long as she can, so she preferred taking "eine Condition" [Ger. an employment] better than remaining on idle with her sister at Dresden, whose children she has brought up. She is 42. and in every way most exellent & conscientuous, & willing to do all manner of work – I have flitted her bed into the nursery now, so that she may have surveillance over the wetnurse, with whom we are up to this date quite satisfied. Of course poor Ida, has sometimes "Heimweh" [Ger. homesickness] especially now, during this long long, rainy dull and dreary season; & I am sorry for her – but she never complains; she is very fond & gentle with children – in no way rude and vulgar – but able to converse on many subjects, & above all a good christian, reading her Bible which has the date of last century in it, having belonged to her Uncle I suppose. I asked her to read & pray with me, when I was ill & not able to do so myself. –

Wednesday ev[enin]g Feb[ruar]y 8th. Such lovely moonlight nights we have had, I wish you had been here last night. I went out at 9. o'clock and took a few turns round the house. The stars were shining so bright, the heaven was perfectly blue, the full moon shone down in all her glory on the Snow covered mountains, and cast

---

79   Probably Anna means Beamter [Ger. official] as she said in No. 28.

a soft reflection on the calm sea, which came gently splashing in against the stones, making a mysterious gentle murmuring. My thoughts wandered home to you & my Sweet Sister, & I imagined you were perhaps gazing upwards too, & our hearts met above in love & gratitude. O! how wonderful, how exquisitely beautiful, are all the Creators works. You would have admired the scenery much – to the left rose the large mountain covered with firs, which you see on the views of Sitka, & beneath it lay Sitka itself, the very picture of calm repose. It was most lovely. Then my heart turned to all the Blessings I enjoy – I thought of my Husband, my Child, and all the comforts which surround me, & I felt inexpressibly happy, and came in, to tell it all to Hampus. –

My own Hampus is suffering from one eye; a tiny tumour or fleshy substance has appeared in the inside of the lower lid – it has often been touched with caustic, but without any good coming of it – now he is using Jodd ointment rubbed on the outside – I am so anxious about it – He cannot read or write without experiencing inconvenience – & O, how precious one's eyes are. God grant of His infinite mercy the remedies used may be of use – but I am terrified to employ proscriptions given by a person who understands little or nothing! – & especially for the eyes, which can easily be made worse – He was quite out of spirits about it yesterday. –

Sunday 12th […] O Mama darling! Now I feel doubly how infinitely much I owe you for all all you have done for me – now, that I have the happiness myself of being Mother; and from the depth of my heart I thank you darling Mama. How I wish you could see your little Grandchild – I will talk much to her about you, and make her quite at home with you. How I long to hear from Florence – I suppose you have letters every week, which would be such a pleasure. How time flies, she has already been married five months, & may already have pleasant and precious expectations! May she be more fortunate than I in nursing. –

If you go to England, what will you do with y[ou]r furniture? your pictures? your books? I hope you will be able to sell the piano, as you wished to do so. By this time I hope you have safely received the small packet I sent by Admiral Woewodsky and were pleased with its contents. I fancy you must soon be receiving my letters sent by Hampus to California, and this letter & the one sent over China, will perhaps arrive at the same time. How did you like Ida's letter? – I did not see it of course. It will be delightful to see Capt[ain] and Fru [Swed. Mrs] Krogius, & to receive verbal messages – also the Cadettes – & how glad I am to get a letter from Moster Lisette. Constance has unfortunately been very ill again – but now she has again been 3. weeks without an attack. She had as many as five in 18. hours, but I never saw her then, she was always alone in her own room. She was so happy to hear about Palsi, and that you like Esperance – What will become of her poor girl, when you leave Finland. […] By & bye I must send you a new plan of my room, it is now quite changed and looks much better. Next autumn "Garitza" returns to Finland, & I could have sent verbal messages – what a pity you will be gone. And pray darling Mama send me your english address in time.

Now I must finish – I have written myself fairly out and have nothing more to say. Baby darling sends a kiss to dear Grandmama. She has such a nice nursery – the sun shines in so beautifully in the afternoon. There is not a corner of the house, which is not occupied now – we are quite stuffed. Constance "ber att hälsa så hjertligt och tacka, om hon vågar, att hon varit så god mot Esperance, äfven att pussa henne på mina vägnar" [Swed. sends her love and thanks, if she dares, that you have been so good to Esperance, and asks you also to kiss her on her behalf] – And now Farewell my own Mama. God bless and keep you, and may this letter find you well & happy.

With fondest love Ever Your own loving Child

Annie

No. 33   Annunciation of our Lady
32 lost in the wreck of the Codiac.   Friday 6th *April*/25 March
dated 24th Feb[ruary][80]   *Government House* Sitka 1860

Thus, I again commence writing to you, my own beloved Mother, & am able to thank you for No. 18. of 3rd Jan[ua]ry last, which I had the inexpressible joy of receiving on the 1st. It seemed to me almost incredible, that y[ou]r letter was of so recent a date, & begun whilst I was "eine Wöchnerin" [Ger. woman in confinement] I looked at it over & over again and still could scarcely satisfy myself of the truth, happy though I was. As yours has come so fast, I trust mine to you, has gone equally so and that you are now in possession of my letter of *11th Dec[ember]* the last few words of which were written after I was taken ill, & will soon too receive my long epistle of 31 Jan[ua]ry, which will make you happy I know. One thing only distressed me, which was: "now Farewell till March, when I will write again by the Company's vessel" – So I am to be disappointed time after time, when our ships will return from San Francisco empty handed! – O you cannot imagine what a bitter disappointment it is here, locked up from the rest of the world as we are, & when the advent of a vessel is already hailed with delight & curiosity by all inhabitants, & sets everyone on qui vive, even whilst it is only to be discerned[?] on the horizon. Judge then, my own Mother, what sorrow you will be causing me. A few lines from you, is better than nothing at all – & there is always so much I want to know half of which I never hear. As regards Florence I know not what to say. I have been disappointed so often, for not a word have I received from her since *April 2nd 1859*! We know nothing about her except thank God that she is married; not what Carl's place is, nor what salary he gets, which particularly interests us – in fact nothing at all, & I must say it vexes me not a little to see that in her happiness she forgets & neglects her sister. I am notwithstanding writing again to her, & hope it will bring me a long letter in return.

---

80   This sentence has been added by someone else, probably Anna's mother.

By the same post I received a long and most welcome letter from Mrs Hawthorne
& one from Uncle Eduard – his was very old though. It astonishes me very much
that my letter of *23rd Sept[ember]* had not reached you yet but I guess it must have
come a few days after you sent yours –

Palm Sunday March 27th. I was at the german church[81] today, & heard a very
good sermon from Pastor Winter – it was Communion Sunday. Ida & the Cook
went – next friday Hampus and I will go, & then the whole house, all our servants
included will have received the Holy Sacrament before the joyful Easter fête. [...]
Later. We have just finnished the "beaux restes" [Fr. what was left over] of a sucking pig at which occassion I remembered the "gourmand" Mr Peter Burnet, & the
delicious sauce he taught me to eat with cold pork – I wished to win my Hampus
over to my taste too, but could not succeed; – since I wrote the last words, I have
taken down an english letter of business for my Hampus, & now I will still write a
few lines to you my precious Mother. Baby is growing sweeter & fatter every day
– I spend much time with her, she is so droll and amusing. We have been obliged to
wean her, though still so young, but the wetnurse's milk did not agree with her, &
I would never try another in Sitka. It caused many tears on both sides – mother and
child cryed; but now thank God she is again quite reconciled to her feeding bottle.
I have been able to take her out a little 3. or 4. times, & she liked it much, but now
it is again too windy, she must consequently content herself with being carried up
& down the Ball room, where she admires the large chandelabre & the portrait of
the Emperor. She laughs quite loud now & speaks her own little language, which
of course Mama understands! – I would not be without a child for anything in the
world – You should see how anxious Hampus is that she is comfortable and well &
happy – he is so fond of his little daughter. If you could but see her darling Mama
– & I see you with Baby, your first Grandchild in your arms! it would rejoice my
heart to witness your happiness.

Monday before Easter! On Wednesday this letter will go, so I must hasten to
finnish it. I want to write to Moster Lisette too, and ask her for the pill receipt, which
she has recomended to so many, & with good success I believe. It seems that cares
never come singly – one breeds the other. First my darling Hampus' eye caused me
anxiety & now I have another still greater one; he has never in all his life suffered
from breast or lungs, & feels & looks perfectly well – still of late, sometimes in clearing his throat, he has observed a little blood mixed with the saliva – what can it be?
He has heard before, & now was again told by the Pastor, that Hemoroydes show
themselves in that way, & that it is nothing else. Hampus occassionally feels pain &
stiffness in his back, & always uses ice then, which seems to do him good – But he
himself, is always easily frightened, & thinks it must be from the lungs – O Mama!
can you not feel for me? – but God is merciful & will spare his health, O! surely for

---

81   Anna is referring here to the Lutheran church, completed in 1843 (Varjola 1990, p. 41).
      In her letter No. 39 she calls it the Swedish church.

His blessed Son's sake. *Amen*. None in his family suffer from anything approaching to consumption, & I never heard of anybody getting it at his age – Tell me darling Mama, what you think about it – & if you think it can be Hemoroydes – or perhaps as I think, only occassioned by the constant fricture in his throat – having been a smoker, he still clears his throat often. Thank God, he has quite left off smoking, and owns himself he is a thousand times better without it – smoke had the effect of poison upon his whole frame & kept him in perpetual nervousness & unsettled spirits – he is quite another man now – I cannot say how happy I am he has left it off – Being without a proper medical attendant, & without the reach of any, is a fearful drawback – God mercifully preserve us from *real* sickness. –

When you read these lines, I shall again be alone – "eine einsame Strohwittige" [Ger. a lonely grass widow] – in the end of May Hampus will leave me to make a tour through the Colonies, and will perhaps be absent 4. months. O! it is so dreadful, always to be obliged to part, and especially when you must be without news of eachother the whole time. It seems to be my lot, like dear Marie's – unfortunately I am not so brave as Florence; but then she does not know what it is to be separated from your husband under the circumstances I was, & without the slightest communication. Four months! it is a dreadful time – but the Lord will help me to bear it now, as He enabled me to do it before and may He graciously reunite us in happiness and health. – – [...]

Tuesday. We have such dreadful misfortune with our fowls just now – In five or six days we have lost about 30 – each costing 1. dollar – Some infectuous disease called "roup" brought over by some hens we ordered from San Francisco seems to have attacked them – I am afraid only a few will remain if it goes on like this. We seem to have decided ill luck with our farmyard, which is very down heartning.

After tea. I have this minute finished mixing a receipt recomended for hens affected by the abovementioned dreadful disease, & sincerely hope, it will thus be checked – 8. have died today – & just now Hampus has been building a new charming poultry house, & we were reckoning on at least 300 chickens this season – again "l'homme propose et Dieu dispose" [Fr. man proposes, God disposes] – – –

It was indeed wonderful for me to read about the Christmas Eve, which you spent once more at the hospital, so lonely, and so different. My own own precious Mother! but y[ou]r children's hearts were with you, & their thoughts and their love too – just as yours were with them. [...]

Our darling Baby is four months old today – thank God she is well fat & bright; it is wonderful how much sleep she requires – God bless her – she thrives so upon it – Tonight when I was going to bathe her, her little head felt so hot, & she seemed suddenly to have become so restless, I refrained from bathing her – I am confident die Zähne sind mit im Spiel [Ger. the teeth play a part], because much saliva runs from her mouth – & in the middle of the underjaw, you see distinctly white marks, as of teeth. God of His mercy, help us safely through that anxious time. Hampus will be away then, & consequently my anxiety increased. But she is such a patient little lamb. Aunt

Mary knows how to give fine names to her children. I wonder when we shall meet again. Darling Mama, if you are still in Finland this autumn, please send me by the provision ship, which leaves S[ain]t P[eter]b[ur]g in October, a few strips of cambric with printed embroidery patterns, suitable for trowsers for little Annie – Everything is so dear at San Francisco – also my own english spelling book from Grandmama, which [..?] afterwards had, if you can find it, & my little Watts hymnbook & any other childs book – we may happen to have. A few flower seeds – also parsley, carrot & beetroot seed would be acceptable and a few yards of some good nice warm soft woollen stuff for a frock for little Annie. It is not to be had here – only ugly coarse Orleans, or scarlet & crimson spotted bad muslins de laine's. Hampus just tells me, you need not wait till October, but through Sturm, the R[ussian] A[merican] C[ompany's] Agent in Hamburg, you can send a packet over Panama. O! how nice it will be to get anything from home! Remember darling Mama, you need never pay your letters or packets to us – we have free postage – In fact, if we count all we have free – a house of this size, furniture, wood, light, servants, washerwomen, soap, food for hens & pigs, milk, fish, paper, lampoil, & anything we chose to have made, Hampus place is certainly equal to 4000 £ per anum, & still it is perfectly incomprehensible how high my monthly bills are. Living is exceedingly dear, Hampus calculates that when our debts are subtracted (for we bought up sundry provisions for 5. years, & equipped ourselves in every way) but a small sum will this year remain from the 35.000 R[oubles] banco he receives – You will scarcely believe me, when I tell you that my bills amount every month at least to 350 R[oubles] equal to 100 R[oubles] S[ilver] though we have wine, brandy, sugar & almost every grocery from England, even vinegar & oil – we have not bought a kopeks worth of anything for ourselves – the money literally all goes in our mouths – about 20. mouths each day. Of course I have extra's too, which are not counted in the abovementioned sum. – [...]

Baby is, thank God quite well today – but she had a rather restless night, to make up for which she slept this forenoon from 9 – 1. without moving. She sends a dear kiss to darling Grandmama. Tell me, if Babette was glad to hear about her – Now I must bid you goodbye my own precious Mother – I must hasten to finish my letter to Florence. Hampus sends his fondest love – he has very much to think of just now & cannot write. Kind love to Esperance also from Constance, who is as usual – she is generally well 6. weeks.

Dearest love to everybody, who asks for news. Did I tell you about my sewing-machine, which darling Hampus gave me? Work flies in it – I will soon send you a little specimen. With fondest love my own beloved Mother

Y[ou]r ever loving Child

Annie F[uruhjelm]

P.S. [...] Will you also give my love to vår älskade Moster, till hvem jag haar villat sjelf skrifva, men nu hör jag brefven måste genast vara färdiga och be henne vara så god gifva mig receptet för de piller hon recomenderar åt sina vänner, och som skall vara bra för hemoroyder [Swed. our beloved aunt to whom I had intended to write myself, but now I hear that the letters must be ready at once. Please ask her to give me the recipe for the pills which she recommends to her friends and which are supposed to be good against hemorrhoids]. You could have them made darling Mama, & send them as all ingredients might not be to be had here. Excuse me darling Mama, asking for so much, but I know you will be happy to do it for me –

Once more Goodbye – our hens are better – The medecine helped to check –

Y[ou]r own A[nnie] F[uruhjelm]

No. 34   Government House
                                                  Sitka April 14th/ April 26 1860

Good evening, my own Beloved Mother! I wish I could this minute peep in upon you, & see what you are doing. It is 8½ with us, consequently with you the day is beginning, and you are most likely just now sitting at the breakfast table, and I doubt not, but that you have already sent a morning kiss to your absent daughters. It is Thursday, perhaps the post of last night brought you the letter anouncing y[ou]r first Grandchild's birth, for I count upon that letter reaching you about this time.

I am now writing these few lines over Vancouver Island, from which place, or rather from "Victoria" we received english newspapers today. It is a pity we have no direct communication with Brittish Columbia, as our letters would then come and go very fast. Nothing new has occurred since my last long letter of 30th March, and we are all thank God well, except that our precious Baby has again got a cough & the whole servant department is coughing. I think she will soon have teeth; God grant she may get over that time well. You will be glad to hear, that I shall after all accompany my Hampus to "Codiac". It was a project long talked over, but I gave it up at last, as there seemed to be many hindrances, however, no sooner was I resolved to remain alone here, than my generous husband cleared away all obstacles and hindrances, & sent some pieces of furniture by the last ship, to await our arival, & even told the Capt[ain] to bring any letters there might be for me at San Fr[ancisco] immediately with him to "Codiac" – had I remained here, I would only have got them next autumn, as "Garitza" makes [..?] journeys from & to San Fr[ancisco] before returning to Sitka. The climate is said to be much better there, & you can go anywhere, unmolested by Indians, which is not the case here, & you have plenty of excellent cowsmilk, all of which things will benefit our little Angel. It rains much here, & when it does not, it blows, especially up here, & there is a draft on the long staircase down. At "Codiac" the house we shall inhabit lies on plain ground, & though not so large as this one, is still large enough for us – as we have no guests to entertain there, nor parties of any kind to give & if it is fine, I shall try to be out as much as possible. Hampus will leave me there, & then proceed further on his tour through the Colonies, & will return for me again. May it be Gods will that all may go well for him & us, & that He will go & come with us, & protect us from all danger.

It is now ½ past 9. I have just been to say good night to my sweet Baby – who is sleeping soundly in her little cot – I took her out & made her comfortable, as I do every night before going to bed, without her waking – she sleeps remarkably well, God bless her the little treasure. It is such infinite Joy to see her smile whenever I come near her, she knows me so well – her Papa she does not know so well yet, but Ida & Natalia she smiles so prettily at, & crows & laughs quite loud. They all love her so, she is such a good gentle Baby. I hope, please God, when Hampus returns in autumn, he will hear her say "Papa & Mama". I have just finished making a little quilted cloak for her in the machine, & must now make a hood for the journey, as those I bought in England wont answer the purpose so well – the cloak is too good & too cold for a steamer & the little bonnet too. I am also making a pink & a blue frock – I don't know what I should have done, if I had not provided myself with all manner of cotton materials in England – the prints, which are sent here are bad & dear, & finer stuffs are not to be had, as jaconette or Brilliantine, in fact no pretty materials for children's clothing. I am so sorry I left all my things at home – it is inconvenient being without anything old – I have only the pink muslin from Faster Albertina, nothing else in the cotton way – & that I intend little Annie to get for frocks when she is older. Is it possible Elisabeth stole? that would indeed be shocking. What girl have you now in Amanda's stead, & how is Florence pleased with Edla? The working classes here, are a perfectly spoilt race, & good for nothing – they are indolent, careless & mostly depraved – unfortunately this is the case in 9. cases out of 10. I keep a strict look out after the 2. young girls of 19. & 14. I have – the former I have a high opinion of, & trust & pray she is good, as I have never seen anything wrong in her – but the young girl, fresh from school, is not so much to be depended upon, & I lock her in at night – for truly & sincerely & seriously do I consider it my duty to see after the well behaviour of my servants, & try to teach them the sin it is to behave badly – But unhappily it seems to be an utter impossibility to keep the youngest of them pure & inocent. I have heard such sad, sad stories about the school, which have perfectly disheartened & sickened me. The school is now again under my especial care, & I hope with Gods help to bring it again into a better condition. During the last Governors time, no one cared for it – & he did not forbid, *strictly forbid* the young officers & men of the town to pay nightly, shameful visits to the school. Only fancy what a crying sin! poor girls as they are, they are sooner the victims, than the sinners, for they are all so young & inexperienced, what can they do? I cannot conceive anything more shocking, more mournful than the depraved state of these poor young girls – From school they enter service, & rejoice to be at liberty as they call it, & care for nothing, know of nothing, have no shame, nor feeling of modesty, & will do anything in order to be able to buy fine clothes – For they receive no wages – the

Company pays for them in school, & then you pay yearly 7[?] R[oubles] S[ilver] to the "hufvudcontor" [Swed. head office, board of directors] which money they receive when they marry. How I have prayed God to help me, that I may do some good! Hampus has given strict orders, that no one may dare to come near the school – for be he officer or workman, he shall be flogged, if any such things occur again. Is it not a dreadful state of affairs, that when I chose a young girl of 12. years old the other day, to serve in a family here, Hampus was obliged to tell her, that if she dares to dawdle about the doors or speak with soldiers, she would receive such a flogging as she never would forget! – 12. years old, is but a mere child! By this, you can judge in general, what insight I have got into "Life" & the "way of the world" since I am married – & what sad, melancholly scenes have I often seen – It is sometimes difficult to retain any good idea of anybody. And still how lovely, how beautiful is this world! How happy – how perfectly happy, has God made me in it. But who can stand in their own strength? who can resist the devil & his temptations? not the best of us? therefore, what we are, we are by *God's mercy alone* who has graciously permitted us to know the difference between right & wrong. O Mother! on my bended knees I bless & thank you, for having taught me to love Him, & fear to displease Him, to pray to Him continually.

Friday morning. Hampus violently continuing calling upon me, to come to bed, as he could not sleep if I were up, obliged me to stop last night – however as the weather is still bad, the post did not go this morning, & I have time to finish this at my leisure today. I am eagerly expecting *"Nikolai"* & will do all I can for the young cadets as you ask me – but what can I do? ask them to dinner – that is not much. Have them here in the evening sometimes. You see, that is not much either. I turned to Hampus to ask his opinion, & he told me the best thing in the world he knows of "låt dem kyssa Dig" [Swed. let them kiss you] –! –! What do you think of that? – however I cannot say how glad I shall be to see Carl's first "Flamma" [Swed. flame] and a friend of Hannas. But especially I am longing to receive verbal messages from you my own beloved Mother – to hear how you are, & many other things. We have been expecting Nikolai daily, & cannot conceive what delays her so long. By the bye darling Mama, if you could get a copy of the little book *"Hemmet"* [Swed. The Home] which Carl gave Florence, I should be very happy – I never finnished reading it, & indeed do not remember much about it, except that it was an exellent adviser. I believe it is by an American author, but as I do not know his name, I cannot order it from San Fr[ancisco]. Baby's cough is worse today, though she passed a very good night. She is such a little rogue & will have her Papa's pretty dimple on her cheeks, where as the saying is "skelmen sitter" [Swed. the rogue sits]. [...] I am going through all Beethoven's symphonies with Madame Makzutoff, we have played the two first off book – & get quite enthusiastic and enlivened over it – I rather fancy, she has not received a liking for sound music though she plays exceedingly well, but she did not seem to recognize the symphonies, nor to delight in their exquisite harmony as I do –

She comes very often to see me, but unfortunately her Baby is generally restless, & she is anxious to return to it again. Outre [Fr. except] Madame M[akzutoff] I have no one to play with – I am again practising Chopins beautiful Fantasie in cis-moll, & remember you, darling Mother, in so doing – for I never could reconcile you to the end. I hope our child will be musical – I flatter myself she will, we should both wish it so much.

Darling Mama do send me your beautiful poem on Max and Mabella[?]. I have only Mrs [..?] lines, which Hampus admired very much & yours I have always wished to possess. I wish I had all your long manuscript poems here, to read aloud in the evenings to my Darling – It would be so charming, and would make Hampus better acquainted with *our* Mother, of whom I am so proud. "The rough House" too – oh! who of us would have thought it should still only be a manuscript – but nowadays, as I read in the Times yesterday, were you to ask "what is the better part of a book?" the answer would be "Binding!" binding. – And thats why the Booksellers have not the sense to accept y[ou]r book – but are ready to print any twopence halfpenny trash.

I see the Prince of Orange is the accepted suitor for the hand of Princesse Alice,[82] I hope she will be happier, than Queen Mary was with her William of Orange.

I wish I could send you some of the macaroons the cook has just made, I remember you liked them so much. Next Sunday is the Emperor's birthday [17 April, old style] & we must again give a large dinner – it is too provoking the Emperor should have a Birth- & a Nameday, for they always entail heavy expences on us. On Easter Sunday we had breakfast for all the town – & now again we must have "en middag" [Swed. a dinner] – but such are the drawbacks & inconveniences of a high post like Hampus! […]

Darling Baby is rather fretful today. My ownest husband sends his fondest love to Mama. His eye is nearly well thank God – he confesses now himself that he thinks it must be Hemoruydes – don't forget the pills. He has never coughed – *that*, was only one of his melancholly fits which makes him always dread & believe the worst.

Goodbye and God bless you my own precious Mother. This will most likely reach you later than letters of a later date, but I have resolved never to lose an ocassion in writing to you – With my hearts fondest love & many kisses

Ever Your own loving Child

Anna F[uruhjelm]

---

82 Princess Alice (see Index of names) married Prince Louis, Grand Duke of Hesse, in 1862.

No. 35   Government House.
                                                         Sitka May 5th 1860

My own most precious Mother!

It is 7½ eve[nin]g, we have just finnished drinking tea – Cadetten [Swed. Cadet]
Bergenheim is smoking his pipe in Hampus room, all is silent around me – the sun
is sending her farewell rays for today, & casts light & beauty on all the objects in
the room, and [an] inexpressible wish to speak with you my Mother, & tell you all
that delights me & occupies my thoughts, seized me, and so here I am seated at my
pretty little writing table, beginning what will in time increase in size, & become a
large volume to you. I have much to tell you my own beloved Mother, and much to
thank you for. On Saturday, April 16th old style of course, the longed wished for
& much looked for "Nikolai" sailed into our port, and filled many hearts with joy.
It was with throbbing pulses & beating heart I watched her in, & thought of how
my own Mother had been on deck & in her cabins, & how well she could have even
now been on board. It seemed to me, as if some opportunity never to occur again,
had been lost, & I consequently deprived of an infinite Joy. But at least I would get
letters and "mündliche herzliche Grüsse" [Ger. oral kindest regards] which I was
not a little happy at. As the "Nikolai" came into port, we sat down to dinner, my
cheeks flushed with expectation, and on coming down, we found Captain Krogius in
my husband's room The first thing that struck me, was his pleasant voice. I waited
silently and anxiously till Hampus would bring him in to me, & I would hear about
you, & receive y[ou]r verbal messages and greetings. He is a gentlemanly young
man & of very prepossessing appearance as you very rightly remark. I cannot say,
darling Mama, how happy it made me to receive "så många hjertliga hälsningar"
[Swed. so many kind regards] and to see somebody who has seen you, and been in
your rooms since we left you. In the afternoon Mr Bergenheim & young Krogius
came with your packet bowing & looking so bright & gay. Young B[ergenheim] gave
me dear Moster's note, which à propos was addressed to "Välborna[83] Gouverneurskan
[Swed. Governor's Wife] A[nna] v[on] Schoultz" – They had been announced as the
"styrmen" [Swed. first officers] who wanted to speak with me, so that when I went
into Hampus' room to meet them, I did not even know their names & was so excited
& confused & forgetful, that I even forgot to ask them to sit down – which shocked
me not a little when I remembered it afterwards. However we have both been as
kind as possible to them & asked Bergenh[eim] once & for all to come every evening,
which he has also done, & I hope has found himself at home and comfortable with
us. He is a very nice, modest young man, and speaks with great affection of Eugénie.
I devoured the contents of my parcel and send you ten thousand warmest thanks
and kisses for everything. The little shoes are so nice, and will certainly be the first

---

83   Swedish title sometimes prefixed to names of people of a certain rank, literally 'high-
     born'.

our little Darling shall learn to walk in. Faster Albertina sent her 2. littles p[ai]rs of knitted socks, and I had ordered some shoes from San Fr[ancisco] so little Annie is not in want of any more for the present. Many, many thanks sweetest Mother for having anticipated my wishes, in sending those books – I hope to teach little A[nnie] her A.B.C. out of that one dear Grand mama gave me. My most especial thanks for the 2. books on education, which I have read with the utmost interest and delight, & in much of Miss Hamilton,[84] recognized my own Mother, & thank God daily for the Mother we have had and have. "Hints on education" is in truth a most valuable exellent book, easily to be understood, and most sound in every respect – Miss Hamilton requires deeper thought & study. I have lent it to Mrs Makzutoff now, & will send her the other one too, before we leave for "Codiac" where I purpose taking them with me, & studying often. I am so thankful to have got them so early, for I see education has its beginning in the cradle. If our precious Child remains as she is & has been from her birth there will not be *much* trouble in bringing her up, with God's divine assistance & guidance for truly a sweeter tempered Baby I have never never seen, she opens her eyes to smile on all around her. Most earnest & ardent is my daily prayer and thought, that her temper may never be spoilt or ruffled through impatience and hastiness from my side – & that we may both be wiser & understand our duties towards her, & her future wellfare better, than to *spoil* or *indulge* her – I may truly say, I have as great a horror of spoiling her, or any other Child, as ever you can have had in educating us – Those are certainly the most fortunate & happiest, whose will has not in every way been tempered and given in to, and who have not been brought up to be a drawback upon their own happiness, and a tormenter of their own selves. But in educating, or rather, in wishing to begin this great work of education, you must continue y[ou]r own education, so that our children may never see us contradict in deed, what we preach in words. May God of His infinite goodness thereto give me His assistance, & enlighten my mind, & give me strength & perseverance. In "Hints on education" there is only one point on which I do not exactly agree, which is to punish a child by keeping any article of food suitable for its age & meal, from it – I think such a plan easily generates greediness, which is in itself a horrible thing. Don't you think so too darling Mama? I am thankful to have found Ida, who, being an educated, well principled, well behaved & in every way good person, will never teach or encourage deceit in a child; or instill into the infant mind "I will not tell Mama", but rather will try in every way to carry out my wishes, and see that they are not infringed upon during my absence from the nursery. She is already an exellent person, and quite attached to us – we get on so well together, I am happy to say.

At 7. o'clock the same evening of the day the "Nikolai" arived, I had the pleasure of welcoming nice little Fru Krogius, having asked her to tea. It was quite strange,

---

84 Probably *Letters on the Elementary Principles of Education* by E. Hamilton, published 1801-1802.

such a wonderful feeling, half pleasurable, half sorrowful filled my heart, when I saw her and heard of you from her – she told me you would have liked to come so much – Oh! if you had but been on board, it w[ou]ld have been *so so* delightful, how happy and proud I would have been to welcome my own Mother here – and then you would not have been so lonely as you now are. And if you had not liked to remain with us, or had found it cold, damp and gloomy at Sitka, you would have had the same good opportunity back again; but it was not to be so – none of us ever knew any ship would sail for the Colonies right from Helsingfors. We spoke about you much, and I asked questions without end, to some of which she could of course not answer, having only seen you once – She remained till nearly 10. and I hoped to see her often again – but unfortunately she has been very ill – at one time so ill, that it quite frightened me. She expects her confinement at the beginning of August, and as all has gone well till now, it would have been sad, should anything have gone wrong. She had Diarhea, with violent pain in the back & stomach, much fever & perfect loss of strength & appetite. We all feared for a miscarriage, indeed Pastor Winter, a cousin of her husbands, feared more and alarmed me so, I went immediately on board to see what I could do – She was very anxious herself, as the mixtures prescribed by our 2. clever doctors, made her worse. I took her little Alice home with me, to keep her out of the way of making a noise. She is such a very good, sweet little girl, and her Papa's darling "Pappa's sockergryn" [Swed. literally 'Papa's small piece of sugar'] as she says. Fortunately Capt[ain] Krogius insisted upon taking a midwife, or nurse with them on this voyage, who has studied at Helsingfors, & seems to understand her business well; as the doctors could not help she did what she thought best and now thank God she is quite restored again, & spent the afternoon and evening here yesterday. Thus you see greater part of her stay here, has been spent in bed – next week "Nikolai" is to sail Hampus tells me. I shall recommend her to Ludmila's particular kindness & care, & young Bergenheim too, and to L[ieutenan]t Elfsberg. It will be so pleasant to see them all again next Sept[ember] when we please God return from our Summer trip to "Codiac", and hear about *Monday 9th* – Ludmila. My own private idea is – she is not happy! – an inward feeling tells me, I am not wrong though I would wish to be so. A letter to Constance written two months after her marriage proves it – for she complains of being lonely, "there are so many things one can tell a sister, but not a husband" she says – how is it possible! – there is no one on earth to whom a Wife can so freely speak, speak all & everything without the slightest secrecy, as to her husband; and thus it ever ought to be. To feel that you have the whole and entire confidence of y[ou]r husband, as he has of you, is such happiness – such Joy, to be deprived of it, would be to be deprived of the foundation, on which happiness in married life is built. I have been making a few patterns of my Babylinen for Ludmila, in hopes they may be of use to her, though we have not had time to hear of her prospects, or if she has any. Constance has also made a few things. Hampus had given orders to buy several books at an auction, this morning Mr Koschkin brought them, and I will give you a list of them, to show you what

pleasure my husband takes in providing his Wife with such books as must improve
and instruct her mind.

1. *Éducation Maternelle*, Simples lecons d'une mère à ses enfants par Madame
    Amable Tastu.
2. *l'Éducation progressive* par M[ad]ame Necker de Saussure 2. vol[umes].
3. De la Démocratie en Amerique par Tocqueville. 2 vol[umes].
4. Souvenir d'un voyage dans la Tartarie, le Thibet et la Chine par [..?] Huc.
5. La vie de la famille dans le nouveau monde. Fr. Bremer
6. La Mare au Diable et
7. La petite Fadette. G[eorge] Sand.
8. Conquest of Mexico – 2. vol[umes] and
9. Conquest of Peru – 2 vol[umes] Prescott.
10. Le roi d'Oude, Moeurs de l'Inde. Révoil.
11. Voyages et aventures au Chili Dr F. Maynard.
12. Souvenirs de L'Amerique Espagnole. M. Radiguet.
13. Huit jours sous l'Equateur. E. Carrey.
14. L'Empereur Soulouque G. D'Alaux.
15. Jérome Paturot à la recherche de la meilleure des républiques. Reybaud.

By this list you see they are mostly french books, which gives me an opportunity of
studying that language properly. I think it will please you to see the good selection
my darling has made. Besides these books, my bookshelf contains others of equal
merit. Byron, Shakespeare, Washington Irving 16. vol[umes].

3. Leighton, on S[ain]t Peter's 1. epistle recommended by dear Mary, an exellent
    book.
4. Macaulay's History
5. Information for the people
6. History of Civilization. Guizot.
7. Robertson's sermons.
8. History of the reformation D'Aubigné.
9. Websters domestic economy
10. Henry's commentary on the Bible in 3. large vol[umes] a beautiful work, with
    illustrations.

Besides these various Encyclopaedias, Longfellow's and Tennyson's poems, Living-
stons travels in South Africa, Life of Charlotte Bronté etc – etc, a few practical house
& cookery books, and I think, though but a small beginning to a library, the beginning is good. I like to initiate you my own Mother, into everything about me, and I
know you will like to know I am not feeding on novels, of which we only possess 4.
and of which I used to be a passionate lover, though now, when nothing & nobody
would hinder me, I never read any so to say. My whole heart and mind is filled with
the desire of improving my own mind & conquering my besetting sins, & to educate
our Child as a grandchild of yours & child of my Hampus' ought to be educated.

I think, my own Mother, my letters of last summer will have shown you, I have never got into the habit of lying up on the sofa, "vegetating" or spending hours of idleness & I am grieved you should ever have entertained such fears – I never did it when it was a temptation & I felt tired and uncomfortable, and I pray God I may never do it in future, for it is the loss of valuable time, and of spirits too. But I am so accustomed to be in bed by 10. & up at 7. or 6½, I can hardly keep my eyes open if my usual time is inflicted upon, which I hope is not laziness. But now it is high time to stop speaking of self. It was delightful indeed to get some extracts from Florence's letters and to hear how kind & friendly Otto and Olga [Furuhjelm] had been to them, & above all, to know Carl had got so very good a place & income. There is a freshness and life in Florence's letters, which is quite delightful, and her descriptions are so graffic. I wonder if she is again in the "wilderness" with Carl now, or if she has been obliged to remain in Moscou. I wonder too when she will write. Soon we have been here 1. year, and our Baby will soon be 6. months old; the little darling is quite well thank God, and has no symptoms of teething yet. She stretches out her little hands after everything you hold before her & smiles when she gets hold of it. Florence & Carl would love the little thing. You must be in the middle of packing up for England – what do you do with your furniture & other household goods. Remember darling Mama, when we please God return home, we hope to be welcomed by you – How can you *for ever* bid farewell to the country, where both your children are married? that will never do my own Mother, for they count upon the great happiness of often, often seeing you an inmate of their families. I shall be so anxious to know where you will settle; and where Uncle Hannay & Aunt Mary will live. Would you live with them, if they should wish it? Many thanks for that pretty little sketch of Palsi – Hampus was glad to see it again, he has had it copied for Ludmila, & I made a copy for Constance who was delighted. Poor Esperance, what will become of her? She writes so warmly about you, I am so happy, she has learnt to know and love you. It would have been much better, had Constance been in Finland, living at Palsi with her sister, who would then not have been so lonely, & had something to interest her. We must see what can be done.

Tuesday 10th/22. I forget whether I ever answered y[ou]r question about my pink muslin – I left it at home, but Faster Albertina's I have with me. I would have been glad to have had some of my old dresses here, they could have been cut up for Baby by and bye. –

Did you hear Lindholm play last winter? I saw by the papers he had been at H[elsing]f[or]s. I still hear him play that exquisite Scherzo by Chopin, which I am most assiduously practising now. What have you decided about the piano? It was well it was not sent here, for I suppose it would have been equally badly packed as the Makzutoff's was, which arrived here completely ruined & done for, they at first thought, but our tuner seems to be getting it into some sort of trim again. It was not hermetically fastened up in a tin case, as ours was in London, but merely packed as if it were going on a journey from P[eters]b[ur]g to H[elsing]f[o]rs, which shows the good people in first name town are not accustomed to send their instruments on a long seavoyage & through the tropics, which is the most trying for them. I still hope to have it *at home*, when we have one – so darling Mama, pray keep it, unless you are in want of money, & then *pray pray* sell it – though I fear you would lose much, & would perhaps not get more than 200 R[oubles] S[ilver] for it. The Maksutoff's is purchased second hand for that price, & was only 1. year old. [...]

Hampus made me speak to Mathilda [Mrs Krogius' servant], as she is called, seeing I have ever since my confinement often been suffering from a disagreeable complaint, which I began to be afraid, I might carry with me through life. However it seems, it is a thing which easily & often occurs after a first confinement, if there has been much exertion, & confined bowels and I trust soon to be quite well. When I described how my confinement had been, & told her about the fever & dreadful pain, want of milk, weakness & the means adopted by nurse and D[octo]r, she lifted up her hands in astonishment, & said I had had the real "Barnsängsfeber, och det var en lycka det gick som det gick" [Swed. childbed fever, and I was happy it went so well] – God mercifully helped me through it all – & now it is all past & gone, as if it had never been. If you my own Mother, had been with me, it would have been better. I thought you would at least remain in Finland till you heard if there were no prospects of our darling Florence soon becoming a Mother, & that you would then have gone to her; you know how utterly ignorant she is about babies – more than I was, because she never cared for Baby's, but I always had a passion for them, & was interested to see how they were managed. I fancy Carl's exstacy! Long ago he asked me to be Godmother to their first son! The pots and pans for Ludmila arived quite safely and one was not at all rusty, the other only a very little. I had them smeared over again immediately. Now darling Mama, I must ask y[ou]r pardon, in case this letter will be an expense to you, for I have all the time forgotten you would be in England, where our Company unfortunately has no agent. As this letter goes with all the rest to P[eters]b[ur]g I can't say whether the Company will be generous enough to prepay it. The next time however I will write on as thin paper as possible; I could not copy it all over again sweet precious Mother – are you angry? – this question puts me in mind of a book I am reading "Heartsease" [by C.M. Yonge, published in 1854], where I have found in the heroine "Violet" a great deal to set me thinking of myself & my ways & faults – so, even a novel, can do good. –

[...] Oh yes – it was fortunate indeed, you could not persuade Uncle Adolf to send Gustaf to Sitka, for Hampus, who is anything but proud or haughty, so that is not the reason, said it would have been most unpleasant. Any relation of mine or his, coming as a sailor, even though a born gentleman, would be impossible for the Russians to believe true – they would say: "Gouverneuren är af låg härkomst, vi behöfver icke lyda" [Swed. The governor is not a nobleman, we don't have to obey] – for Hampus says, it would never enter into a russian nobleman's head to send his son on such a journey, he would lose cast, & be treated like a common sailor. They make an enormous difference in being noble, or not noble, & are exceedingly proud

& haughty. So you see, it might have inconvenienced Hampus not a little, though we would both have been kind to him, & had him with us – But I hope he may not come while we are here. Hampus says Ad[olf] Etholén knew very well why he refused sending him – & if so, that was very considerate.

Ascension Day. We have now had several days perfect summer weather; all the trees are green, & have been so, though not fully developped, since the end of April, which shows that we are much before Finland. I have on a pink muslin, or rather batist, for it is linen dress, bought & made on board the large steamer "Golden Age" where I wore it last, so you may fancy it is warm. It is so exquisite – it is difficult to keep indoors, such days are not good when you have many letters to write. I was twice in the garden with Baby yesterday. Mrs Maksutoff asked us to coffee in the garden, and we sat there with our work till it was time to come home & bathe the Baby's. I have asked her and nice little Fru Krogius this afternoon – one must take advantage of such days.

Hurah! hurah! a merchantman from Hamburg. letters! letters – wont that be delightful? my darling Hampus is worried very much now with the many ships he has to send; & the ship from China with tea, does not come, so "Amour"[85] will remain without tea. Is not that a darling little hand of y[ou]r own little Granddaughter? O Mama! she is such a precious little thing. *After dinner.* It would be well not to expect too much, as one is sure to be disappointed – No letter's from Mama! no letters from Florence, of whom I have given up all hope – only half a sheet from that darling Mrs Hawthorne, with such an exquisite lace cap of her own making – she is really so wonderfully kind & sweet. It will not fit Annie unfortunately it is much much too small, but she says will do for the 2nd. Through her I have been rejoiced to hear of our darling Florence's happy prospects, so I ardently hope you will manage to be with her, and not leave Carl as the only nurse of y[ou]r Firstborn. How I wonder what it will be – a boy I think, won't Florence be happy – I am so glad. Constance is also in the 7th heaven of delight, having heard that Ludmila is also expecting to be a Mother soon. Now I am quite cross & out of sorts at being treated worse than all other people with letters, & will therefore finish. –

Monday Ev[enin]g 16th/28. I am anxious about Baby – she has had looseness of the bowels for nearly a whole week, & has grown so pale & thin these last 3. days with such blue shadows under her eyes, & loss of appetite – It is I fear the beginning of troublesome teething, for you see 2. in the underjaw, shining quite white in front. *Tuesday.* Baby is not better, has passed a bad night, & looks so miserable, it quite frightened me this morning at 5½ when I went into the nursery. I put her into a warm bath which seemed to quiet her – she does not cry, but frets & sends forth

---

85   Amur, river in eastern Siberia. At this time, Russia's East Siberian Maritime Province, 'the Amur region', was under expansion. With the Chinese-Russian treaty of 1860, Russia gained jurisdiction not only over the Amur river, but also over the territory between the Ussuri river and the Pacific Ocean.

a little plaintive sound, as I have never heard before from her. We sent for the doctor, who insists upon that her teeth are the cause of everything, though she neither thrusts her fingers into her mouth or wishes to drink often, sure signs of teething, but in the contrary, refuses her food. The doctor prescribed a powder which I tasted & think is, Rhubarb, Magnesia, Sugar & Anis. She is again asleep now if she could but sleep several hours running, she would soon be stronger. The Lord help us – for He alone can help – we are both so anxious.

Night. Nearly 4. Oh Mama! thank God with us – our darling is better – & has slept sweetly & quietly in her little cradle since 7. o'clock – the whole forenoon almost she was in my arms, she dosed 20 minutes or so, & then awoke pining, & with such an expression of suffering it was dreadful to see. How she has changed! one would not know her – but now! O if it be the Almighty God's Will, I trust she will mend speedily – I lay down tonight with a lighter heart – & I can never say how infinitely grateful – it is dreadful to see your little precious infant suffer – I could not go to bed, before having told you she was better. O Mama! are you not happy. "The Lord is my shepherd I shall never fear" – Amen – and God bless you my Mother – & good night –

Wednesday 18. Baby has thanks be to God passed a very good night; she slept from 7 – to 2. in the night, and then till 7. in the morning; her appetite is bad still, but we must not expect perfect recovery in one day – I have now bathed her, and she is again quietly asleep – the doctor found her much better.

Now, that my mind is more at ease, I can tell you about the beautiful present Hampus has made me. He ordered several things from China, by the ship which came on Sunday night, and amongst other's a chinese worktable for me. Well, it is indeed a magnificent one, covered all over, as closely as possible, with pictures, arabesques, flowers etc, in gold like the workbox Florence got – Inside the lid is in the same way one large picture, & all the fittings are carved – but though much larger, again as large almost as Florence's it is arranged exactly in the same way. It stands on – but I have tried to sketch it for you – & though badly done, it will give you an idea. It is all gold & the most exquisite thing possible; also a carved ivory card case which is very fine, & 4. pieces of satin 1 ¼ y[a]rd broad. We have also got a splendid chessboard & set of chessmen, & a box of letters for Baby. Is not my Hampus a kind kind husband? I was as happy as a child about the table.

On maux faux ['at random', probably Anna's false interpretation of the Swed. expression 'på måfå'] I will send this to Moscou, in case you are there, or if you are not there, Florence will forward the letter. Nikolai goes to Ajan tomorrow, and all our letters with her – Soon too I trust we shall be on our way. I am writing these lines in the nursery – Baby is lying awake on her cushion, & has been crowing a little – but now she seems to be becoming impatient to lie there alone. It was so nice you had the 2. announcements of our marriages entered into the same paper. I had often, often looked for mine, & as I never found it, I thought you had forgotten it. […]

I have just had the farewell visit of a young officer, who has dined 9½ months at our table, & who has I am afraid quite carried off the heart of Sophie Klinkowström, daughter to the lady who nursed me, & Tante Margerets Goddaughter; she is not yet 17. rather goodlooking & a good girl – her mother has permitted him to accompany her on long, daily walks alone, & the end is that she is perfectly in love – he has nothing – and is not[86] sent to Amour for 2 years and a half – I fear there will be bitter, bitter tears. –

I must now finnish darling Mama with fond love from Hampus, who cannot manage to write this time – he has had so many other letters to attend – he desires his best thanks for the view of Palsi, and all that is dear & fond –

God bless you my beloved Mother – Baby is asleep – I hope to hear from you by return of Nikolai – With love to dear Babette

Ever Your own loving Child

Anna Furuhjelm

No. 36   *Codiac. June 8/20th 1860*

My own beloved Mother,
As you will see by the date, we are no longer at Sitka, but have been in this lovely place since last Sunday ev[enin]g 5th June. We left Sitka by steamer "Constantin" on Wednesday ev[enin]g and had thank God a prosperous voyage, though slower than would have been the case, had we not had a head wind all the time. Our little Darling bore the journey quite well, though she too was sick the first day, but afterwards she was as merry and happy as if on shore. Even Hampus was sick the first day, and as for my 3. women servants, especially Ida, they were as useless as if they had been in Europe all the time – So what was to be done – the only person who was well was Constance, & as she is never permitted at home to carry Baby, for fear of anything happening, we were obliged to call in the old boatswain to nurse Annie, which he did admirably. The 2. last days I attended to her myself with Constance help, & we let her hold the child on her knee, sitting close to me. She really was the "Soeur de charité" [Fr. Sister of Charity], ever ready to help everybody. You cannot think how pleased & delighted we all are with "Codiac". We feel like school-children let out for a good long holiday – we live for ourselves, & are able to enjoy ourselves thoroughly, taking long rambles into the wood & over the downs which really remind me of Ilfracombe,[87] picking hands full of flowers, of every possible colour. My Hampus comes out in a perfectly different light here, & it rejoices my heart to see how completely he enters into the beauties of nature & exsults in the

---

86   Anna probably means 'now'.
87   Ilfracombe, a seaside resort on the North Devon coast of England.

freedom of our present life, ever wishing to go out to walk, where as it used to be
his plague at Sitka – & no wonder – I disliked it too – We had there but one single
walk, & that an uninteresting one; every step we took Hampus had to bow, or be
bowed to – then we would meet these dreadful Indians – where as here, we meet
nobody & can walk how & when we like – Hampus has no "uppvaktningar" [Swed.
visits] every day, nor have we any other gentleman, but the secretary to dinner – I
have refrained from mentioning a day on which I would receive the so called ladies
of this place, thereby wishing to show they are all welcome to come at any time, &
that we consider ourselves quite private people here, wishing to be left at peace & not
bothered with any etiquette or formality. – I am alone today – my husband having
left me this morning to make a little excurtion in a "*Bydark*"[88] (we sent you a model
of one). The weather was perfectly exquisite, when he, the Bishop[89] [Petr] & another
gentleman started each in their Bydark with two Aleutians to row them, but now it
is blowing hard, & I feel quite anxious – I ordered dinner for 4. o'clock, but I fear he
will not be home yet. I had a strange fright this morning after H[ampus] was gone.
I was sitting reading the Bible on the sofa in this room, when it suddenly began to
tremble underneath me, & then the house shook & I heard a noise as of thunder
at a great distance. My heart beat, it could nearly have been heard, involuntary I
sprang to my feet & dashed into the next room, where Baby was sleeping – But all
was again quiet & Baby was not disturbed – I immediately went to ask if any other
person in the house had felt the shake, but none had. When I came in & happened to
see my face in the glass, I saw it was as white as a sheet, & I felt quite sick – In fact
it has been an earthquake, such as I hear is often felt here; but you may fancy never
having felt one before, it might create this feeling of fear & terror just mentioned. I
had Lisbon[90] in my mind as quick as lightening, was it not strange. I am curious to
hear whether H[ampus] felt it at sea. I hope he will have had a pleasant day. I am
so happy to have him at last all to myself; I quite dread the sudden announcement
"Annie, tomorrow I am going" – I have not asked, and do not know how long he
will remain. But all cannot be pleasurable – You can never conceive what a dreadful piece of news met him here, communicated to him by the pilot – "Codiac" the
vessel we came to Sitka in last year, dashed in a thousand pieces, cargo, post every,
everything lost – but no life thank God. This is a loss of 40. or 60.000 R[oubles]
S[ilver] to the company, which is not little, & a doleful unpleasant thing to have
to write to the "hufvudförvaltning" [Swed. central administration, board of direc-
tors]. How it actually happened, that is to say, how nothing was saved, is not yet
ascertained. The ship struck on a sandbank, never known of before – but the day

---

88   Bydark ('baidarka' in Russian), a kayak, used by the natives.
89   The diocese of Kamchatka, the Kurile Islands and the Aleutians had been established in
     1840. "The Bishop's house" is still to be seen in Sitka.
90   The Lisbon earthquake in 1755 killed 30,000 people and destroyed more than two-thirds
     of the city.

was calm, clear & beautiful, she did not sink till 2. days after she struck & received a small hole – How was she still not saved? that is the question. The Captain, not the one we had, & all the crew are still here – an investigation will be brought about ere long. This was a heavy blow, & I already thought our whole stay, & the pleasure we had anticipated, would be quite spoilt – But now thank God, H[ampus] is calmer about it, and quite, quite merry & full of fun, when he is not thinking about this sad event. It is not his fault but somehow, Hampus is afraid all will go wrong with him, & that the good gentlemen in P[eters]b[ur]g will never be contented with him. Darling Hampus! his thought night and day, is how best to improve the Colonies – & everybody sees a great difference since he is Governor, still he is never satisfied with himself – But I always tell him, though he has many, many difficulties now, & often all seems to be against him, & we have so many expences, only having saved 2000 R[oubles] S[ilver] this first year, he will some day reap the good fruits of it – for I truly believe, God never forsakes those that earnestly seek Him & pray for His guidance & enlightment in all things. –

Tuesday 14/26th. The last time I wrote, was doomed to be a day of solitary adventures – It began with the earthquake already mentioned. In the afternoon it blew so hard, I felt anxious about Hampus – at 3. o'clock I put my shawl & bonnet, and walked across the downs – the wind blowing about my cotton dress in all directions, & a cold wind it was. However after having walked half an hour without seeing the 3. Bydarks, I began to return, turning round every now and then, but without success. As I approached the church, which lies just outside our house on a slope, I saw at a distance a number of dogs as it seemed assembled in one knot – as I came nearer and they caught sight of me, they all with one accord began to bark & rushed down the slope, up & round about me, pulling my dress to pieces, & then rushed off each one with a piece of it in their mouths. You may easily fancy my fright – I screamed right out & prayed God to help me. I was afraid of running for fear they would begin to chase me, & my voice could not be heard because of the wind. I know not how I got home, not till they had left me, did I hasten my steps, & when I got into the nursery, I was deathpale, trembling & shaking all over & could hardly speak – the tears ran down my cheeks, tho' I did not cry – Ida brought Eau de Cologne and gave me a Soda powder, I took off my tattered dress & lay down on my bed & thought what a good picture for an illustrated paper I would have made, or for a story a novel, except that there, the rescuing lover would have been wanting had I been a young girl. I fell asleep & woke up at 5. just in time to receive my husband all safe & well home again. He was horrified when he heard of the fright I had had – 3. of those dogs were wild ones, belonging to nobody – Hampus ordered them to be shot. Today I am again alone; Hampus went on a longer expedition this morning, & may possibly not return till tomorrow. I accompanied him down to the shore & saw him comfortably seated in his Bydark, & thought it was so lonely without him. Yesterday I was out with my husband – We started in the afternoon in 2. Bydarks, I, little goose as I am, with my heart in my throat all the time – for it is a nervous thing going in those boats the first time. We sent you some models of them, by which you see, one sits on the bottom of the skinboat, with outstretched legs, & seems to be dancing along on the waves. We kept near the shore for my sake, but twice we had to cross the open sea, where the waves were higher, it began to blow & look somewhat threatening. We had gone to inspect the cow establishment. There were not so many as we expected – about 80. with the calves – The old man is a Fin, has been there 28. years, & is married to an Aleutian woman, by whom he has 3. daughters & one son. It was a delight once more to see a healthy looking, pretty, strong country lass of 17. years old – You never see such a thing in Sitka, where women, girls & children are all consumptive & in every way sickly. The dairy was a nice sight – 60 or 80, or still more wooden milk pales, all filled with milk, were ranged round the walls, & a large tub of butter was standing ready to be sent to Codiac. We saw our men catching salmon & a few versts[91] from there, we went to see a catch, made for them in a clear, rapid little river, which empties itself into the sea – Our guide had to carry us both several times over the open places – would you not have laughed if you had seen me? It was now fairly raining & blowing in our faces – and on the way back we got a thorough drenching – my hat streamed with water – dress, petticoats, (I had no crinoline) stockings, shoes were all one pool of water – We entered the peasant "stuga" [Swed. cottage] where we soon became more comfortable – a fire was lighted, my draggled petticoats, shoes & stockings taken off. The eldest girl brought me a pair of quite new white woman stockings, & one of the rowsmen gave me his skin topped boots – after having eaten a little sour milk we again entered our Bydarks, the wind had subsided, but it still rained. I was now no longer afraid, & was able to enjoy myself. We came home at 6½, & were met with the news that darling Annie had not been well – her stomach seems to have been a little wrong. I immediately gave her some rhubarb, magnesia & Annis powder, after which she fell asleep & is thank God perfectly restored. This is such an exquisite day, my Hampus will have quite a "partie de plaisir" [Fr. pleasure trip] & will most likely be home tonight, for I see the wind is favourable. I made up a basket of provisions for him, which I hope he will enjoy. Baby has been out mostly all day it is so fine. I have made a little sunbonnet for her, in which she looks so very sweet. She will soon have her 2. toothies through – they look like little pearls; you cannot think how very sweet & gentle she is – I really never saw such an infant – she never cries, & will lie perfectly happy & contented on a cushion or the bed, talking to herself – she now says: "Ah ba – ba! – bababa. Sometimes it sounds like *Papa*. Hampus gets fonder and fonder of her every day – I think he will miss the little thing much. –

Now I must tell you a little about Codiac itself. It is much prettier than Sitka, though there the scenery is grander – but here everything is so rural – you fancy yourself in the country. The dwelling houses, built of wood, unpainted, lie along the seashore, & straggling backwards along the foot of the mountains, by which we

91   Verst, a Russian measure of length: 1.06 km.

A page from letter No. 36, with the Imperial double eagle and the house of Anna and Hampus Furuhjelm at Kodiak.

are fenced in on one side. Our little suny comfortable house, consisting of 6 rooms & many outhouses, the kitchen with cooks room in an extra little building, lies just opposite our steamer "Constantin" and may be called lying at the end of Codiac – the only building a wee bit further, is the russian church. These mountains nearest us, differ from those in Sitka, in that they are thickly covered with grass & every possible wild flower – violets too, I was as pleased as a child when I saw them – you remember they do not grow in Finland. Hampus and I scrambled up one of them half way one day, and were quite delighted. Further on to the right is a little wood, consisting of popplar & elder trees; the highest hills are covered with snow, & are quite like ours at Sitka. All cattle would thrive well here, & sheep would do so perfectly. We have no want of milk, cream & fresh butter – meat also, whereas in Sitka we have only venison – in autumn you have delicious wild geese, ducks, partridges & other birds – mushrooms & all kinds of berries. We are going to order 100 geese or so to be salted – eggs too we can get for 10 kop[eks] 1. piece, instead of 50! Outside the nursery & our bedroom windows is a nice little garden, with an arbour where we have been sitting all the afternoon, & have planted spinage & salad. We get up at 6½ or a little later & breakfast before 8. Hampus has had levées each forenoon – all the men & women in the place I think have put some petition to him – it was so amusing to see the Aleutes – You know, or do not know – they were also savages at first, but are christened now, and are a very quiet, harmless set of people now – quite unlike the Kolosches, who are as savage now as ever – they are yellow brown, very high cheekbones & ugly, wearing a peculiar kind of long shirt over their trowsers, & skin boots. their language is very like the K[olosh] language,[92] in fact I can hear no difference – there is generally before every word a sound like "kl" – when they were here with the interpreter & wished to signify their pleasure and approval at the answers Hampus gave, they said "Ah – h" ah – h, & the secretary afterwards told us, that they had all said "that must be a good man; he listened to all we had to say to him, & asked us what we wanted & let us talk out, & then gave us sugar, tea & flour, & a 'sup' [Swed. shot of] brandy –" No wonder they said so – my husband speaks so kindly to them & is so attentive to all they say – the old infirm men he bids sit down, whilst he himself is standing – O! if anyone knew what a jewel he is – The flag has been wafting from the flagstaff all day, showing Hampus is away. He makes himself thoroughly acquainted with the colonies – & knows much more *now*, than many another one knew at the end of 5. years; perhaps Etholén excepted – swedes are more conscientuous than Russians – In how many instances I have seen that. O Mama there are so many many things in Russia you cannot help deploring – where is truth – integrity, sincerity, honesty? – but you will see plenty of flattery – polished manners & amiable conversation – & alas what a mournful state of blind-

---

92 Actually, Alutiiq, the language of the inhabitants of Kodiak, is related to Eskimo. The language of the Tlingit Indians or Koloshes belongs to another language family, the so-called Athabascan-Eyak-Tlingit.

ness the clergy puts upon the congregation – what ignorance – what superstition! it makes me quite sad.

Friday 29/17 June. Another post without a line from you or Florence! though thank God I was not left totally without news from you – That kind, kind Tante Margeret sent me a wee note from you to her of last March, and a long happy sweet letter from Florence to her – by which I learnt you were all quite well. Hampus does not now exactly remember the reason why he kept y[ou]r letter so long before posting it, tho' darling Mama, you may be sure, it was from *some* well meant, good intention – he is however very sorry to have occassioned you so much anxiety darling Mama. – Though I have been deprived of an anxiously expecting Joy by this post, my heart has nevertheless been filled with real gratitude & joy on my husbands account. You know he was sent on a negociation to San Francisco, & he, as usual, thought the "hufvudkontor" [Swed. head office, board of directors] was displeased with him, & the contract he had made. He told me last this morning "I hope "Garitza" will not come before I go, as I am afraid of opening the post – all seems to go wrong with me" – however I as usual tried to make him join in my sanguinity, feeling assured the Company could not otherwise than estimate his unwearied efforts in their behalf – And so! a most kind letter from Uncle Adolf, & ditto one from Ad[miral] Polimkoffsky *thanking* him heartily for all he has done, & both expressing their entire satisfaction. How his eyes glistened – & how glad he was! I knew it would all be right, & thank God for all. Uncle Charles, Tante Albertina & Tante M[argeret] have all written such kind welcome letters – oh, it does warm up one's heart so to hear something from home. My father in law wrote a long letter to my Hampus, which has made us all very happy & it makes me feel convinced, my daily unceasing prayer will be heard & all family feuds be put an end to, & his heart once more soften towards his children. Hampus has ever been a good son, & tried to make his brothers as soft as himself – & please God, he may reap the reward. It was also a delight to my poor Sister Constance, to be this time so affectionately written of, & such kind messages sent to her by her Father, whom you know she left without his leave – She repents it sadly – but it was Otto's doing, & very wrong in him it was. She has such a warm affectionate heart – though her mind has suffered through the sad disease God has laid upon her to bear – She is in no way "bortblandad" [Swed. mixed-up] – not like poor Emmy – but still she cannot think, nor can you converse on anything but household affairs with her – in this, she quite delights – & is an exellent practical housekeeper – I let her help me a little sometimes as it amuses & diverts her. She, for instance has the management of our dairy, & collects sweet & sour cream, of which we have plenty here. I would like to give you a cup of the coffee I make in the morning with cream like a porridge. But "aufgeschoben ist nicht aufgehoben" [Ger. literally 'postponed is not cancelled'] so please God it will be some day 4. years hence.

Florence's letter to Tante M[argeret] filled me with delight, & my eyes with tears – So fully do I enter into, & understand & appreciate her blissful feelings & sentiments over the coming event. No one can know the inexpressible Joy a child can give, till you actually have it – how often, just like her, did I fancy I *could* already feel it – how I wondered – how I prayed – how I rejoiced! & how holy & serene a feeling it ever was – To work Baby linen for y[ou]r first child, those tiny fairylike articles, what happiness does it not afford! what pleasant company such occupation afforded me in my loneliness when Hampus was out or occupied – what thoughts, what prayers what not to be expressed feelings you work into them! and then, when everything is ready for the "welcome little Dombey" what childlike Joy to view each piece, to take it up & wonder if any living creature could ever put its head into so diminutive a thing to call a cap for instance. Oh! I feel it all anew & over again with & for my precious sister, & cannot cease imploring our Heavenly Father to be with her in that fearful hour of pain, & to bless them both. There is such true, deep piety in all Florence's letters – too deep to be put into many words – but still immediately *felt* by the reader – How wonderfully & beautifully "God's grace to will and to do" has worked in her. I have always loved her dearly, I have always as you know admired & looked up to her – but I have never loved her as I love her now – Carl must be truly, truly happy – & he deserves to be so. –

I now forget, if our precious Baby was already recovered when my last letter went – but Mama! one day & especially the forenoon, she was very ill – my very inmost heart beat – & I felt what an awful blank it would be to lose her – but, the never ceasing power of comfort, *nothing can happen without Gods Will*, never left me all the time. And through His great & wonderful mercy she became better, & now this is the 3rd day since she has cut her first tooth. If you could see her Mama! if you could feel her little hand patting your shoulder – tell me would you not be happy? how happy I am you will be near Florence, & that she will have the joy of seeing their child nursed by you. – I fancy you as now on your way to her – or perhaps already there. How I envy her. –

By this post we have had 2. interesting books sent us: the *correspondence of Alex[ander] v[on] Humboldt,* and "*the fate of Sir John Franklin discovered*". This latter work reminds me of our juvenile enthusiasm for him, & wishing & even trying to dream of him & where he was to be found.

Monday July 2nd/June 20. Today we have been one year in the Colonies! four only remain! how wonderfully fast this year has gone, & how fast the rest will go – when they are past, they will seem like a dream. I have written long letters to Tante Margrethe & Wilhelmina Grancy. How I wish you had sent me the Schäffers, Frau v[on] Bockelbergs & Tante Louise's kind letters to read. I feel as if we were quite cut off from all former associations, so little do I hear about anybody now a days – All the news I get, is so interrupted & inconsecutive – If you would be so kind darling Mama, to send me now & then some letters to read, I would be very thankful. I am thinking of Carl & Florence every day now. In a few days she will have been married 10. months. I have tried to calculate when she might possibly be confined, & think perhaps any day between 8th and 15th July. How happy I am you can be with her

I cannot say. I hope you will give me a full account of how it all went – I trust all well, & that she can nurse her little one herself. I fancy dear Charlie in one extasy of delight – I think the first few day's, "the byrå" [Swed. office] will be none the better of his presence. I am astonished he too has proved so bad a correspondent – In fact we are quite forgotten. To everybody my sister can write, but to me, and I need not try to disguise the pain it costs me. But no more about that.

I am longing to hear you have received my long letter of *11th Dec[ember]* over China, & mine of 5th Feb[ruar]y & that you are happy to be Grandmama. Though you cannot see our Child, don't forget she is your first Grandchild, and don't let "her nose be put out of joint" by Florence's little darling, whom you will see. It is marvelous to me, not to hear of the arrival of Ad[miral] Woewodsky, I tremble for the little brooch with my portrait, which I sent you. I am now afraid you may have written over Ajan, & not at all over San Fr[ancisco] in which case I shall be without letters till October. I fancy *No. 30. & 31.* must arrive at the same time in April. *No. 32* is lost & was not a long letter I think. *No. 33.* ought to have reached you at the end of June a few days ago. No. 34. ought to reach you end of July or beginning of Aug[ust] & *No. 35* was enclosed to Florence & I hope will find you there in Sept[ember]. This is No. 36 & ought to be with you beginning of October. As you have not written, I send it too to Moscou, having no idea what you are going to do. I have received from you, *No. 16*, which is the last I have. I am curious to see if I have reckoned right. I have just read through my letter, & am grieved to see it is so dull & uninteresting, joined to which it is badly written, and I am afraid you will be vexed. I know you would like a full description of the scenery around us – but that is just what I cannot give and never have been able to give. Florence or you, would do it admirably. This is another lovely day. I had Baby out in her little carriage, just come from San Fr[ancisco] but now she is sleeping in the nursery. If you go to England darling Mama, would you send me some socks, and a little white straw hat, quite plain and cheap. To order anything from San Fr[ancisco] is so dreadfully expensive, and at Sitka one cannot get any single thing for a child. How did Florence get paterns from England? they could not have passed the customhouse – perhaps she brought them with her; I suppose they are the same as mine, better & prettier one's I never saw, everybody likes them. I have commenced taking cold sponging baths, preparatory to sea bathing. The sea is only 8 degrees warmth, which is too cold for me to venture, though Hampus & Constance go every day, & enjoy it exceedingly – but they are both accustomed to cold baths & ice all the year round. Baby enjoys her salt baths of 16 degrees, & thrives wonderfully upon them thank God. Cold water judiciously employed is really one of the finest things I know, & the best preservative against colds and coughs.

Wednesday Ev[enin]g June 22/July 4. I am again alone! You know what these words mean – my precious husband left me one hour ago – May the blessing of God accompany him, as my hearts fondest prayers will, & may it be the will of our Heavenly Father, that ere 2. months have passed, we may meet again. It is a heartrending this *parting*! to be torn away from your hearts dearest treasure – & especially when one must remain without the slightest means of communication, as is the case with us. I should be in despair, utterly miserable, had I not my God to trust and hope in – I felt serene peace in my soul, when we parted an hour ago – though every pulse in my body beat & my heart throbbed & heaved; and oh! how infinitely grateful I am for *that* great, great Mercy. The Lord will be with him! the Lord will go with him & let his angels watch over him – near or far, the Lord will ever be with those who seek & call upon Him. We knelt down & prayed – he blessed me – and then kneeling on either side of the cradle, with our treasure asleep inside, & our hands folded over her, we again prayed, & implored God's protection over us all – over those who remain & him who goes. O Mama! what cause of infinite thanks, that we are united in prayer – united in one religion, filled with its blessed hopes & promises – & both professing one Faith. How good God is towards me now. I am not so lonely as I was last time we parted. I have *Hampus child* to comfort and console me & fill me with Joy – I have her to nurse & tend & occupy my solitude with. When his heart & thoughts dwell upon Home, they dwell upon her, our little precious child too. She is to me a piece of him. How he will miss her sweet little ways & darling little voice, her crowing & laughter. O! may he find her quite strong and well on his return.

This is a lovely ev[enin]g. Not a breath of wind stirs – & though a thin thin rain has been falling, the air is perfectly warm. You know, I cannot take leave of, or receive my Hampus in public. We took leave in our room – I could not accompany him – Crowds of men, women & children assembled outside our windows – I went afterwards to the house door and watched him down the road, then I went in & remained at the open window – The bay was as smooth as a mirror – silently, mysteriously the boat, containing my Hampus & the Bishop with 4. men in red flanel shirts rowing, came gliding along – the little battery saluted 3. times & the rows men lifted up their oars in one line – then the church bells rung for the Bishop. It was a solemn moment & I prayed all the time, not taking my eyes from my Darling – As long as I could see the boat, I remained & soon afterwards, put on my cloak & hood & walked over the little hill to the battery, just in time to see the stately "Constantin" slowing getting up her steam; soon she was out of sight too – & then I felt myself thoroughly alone. Thank God for this exquisite weather. Tomorrow by 10. f[ore]n[oon] Hampus will please God, be in Kinaj[93] with Hjalmar – & he will have someone to talk to. How I longed to go with him! But oh no. I would not pine or grumble – that would be weak unreasonable & ungrateful. I feel as if I were much nearer to him *here*, than had I remained at Sitka. How good it was of him to bring me, & the whole household here – what an inconvenience we were to him in the small cabin, though *he* never complained. Mama! never was there a finer, nobler, more generous heart & mind than Hampus' – he is gentleness & peace & love personificated. God has been more

---

93   The Kenai Peninsula, where a coal mine had been developed by Hampus Furuhjelm's younger brother Hjalmar.

than inexpressibly good towards both your children – we can never cease thanking Him. –

I do not tire you, darling Mama, do I? I could for ever speak to you about Hampus & my love for him.

Saturday morning June 25th. This is the 3rd day my husband has been gone, and I am thankful he went on the day he did for the very following ev[enin]g the weather changed, and has been blowing and raining furiously ever since. Please God Hampus reached "Kinaj" on Thursday forenoon 10 o'clock, and will remain there till Monday or Tuesday. He could not have gone to sea in such weather as this, & any delay here, would in consequence have delayed his return. So indeed "everything is for the best" & I rejoice he got off so well and comfortably. I have not yet told you of a dreadful fright I had the last morning he was at home. Whilst we were sitting at breakfast Mr Koschkin came in, & he & Hampus began talking of the journey. Presently I heard Hampus say: "Be that, how it may, I will go". I did not understand what he was talking about, but he had told me that morning, not very far from one of the places he would visit, was a valuable copper mine, and somehow I fancied, that might have been what he was alluding to. Hampus left the room, & I immediately asked the Secretary if it was connected with any danger going to that place? "O! il y a beaucoup de danger Madame!" [Fr. Oh, there is a lot of danger, Madame] he replied: "les hommes là, sont encore sauvages, et on ne peut pas aller sans avoir 40. hommes bien armés" [Fr. the men there are still savages, and you cannot go there without 40 well-armed men]. You may imagine, this intelligence made my heart beat, & I recognized my Hampus in never considering danger, but resolved to entreat him to abstain from going there. Three years ago a clerk was sent there & was killed by the savages. Of course I felt why Hampus wished to go; it would be such an immense gain to the Company who send copper out to the Colonies every year, & you know copper is very dear – consequently, should Hampus gain victory over the savages, it would most likely bring 10. or 15000 R[oubles] S[ilver] into his pockets. As soon as Koschkin left us, I asked Hampus, if it really was his intention, he said "Yes"! At one moment I could not speak, & hardly knew what to reply – but when at last my words & looks bespoke the utter misery I was enduring, & I represented to him, how it was his duty to take care of his life for *our sakes* – how could he with a handfull of men venture amongst those savage tribes, whilst I should be sitting here without any possible means of communication, kept over a torture, not knowing where he was, or what had become of him – he desisted & looking into my face said: "before God I promise you, I will not go – I would not cause you misery for my life – I see now how rash it was of me – I never considered the possible consequences, and though I believe God will take care of me, he never wishes me, heedlessly to expose my life, when I am a married man" – Oh! I was so happy & thankful. Had he gone, I should have had no peace. Was I not right darling Mama? & what if he would have succeeded & thereby gained the trumpery money –? it would have been an awful risk at any rate. I never before knew, we had savages so near us. We heard lately from San Fr[ancisco] that there is a general rise amongst the indians, whose hatred for the white men is so great, they have resolved to destroy them all. It is much feared, this spirit might spread to Vancouver and so along the coast to us.[94] I pray God we may be spared from any such calamity. The Kolosches are very afraid of Hampus. Woewodsky spoilt them, & allowed them too much liberty, the truth is he was afraid of them, but Hampus is a different man, & is gradually subordinating them. Some 20. or 30. were called up to breakfast the day before we left Sitka – the expression of their countenance is frightening – I am just now deeply engrossed with poor "Sir John Franklin discovered" it is most interesting. During all the long years his widow was looking for some news of him, he was dead, for he died already the *11th June 1847*. It is wonderful to read how a small yacht like the "Fox" could make the voyage she did, and with such success. You must by all means get the book and read it. Florence will be delighted with it too.

Yesterday afternoon a poor, poor woman, the mother of one of my young maidens who arrived the day before from a neighbouring island to see her daughter, came to see me, by my especial wish. I had never heard of the utter poverty she was in. Her 3. husbands, for she has been married thrice, are dead, the last died one year ago, and she is left with a Baby of 10. months & two others besides Lisa, the eldest who is with me being 16 years old. The poor woman was so weak & looked so miserable, she told me they had no money and only fish to live upon, & that the clothes she had on were borrowed in order to be able to come to me. It was truly a picture of misery. Constance immediately gave her an old shift, a p[ai]r of stockings & some stuff to make a shift for the child, & I bought a nice warm blue baize petticoat, woollen shawl, or rather very big hankerchief and cotton gown for her – It was delightful to see the poor woman's joy – my heart was so happy for her, & I thanked God for having given us sufficient means to be able to help those that are in need. I hope she will be better now – tea & bread & butter warmed her body too. She made the sign of the cross, and said she would pray for our house, for which I thanked her. I had at first intended to send Lisa on a visit to her mother, but since I have heard of their poverty, I told Lisa she could not go, but that her Mother could come to her every day, which plan she thought herself would be best.

Today our little pet has cut her second tooth. I think I must begin to give her a little more substantial food now – for instance pounded rusks boiled with milk & strained through a seine with a little sugar and salt added.

Sunday ev[enin]g 8½. Baby slept unusually long this afternoon, from 3 – 6, which has made her bath & putting to bed much later, so that I have only now returned from putting her to sleep. If you had seen her this ev[enin]g when she woke! from that sound sleep, she opened her bright eyes, saw me sitting beside her & immediately smiled, & when I stretched down my face to kiss her, she took hold of it with her dumpy little hands. She looks the picture of happiness when I hold her in my

---

94   The rise did not reach the Russian-American colonies.

arms, & gaze into that sweet, pure innocent face, it is sometimes almost impossible to believe, Sin is upon her too! she who has never done anything wrong, but is an angel itself, is stained with original, hereditary Sin! is it not sad & melancholly? How you would love her darling Mama! I would give anything to see her in your arms. If you could only see her delight when I give her your picture! she gazes at it – holds it firmly clasped between her tiny velvety fingers, & bursts into loud exclamations of delight. It makes me laugh aloud; she is so droll. How lonely I should be without her – O! what heavenly happiness it is to have a child – what a rich blessing from our Father. Hampus is quite wrapped up in her, and likes to hold her on his knees.

Thank God, the rain & gale has left us, & it seems to be clearing, so there is every chance of my Hampus having fine weather to start from Kinaj with tomorrow. [...] I have nearly finnished "Sir John" & with greater & increasing interest have I perused that well told, simple tale of those 2. years in the arctic regions crowned with such glorious results. It was wonderfull, that though M'Clintock found evident traces of the 2. ships "Erebus" and "Terror" in different parts, & bought spoons & forks with Franklins crest from the Esquimaux of Cape Victoria, none of these people who constantly roam about, should have reached Cape Felix [King William Island] & carried off all those precious relics, which M'Clintock & L[ieutenan]t Hobson found there undisturbed 12. years after the ships had been wrecked. What feelings of delight, though mixed with mournful contemplation, those scenes must have afforded him. I really read the book with mouth open, so to say, for how is it possible for a vessel to sail through an oceans drifting ice & huge icebergs unmolested? and how, when she has been frozen fast during the winter, is she not crashed when the ice breaks up & surely must come down & about her? these questions I should like answered by Capt[ain] M'Clintock himself. After all, Sir John Franklin discovered the North West passage, & died having achieved this great act.

I am thinking daily of our Florence, and what she may be doing now – She little knew what she had to go through I suspect – tell me if she went through it courageously & quietly. God grant she may be able to nurse her Baby – Did Tante Doris or Costi visit them last February? I hope not – they are better separated for some time to come. It is going on to 10. and I am still writing by daylight, but will bid you goodnight now my precious Mother.

Tuesday 28th. Baby is 7. months old tomorrow, and I think she will celebrate the day by having her 3rd tooth through. God bless the precious infant – & thank God for His mercies towards her, for I cannot say she has had difficult teething. I think it speaks well for a child artificially fed from its birth having 3. teeth at the age of 7. months. I have been wandering over the flowery carpet along the hillside this evening, & had such Sehnsucht u[nd] Herzensverlangen [Ger. a longing and desire in my heart] after my husband – I thought of the day after our arrival when he and I took a long afternoon ramble, & sat down on the soft grass, Hampus with his arm round my waist and were so happy together. I wonder where he now is – I hope he has had as fine a day as we have. Baby was out from 11. to 5½, and is now lying beside me (it is not 7. yet) playing with the cape of the blue dressing gown you sent me. I do not know how I should get on without it – it is in daily use.

Well darling Mama, are you Grandmama again? this is the 10th July & what is my Florence about. I am so hopefull, & pray God all may go on well. How I shall long for the first letter. I have just put Baby to bed; it is so nice to occupy myself so much with her – & indeed *here*, it is a perfect necessity – I never dare leave her alone with Natalia, the nursery maid, who is a good girl, but still you cannot trust any of them alone with children – they are but a little better than the indians. Ida is an exellent and trustworthy person & so fond of Baby. Will you please tell me what the english fashion or mode is for keeping Babies dry – as you cannot always change petticoats & dress. I have used a flannel cloth laid under her, & besides a flanel and linen napkin, which are changed each time she is wet, & very very seldom it goes through, but perhaps you can tell me some better way. – You cannot conceive what a quantity of clothes she requires, for I keep her as clean as an angel, & change linen twice a day after the bath – I have a young girl, who washes each day of the week for Baby, & still I have by no means a scanty wardrobe – but I remember always disliking Babies who were not kept sweet & clean, & therefore am scrupulously particular with ours. Baby sends Grandmama these wild flowers. You would be charmed could you but see them. Thousands & thousands of them cover the ground, & such lovely ones – some are like garden flowers. [...]

God for ever bless & preserve you & grant you good health precious Mother, is the sincere prayer of

Y[ou]r fondly loving child

Anna Furuhjelm

No. 37   Codiac July 24/12 1860

My own, dearly loved Mother,
Though my last long letter of 28 June is still in sight, if I may so call it, seeing the "Garitza" has been lying waiting for wind to carry her off, exactly one week now, I still begin again, wishing to have a long journal ready by the next mail. It is most distressing "Garitza" cannot get off, as she must consequently arrive after her time, & what is of more importance, the ice[95] will have melted very considerably, for we have had unusually hot weather; the thermometer showing sometimes 32! – My darling husband would be very sorry, could he see Garitza still lying here; but what is to be done? none of us can make the wind to blow –

---

95 Ice was cut and stored in ice houses both at Sitka and at Woody Island, 2.6 miles east of Kodiak and sent to San Francisco. It was the most important export item of the RAC in this period (Otchet 1864, p. 63).

How I have been longing for you darling Mother –! now, that I am again alone, I could enjoy your society & conversation without interruption – it would indeed be a happiness in my solitude. And there is so very much I would wish to ask your advice about, & hear your opinion on – foremost on education. I am studying "L'Education progressive" which I wrote to you about, and am much pleased with it – I would be inclined to call it an enlargement & continuance of Miss Hamiltons work, which Mme Necker de Saussure calls *"cette admirable ouvrage"* [Fr. this admirable work]. In the 2nd vol[ume] there are a few chapters on marriage and happiness of first maternity, which I have been reading today & yesterday. The chapter on marriage, contains according to my humble opinion, much that is exellent, but at the same time much, that you must be a frenchwoman, to agree to it – for she evidently considers marriage as generally having been entered into, more on the wish of your parents, than on your own choice, and I believe a french girl, is not always permitted to follow the voice of her heart, but is obliged to accept the husband her parents select for her. […] By whom is your *"Marriage"*. I remember you read & liked it I believe. I wish I could read it too.

When you have entered upon marriage that holy, solemn office, knowing what holy duties will be involved upon you, & having thought earnestly, & prayed ardently *before*, & have felt in the depth of your heart, that your whole hearts love will ever be your husbands, the world, which before bore so bright an image, in your mind, is indeed changed & you feel, you have your *own World*, your husbands heart! your Home! your children! there is your new world; your *real* world! & a world, which with Gods blessing and help, will ever be a world increasing in brightness; –

I often think back with astonishment on myself, four & five years ago! – I am no longer the same person. Then, an invitation to a Ball or any soirée, was a source of infinite pleasure to me, perhaps the mere thought of such an amusement in perspective was pleasure enough – when you refused an invitation it was a matter of great regret on my side. I had not yet been long enough in the world to feel its insipidness & emptiness, perhaps I was determined *not* to find it out or believe in its existence. I think I was one of those characters, who when going into society, must always have an object for so doing, that I would always single out some person to be worthy of my particular interest – & you will be ready to own, that consequently society must ever have had a charm for me. This tendency might easily have led me into mischief, & unhappiness, instead of the great Happiness God has mercifully given me, might have become my lot. I count it therefore a misfortune for a young girl to be of such a disposition, especially when the *heart* is not *really* engaged, but only imaginarily so – for, were the heart with all its depth of love engaged in the matter, it would but be *once*, & never more. Now, though almost all young girls, before they marry, have been once or twice *in love*, I can truly say, I have never, never loved before now, before I was engaged & married to Hampus, nor ever before understood *loves true meaning*. I cannot say I was a "flirt" as a young girl, & I do not think you would call me so either? would you Mama darling? & still I wonder, wonder without ceasing, how *such* a lot of true blessed happiness could have been reserved for me, so perfectly undeserving of it, as I am. Oh! it is God's infinite Love & goodness alone, that has given it to me, He who ever "giveth before we ask it", & ten thousand times more, than we ever deserve; & to know, and feel, that though undeserving, God has *given* it, as He giveth all good things, makes you still happier. Constance has several times asked me, if I do not miss society, & is astonished I do not; I cannot deny I miss the intercourse of friends, and would give much to hear your instructing conversation, to hear Florence, Mary Cautley, Mrs Hawthorne; O! very, very much, still the *world* is as indifferent to me as if I had never been in it, and no one thought or wish, has since my marriage gone that way. To live for my Hampus, he, who is my *all in all*, who is the most perfect & noble in my eyes, & for *our* children, is not that already so overpoweringly lovely, O! so infinitely much to have received in so short a time? I often, often think over the beauty of a womans mission & sphere, I think nothing is more beautiful; very, very much hath the creator put into our feeble hands, and we shall all have to give account before Him, of how we have fulfilled the lot assigned us. Darling, precious Mother! pray for your child, your youngest one, that she may ever, ever strive to act according to Gods will – […] and doubtless in bringing up your children there will be many anxieties & troubles, but if we seek Him, & lay all before Him, He *will* guide us. Is it not a weighty, an exceedingly important thing, to have souls committed to your care, not only to educate so as to become in their day, useful members of this world, but to educate them for Eternity!? O, it is so much, I tremble to think of it. – Now, all these things, how I would wish to have you my Mother, to speak to about. But you will at least write as much as you can. My Hampus will help me – for we must work hand in hand.

If you knew how lonely I am without him – but still, I have even reason to thank God for the separation, as it teaches me more to look into myself, to study my faults, & O, to pray for strength to combat them – so truly it is said "all things work together for good to them that love God" [Romans 8:28] – Hampus will have been gone three weeks tomorrow – 4 more! & I may expect him home. –

I have been thinking of you, Florence & Carl every day – & take it for granted, my darling little nephew is born. When shall I hear of it all? Oh! how I do long for some news again from you. Your latest letter is of Jan[uar]y 3rd; 6 whole months have passed since then, & 2 mails brought me nothing. God grant darling Florence may be quite strong & well again, & the Baby thriving to her hearts content; dear Carl! how supremely happy he will be. But now it is dark, so goodnight, and God bless you my precious Mother.

Friday 15th. Only fancy darling Mama, "Garitza" is still here – no wind has stirred since last Tuesday week, at least very little, & that [h]as been contrary. However today I think she will be able to sail, which would be a comfort, for her delay may already be of serious consequences to the Company. We are enjoying a perfect European summer – such lovely warm weather! & we have had it all the six weeks we shall have been here next Sunday, with a few days exception after Hampus left. Still, I have not braved the sea – & see I shall not be able to bathe at all, as the water does not rise more than to 13! I tried once – but when half way in, came out again, it was too, too cold; but I take a cold salt sponging bath every morning, & like it very much. How Hampus would have enjoyed bathing; it is such a pity his journey put a stop to the baths he had taken & delighted in during his stay here, but if he returns soon & O! how I do long for him, he may still continue with them. My letter going by the Garitza was closed on *28th June*; it is a great pity it should be lying getting old under my very eyes. If G[aritza] has a prosperous journey to & from California, she may be back by 30th Aug[ust] & then off again by 15th Sept[ember] so that this letter will not be very long after the other. If I only knew *where* you are my own Mother, and what your plans are. Though you say in your last letter No. 18. closed 3. Jan[uar]y you do not intend writing again before March & then over Ajan, I cannot believe you would not immediately answer the letter announcing our childs birth, & that over San Fr[ancisco]? surely you have done so darling Mama? You will be talking over last summer together, your pleasant sojourn at Palsi; and all the hopes & fears which alternately filled your mind, and which have now with Gods help been all cleared away, & replaced by happiness & certainty on dear Florence's account. Now first, that she is, as I ardently pray God may be the case, the Mother of a healthy thriving infant, now first she will feel "lifes earnest", and the highest stage of happiness she can gain. Tell her Mama, she must send us a photograph of herself with the child in her lap. Do ask her to do so.

I wonder if our children will have any resemblance, & if they will be like their father's or mothers family. Our Annie, will decidedly resemble her father; she is such a lovely dumpy precious little Baby; if you could but see her – You would love her so dearly. She has long since cut her 3rd & 4th tooth. Wonderfully fast and well it has gone, & I cannot sufficiently thank God. Do you know if Florence has that invaluable book "Bulls Hints to mothers" & ditto "Maternal management". I should like to know, and personally thank Dr Bull, for the help & comfort his exellent advise has been & is to me; without it & with my utter inexperience Baby would surely never have been the healthy child she is. –

What do you think we dined upon today? trout! real fresh water trout & roast snipe! Was not that a dish to set before a King? our cook Mr Carl Bruno Triebe caught both fish and flesh, or rather shot the latter. I am going to let him show me where he found the trout, & will take my Tavastby hook which has lived in my little pocketbook ever since Uncle A[dolf] sent it from P[eters]b[ur]g, & try to catch some. They were delicious, he caught them with his hand, there are such immense quantities, he said. I would advise some of the rich young english noblemen, who have nothing to do, to spend a summer up in our quarters, where they w[ou]ld find salmon enough to satisfy them. We have so much of it, we get quite tired of it – the halibut is better, and also considered a very rare dish in England. It only shows that all so called *dainties & delicacies* can become "de trop" [Fr. too much] when you *only* have them to live upon. A piece of engl[ish] beef or mutton, or a boiled pike! would according to my taste be a delicacy now! –

Saturday 23. Again several days have passed, & Garitza has sailed thank God. She got out at last on friday afternoon, & is now, as we hope, halfway to San Fr[ancisco]. A few days after her departure, the weather changed from sunshine and heat, to rain, wind and cold, and we have not had fine weather since. I often look at the map where Hampus has marked his rout & wonder where he can be. Thank God he was well on 7th July – a post came in from an island near Kinaj, with papers for the office, wherein was mentioned that on that date Hampus was to start again from Kinaj on his further voyage. I was very unhappy not to have heard from him, but it was impossible. –

Has Esperance spoken to you freely about her home, och förhållandena der [Swed. and the conditions there]? we used to think we were poor – but in comparison with their home, I see we had no reason to call ourselves so – my poor mother in law! she must have suffered much, & how often it was difficult for her to make the little money last – it was a sad home, and she so ill, and that poor Constance too. We were speaking of her last illness the other day. It made a melancholy picture – those poor, poor girls! and they were quite alone when their darling Mother died; – in her they lost the last & only link, which held the family together, and were left alone & destitute in the world. Esperance is the one most to be pitied, for she is separated from all she loves, & I often wonder what will become of her when you go to England. It was indeed a wild & foolish advise of Otto's sending his 2. sisters to America, for as it was done in the absence of their father, though they wrote to ask his leave, & he replied: "de må gerna fara, bara jag få behålla Constance" [Swed. let them go if only Constance stays with me] she went too, & since that it is natural the father should be offended, & say his daughters have forsaken him – He can never forgive Otto's medling. – Ludmila is married, & will be happy I hope – Her brothers & her father were against the marriage – I cannot say why; – but I fancy his aristocratic feelings disliked a union with an "ofrälse" [Swed. a commoner] – There is no great choice in the colonies, & I am sure Otto sent his sisters in hopes of Ludmila be married. I pity Hampus father. That is my feeling on the subject. His children are & ever remain his children, & had they remained with him as they ought, he would never have left them on his then unmarried son's hands. Now he is old & alone! this often makes me sad, & Hampus too. Please God all will still be right & smooth when we return D[eo] V[olente]. […]

Wednesday 27. Only fancy Mama darling, I have had the inexpressible happiness of receiving a treasure of a letter from my own Hampus! A letter full of love and longing to come home again. I cannot tell you how very happy it has made me. His journey has thank God been very prosperous – sunshine & calm weather all the time. His tour was nearly finnished, still he does not think he can be home before *20 Aug[ust]*. Nevertheless I expect him about the 15th. O! that will be such a happy, happy day! He misses me every where & longs for his little Darling – I was quite wild with Joy over this unexpected surprise especially after my Sore disappointment last Thursday. On that very day his letter was written, & I received it on Sunday,

by which you may judge how near he is. He sent me too, a little tub with salted
reindeer tongues, a bag of smoked salmon, & 6. tins of preserved pineapple. Darling
Hampus! he is ever so thoughtful and considerate. I was so thankful for this break in
my loneliness, for it is truly a sore trial to be separated, without even the common
means of communication. I wrote to him immediately by the same boat, tho' it is
not certain whether it will reach him. I hope it will, because it will give him such
pleasure. I must copy out a part of his letter for you, where he describes the grandeur
& beauty of the Scenery:

" – I Nikolaeffsky[96] redutten tyckte jag mig vara i Finland, om icke omgifvningarna
varit lika så storartade här som de äro småaktiga der. Föreställ dig en jemförelsesvis
trång vik, hvars ena sida utgöres af ett oöfverskådligt slättland bevuxet med den
herrligaste matta af blommor samt öfverströdd med just så många grupper af trän,
som behöfvs för at gifva omväxling åt taflan hvilken för öfrigt var en bild af yppig
grönska.
I motsats härtill "imaginez vous" på andra sidan det mest storartade Alpland på hvars
kusliga, dystra och af tusenåriga snöar tyngda rygg, stå 2. 13.000 fot höga Coner,
hvilka högt öfver molnena ibland utkasta den rök som blott nu tycks återstå af fordna
bättre tider då de sprutade eld och lafva öfver den kringliggande nejden." – [Swed.
In Saint Nicholas Redoubt I felt as if I were in Finland, only the surroundings are as
great here as they are small there. Imagine a rather narrow fjord, where on one side
you have an immense plain overgrown with the most wonderful flowers and exactly
so many groups of trees as are necessary to vary the scenery, all in lush green.
On the other side, the greatest alp country whose sinister, dark back is weighed down
by thousand year old snows and surmounted by two cones, 13.000 feet high, which,
high above the clouds, sometimes emit smoke, all that is left from earlier, better
times, when they emitted fire and lava over the nearby country.] Must not that be
beautiful? How I wish I could have stood by his side, whilst he was pointing out
each spot more lovely than the other to me. Hampus has great facility in describing
– he does it so well, & I like his written pictures so much. How much he will have
to relate when he returns please God very soon.
I am just now deeply engrossed with Washington I. Conquest of Granada – It is most
interesting; but still I cannot help feeling for the poor Moors, who were driven out
of their lovely homes, vales & mountains, to be massacred by the Christians, though
at the same time you cannot help rejoicing that the war was undertaken for a Holy
purpose. At one of the numerous battles an english Earl with his followers were
engaged, & he won the victory – there are some of his pleasant speeches recorded,
& my heart beat with delight when I read the words: "Remember my merry men
all the eyes of strangers are upon you; You are in a foreign land [Four pages are
missing in the original letter.] the waist. You cannot think what an effect smoking

96   St. Nicholas Redoubt, also known as Fort St. Nicholas, was situated on the west side of
the Kenai Bay.

has upon him. He has now left it off altogether since the 1st January, & sees himself how much better he is without it. As soon as Hampus smokes, and you must know, he *swallows* the smoke, he becomes nervous and out of spirits, & fancies all manner of ills must come over him. I can never say how thankful I am he has stopped it, and will now never recommence again. It has however not been accomplished without an effort, for no one knows how immoderately he has smoked formerly, and how passionately fond he was of it; and though he would still sometimes like a pipe, he never indulges himself, which is having shown great strength. We intend trying our hands at archery when we return to our residence, which will be amusing and strengthening. Hampus made me try to pull out one of the indian bows he brought home, and was astonished I could pull the string out so far – but when we came to investigate the matter, we saw that I held the string with all my fingers instead of with only forefinger & thumb, which changed the whole affair. *Thursday 2/14. Sept[ember]*. In a few more days, we shall be leaving this pleasant little place, where we have had a so peaceful and quiet undisturbed séjour [Fr. stay]. Everything around us reminds of autumn, and approaching winter, & it behoves us to decamp before the equinoxial gales begin to blow. We are however without our steamer, which Hampus sent to Kinaj for coals, but which we are daily expecting back again. I think with horror of the seavoyage, knowing beforehand how sick and miserable I shall be. Darling Mama, having yourself set me so good and example, I can but follow it, & therefore it must not surprise you to hear, that we are again expecting an increase to our family! and that, please God, all goes on well, about *16th 18th March* (n[ew] sty[le]) If we could have any power in hastening or retarding such things, I should gladly have waited a little longer, for precious little Annie will scarcely yet be on her feet, when this 2nd little being will be ushered into existence – but – as we can do nothing, I am happy for this new blessing and thank God. It pleased Hampus exceedingly, to hear this piece of news on his return – for when he left, I did not yet know it myself, though I had a presentiment of it. Thank God I am quite well, tho' I am occassionally troubled with various unpleasant "diseases of pregnancy" where "Bull" again is my right hand, for nothing on earth could ever make me consult the young doctor. I really don't know what to have done without that book. I have only one ardent prayer & that is that I may be able to nurse myself, & hope, my prayer will be heard – I shall now be thankful to be at home, for Constance sleeping next door, often frightens me at night, when she gets an attack, so that I go to bed quite nervous. But thank God, for His providential care, I have never yet witnessed an attack, & pray God, I never may. Poor, poor girl! I cannot say how sorry I am for her, & how I pity her, for when she has been well several months, she brings herself up in the vain hope, she is quite well, & therefore feels perfectly unhappy when an attack comes on again. It is so painful too, both for me & for her, to ask her for instance *never* to go into the nursery – when she is well, she thinks it unkind to remind her of her illness, & still I have no peace of mind when she comes in; especially as I see darling Baby is so easily frightened. Any loud noise makes her start, & she cries when the church bells ring, or even I tare [i.e. tear] a piece of shirting in her presence. Constance is a warmhearted girl, & never takes anything amiss I say to her, but she forgets, or thinks it is of no matter, when she is without her fits. I am often afraid that it is unkind & unchristian of me, to be so careful of myself – But, then it is my holy duty surely? what awful consequences might ensue on the innocent Babe still unborn? O! it is a dreadful affliction the Lord has laid on her. – –

It is wonderful to me, I feel so perfectly calm at the prospect of what I am again to suffer – God has arranged those things most wonderfully and beautiful – Fear is so completely swallowed up in Joy, you seem each time to forget the pain. This time, thank God, I shall have my own Hampus to nurse & look after me, & hope it will consequently be a more comfortable confinement. By the time you receive this letter, there will only remain a few weeks still. If you could only be with me precious Mother. When shall I hear about Florence? and what she has presented her husband with. And when, when shall I receive answers to all my many letters? – it is indeed hard to be deprived of them so long. Darling Baby thrives, God be praised, wonderfully well – if you ask her in *russian*, "where is the stove" she immediately turns her head and gazes at it – her russian nurse taught her this, & it makes me quite uncomfortable to think, she will perhaps speak russian first. I am astonished she does not crawl yet – but I remember you often told us, I too was very remiss in such things, & only began to walk at 18. months. Hampus grows fonder & fonder of her. I am continually obliged to make new frocks; she grows out of them so fast – at Sitka I cannot get anything I want unfortunately and I cannot bear to dress her uglyly. I am sure Florence will invent all manner of pretty shapes for her child, of which she could send me the patterns. I hope we shall get a little son this time – I always speak of it as "he" to Hampus. He hopes for a boy too. But he prophecies Florence will only get girls at first, & then a boy! I say, she has a Boy! –

Hurrah! hurrah! a ship coming, *O! shall I get letters*?!? now I am quite "aus dem Häuschen" [Ger. beside myself] so goodbye for the moment –

3. *Sept[ember]*. The ship which made me so happy in anticipation yesterday, turned out to be only our steamer, as you may perhaps already have guessed. On Tuesday Hampus hopes to be ready, & please God – may be permitted to have a speedy and safe voyage back, & that Hampus may find all right & according to his wishes, at Sitka. We shall then have to settle down into regular tedious uninteresting winter duties: viz: giving weekly soirées, and a Ball before Xmas. But I have much to do; Baby requires many new clothes, so I must be busy at the sewing machine before it becomes too fatiguing. I wonder if I ever told you of a little orphan Jakuty[97] girl Hampus, ever kind & good, took in Ajan, & who came to us last year with my sister in law? She is 7. years old we suppose, the mother when she died, could not tell her birthday, & rejoices in the name of Palascha – she was rather spoilt by Ludmila & C[onstance] & has an enormous idea of herself – otherwise she is a good little thing,

---

97   Yakuts, a people living in North East Siberia, by the Lena river.

& I hope to train her up as a good servant. She knitts stockings very well, & has a pleasant voice; she will be able to play with little Annie when a little older. Wikström, that incomparible servant, has committed the folly of marrying Wendla, the swedish maid my sisters in law brought from home. We all tried to disuade him, but "um-sonst" [Ger. in vain]; he is indeed an exellent servant; you would never recognize in the sprightly attired servant, the clumsy Wikström you saw at H[elsing]f[o]rs. I too have learnt by this time, that servants are a "pack of troubles" & as Montaigne very justly observes "plus de valets, plus d'enemies" [Fr. more servants, more enemies]. But this is a subject far too menial to touch upon in letters. *Saturday. Sunday.* I must now make haste to finnish; it is a great disappointment having no letters to answer, but the S[ain]t Fransisco post has unfortunately not arrived yet. So I have no other address for you but the old one, & suppose, should you have left Finland, the Langenskiolds will know how to forward my letter. I am afraid there will be no further opportunity to S[an] Fransisco for a long time. But I will write round the world by the "Nikolai". [...]

Our things must go on board tomorrow so I cannot add anything more. May my earnest prayers be heard, and you my precious Mother, be quite well and happy. Give my dear love to Uncle Charles & Aunt A[lbertina], tell them I had written a long letter of 4. sheets. But when I asked Hampus to read it through, he told me, there were so many faults, I tore it up again. But here are the flowers & view of our house at Sitka. We are all quite well thank God. My own Hampus sends dear, dear love; he is asleep just now; give our kind love to Esperance –

God for ever bless & preserve you, darlingest Mother, prays

Y[our] own fondly loving child

Annie Furuhjelm

Love to all dear friends. To good dear old Babette and Ormelie. God bless you my own Mama.

No. 38   Government House. Sitka.
                                                          Sept[ember] *18th 1860*

You will be quite astonished, precious Mother, when you read this letter full of news. I had no idea when we left Codiac on 8th Sept[ember] that I should so soon again have an opportunity of writing to you; but, though my letter will be very short, seeing it must be finnished by 6 o'clock, & now it is soon ½ past 4. I must make all possible haste to tell you about the unexpected pleasure which awaited us here. After a dreadful storm, which even did some damage to our steamer, and was nearly washing a man over board, we reached Sitka with deeply grateful hearts, I can assure you, this day week at 10. o'clock at night in a perfect downpour of rain.

The night was dark, & our signals had not been seen, which made us rather anxious – however at 8. o'clock we were thankful to see the light in the lighthouse, and to see a rocket, which assured us all was right. What was our surprise and pleasure, to hear an english man of war, was lying in the harbour! Her M[ajesty's] S[hip] "Alert" commanded by Capt[ain] Peirce. She had been here since 3rd Sept[ember] creating great sensation, & giving pleasure to all the inhabitants. On the Tuesday before we came, the town gave a Ball at the club, where all the young officers amused themselves exceedingly. I have no time to enter into particulars; I have had no time or leisure to write before this, for the Capt[ain] & his officers have been our continual guests. Some are upstairs just now, while I write. On Tuesday f[ore]n[oon] Hampus received the Captain, & brought him down to me. I cannot tell you how much I was pleased – not only with him, but with all the officers – honestly spoken, I never saw such pleasant englishmen before – charming manners, easy conversation – no prejudices, pleased and delighted with everything, *perfect gentlemen*. The next day Hampus returned the call, & was received in state – The "Alert" was "en gala" – All the officers & men (160 in all) were ranged round the deck, the sails were manned, & when he left all the guns sent forth a volley of smoke, our batteries returned the salute, it was a fine sight. The Capt[ain] hearing I should like to see the ship, very kindly came for me at 2. o'clock & showed me all over. It was a great pleasure to me – & I could not help admiring the perfect order every thing was in. We invited the Capt[ain] P[eirce] & all his officers to a soirée next evening, which turned out a very sucessful affair. You may fancy we did our best to receive them with every honor, & our Cook turned out a splendid supper. At 2. o'clock on the same day, we were invited to a Ball on board, which was capitally got up. The deck decorated in every possible way, a good cold colation laid out, & the officers made "les honneurs" [Fr. the honours] splendidly. Since that we have had from 3. to 7. every evening, & today 2. to dinner. It is indeed pleasant to see how satisfied & pleased they all with one accord are. I made out a living "Hedley Vicars" [see Index of names] in the first L[ieutenan]t Mr Stubbs; it was indeed delightful to hear the young man speak with such earnest conviction & such heart & soul interest. He is the son of an irish clergyman. He sent me "Cuming on the Apocalypse" to read; unfortunately I have not time enough to get through it, but will certainly order it from San Fr[ancisco]. To meet a young man, whose soul is filled with thoughts of, & love for our blessed Saviour, is something so gratifying and at the same time astonishing, for after all, there are but few, who think seriously whilst they are young, & surrounded by the gay & alluring world.

The evening of our party, the "Alert" was illuminated with blue lights, unfortunately it blew so hard, the rockets were not seen to good effect, still it was a very pretty sight. Tomorrow afternoon at 2. the Capt[ain] intends returning to Vancouver from where he will go to the Sandwich Islands [now Hawaii], & hopes to be home, this time next year. They are all very home sick. They all say they will never forget the kindness shown them here, & that they will carry home most delightful reminiscences. One thing has pleased me mightily, which is that the Capt[ain] said, wherever he had met me, he would without hesitation have addressed me in english, & all think I look quite english. He said, he had been rude enough as to try if he could detect any particular dialect or accent in my english, but had not been able to do so; of course I am flattered. We shall miss them very much – it is so charming to be in english gentlemen's society again. The master, Mr Boxer an irishman too, thinks his family is intimately acquainted with Mrs Hawthorne's brother Mr Russell, but being sent to sea at the age of 12. he cannot so well remember. Dr Leonard, a scotchman, is a very pleasing person – in fact I cannot speak too highly in praise of them. I heard to my astonishment and regret that Mr Scott Russel is dead, that the queen [i.e. Victoria of England] has had her 9th child, & several other new things. Our ships from Ajan or San Fr[ancisco] have not come in yet – we are all anxiously expecting letters. God grant no accident has happened in these storms. O Mama! that 30 hours furious storm, we were out in was dreadful. One crash still sounds in my ears, my heart jumped into the soles of my feet – it was Gods providence that saved me from a miscarriage, for the fright shook me so, I could neither speak nor move, & felt as if all strength had departed. I was very sick, & slept only one night out of 5. As yet I am not rested, for since our return there has been so much to do, & to put in order, we have not been in bed till 12. o'clock. Baby darling has 6. teeth now – she cut 2. in the storm, & looks well & healthy. Hampus grows fonder & fonder of her. We returned to a clean house – everythings looks so cheerful & nice. It is indeed a comfortable home. Darling Mama I must finnish, for the secretary has called for my letter. This will scarcely be more than 2. months & a half old when you get it, perhaps even before my long letter from Codiac arrives. Soon I shall again be writing round the world. O! that I could get letters from you.

God bless you precious darling mother – I send you many warm kisses. My Hampus sends fond love – dear love to Florence & Carl. I will send this to Henry, he will know where to find you.

With fervent prayers, I ever & always am, darling Mama's own fondly loving child

Anna Furuhjelm

[The following program is attached to the letter.]

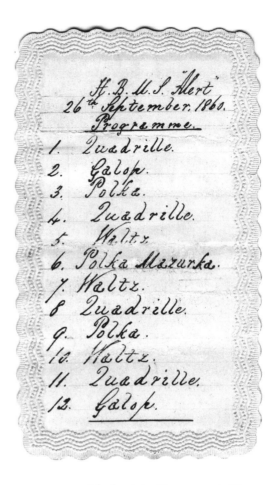

No. 39

12 o'clock *night* Government House.
Sitka Oct[ober] 4/16 1860

My own most precious Mother,
I cannot go to bed tonight without beginning a letter to you, to thank you for the
4. letters I have *at last*, & praised be God, had the inexpressible joy of receiving,
– […] You ask me who & what are the Creoles – they are by rights Mestizzos,
being mixed blood – & an unprincipled people they are. O Mama! the life these
men & women lead would shock you, & by this word I mean not the trivial sense of
the word, but the deepest – it affects y[ou]r heart & soul. Over & over again I ask
myself, can nothing be done to "turn them from unrighteousness" – but here the
grand obstacle arises – the intolerancy of the greek church. You may not distribute
Bibles, the clergy would be upon you, & especially the Bishop, who would stop any
interference at once. When I wanted to suggest something about the religion instruction for the school, I was told, that is a thing, in which none of us can do anything

– I only pray God ardently and earnestly, the day may not be far off when the greek church will be cleansed from all her imagery & idolatory, & when our Lord Jesus will reign supreme, & His word be read & studied, and out of Love for Him, men will go forth into the wilderness & amongst these heathen preach His blessed Gospel. Many Kolosches have been *christened* outwardly, but that is all they know, & their darkness is as great as it was before. What can you expect from clergymen whose whole soul & heart is not full of the holy office they represent – no heathen was yet converted if the preacher was not impregnated with Holy zeal & love, for the Gospel he came to teach. This is a sad & melancholly thing, is it not? We must pray for them, & at last our prayers will be heard & they too will glory in the "good news". It is my firm conviction that the world is not yet so near its end – for first the heathen, those millions of souls who are still in darkness, must be converted, or at least must have the opportunity offered them, of being converted, tho' it is not said they will all receive and accept the Truth. [...]

Thursday f[ore]n[oon]. The Ajan post will be in very soon, we were all delighted to see the long expected & anxiously waited ship "Schelikoff" appear on the horizon a short time ago. But we are all anxious to hear what news there will be of poor Ludmila. My Father in law, who wrote me such a kind, warm hearted letter of congratulations on our precious Baby's birth, it made me quite happy says, Ludmila had miscarried & been very ill in bed nearly 2. months. I am so very, very sorry for her disappointment – she will look at the Baby clothes we sent by the "Nikolai" with tearful eyes & aching heart. But, please God she perfectly recovers her health & gains strength, she may soon again have her heart full of sweet hopes. Now, I think I have answered No. 20. perfectly, & will hope in the afternoon to be able to answer Nos. 19 – 21 which I expect by "Schelikoff". So long darling Mama goodbye. Yesterday morning, when I went into the nursery before breakfast, and took our blooming, lovely little child in my arms, I held your letters before her face, & said: "Kiss Grandmama's letters Baby" several times, she stretched forward her wee little rosy mouth & did so. I am perfectly enraptured to see she understands *english*, & that her young nurse, a very nice, good girl, Natalie, catches up all I say to Baby, & goes on repeating it to her. "Where is Baby's nurse – where are the flies – where is Baby's bath?" All these questions she understands, but at the same time, she understands some russian ones too. If you could but see her darling Mama! If but for one moment I could run in to you, & clasp her in your arms! But you will sometimes think you have her, when you look down upon darling Ponnies [Florence's term of endearment] little angel. When shall I hear about it? I cannot describe *how* I long to hear of my own little nephew or niece. God grant, & with His help surely it will have gone all right with Florence; she has the comfort of skilful attendance, we have not. I am so happy, she has asked me to be its Godmama, & my Darling to be Godpapa. I love it so dearly, tho' I have not seen it. Won't it be a little precious angel? won't it be a clever child? But above all things, may it be *a good one*; & may the peace & grace of our Lord Jesus Christ ever abide with it.

*Government
House, Sitka.
From a letter-
head in letter
No. 29.*

It will be a happy, happy day that "we 3. meet again" with our precious husbands &
"little sixpences" – I often get quite elated when I picture *that* meeting to myself. –

Friday. Well many, many warm loving thanks my own darling Mama, for *all*
y[ou]r sweet precious letters, 5. in number, not counting the few lines with that good
Professor L[illes] beautiful verses, full of feeling. Nos. 19. & 21 came yesterday from
Ajan as I had hoped, [...]

When I read over your letter of 25th Feb[ruar]y, it makes me still sorry, though
you have the wished for good news, long since. But I can so well understand how very
painful it was for you my ownest Mother to wait for my letter over San Fr[ancisco]
with my Hampus so long. Darling husband! he thought he was taking away from
y[ou]r anxiety by letting *that* letter, and the one which would contain our childs
birth, come close upon one another. As it however turned out, you received the latter intimation only dreadfully late. I hoped it would reach you in April. I have now
ascertained for certain, that my letter by the "Codiac" which was lost was of 24th
Feb[ruar]y & *No. 32*! So I am satisfied to think Florence's was not lost. It does not so
much signify however darling Mother, as you had one letter anyhow in Feb[ruar]y
which you have now already acknowledged. But after all I have been disappointed
in answers to my letter about Annies birth & christening, for it arrived just as you
were finishing your letter of 24th April, & there promised me an answer over California. But when you came to write *that* one, you were in the buzzle [i.e. bustle]
of packing & very little you said either about Annie, my confinement or your Joy
at being Grandmama. You have never taken the slightest notice of our petition you
would be its Godmother, darling Mama, though you are entered in the "kyrkobok"
[Swed. parish register] as such. I thought you would choose a verse out of the Bible
for Annie & send it to us. On the whole I thought *such an event*, the 1st Grandchild
in both families, would have been more fully dwelt upon by my own Mother.

(You must forgive my unsteady hand, but I gave my thumb such a deep slash this
morning at breakfast, it is quite painful.)

We are invited to a Ball at the Club this evening, given by Capt[ain] Jorjan in honor of his Wife's Birthday. We are asked at 6. & shall certainly be punctual; Hampus is very particular on that score. You are afraid I might become extravagant. Certainly 10000[?] a year is a great deal, but you surely never imagine we spend the whole or even half sum a year? My Hampus is I am happy to say very pleased with me as housekeeper. You know he gives me the entire charge of the money, we only take out, when we require any. Hampus will not give me pinmoney as it is called, he says it is all yours, & "use as much as you require", or rather "don't buy anything, but what is absolutely necessary" – Still, you must not think he is the same headless spender of money, the unmarried Puxti [Hampus' term of endearment] was – O no! I am thankful to say, he is very particular & careful now, tho' always ready to pay the larger part. He is truly generous & noble, & God will bless him for all the good he has done. Don't you think he might have saved a great many thousands of the 5000 R[oubles] S[ilver] he got yearly at Ajan for 3. years? But he gave his sisters all & more than they wanted, & told them always "don't spare the money". – Now he is often vexed at the unnecessary expences he then incurred upon himself, but I always tell him, don't grudge a penny you have given away – it will bring its Blessing – certainly it does not vex me. On the contrary I am glad.

¼ *to 3. after.* I hope you will believe darling Mother, that I am wise enough to remember this is Sitka, & there is no necessity for fine clothes. I have of course got so many good things, because we were in England, Germany & P[eters]b[ur]g immediately after our marriage, but during our 5. years here it is my earnest desire to buy nothing for myself – neither dresses, bonnets, cloaks or anything else. Shoes & gloves you require oftener. But I have not bought anything but a few tiny neckerchiefs & a black silk "herrencravattentuch" [Ger. man's scarf] to make myself an apron of, since we have been here. My pink silk dress lies unpicked in my tin box, I shall never wear it here. Besides that I have a black silk & the lovely blue one you gave me. To show you how I manage I will tell you that this evening I shall wear the green silk Aunt M[argeret] gave me, to which Ida has made a low body white tulle fichue & sleeves. The under silk shirt on which the flowers were sewed was too narrow, so I sewed all the flounces together into one long flounce & only added a piece at the top to have the proper length. The Furstin [Ger. princess, Mrs Maksutova] has many more dresses than I, but I do not wish for more, & don't think I can wear out all mine. I wore cotton & jaconette dresses all summer, & when colder my woollen dress of the last happy Xmas at home. But till my bodies grow too tight, I seem to be continually obliged to *let out* & then *take in* – but am changing many dresses into so called "Morgenröcke" [Ger. dressing gowns]. Ida works very well, & my machine finishes work in no time. I have only 1. headdress which I put on on all occassions. You will not think precious Mother, I wish to *justify* myself in your eyes by telling you all these things; but as you speak of economy and extravagance in one of your dear letters, I tell you all this, that you may see how it is. Nothing can ever annoy me in y[our] letters – You are my own most beloved Mother, & I *thank* you for every word of advice you can give me. No. 20 is the only letter that *grieved* me, & made me cry bitterly. My Hampus came in, in the midst of it, & kissed them away. I was grieved, because I felt you were *too* hard upon me, & judged me a little little bit unfairly. I may tell you so, may I not darling Mama, without hurting you, which God forbid I should ever, ever do.

I am so sorry for poor Esperance. Is it possible, it is the *Frenchman* she still thinks of? in that case I am afraid there is no possibility of her wish being accomplished. Hampus & Otto say, *he* was never serious. I wish indeed she were happily married. We had thought the best plan would be for Constance to return home & live with her at Palsi, the 3. brothers uniting to pay yearly a certain sum for them to live upon. Hampus is the one who has done the most, & says he has now a family to provide for. Otto is rich & without children, Hjalmar has already saved 12000 R[oubles] S[ilver].

Poor Constance! I am almost sure Epilepsy can never be cured. But a mercy beyond measure it is, she does not suffer herself in any way. With her the disease comes from the spine I think. She is a very sweet & amiable dispositioned girl, ever ready to help – but of course being all her life thus afflicted, no companion. The only subject she is at home in is cooking. I am often afraid to make any remark on food or housekeeping before her, as she almost always brings on a cooking conversation, & recitation of different receipts. It rejoices me to hear her say she is so happy & contented with us – Papa writes to thank me for it. But how often in the silence & secrecy of my heart, have I sighed at never being alone with my beloved husband. I have never mentioned this subject before, but tell you now, you can never imagine, the tears her arrival cost me. I prayed God to help me that I might ever be a true sister to her, & to give me strength not to complain, or ever be unkind towards this poor sick girl. To take it patiently. At first darling Mama! it was a sore trial & a daily sorrow; but she never has, nor ever shall know it. It was so heavenly to be alone with my Hampus; and we were so newly married – when he went out, I delighted in silently thinking about him over my work. We read much together – Now there is always a 3rd person, & it never, never is the same sweet privacy. When I read the Bible with explanations, & see how it is the lot of *every* man to have *some* trial, be it great, or be it small, I think this is *my trial*, & I must submit; I pray God humbly to make me more *charitable*, less selfish, & to forgive me the many times I have been annoyed. Pray for me too darling Mother. […]

Two new officers have been added to our table, so now we are 12. people every day, & soon shall be 14! Is it not dreadful to provide for so many? everything is *so* dear here. And now I will tell you an unpleasant piece of news –

Sunday Ev[enin]g 9 Oct[ober] – which Hampus received by this last post, which is, that the russian Government is sending "en revision" [Swed. a committee of investigation] to inspect the Colonies. There are 2. very high men coming – one, a "Stadsrådet" [Swed. 'State Counsellor'] the other a protegé of the Grandduke Constantin, who, as you know, is the chief over the russian Navy. This later personage has no good renomée [Fr. reputation] & is known to have made mischief very often. It is most unpleasant to have this kind of secret police watching over you, & marking all you say. It has put out Hampus a great deal, & causes him much anxiety. God grant all may go well for him. The Stadsrådet will live with us. We are preparing 2. rooms for him upstairs. The blue drawingroom to be his cabinet, the adjoining ci-devant office, wh[ich] my Hampus has been obliged to remove on his account, his bedroom. It has had to be papered, painted & repaired. There are curtains being made for 7. windows, a dark blue cloth carpet for the floor, & some of our furniture from downstairs, must also go upstairs. Fancy also the expence it will be to us – I am sure the Company will take this into consideration. His manservant must live with Triebe – The other gentleman will live in another little house. It may bring good to my Hampus, and it may not. Thank God! he has a clear conscience, & I can say, no one's interest lies nearer his heart than the Company's; his own often gives place to it.

The cause of this inspection is, that in 1862. the charter of the privileges of the R[ussian] A[merican] C[ompany] is out, tho' it is generally supposed it will be renewed again, & consequently Government sends a select comittee of investigation, to see how the Indians are treated, & what progress the Colonies have made, during these 60. years. Hampus has commenced his reign with many troubles & disadvantages, for his precedent did not do much to further the interests of the C[om]p[an]y he was serving. But, far be it from him to complain – and God will help in this matter, as in any other. I am not afraid of the Stadsrådet, but the other gentleman can if he wills put things in an unfavourable light, as as "gunstling" [Swed. favourite] of the Grandduke C[onstantin] will be believed. Well, in my next letter, I shall be able to tell you something more on this subject. And now I will return to the answering of your letters. Many, many thanks, darling Mama, for the pictures, cups, books, etc – etc. I could like Florence, never bear the thought of our dearest "home treasures" being scattered to the winds, & rejoice to think Florence & Carl, will have greater part of the furniture. I should have liked something of it myself; but there scarcely remains anything now. I am very glad for dearest Grandmama's wash handstand however, & the dear old chest of drawers, where I so well remember Grandmama used to keep nice, ripe pears for us. I am afraid I carried away the key of it. You have had much trouble & worry, & many a headache I fear – But when you got to Moskva, & Florence & Charlie, everything was forgotten. That lucky Ponnie! O, how inexpressibly happy she must have been to receive you in their own little home, & keep you there so long. To put your mind at rest Mama dear, let me tell you, I have all your letters, none are missing. […] I am writing this by lamplight, at the oblong table before the sopha, which now stands in the middle window. Constance is reading & Hampus is thinking. He has many letters to write. We were this morning in our little swedish church.[98] Pastor W[inter] preached a very good sermon on the gospel for the day – on forgiveness of sins. He told us, when we pray for the remission of *our* sins, we must also pray for the forgiveness of

---

98   Anna has in mind here the Lutheran church, completed in 1843. In her letter No. 33 she
       calls it the 'german church'.

other's sins, of our christian brethren's sins; this I liked very much. I think he is a real clergyman, & preaches out of love & from conviction of the truth of what he tells the congregation. His sermons are not meant to touch your feelings but to go the heart, & convince you. It is a sad pity his chest is so weak, & though not consumptive, I fear his lungs are not very strong. He leads a dull & lonely life here – but an exemplary one. I wish he had a nice wife & children to cherry him.

Tuesday 11th. I must write busily each day, for the mail is expected to go next Saturday via China. Hampus and I were talking about your prospects in England. We think for 50 £s per annum, you ought to get very comfortable lodgings, now that you are alone. The Landlady will cook y[our] dinner & good old Babette will manage the breakfast & tea; and in that way you will have no household "bestyr" [Swed. cares (of the household)] & Babette will not be overworked. [...] It is indeed wonderful none of our Darmstadt young friends are married yet – Ellen will never be married now I think – she is already 28. O, it is indeed marvellous, that we, Florence & I, the poorest amongst them, should have been married at all. I am sure, I never thought I should be married. The first year of my marriage, & even now still, though not so much, I could never bring myself to feel as if Hampus' money, was mine also. I could never buy anything without asking him; if he seemed not to think this or that necessary, I thought I mightened & could not buy it. He often asked me not to ask him, as it was all the same to him – Whatever I required I should buy, how could he judge? Still, I always tell him this or that I think of buying, what do you think. Is it not strange. You don't know darling Mama, *how* glad I should be to send money to this & that person. But I could never, never ask Hampus, tho' he would never say no – But I feel as if it w[ou]ld be inconsiderate. When we get home, & my Darling fixes a certain monthly sum upon me, then, I can do with it exactly as I like, and God knows, & may He ever, ever help me to do so, I truly like giving. It is one of the greatest Blessings money affords, being able to help others who have less than we, not "grudgingly" but according to the means given us, & with all the heart. Hampus also says, whilst we *are here*, it is our duty to save as much as we can. Out of our first year's pay, we only sent home 2000 R[oubles] S[ilver] For we paid 3400 for our engl[ish] provisions, I mean wine, sugar etc – etc – & nearly as much for those from California. Our journey here entailed many, many expences upon us, for altho' the Company paid all the travelling expences to the amount of 10000 R[oubles] S[ilver]!!!, we spent 7000 ourselves, & I am quite sure, paid many things the Company ought to have done. We had carte-blanche from the C[ompany] for our journey but had to pay our living. Now you see, other people in the C[ompany]'s service get a certain sum, for instance 500 R[oubles] S[ilver] on which they not only manage to live, but, like the Makzutoffs to save a few hundreds. Being 4. weeks at San Fr[ancisco] where we only paid 57. *dollars!! for our washing*, was a dreadful expence, & Hampus has as yet not got any gratification, as he hoped & expected he would. Now, suppose the C[ompany] had fixed 15000 R[oubles] S[ilver] for our journey – don't you think we should have managed to save upon it too? but having "at libertum" [i.e. ad libitum], our *own* money went unknowingly at libertum too. A few months after our arrival here, after all the 1000's Hampus had given Ludmila, comes in a bill from Ajan for 1600 R[oubles] S[ilver] & soon after from the Capt[ain] who brought the 2. sisters out *4. years* ago, a Bill of 160 R[oubles] S[ilver]. Then Ludmila sends Wendla to me, with 10. months wages due, there were again 50 R[oubles] S[ilver] *for nothing* – Don't you think this was *not* pleasant? So you see, darling Mama, Hampus must save a little first, & Esperance has still got her rich, childless brother Otto, besides Hjalmar. We have Constance & give her 15 R[oubles] banco a month. We have also that orphan Palascha from Ajan, & Ida gets 120 Th[a]l[ers] a year. Now sweetest Mother you are initiated in all our affairs. Our family is increasing, & though Baby is certainly not dressed in finery, only kept perfectly sweet & clean, she at least requires many clothes, linen I mean – for the women do not work *here*, as they do in Europe. My own washing is washed every 4. weeks. Three women can not finish it sooner than in a fortnight – during that time I must give them daily twice sugar, tea & black bread, & pay for *one* washerwoman 20 R[oubles] banco monthly. The C[ompany] pays for the other 2. All our servants get 3 lbs[?] white sugar each per month, & ½ lb[?] tea in common – In fact we have many outlays as you may judge yourself. [...]

Many thanks darling Mama, for the photograph of yourself, which certainly is not fit for *that* house any more. I shall be very happy for it, though I wish you had had one made *on purpose* for me, whilst at S[ain]t P[eters]b[ur]g by the man who made our beautiful one. This is, what I have all along been wishing for, & thought you would do, if ever you got to Russia's magnificent capital. For all the other things you are sending me, 10000 thanks & kisses already before hand darlingest Mother. It is such joy opening a parcel from Home.

Thursday 13/25. [...] To Tante M[argeret] I wrote from Codiac a long letter, & told her about both schools,[99] asking her advice. In my last letter from Cod[iac] I said I should not for long have an opportunity for writing but lo & behold, besides this letter, I shall write 2. more this year. This one goes over China, the next by "Nikolai" over Honolulu & California, & the 3rd most likely direct via San Fr[ancisco]. I will send them all to Henry's address, who is sure to know where you are. Were you not charmed with what you saw of S[ain]t P[eters]b[ur]g? It is by far the most splendid town I have ever seen. The Isac's church pleased me exceedingly, & especially the outside – it is such a solemn, serious looking building. How happy you must have been to go to the english church again. Is there one at Moscou,[100] or which church do Florence & Carl attend?

---

99 One of the schools Anna refers to is the school for girls of mixed blood, the so-called Creoles, and female orphans. The other one might be the new school for "daughters of deserving parents" that was to be opened in 1861 (Otchet 1864, pp. 10, 57).

100 In 1814 an Anglican Episcopal church (name unknown) was established in Moscow, Briusovskii pereulok 5. In 1882 St. Andrew's church was erected on the location of the old church (Palamarchuk 1994-1995, 4, pp. 442-443).

I am so sorry you did not take the view of Ajan with you to England – Surely some where you could have found place for it – But it is framed I suppose. Neither Hampus or I, have ever heard of any relief view of Sitka which you speak of; it must be very pretty, & now at least you know what Sitka looks like. Hampus has built a new magazine, beside the old one, facing the sea, & 2. little houses beside the Makzutoff's house. He is now pulling down one of the old tumble down barracks, & will build a large, airy, healthy one instead. All the houses are old & rotten och många hålla på att ramla ikull [Swed. and many are falling apart]; Hampus does not know where to begin – It leaks in almost every house, & one person petitions for a new roof, & another for a new "quartier". There are so few workmen here now, it is really a difficult thing to do all that is wanted. I wonder how this tiresome revision will pass, & what the good gentlemen will find faults at & complain to Government about. We are naturally very anxious – But with God's help, all will go well. […]

I hope the finnish servant you brought Florence answered well & understood her office as nursery maid. I am, thank God, fortunate with mine – But what shall I do when there are two children, both requiring constant attendance? that is a difficult question. How I wish I had a regular good, *old*, english woman as upper nurse. The Fürstin was here last night, & was telling us about the inconvenience of travelling through Siberia. I don't know *how* you get on with small children. It must be dreadful – And still it is almost certain, we shall return that way; and who knows how many small ones there will be. What others have accomplished, we must do too. Anyhow a *land*journey is better than a 6. months seavoyage & constant seasickness. There is no choice – "out of the frying pan into the fire" – In my last long letter to Aunt Mathilda I asked her to be so very kind as to send me a few paper patterns for boys & girls clothes, thinking you would not be in England. I hesitated a long time whether I should ask Aunt M[argeret] or not, fearing she would perhaps buy some expensive things as a present – But afterwards thought, no I may ask her & did so. Now I would ask you darling Mama, & to send me a hymn book with music; it w[ou]ld be so pleasant to sing hymns together with our children. And if you ever feel inclined to knit any small sofa socks, darlingest Mother, in the winter evenings for y[our] grandchild, I would kiss all y[our] sweet fingers in turn & thank you gratefully. A parcel addressed to the R[ussian] Consul at San Fr[ancisco] would reach us safely, & I do not think it would need to be prepaid.

I have made you a new plan of our sitting room. As you see it is quite changed & I think looks very comfortable. The paper is dark brown which makes it difficult to light well, but the whole house has been painted & cleaned & looks so nice now. Perhaps you will send it to Carl & Florence. I hope she will send you my letter, for there I have given her a detailed account of our doings whilst the english man of war was here.

It has been raining in torrents for a long time & today we had 2. heavy showers of hailstone. Darling Baby has got a cold in her nose, & seems to be uncomfortable today. We are thinking of having her vaccinated[101] soon; it is not well to put it off too long.

You hope that amongst all your Grandchildren, some may have the *"passion"* for books & drawings you have. Now darling Mama, will you think me a very prosaical sort of daughter, when I say I would not wish my child to have a "passion" for fine arts or even music? – but a decided taste for one or the other, or even both, yes. – Look at Ellen B[echtold] & her Mother. Does it give a person a peaceful, quiet mind, having a passion, an *overlove* for such things? I think not. And as we cannot always either be in the society of artists or artistic minds nor is it desirable we should, for we have more to live for than that, I think it better only to have a quiet liking & taste for such things, so that I should not feel myself unhappy were I in a place where they were neither appreciated, nor understood. I wonder what Florence thinks on the subject.

Friday 14. Our little treasure is cutting a double tooth. I rather think, she has not been quite cheerful these last days; yesterday she was feverish & irritable, & today she has no appetite. Still she plays & kicks with her little fat legs in the air. A strange love of hers, is to draw everything over her face – the first thing in the morning on awaking is to pull one of her small cushions over her, then she kicks for joy, & pulls it off again to begin over again. Hankerchiefs, frocks, petticoats, everything she covers her face with & is so delighted at the fun. I think she will be a clever child, for it is with great pleasure I notice how well & soon she remembers anything I show her. How you would like to see her, & keep her on your knees darling Mama. If there was only an opportunity of having her picture taken for you.

The evening sun is shining so beautifully into Hampus room, & the silvery cloud on the horizon so completely deceived me, I was perfectly sure it was a ship I saw. We are gradually getting the rooms in order upstairs for the reception of the "Statsrådet" & hope he may not come before we are quite finnished. I hope he speaks some foreign language, otherwise we shall not exchange many words.

The Fürstin came in with her work a few days ago, & I promised I would do the same soon – As it is a fine evening. I am thinking of going tonight, after having put my little Angel to bed. You cannot think what an exertion it is to go out – We are always at home, & therefore grow more & more disinclined for leaving home – & I do not like leaving Hampus alone for tea – but I must not be selfish & he wishes me to go. Those dreadful staircases of ours are a dreadful pale, especially now. – Good-night darling Mother, it is perfectly dark, tho' not 5. yet.

*Saturday 15*th. I spent a quiet pleasant evening with the Fürstin last night. She is a very amiable, well informed & well educated person. Her father Mr Bushman, is an englishman but has lived in Russia since 1825. He gives english lessons, & is Professor of the english language at one of the corps in P[eters]b[ur]g. His wife is a german from the Ostsee Provinzen [Ger. Baltic provinces], the daughter of a

---

101 Vaccination against smallpox was introduced into Russian America in the 1810s (Kan 1999, p. 95).

clergyman. I saw them both at the Fürstin's wedding, but do not remember their appearance. She was telling me much about the horrors of the administration in Russia & said "everything is false in Russia, from the greatest to the smallest thing – Everything has a splendid outward appearance – but don't look too deep – the beautiful, elegant drawingroom with well dressed ladies & gentlemen, often adjoins a *filthy* nursery, kitchen, children etc – etc." – She was telling me some dreadful cruelties practised by the slaveholders on the poor serfs[102] – & said "Russia is not a bit better than America with the poor negroes". There is a russian newspaper given out by a russian in London, called "the Bell".[103] I wish I could read it – *there*, everything comes to light, & you get behind the scenes, whereas the system in Russia is to hush & silence up everything that happens, & to put it forth in a false light. It is really deplorable to think of – when will it be changed? When will there be a *truthful, honest* Government and healthful administration? Russia is not ripe for it yet I fancy, but by degrees & perhaps still in our Lifetime, her sons will rise at a rush, & a dreadful revolution & cleansing will take place. This is my firm belief. What does Florence right [i.e. write] about the country she lives in – or has she only to do with french people.

*Monday 17*th. My long epistle must be closed today – I hope you will be pleased with it darling Mama. I sat up late last night reading it to my Hampus; when I had finnished he kissed me and said: "All right. It is a charming letter & Mama must be pleased with it". – Our little darling is still not quite the thing – her tooth will soon be through, she bites her little tiny fingers & seems to feel pain in the gum. I have this moment received a farewell visit of one of our young officers Mr Baranoff, who is returning home to Russia. I am giving him a little note of introduction to Carl, in case he goes to Moscou & would feel inclined to make a trip to them. I am sure he will receive a kind welcome from them both, & they would be delighted to meet somebody coming from us, who can tell them at least that he saw us in health the very day before he left our Colonies for ever. [...]

When Baby is a little older, I may perhaps send you an order for 10 £ asking you to make up a box of useful clothes for the children – Wont it be nice darling Mama. Hampus is intreating for music – Goodbye. So long. –

After dinner. Rain, rain! there is no end to this dreadful weather. I hope you will receive this letter soon – It is not going over China, as the Captain must touch at Honolulu. I suppose it will be 3. months or 3½ old by the time it reaches England. I am so glad for the pin you are sending Ida, & the brooch for Constance it will give them both much pleasure. The doll for our little one, too I am so thankful for. Did you get the Colibris & skin bags & how did you like them. My Hampus wished to write, but cannot manage it this time. By "Nikolai" however he hopes to do so – in

---

102 Serfdom was abolished in Russia in 1861.
103 "The Bell" (in Russian *Kolokol*), published 1857-1867 in London, afterwards in Geneva, was brought illegally into Russia.

the meantime he sends his fondest love to his "dearest Mama" & prays God you may
be well & happy, as we are too. How comfortable the Lille's house must be – O! it
will be nice to see H[elsing]f[or]s & all friends again. Marie said nothing about her
husband having been made a Baron. I am sure he will be the russian minister[104] before
we get home – His new title is only a for runner to a higher honor still. […]

   Now Goodbye my own most precious, precious Mother – May the peace of God
abide with you & your children for ever – With fond love to dear old Babette. I hope
she is strong & contented to be in England & a kiss to darling Ormelie.

   Ever & ever my own darling Mother's
   Fondly loving & dutiful Child

                                                                Anna Furuhjelm

No. 40   Sitka Nov[ember] 25th/Dec[ember] 7 1860 –

My own most precious, beloved Mother!
A few hours ago, I was made happy by the receipt of your last darling letter of 31st
July, with the anxiously looked for news of our precious Florence's safety and happiness. O! the good Lord be praised for His wonderful, wonderful mercy and loving
kindness, towards her; and you all! My own, own Ponnie! My heart was bursting,
whilst I read your account of her dreadful confinement – to think she should have
suffered such agony, & that the little angel, *might* have been dead! O Mama! it was
indeed awful, & I am glad I read dear Charlie's letter first, in which he only told
me the joyful news, without mentioning Florence's sufferings. I cannot be happy
enough you were with her, & that poor Carl was not alone during that long period of
awful suspense. I all along dreaded Florence's confinement & often told Hampus so
– it was strange too, that for 3. nights following, in the 1st week's of July, I dreamt
such dreadful dreams about her, & sobbed violently in my sleep. Since that I have
not had distressing sights of her. What must it not have been to Florence, who was
only delivered on the 3rd day, when 14. hours in all, seemed so dreadfully long to
me, & especially the last 4. hours, like an eternity. But then, the precious, precious
Babes scream, does away with all sorrow, & fills your heart with a whole sea of Joy
& gratitude! Dearest Ponnie did not hear this, and must have thought her child
was dead! O! what an intense agony, on the top of all foregoing one's. My own
Hampus' eyes filled with tears at the account, which I could scarcely read audibly or
intelligibly, & we both praise and thank God from the depth of our hearts, for His

---

104 In spite of Anna's expectations, Fabian Langenskiöld was never made 'Russian minister', i.e. 'minister-secretary of state' (a person who submitted the resolutions of the
   Finnish senate to the Russian Emperor). He died in 1863 (Carpelan 1954-1965 2, p.
   690).

merciful preservence of mother and Child. And that all went well afterwards, and she was able to nurse the Baby itself, was joy upon joy. – And she remembered me too, darling Sister. Yes, truly the Almighty Father was good towards me – What would have become of me without Mother or Husband, had I been in her case? May it please the good God, to help me through the 2nd confinement, equally safely, if it be His Will. What can have been the reason of her slow delivery? I always trembled for her, because she is so narrow across the hips, but Hampus always tried to assure me, all would go well.

I am sure little Mary, must by this time be a fat, rosy, dumpy, lovely Baby. Indeed your description of her, exactly suited our Baby, except the brown hair, which with our little bonnie, blue eyed fairy is, golden, & promises to curl. If you could only see her now, as she is sitting in her high chair at the table before the sopha in the middle window of this room, & hear her little, sweet musical voice, & see her dimply rosy elbows, round arms & fat pointed fingers, her beautiful eyes & tiny mouth, I think too you would be enamoured of her. She has cut a double tooth now, & eats chicken broth every day once. Thank God she is quite well, but neither crawls, nor stands yet. I have been busy making a little frock for the 1st anniversary of her Birthday; unfortunately you cannot buy anything but coarse bad prints, or still worse *half* merino's here, which "färger af" [Swed. (from which) the colour comes off] dreadfully – when the frock is dirty it is good for nothing & must be thrown away as it cannot be washed – still the y[a]rd costs 2/6!! – I am now going to make a list of things, which please darling Mama buy for me in England – & having made up a box, send it with a german letter to our agent *Sturm* in Hamburg, to be forwarded by the 1st opportunity. The box ought to be in Hamburg in *September 1861* and will then come by the "Nikolai" in spring 62. Hampus will through Kostromitinoff send an order for 20 £. It will be so nice, opening a box of things, bought & chosen by my own, precious Mother. You cannot think, how badly off we are here for children's things; not even a skein of wool to knit stockings! – bad russian shoes, & worse shoemakers. But more about this further on. I cannot conceive how my letters of *30th March* & *14th April* had not reached you before your last was despatched – & sincerely hope they may not have been lost, but have long ere this made their appearance, and given you the pleasure I hoped they woud. I must now take up my narrative where I left it on *17th Oct[ober]*. Nothing of any consequence has happened since that. The "Nikolai" arrived on *26th October*, and has been lying waiting here ever since. As I told you before we expected our *unwished* for guests would be on board – but such was not the case – the news came, they would come over San Fr[ancisco]. We were glad to be alone, & free from watchful glances a little longer, and had also more time to prepare ourselves. Today however they arrived by the "Garitza" & are now installed for *5. months!* in the whole of the upper story. I cannot tell you how unpleasant my Darling husband's situation is – & how painful the whole restrict is, which is laid upon us all. I am now beginning to understand a little, the ways of Russia – the underhand dealing, and falsehoods used every where. When my Hampus went on board to meet these gentlemen today, my heart beat, & my eyes were full of tears; I felt *this* day, was the commencement of a result we still shall see – it may be for his good – it may be the reverse. God, who sees into our hearts, & knows all our motives, can alone protect from slander & an evil tongue, and He will be with & protect my honest & righteous husband, who hates all double dealings. – The expence will be great to us, though I never can think the Company will not renumerate us. Mr Golovin is a great "spion" [Swed. spy] & has made mischief in diverse ways, as is known. – God preserve us. –

We have had rain & foggy weather, almost incessantly – my walks have very often been obliged to be taken up & down the rooms, or at the furthest, round the house. I have thank God been perfectly well; – my back however begins to ache & it is fatiguing to sit long up right – But I have no sopha on which it is possible to lie with any degree of comfort – I have often longed for our red divan. My Hampus is now having one like it made for me. I have much to do – I am working a cushion for my Hampus to Xmas, & wanted to make a few trifles to send to Esperance, Dascha & Hanna, but now I fear time will fail me. We have had young Bergenheim almost every evening since he returned – he is such a nice young lad – Fru Krogius has a little son; – all went off well, in *3 hours* the whole affair was begun & ended! I like them much. The other day there was given the 1st so called "Wasser Ball" [Ger. Water dance] at the Club, to which we had to go – It was an arrangement of Ad[olf] Etholéns, & has not existed since. The meaning is to go with your work, and meet en famille, with dancing and games to amuse you. The refreshments are plain, & wine is not at all provided. I took my work, as I only danced quadrilles – the evening went off very well, & we came home at 10½. We had intended giving a soirée dansante next Thursday our usual winter reception day, but now the rooms are otherwise taken up. I am sorry the Capt[ain] and young cadets of Nikolai will lose the entertainment, being passionate dancers. Perhaps at Xmas, we shall be obliged to give a Ball. –

The Fürstin & I, meet now regularly each Tuesday, alternately at our & her house, to play Symphonies à quatres mains [Fr. four-handed] together – I made the proposal & she gladly agreed & I cannot say the pleasure it affords me. But these evenings excite me so, especially those at home on our own beautiful piano, I get quite into a fever, & spent a wretched night last time. I know you will rejoice to hear of these réunions. Last night I was with her, & spent such a pleasant evening. We meet at 6. play till 8. & after tea work & talk. I was talking about you, she about her father – also a highly educated, cultivated mind. It was so nice. The Fürstin is the only society I have, & I am glad she is here now.

Next Tuesday is our precious little Annie's Birthday! How wonderfully fast the time has flown – I can scarcely realize it. And in 3. months, please God, I shall be the Mother of a 2nd child, as you all unanimously have expected. This one is very lively – much more so than Annie treasure; but I am not larger than the 1st time, & to myself appear wonderfully small; but perhaps that is a mistake, & you would think otherwise. I am now, & shall be very anxious for your next letter, to hear that please God all has continued to go well for darling Florence. I can never forget her sufferings. […]

I am sure you will feel so well & comfortable at Nettleden, that lovely little spot. But where will you eventually settle? O! that such miles and miles of sea should lie between us, & hinder our correspondence.

Saturday 26th Nov[ember]. Good day darling Mother! This morning, just as I was out of bed, Hampus came in with a very roguish smile, holding something behind his back, & saying "hvad får jag" [Swed. what do I get]? I guessed immediately it must be another letter, & was truly happy to find after a few seconds delay, that I was not mistaken. By the date outside I rejoiced to know I should now hear how darling Florence had progressed. My surprise & Joy was great when I saw her own handwriting, though I was disappointed to find nothing from my ownest Mother. Thank God for all the good news it contains. O Mama! how I envy that creature Florence, though I also rejoice intensely for her sake, that she has had you with & near her so many months; & that she has seen y[ou]r happiness over *her* Happiness, & y[ou]r little darling Grandchild. I quite like that place "Troitskoie"[105] & think there [i.e. their] little house is charming, tho' it must be very tight, & may be still more so, before the two years are out. Hampus cannot cease wondering at Charlie's most wonderful luck & good fortune; I cannot say how glad we both are. After all Uncle C[onstantin] does not appear to have been at the christening. Will they never be reconciled in heart? – O! it is so mournfully sad! –

This is a splendid day! Clear, bright, hard frost. The sun is shining on the snowy mountains, & the cross on the greek church towers glitters beautifully – My Hampus has had no time to walk with me, & alone I never go, as I can't bear it. Precious Annie is asleep now, but will be taken out as soon as she wakes. She is growing so merry, & screams right out in her delight. She tries all manner of sounds, & seems to be relating long stories – she shows where *our* noses are, when you ask her "where Baby's nose is?" gives her little hands to kiss, or stretches her little arms towards you – but what she never tires of is saying *"Pappa"*. You would rejoice to see the high, good chest she has – a good sounding board for singing, & is a sign of good lungs – I think she will be a funny droll little creature, & a docile, gentle child. She knows your picture quite well, kisses it & says "Ma-mama".

Nov[ember] 29th/Dec[ember] 11th! Before going to bed tonight, though the clock has struck 11. I must send you one line my own precious Mother, on this our little darling Treasure Annie's first Birthday! I know you have remembered it, & sent up your warm prayers for her, & have blessed her in your spirit. O Mama! what an inexpressible Joy she is to us, & what a sweet, lovely little thing. May the good Lord bless & preserve her, & make her year by year more His child – how merciful has He not been towards us! what gratitude do we not owe Him – our angel has been permitted to spend the 1st year of her life in health & but little sickness, & He

---

105 A small place not far from Moscow.

has made her a strong & robust child, notwithstanding all obstacles. O I am so very happy! and all my happiness comes from God, who blesses me so undeservedly. May He watch over us for ever, & may we never, never be forsaken by Him. – My precious husband is in the midst of much trouble – his future lies dark before him, but God will help us & be with us, & grant us what He thinks good. – –

You cannot think how unpleasant our situation is, & what inconsiderate, indelicate persons Hampus has to deal with; he has no rest or peace more, and must still put on a smiling face, & be ever ready & willing to converse. I hardly see him now all day, & at night he is perfectly knocked up & worn out. But I know, come what may, *"our time is in Thy hands"* & what is good for us will happen. The Lord rules over all men, & will not leave those that call upon Him faithfully. And now Goodnight beloved Mother! pray for your children.

Friday ev[enin]g 2/14 Dec[ember]. After all this letter will not go by the *"Nikolai"*, as I think it best to send it by the vessel which will go to San Fr[ancisco] in Jan[uar]y & may arrive before the uncertain mail from Honolulu. I hope you will receive it in time to purchase the list of things I send, immediately, so that the parcel may be sure to reach Hamb[ur]g in time for one of our "verldsomseglare" [Swed. circumnavigators] to pick it up. We are sending 20 £ – & hope it will be enough – if not, you must diminish the list according to your own opinion darling Mother.

We have had several days of splendid frost – but the climate is so changeable here, it has now turned over to rain & thaw again. Yesterday afternoon we went on the lake, Pastor Winter having asked me at dinner, whether I should like to come, as the chairs were in order, & the ice 3. thumbs thick. Accordingly at 2½ Constance & I were ready dressed to go. My Hampus was going to accompany me there, but as we came out we noticed a thin rain was beginning to fall & therefore thought of giving up the whole affair – however being dressed we went down & soon met the Pastor coming from the lake to tell me it was raining & the ice rather wet – Hampus, who anyhow had but little time to spare & who was in no ways disposed to walk, made us gladly over to the good Pastor, who led me safely across the slippery planks leading to the lake. Arrived there, we saw Mrs Krogius coming towards us in a chair with Alice on her lap, she got out & persuaded me to take a turn – her husband drove me across, but lo & behold! when we turned, the rain was fast beating in our faces – Nobody had an umbrella – we sent men home after some, & whilst Constance & Miss Klinkowström were driving, stood quietly looking on. It seemed to clear again, & young Bergenheim would nolense volense drive me too, so I got in, but before we came back it was raining very heavily, & with much laughter at our "Wasserpartie" [Ger. water excursion] we picked up our petticoats & came home such dripping spectacles, as fast as our legs would carry us. Still no umbrellas came to meet us – the rain cleared as we got back into Sitka, & were met by umbrellas pouring in from all sides, no one knew whose they had over their heads. Well, I had my Puxti to laugh too when I came home, & that was already some thing gained, seeing he is so troubled & harassed now. Next Tuesday being Ball night at the club in honor of the "herrar Revisorana" [Swed. inspectors] I am going to the Princesse tonight instead. We intend playing Mendelsohn's "Schöne Melusine" & Verdi's Ouverture to "Scicilianische Vesper". On Monday evening the two gentlemen spent the evening with us, on Tuesday the Princesse was here & we played, on Wednesday Mrs Krogius Pastor, Thursday alone & tonight I am out. Young Bergenheim is with us tous les jours [Fr. every day], & we like him very much & receive him without the slightest ceremony, still, I don't like never being alone. We have had the french & english illustrated papers sent us – They are full of interest now. What a critical position Europe is in – & what shall one think of the dreadful massacre of the Christians at Damascus?[106] Surely these revolutions & battles, that are going on everywhere now, mean something very important? I cannot help thinking a new page out of the Book of Revelations is being fulfilled. *Sunday 4th.* Still the clear, fine weather continues; we had several nice turns on the ice yesterday. I sent in the forenoon, to ask if the Pastor intended going to the lake, in which case I would ask him to accompany me, Hampus having no time. Constance & I went down at 11. & met him at our gate; I had also sent to the Fürstin to ask if she would like to go – so we were a nice party. Capt[ain] Krogius, Bergenheim and young Kr[ogius] were there already. The wind was rather cold on the ice, or rather the air, as you returned in the chair across the lake, but the sun poured down her warm rays upon us, & we enjoyed it much. I have little time either to play or read just now, as my work for Hampus is quite en arrière [Fr. delayed], & I want to make several things for Baby, & have many letters to write. What do you say to my having yesterday bought a sky blue silk dress, all ready made? & from whom do you think? – from Constance! who received it as a present from Ludmila, who received it from Otto with several other silks, but being too tight in the body & too light for her years! – as she says, besides which such things being perfectly useless at Ajan, she sent it to C[onstance] who was quite distressed at the present which neither gave her pleasure, or would be of the slightest use to her, as she never goes to the Balls, nor requires any thing of the kind at home. Since she received it, she has been asking me over & over again if she could not sell it, as she requires many other useful things instead. Of course Hampus would not allow her to sell it to anyone but myself, so I thought I might as well take it off her hands, & she jumped for Joy, tho' I told her she had made a very bad bargain, but she declares she has had "en stor Julklapp" [Swed. a big Christmas present]. Will you darling Mama, buy a largish print Swedish Bible, nicely bound, at the Bible society in London, for C[onstance] which I want to give her, & a few russian testaments bound in calfsleather. She is using the swedish Bible Scott gave, but the print is dreadfully small, & as Scott gave it, Hampus would rather keep it.

Friday Ev[enin]g 9. Dec[ember]. Last night young Bergenheim took leave of us. He has been like one of the family, and seems to have liked our society much. Poor boy!

---

106 The massacre of the Christians at Damascus in 1860 was instigated by local Ottoman officials.

he was so sad & affected at bidding us goodbye; his lips quivered & voice shook, & his eyes were full of tears. I was quite touched myself. He had been quite out of spirits all the afternoon, and as the evening drew to a close, I remarked how he sat on & on, postponing the moment for saying Farewell. At last, at 10½ he rose quickly with a sigh, & could hardly bring out any words at all. I cannot say what great pleasure it gives us both to think he has had a home with us in this strange country, & that he carries home such an affectionate remembrance of us. We grew quite fond of him – he is such an exceedingly well behaved, modest, amiable young man. I stuffed his pockets full of apples, & sent him & the Captainskan [Swed. captain's wife] each a large "kringla" [Swed. cake] on board this morning. The Pastor told me Bergenheim had said no parting yet, of course with exception of the one from his own home, "hade så mycket kostat på honom, som denna" [Swed. had been so difficult for him, as this one]. We shall be happy to welcome him back again, if we should ever meet at Sitka, or anywhere else. It is always most pleasing to find heart & feeling, and especially in a young person. By him I wrote a long letter to dear Moster Lisette, who will be so glad to see him, & to hear that he liked us. We sent home a box of curiosities by this occasion. By the bye, darling Mama, have you ever received the red colibris, views of Sitka & various little trifles we sent last year? This is Anna day; or rather has been – we have par hazard celebrated it very pleasantly. I went to see poor Schwartz little girl, my Goddaughter this morning, visited the school, having to speak with the mistress about various things belonging to the examination which will take place on the 20th & then called at the Fürstin to ask if she was inclined for a walk. We came out together & met Mr Koshkin, who asked, if we would not come on the ice this afternoon – We were both inclined for it, & I promised to cook chocolate & bring kringla, he immediately rushed off to send a table, chairs, carpet, etc – etc on the lake. At half past 2. Hampus, C[onstance] & I went down, the Prince & his Wife soon followed, Miss Klinkowström a nice girl, in whom the secretary is dreadfully & seriously in love, & all our gentlemen were there. A bonny "jolly" fire was burning on the ice, the table spread samovar smoking, & all ready when we came. The air was perfectly mild & there was no wind. You cannot think how nice it was. After several turns on the lake we sat down & partook of the entertainment & then skated again till 4. o'clock. Every body pronounced it a charming thing – the plan originated with Mr Koschkin. I was so sorry our young friends were sailing on the wide ocean already, instead of enjoying the afternoon with us. I have been working all evening on the cushion for Hampus, & whilst he is walking up & down, warming himself before taking his cold bath, I am writing to you. I wonder where & how you are now precious Mother? my letters ought to be always of very recent date now that you are in England. It was a pity you could not meet Fru Krogius who had seen us & our Darling. It would have given you such pleasure to hear about us. *Sunday 11/23.* This is little darling Ormelies Birthday, though he can, & ought, no longer to be called "little" – He is 12 years old today if I am not mistaken? he will be a tall youth of 16 when we return – but when shall we three meet again? [...]

Tomorrow is Xmas Eve, though not yet for us. Here we must celebrate it after the old style. In our hearts, & in our prayers, my own Hampus and I, you & Florence will remember tomorrow – that day, on which we first met! O! that we might *all* be permitted once again to be together on *that day*. Where are you my precious Mother? with dearest Mary & her bright husband I hope – you will have a merry, happy Xmas I am sure. There will be letters from Charlie and Ponnie, perhaps from Puxti and Annie too? – Perhaps my long, long letter of *6 Sept[ember]* or even that of 18th Sept[ember] sent by the english man of war, may reach England in time to bring you the deepest, fondest, lovingest wishes & kisses from your R[ussian] American children – that would be nice! the first named letter would please you I hope, for it was enormously long. Florence's letter & your few words at the end of it, of 12 – 22nd Sept[ember] reached me on *26th Nov[ember]*, the shortest travelled letter I have yet received. If you counted new sty[le] it was a little more than 2. months old, & if old as we do, just 2. months. It was a pity you did not send your own too. Please God I shall hear of your safe arrival in England, & much else I want to know, by the next post. We have been driving on the Ice today – our sledge & horse was a funny concern, but notwithstanding we enjoyed it much, except that I do not like going on the lake on Sunday, there was such a crowd – Hampus does not either like it, & we do not intend going again on a Sunday. It would be pleasant to have such fine, clear weather over the holy days. I am so unhappy that here too there must be a newyears Eve Ball. I do not wish to go, & still less wish to be separated from my Hampus when the new year enters. It is not only that sitting up so long fatigues me so very much, but that I do not like spending the new years Eve, & morn, at a noisy Ball. What is to be done in our case?

Christmas Eve. Own, darling Mama! many, many happy returns of the day to you – may happiness & Peace abide with you for ever, and with your children wherever they may be. – [Hampus:] A merry, happy christmas and many happy returns of the same! – iz the sincerest wish, dear mama, of your much affectionate son. – Hampus says he will write a real letter to you, these lines are only to be considered as prelude & Impromtu! We shall soon be celebrating our Xmas; I wish I had many presents to give, but you can't get anything here. We intend eating finsk julqvällsvard [Swed. Finnish Christmas evening meal], & I want to have a table spread in the kitchen for all the servants. There are no real poor here, for the company provides for all; no destitute orphans, for they are immediately put into the school. We have our little orphan Palasha at home – unfortunately I have been any thing but satisfied with her; – she is neither obedient, nor careful of her things, nor does she try to remember what I tell her.

To Constance we give 2. summerdresses, a black silk umbrella, blue ribbon for her neck, & several other trifling presents. I am so happy to be able to give, at least. For Ida a sable muff & muffitees; the other servants get gowns, aprons, hankerchiefs etc – etc. We have our own hams this year, & the meat is very tender. Our 2. gentlemen upstairs are quiet enough, except that I hear them walking above head, and meet them at dinner, I know nothing about them. They praise our cook, & say it must be a difficult thing to variate dishes at Sitka, which indeed it is. But I am now quite without eggs which is a dreadful thing; there are none to be bought – we have to find out sweet dishes in which eggs do not enter as an ingredient. *Sunday 18/30.* I must write a few words darling Mama, before our two gentlemen, who announced their intention of spending this evening with us, come. Hampus has invited a few other gentlemen to meet them. It is the first time we have had company on a Sunday – I do not like it at all – but it can't be helped. We have read our evening service & prayers, which makes me feel more happy. I think I must have said at the beginning of this letter, that my Hampus feared the worst consequences of the revision, & that his conviction was, 1862. would be the death of the Company. He has spoken of packing his trunks too; – but now his opinions have changed, or if not that, he is calmer, & seems to view every possible occurrence with his minds eye – so that he looks at the worst for us individually which may follow, or the next extreme, the best. – A few nights ago he said. "Annie, suppose the Company should offer me to retain my place 3. years over the five, & they should at the same time increase my pay by 5000 R[oubles] S[ilver] yearly, I should feel very much inclined to accept their proposal – What do you say?" – I said no! I should not like it at all, though the proposal would be tempting. Darling Hampus! he told me I should go home for one year & a half, & take the children with me, to pay you a visit; and he would remain alone at Sitka! parted from wife & children. No! I could never, never do it – I could never leave him for so long, with all the big ocean rolling an inseparable gulf between us. – Were it only to San Fr[ancisco] I could make up my mind, but not to Europe –

Monday Ev[enin]g. I was interrupted last night, by the arrival of our guests, & have only found time now to continue. I must relate part of a conversation which passed between Statsrådet, a young pole Dr Markoffsky, the Princesse & myself last night. –

Mention being made of an elderly couple, who are very much attached to each other, so that the husband, who is a seafaring man, will not go to sea without his wife, who again is exceedingly delicate & suffers from some interior chronic complaint, Dr M[arkoffsky] observed: "Mais Madame, c'est vraiment un peu ridicule – toujours ils sont ensembles, ils ne peuvent pas vivre sans être toujours l'un auprès de l'autre, comme deux pigeons! – elle est vieille et malade, quelquefois même lui il faut la soigner 2. ou 3. nuits de suite, sans pouvoir dormir. Si elle était encore jeune!! –" [Fr. But Madame, it is really a little ridiculous – they are always together. They cannot live without being next to each other like two pigeons! – She is old and ill sometimes he must tend her two or three nights in succession, without being able to sleep. If she were still young!!] Mr Kozlizeff answered: "C'est perdre aux yeux de sa femme, je trouve, d'être toujours amoureux d'elle! les femmes aimes la distraction, les changements, *la constance n'est plus à la mode*" – [Fr. It is declining in the eyes of your wife, I think, being always in love with her; women love distraction, change, stability is no longer modern.]

Such alas, are the elevated, pure & noble ideas, russians & poles have about the most sacred tie on earth! – *marriage*. I answered not a word to Mr K[ozlizeff]'s latter observation, but was afterwards sorry I did not say to both, that woman is to be pitied, who is married to a man entertaining those views. It made me quite uncomfortable to be in company with such lose principled men. O! how I deplore their utter ignorance of integrity; – of generous, noble, *christian* views & opinions – likings & expectations of married life. A woman, a wife is good enough when she is young, but though she is the mother of your own children, she may be thrown off & put aside like an old, dusty book, when she is old, & may be delicate & in want of care. – The Princesse, who is born in Russia, & has never been out of it, tells me, few, few are the really happy russian marriages & that principles & morals, sit but very, very lose on both men & women of all classes of society. It is a standing marvel to me, that she, a woman of heart, sense & education, could, *knowing* what the russians generally are, and what expectations they have of married life, could ever make up her mind, or have the courage to wed a russian! But, she has made a convert to her own opinions of him, & they are really an attached & happy couple. What I have said only shows, where religion stands on so low a standard, & is a thing easily put on & cast aside, where y[ou]r sins of one week, can be perfectly blotted out & forgiven by the priest, by burning a couple of wax candles before one of their 365. saints!, morals, cannot be expected to stand much higher. –

Tuesday night half past 10. This is New-years day with you my own darling Mother, & I cannot go to bed without sending you my fondest, warmest, truest love & well wishes for this new year. May you my darling Mama, have entered & begun it, in Peace, Health and Happiness, & may it please our Almighty Father to let you continue & conclude it, & still many, many others, in the same way. Your picture is standing before me, & I have kissed it many times, wishing it were yourself. O! how happy that day will be, when we may, please God, meet again! I fancy you have today been writing to your children, & have I hope had quite fresh letters to read over again from them both. This day last year, I was weak & ill & could not write, but you wrote to me. It has been another blessed, precious year of peace & happiness to me. O! how can I ever, ever thank my Father enough, for all he has done for me. I have not been able to write today before now. The forenoon was taken up with the examination at the girls school & sale of their works, the afternoon with walking & working. In the evening I was with the Fürstin. Last night, on returning from school, where I had gone to see that all was in order for today, I fell on the street. Thank God, there have been no ill consequences of any kind, for which I feel deeply grateful – for it frightened me much to think of a premature confinement. This is the 4th week of fine, clear, frosty weather; it is indeed delightful. The ice is being cut & immediately brought on board the "Nakimoff" which will leave on Saturday. It is beautiful ice, clear & white as crystal, & will I hope arrive in good condition at San Francisco. Have you seen any of the volunteer parades? the papers are full of accounts about them, & I saw Lady D. Gordon's name mentioned, as one of the ladies

The flag of the Russian American Company with the Imperial double eagle.

who had presented a silver bugle & held a speech. What a glorious man Garibaldi is. What reward will he get, he is the viceroy of Italy to all intents & purposes – How happy he must feel forwarding the freedom of so lovely a country.

Friday 23th Dec[ember]/4th January 1861. new style. It is indeed most un àpropos, that "Nakimoff" is sailing tomorrow, as Christmas week every where brings a great deal to do, & my letters have been thrown back by a good deal. Fancy darling Mama, it is the first Xmas, Hampus and I are celebrating together as man and wife – It is the first one we are together since Xmas 1858. when we met & saw each other for the first time. I cannot express, how happy I feel to celebrate this blessed time together with my own husband, and our precious little Firstborn daughter, though she is still too young to understand anything about it. We are going to have a large, fine tree; Constance & I were up till 11. last night tying strings to the cakes, apples, silvered nuts etc – etc – She too is so glad, for these last Xmases have been anything but bright or merry ones for her. My darling Hampus has not celebrated Xmas for years & years, & he says it is indeed a joy & a Blessing to be permitted to celebrate one in his own family. My cushion is finnished and looks very handsome. Constance will I hope like her things too; The servants will all be pleased, & have a merry dinner, with Ida, in the kitchen.

The examination at the girls school went off as well as could be expected considering all things – their masters are bad, & not made for teaching – the best thing they had to show was their work, mostly consisting of Baby clothes, which were very well done, & brought in a good deal of money into their Bank. We bought for 76 R[oubles] worth all of which things, except 6 p[ai]r stockings & a ball, I am sending incognito to my little Goddaughter, Anna Schwartz, whose parents will be pleased I hope. They are very poor and have 4. children. Hampus says he will be obliged to ask the revisors down on Xmas day, which is not pleasant. On Monday there will be theatre at the Club. It is delightful to have such exquisite weather the sun shines, & the heaven is clear & cloudless, such a very rare ocurence in our part of the world. O darling Mama! if you could but see our little angel Annie; she gets sweeter & sweeter from day to day, & is indeed the delight of our hearts & eyes. She can stand, but not walk, & will I fear scarcely do so by the time our second child will be born. This letter ought to reach you in March, when your thoughts will be with me; I pray God, all may go well this time too. I hear from right & left that so many of the married women here, suffer from the fall of the womb, which I entirely contribute to the ignorance of midwife & doctor – for they make you get out of bed on the 9. or 10th day, to walk on y[ou]r feet, & sit upright, insisting that you will never regain your strength otherwise! This time we do not intend following this plan; Hampus has had a comfortable sopha made for me, on which I will be removed from bed – last year I had nothing. What deplorable consequences a mismanaged confinement can have; – the loss of health & strength for Life. What shall I do for a nurse? the woman we engaged at Codiac, is consumptive & coughs much, & there is no one to be had here. Indeed I should not like to remain longer than 5. years, for you cannot think the many troubles you have. If you could see how Annie loves her nurse – she calls her "nana",[107] & puts her little arms round her neck, kissing her over and over again. God grant she may grow up as gentle and good as she now really is – Everybody will love her then. [...]

One of our Captains, Mr Ridell from Åbo, is now returning home over Panama & London. I will give him a letter from[108] Henry, to whose little Mary, we are sending some Sitka made toys. I will ask Henry to let you know of his arrival, in case you would like to meet him, & speak face to face with a person who knows us & has often dined at our table. I don't know him of course, but he can tell you many things you would like to ask – and it will always be a pleasure to meet a person coming directly from us. He expects to be in London by March. By him you can send messages to our dear friends in Finland. Darling Mama, I must now finnish. In Henry's box, is

107 'Niania' is Russian for 'nanny'.
108 Anna probably means 'for'.

a little bag of real eider down for you, which you will find some use for I hope. God
bless you my own most precious Mother, & keep & preserve you unto us, in health
and peace of mind. Perhaps this ship will return with a letter from you, to welcome
me a few days after my confinement. […] My own husband sends Mama his fondest love, he is so harassed in mind, & could not write, but he loves you never the
less. – Our own bonny little Darling sends many kisses to Grandmama & to Aunt
& Uncle Charlie. Praying for Gods blessing on us all, & our homes, I ever ever am
Y[ou]r most truly loving, devoted child

Annie F[uruhjelm]

No. 41   *Sitka. New Years day 1861.*

My own beloved Mother! A few words on this day, before going to rest, I must still
send you; though with you this is the 13th Jan[ua]ry, I cannot refrain from once again
sending you my hearts warmest & fondest wishes & prayers for this new year, which
lies veiled in uncertainty & obscurity before us. May it be our Fathers will, that it may
be another Year of peace & happiness to us all, & that we may one and all of us increase
in Love for Him, who is Love personified, & may grow in grace & knowledge, faith &
charity. It has been a pleasant, happy year for us. Hampus and I have been reading,
praying and talking together – We are reading the history of the reformation, which is
a most interesting & cultivating work. The dear, old year has left us for ever! behind us
now lie all the joys, all the sorrows we have felt in the same. Thank God, the sorrows
have been small, & the joy of health & happiness, great. May our Fathers Blessing
have followed us into this new year, & may it for ever continue with us; may we pray
Him for truly grateful & contented hearts, leaving our Future in His divine hands,
who ordains all things for the best, & alone knows what is good & necessary for His
children. – *Sunday morning 8th.* Every day of this new year I have been wishing to
continue my letter, and now the first week is already for ever & irreparably gone. How
I am again longing for letters from you my darling Mama. I have had on the whole so
few only. I hope to make a long post ready for the next mail, which Hampus hopes to
expedite on the 1st April. Please God I am quite well again by that date, I shall be able
to write myself a few lines about the new wonder child God has given us. Our little
Annie is making daily progress; she stands so firmly, & even alone at a chair for half a
second; we do not expect that she will crawl at all, but walk immediately; two points of
the 3rd large grinding tooth is through, & she eats a soft boiled egg with great gusto.
Today, I will give her some "hafvresoppa" [Swed. water gruel] for the 1st time. I send
her out every fine day, though there may be for or five degrees of cold, but never do
so if the air is at all damp or foggy, though her papa would even then wish her to be
carried out. She understands so much, & shows you "how Mama plays" by tapping her
little hands on the table, or "how Baby dances" "where little Annie is" by pointing to
her little chest, etc – etc. I am so curious to see what impression the sight of a brother

or sister will make upon her. O Mama! how you would love your little darling Grand child. Last night we had 10es cold at 10. o'clock, & still more towards morning I suppose; it is so pleasant having got back this clear, healthy weather again. It blew such a furious storm on Thursday last, that Garitza's 6. cables were broken, & she was driven on shore. Hampus was quite unhappy; towards evening when the tide was full, she got afloat again, without having received any damage, which was indeed a good luck. Today, whilst I was dressing, the alarm of fire was given, & again my poor Hampus received a great fright – all men turned out instantly, but it proved only to be one of the bishops chimneys which had caught fire, & nothing worse came of it. Meanwhile my Hampus is really placed in a most unpleasant situation now; – you cannot think darling Mama, how worried he is; every day almost brings something unpleasant. Our opinion is, that these gentlemen upstairs are false; with all their smiles & fine words their hearts are against us, & they wish the company no good, on the contrary would willingly see it quite anihilized. They have given questions to be answered to all the gentlemen here, & make a minute account of all complaints brought forward. My Hampus is often very out of spirits, & says "it is because I am the 13th governor that all these troubles crowd around me" – but I try to encourage & comfort him, & to make him trust in God, who will certainly protect us, and help us, if we but faithfully seek Him, & believe that "not a hair of our heads can fall without His will" – Should 1862. see the end of the company, it will still require a couple of years before all is arranged & sold & disposed of in another way, & an honest man & an esteemed & well known one, can always get some other employment. Mr Kozlizzeff said to Hampus "it is not the minister of foreign affairs who is against your Company, but the Grand Duke Constantine cannot abide it" – This very G[rand] D[uke] is as you know, chef [Fr. commander-in-chief] of the russian navy, & is a man who meddles in everything, & has great influence. He is a perfectly unprincipled & vicious man, of whom you read so many harsh acts, in a russian paper called "the Bell" which is published in London. Our two gentlemen upstairs, are exceedingly clever, & have great influence too; consequently it entirely depends upon *how they choose* to put forward the company, & in which light they will place it – for their reports will be perfectly believed & acted upon. *All this is of course private & confidential*, Hampus wishes me to say. –

All the respectable families here have been giving card playing parties for them, & they evidently wish to make themselves very popular. In return they are going to give a Ball *for me* they say – next week! Is it not a farce? They and we put on smiling faces & seem charmed! – Such is the world. I am thank God of a sanguine temperament. Except when I see Hampus out of spirits, I must say, all these things do not distress me, or make me anxious, for I *so certainly* believe that Gods Will, will be done in all things.

Sitka has been exceedingly gay. Monday, Tuesday & Wednesday nights, we were obliged to attend the theatre at the club. Some of the men showed decided talent for acting, but the 2. ladies were awful to look at. Each night 2. pieces were given; during the pauses, we, viz: Hampus, Annie, Fürst, Fürstin, Klinkowströms & revisors, retired to Mr Koshkins very comfortable room, where he served tea & preserved pine apples for us – the 2nd night after the play was over he gave us a very fine supper with champagne & drank "dla storovia Anna Nikolaivna" (to the health of A.N.). I was so tired on Wednesday, & besides which ennuyée, that I intended to stop at home, but Hampus who was oppressed in spirits that day, & therefore wanted to stay at home, wished one of us to be present, so I went & laughed very much, for the pieces were ridiculous & the chief actor played very well. On Thursday night we were all asked to the Maksutoffs, where I always like to go, for we spend pleasant evenings together. I like the Fürstin more & more, the more I get to know her – We are neither of us inclined for making sudden & passionate acquaintances & have therefore gone on progressively in our friendship. She was again speaking of her father, & was telling me about the many trials & hardships he has gone through. He has lost his health, & never been quite well or strong for 7 years now. His family is large, & his purse not at all heavy. He was at last obliged to give up his place as professor of the english language at the Rechtsschule[?] [Ger. law school] in Petersburg, & all the money he has saved, went to try to restore his health. At this time the Princesse said, the idea arose in her mind to perfect herself as an artist, having both talent & love for paint-ing. But her father would not hear of it, so she accepted a situation as governess at a rich russian merchants, & was there 3. years! She said "but if you knew *how* difficult it was, & what it cost me" & spoke with such feeling & such emotion, I was quite touched & felt that I knew & esteemed her more for it, & having told it me sans gène [Fr. unconstrainedly]. She said at this time, her father generally wrote once or twice in the week to her, which letters she treasures like gold, & says she can never be thankful enough for all the good advise they contain, on various & all circumstances of Life. It was when her father gave it to be known, that if any young officer, wished to learn the english language & take his meals with them, he would find such accommodation at his house, that the prince presented himself, & there she met him on Saturday & Sunday evenings, but hardly had any time to speak with him herself. They had seen each other only 5. times when he proposed to her father for her, & then to herself. She is truly happy – & he is a fortunate russian to have got so educated a Wife. He too is a very exellent young man, & a very good husband. *She* has got the *head* though.

Tuesday forenoon 17/29. If you could only see how splendidly the sun is lighting up the snowy mountains, & how bright & brilliantly the reflection falls over our little Sitka. We have still, or rather over again, the most exquisite clear, cold weather, which is so rare here. The roofs of the houses, & the streets are covered with snow. Yesterday afternoon the secretary drove me in a sledge, & this afternoon we are going again. I cannot persuade Hampus to drive me, he says he would not venture; that a sailor cannot manage a horse! This day 2. years ago, was the soirée given by Achates Gripenbergs for us; – how very fast the time has gone. Hampus says: "have we only been married 2. years? it seems to me as if we had *always* been married, & I had known you for years!" – I say the same thing – the actual 2. years of our married life, have gone wonderfully fast, but husband & wife are so entirely one, & so it is thank God with us, that we both cannot fancy we ever did not belong to, or know each other. I cannot think it is 2. whole years since we parted from you, my ownest Mother! Still 3. more, or a little over 3., & then please God, we may meet again, & that moment will be full recompensation for the 5. years separation. I daresay the time has not appeared so short to you, & you are still looking forward to the time which remains before we can meet, as an Eternity. But – when we do see each other face to face once more, I think the Past will seem like a dream, though our little ones will remind us of the reality. I know, that I shall ever entertain an affectionate & fond remembrance of Sitka, this my first Home & the birthplace of some of our children; I can never forget it nor feel indifferent for it, & shall ever be interested in hearing about it, & meeting any one coming from Sitka. What a peaceful, quiet Life we have been permitted to lead here, thanks to the great & infinite Goodness of our Lord. Of course life here, has its drawbacks & trials, but where can it be otherwise? Every place under the sun has its advantages & disadvantages & we must never expect to have everything quite smooth & without the slightest difficulty. The greatest drawback to Sitka, & my greatest difficulty, is the impossibility of getting clean & proper & above all *busy* women servants. Do not think I worry & fret all day long – oh no! I have long since found out, that it is an irreparable evil, on which it is useless ever to spend your vexation – or at least, as you cannot help feeling annoyed, no use speaking about it. The women are worse that the men – They *will not* work, & that only because they can always gain money on other paths, without the necessity of working. The poor children are spoilt from the birth – they see & hear nothing but what is wrong around them, & grow up equally bad as their poor mothers. The greatest vice of both sexes here, is the insatiable love for liquors. One of my washerwomen was at last obliged to be sent quite away from Sitka, because she was such a dreadful drunkard, & made such a row in the barracks, the other women could not live with her. The fall of this poor woman is entirely to be laid at the door of the former adjoint, who first began by giving her a little porter, then wine & brandy, till she attained love for strong drinks, & now cannot do without it. She was young & beautiful, & that is the end of her, poor, poor thing! They are all more to be pitied than blamed. What can be expected of people who hear & see nothing better often in their superiors, & in their clergy to whom they ought to be able to look up? the russian priests, & especially the monks, are the worst set of men, round whom a cloak of holyness is thrown – you can truly say of them "they go about in sheeps clothing; but inwardly they are ravenous wolves". – It was indeed a painful pulling open of the eyes, to come straight from a happy, innocent Home, where nothing impure or unclean ever entered, nor of which very existence I never knew, to this place, where it is impossible not to see, hear & know much that must both shock & pain. The world is nowhere any more a paradise – Sin, in some form is predominant everywhere – to begin with, in our own hearts – but still you will see a striving after what is right, & a baffling against what is wrong, & can never come so closely in contact with Badness as in a small place like Sitka, & especially in a colony. I often think, surely Russia must be much, much worse than other countries; and I am sure of it too. –

Ida just brought in my little Annie, who had woken from her sleep & looked so rosy & fresh. She went away with Grandmama's portrait in her hand, which she kissed several times. I will send her out now, it is so fine. A couple of days ago our guests upstairs gave a Ball for us. I was obliged to walk through 5. quadrilles & sit up till ½ past 2. which was not at all according to my taste. The consequence was that I woke towards morning with dreadful cramp in my leg, I screamed aloud, & feel the part still painful. Otherwise I am thank God quite well & feel wonderfully light on my feet. The only fatiguing thing is the long staircase from the street, which is really more than I know how to manage – I must literally creep up. The Ball was a very animated one & everyone seemed very pleased. Hampus was distressed to see how luxury is gaining ground here, which led us to a serious conversation last night. I have therefore determined henceforth to dress as plainly as possible, letting black silk be the best dress – It is only now I begin to think over it; I see, that though I do not spend money on my dress, wearing things in reality too fine for Sitka, only because I have them ready made, excites the wish & desire in every one else to dress extravagantly, & I am consequently putting a thorn in my poorer neighbours eyes, & encouraging a liking for fine things which they cannot afford. Hampus has not either before come to think of it seriously, but now he sees the Creoles in flowers & fine bonnets, though they had them before we came, he is annoyed at it, & says that one of the Company's laws is that the Governor must watch over & subdue the unnecessary introduction of luxury. I know I am not the only lady here who has expensive dresses – Mrs Klinkowström, having lived several years in San Fr[ancisco] where ladies really dress most extravagantly, came here with no end of fine things, and though [Anna has forgotten to finish this sentence.]

20 Jan[ua]ry/1 Feb[ruary]. I am so happy to be progressing gradually with my letters. I write every day to someone else, & hope by that means to have all ready before I am taken ill. I have just written to Tante Margret, asking her to engage a swedish servant for me, as washerwoman, as I see it is impossible to go on longer in this way. I earnestly hope she will succeed in getting a good & industrious girl. I am writing to Eugénie, to dearest Mrs H[awthorne], to Mina G[ripenberg] – these are all begun, & still wish to write to Florence, Miss Macleans & Uncle Eduard, so you see darling Mama, I have much to do – besides making nightgowns & sheets to little Annie. It would be nothing, could I work in the machine; but now it is impossible & uncomfortable to bend over my body so much. Darling Annie has now been removed from her cradle to a new little bedstead, where she lies so nicely – it would be large enough for 10. years. She grows droller & sweeter day by day. I have taught her to show where Grandmama lives, by waving her little hand far away. If you ask her "Wo wohnt der liebe Gott" [Ger. Where does God live] she looks up in y[ou]r face, & points with her hand towards heaven. Hampus will miss her much, when he goes away in spring, and cannot hear her little voice, nor see all her endearing ways. I think the revisors & Hampus will leave Sitka at the end of April, & though Mr Kozlizzeff says "votre mari sera absent qu'un mois" [Fr. your husband will only be absent one month] I do not know whether I am to believe it or not. It is too sad, that I must be separated from him every summer – I compare myself to Marie L[angenskiöld]. His time is so completely taken up now, I see little or nothing of him during the day, & in the evening he even sits & writes. It is a dreadful annoyance for my Hampus having a stupid secretary – for all the writing falls after all upon Hampus – Koshkin writes everything so badly & without understanding. When Hampus has time, & feels inclined for it, he reads D'Aubigny's history of the reformation aloud to me, it is so pleasant being read to, & the Book is of course very interesting to all who call themselves christians. Yesterday I was reading "the golden legend" again – What a lovely story it is, but what a strange poem – I do not like all of it. This day 2. years ago, was the last day I was at home. I remember it so well. You my own Mother were packing my trunk, & Hampus was coming in & out, & had a farewell supper for his friends in the evening. How we are all scattered who were then together in that suny little green drawingroom! none of us are to be found in the same country! indeed wonderful, marvellous are the changes a short time can produce. [...]

Saturday 2 *February*/21 Jan[ua]ry. At this very hour 2. years ago, my own Hampus and I were united, & made man & wife in the sight of God and man. How I love to think of that day! I see it all as plainly as if it had been yesterday – No one would have supposed, looking at us all, that that very evening we should part; it was a strange thing; I could neither look nor feel sad during the whole ceremony or wedding breakfast – I felt such perfect peace in my heart & soul, & could even then scarcely realize to myself, that I was going away from you my precious fond Mother, & from my Home which had always been a bright and happy one. I had felt it all much, much more the 3. weeks before, & just that last terrible moment when cloak & hood was put on, & we got into the sledge. O! that was dreadful! But I could not, & should not like to have looked sad, or had red eyes the very moment my & all our fond wishes had been fulfilled, and I had become Hampus own Wife. Do you ever think it was wonderful? I often think how very pleasant it must be for you when you think back on our weddingday, to have so bright & cheerful a picture before you, & am therefore doubly glad. This day last year our darling was christened, & I was also writing to you. How fast the year has gone! then Annie was a tiny little thin Baby, & now thank God, she is such a rosy, fat little child, laughing, screaming for joy & talking her own incomprehensible language all day long. That letter is the last I have received an answer to. I was last night dreaming about long letters – perhaps the "Nakimoff" will soon return from San Francisco, with a heavy post for me I hope. O Mama! So much joy is still in store for me. A child! letters from Home! & soon afterwards, your picture! – [...] O! may we be spared to each other still many, many, many years! & if it be Gods Will, may we see our children grow up around us "like green oliveplants". Two years ago the day was clear & fine. Today the sun has hidden himself quite, & the wind and rain are playing hide & seek together. Last year only daughters were born here, this year only sons – one of the german ladies was confined yesterday of a son, so I hope after six weeks, please God, the news may be going from mouth to mouth "I dag har Gouverneurskan fått en liten son [Swed. Today the Governor's wife has given birth to a son]!" […]

Sunday. For long we have not had such a dreary day. It has hardly been daylight, & the wind is still very boisterous; there was no possibility of getting to church this morning. We read an excellent sermon by Mr Robertson, called "the Law of christian conscience" – His sermons are all calculated to instruct, and I think a person belonging to whatever party, might read them without offence. He is really tolerant, and writes in a spirit of true christian liberty; perhaps many find fault with him, just for that very reason, but it seems to me, many people, and all of us more or less, carry their prejudices into their religions. Views even, & quarrels & controversies arise mostly from not wishing to give up the point of an I, though at the ground opinions may after all not be very different. Love, is the "fulfilment of the law" [Romans 13:10] & if true christian love existed in all who call themselves christians, I think there would be less inclination to think those of our friends & acquaintances irretrievably lost, who hold views not quite akin to our own. – […]

I have just come from the nursery, & seen our little Darling before going to sleep. She does not like being put to sleep in the evenings, & would rather wish to play & kick a little longer. Now is the difficult time, when her understanding & intellect is developing itself daily, & she would like to have her own way. Still I hope and trust, we may have understanding to bring her up judiciously, trying to call out & encourage all that is good in her from the very beginning, and subdue the wrong, which of course exists in every child. *Friday*. I have been so occupied with Annies nightgowns, five of which are finnished now, with Constance help, that my letters have not advanced this week. Sometimes in the forenoon the Princesse comes here to practise on my piano, as I have asked her to do, hers, not a good nor a new one, when she bought it before leaving Russia, came here perfectly ruined in consequence of improper packing, so that she has neither use or pleasure of it; her husband intends ordering another for her from Hamburg – I advised them to write for a "Schied-mayer" as I could *possitively* assert that his piano's were perfect and not so expensive as the P[eter]b[ur]g grande piano's. The Princesse hopes to have it here next spring. She plays difficult pieces, & has great execution, but no feeling – only "Vortrag" [Ger. execution]. Still she is very fond of playing & does not wish to forget what she knows. I thought she might come today, but now it is raining. A few evenings ago I played for nearly an hour & a half after tea, only Mozart & Beethoven's sonates for Hampus; – but I paid for it at night, for I could not sleep quietly, nor get rid of an intense heat. Playing now, heats me to such a degree it is perfect discomfort – I get into perspiration all over & cannot sleep quietly after it – I hear the music in my dreams, but generally in form of a nightmare, & I often frighten Hampus with my screams. Generally speaking I am just now suffering mostly from heat. The blood rushes into my head, and I am in a vapour bath, though our room is cool, & the

window is much open. I have not gone down our dreadful stairs for more than one
week now, and I do not think I shall go down any more, except once still to church,
to receive the Holy Sacrament. –

   I told you Hampus secretary was deeply in love with a young girl here? Well, he
is a most undecided character; a very good man as far as heart goes, but very weak.
He comes to me sometimes for advice, what to do – Yesterday he came before dinner,
& asked me if I thought it would be well for him to marry. What could I say. I told
him, in such matters no person could give advise; it was far too great a responsibility, but that certainly I thought it better to be married, than unmarried, & especially
for him now, as otherwise he would grow too old. She is a very good girl, & though
he might marry *richer* & *finer* in Russia (this I only tell you) he might not get a
better Wife, for she has principles, & has been brought up very religiously, & has
some *heart education*, which russian young girls are void of. – I told him, he must
once & for all make up his mind, either to marry, or not to marry, & having decided
this point, to stick to it. He says, this whole week he has been thinking "Il faut se
marier" [Fr. I must marry]. – Well then do you really love her, & will you always
be contented? "Je l'aime, mais je ne sais pas si je serais toujours content" [Fr. I love
her but I am not sure I shall always be content]. The thing is, he is in love, & wishes
to marry, but wants to gather general opinions on the subject first. He wishes to ask
Hampus advise, but cannot bring himself to talk unconfusedly on the subject. I said,
I will begin for you. Just at that juncture, Hampus came in – the poor man blushed,
put his hands up entreatingly & said "Je vous emprie Madame, ne dite rien" [Fr. I
implore you, Madame, don't say anything]! – & so the conference ended. When we
were alone, I told Hampus all about it, & asked him to listen attentively & give good
councils, when Mr Koshkin broaches that subject. Hampus says I will advise him
not to marry for this is just a very critical time – should the Company's privileges
be discontinued, he is without employment, & is a married man, which may bring
troubles upon him. But, at the same time, is he bent upon it, now is the time. Florence often laughed at poor Koshkin, & will remember him I am sure. I think he is
really attached to Hampus, & always would take his part. After russian fashion he
looks upon us as a sort of relation, seeing that Olga Alexandrovna [Furuhjelm] is his
cousin, or Aunt as he calls her. Sitka is a great place for marriages; but it is a great
pity for Europeans to unite themselves to creoles. First they have not the slightest
education, & secondly they never "trifvas" [Swed. thrive] in Russia, but long to get
back to Sitka. As the creole men are faithless husbands, so they are often faithless
Wives, & the intermingled marriages are never happy. The russian, after a short
time, repents of his choice, & feels ashamed of his Wife. The young lady in question
for K[oshkin] is no creole, & her father is a german, & an excellent man. Hampus
is building a new barrack. It is pleasant to see how fast the work progresses. It will
be a strong building, & stand as many years as Etholéns houses have stood. All the
large & well built houses, are Uncle Adolf's doing – the other governors do not
seem to have cared much for *how* they built, provided they only got up some walls.

Hampus always makes stone foundations, which is utterly necessary in our damp & rainy climate, but greater part of the houses are built right upon the ground, so you can fancy how rotten & tumble down they soon become. I have finnished reading the 1st vol[ume] of the reformation – there are still 3. to read. Hampus is just now going through Fredrika Bremers "Lifvet i den nya verlden" [Swed. Life in the New World] & likes it very much. Some parts he read aloud to me, & it brought Florences little suny room with the green curtains, so vividly before my eyes. I like to think of our winter with dear Marie; our rooms were so cosy & pretty, & if you only do not think of what was painful during that time, we have all a happy remembrance of the last winter we were all 3. together.

Saturday. I have been busy preparing a little bedquilt for Annie, to be wadded with down at the school. I bought a foulard morning dress, ready made at Chelten-ham, especially for wearing in the West Indies, though it proved to be too warm in the tropics. It is a very pretty stuff, flowers & small palms on a light yellow ground – I have worn it now quite dirty, & had it unpicked & washed by Ida; it looks quite like new again, & will be a strong & nice material for Annies quilt, it is so pleasant being able to make up something for children, without buying anything new. Of what remains she will get a nice little frock by and bye. This afternoon I must cut out sheets, & then I am quiet, & know that I can abide my time in peace, seeing both children have all they require. Constance is a great help to me now that I cannot work in the machine. You remember how stupid I was at home at cutting out, & always went to Florence for the smallest thing? I see now, "that where there is a will, there is a way" – because I cut out every thing for Annie, & make my own patterns when I have none. I spent a bad night again; my face & teeth were aching. I must have caught cold some time ago, because the whole side of my face aches & the ear too. Now it is better but still one tooth is so tender I cannot shut my mouth or chew properly. Yesterday Hampus told me, 2. poor Kolosch women had been doomed to be sacrificed, in consequence of one of their men having fallen ill, & they were accused of having used witchcraft to make him ill. The Kolosches believe in witchcraft, & when they find out the person whom they imagine to have used that power, he is tortured till he confesses, & is then sacrificed. Hampus let it be known that, if those women fled during the night into our fortress, they would be received. How is it possible to know of such an act intended to be put into execution without doing everything in your power to hinder it. Is it not awful? when, O when will those poor heathens be converted, & brought to the knowledge of the Blessed Truth? Never, I am afraid, as long as they are under russian power! & therefore it would be already much to be wished that England or America had been the possessors of our Colonies.[109] – I hope darling Mama, when you send

---

109 After the sale of Alaska the influence of the Orthodox Church remained weak among the Tlingit Indians in Sitka. "However, by forcing native children into the school and attacking important traditional practises, such as the potlatch [see below p. 221], the

the box, you will put in some new book just published in England. Has Thackeray written anything new? & Dickens? What is Henry painting? Has he finnished the 8. pictures for Lady Walgrave? I never see his name in the papers, & still I always flattered myself he was one of the first artists of England. I have asked him, when he sees you, to make me a pencil sketch, like the one of Henrietta Parker; he could do so, so well, if he only chose. [...] How I wonder if Uncle & Aunt Mary are in England when this letter arrives – how lovely for them to see their child! O! when I think of Aunt Mary & Uncle H[annay] never having seen their child during his endearing childhood, & I look at our little Annie, I feel how *terrible* that separation must be. But still I would not part with my husband either, and am truly glad my fate was not to go to India.[110]

Sunday 5/17 Feb[ruary]. More than one whole week has again slipped away, since I last wrote to you, my own darling Mother. The reason is, that I have not been well at all, and therefore neither had spirits or inclination to write. Since yesterday thank God I feel well again. I have been so feverish & weak, lost my appetite & drank glasses upon glasses of water, without slaking my thirst. I think the whole & only cause of my indisposition has been fatigue. Since the revisors are here, we have generally had card parties for them every Tuesday, and some ladies have been with me. The talking & laughter around me, & the increased heat of the room, acted so upon my nervous system, that I could not sleep in any degree of comfort, & could not get rid of a sensation of heat; my back ached so dreadfully too, & a few days ago, when Hampus went to the "Wasser Ball" at the club, & I was alone & felt so unwell, such an anxious feeling came over me, & such a nervousness at the thought of possibly being taken ill, without any creature being near me. When my Hampus came home, he made me get up & sponge my whole body with cold water, which greatly refreshed me. We are not going to have any parties more, at least Hampus will only ask a few gentlemen, & I will remain alone & at ease in my room. I cannot walk much now, the staircase is too much for me at the end of a walk – But with God's help I hope to go to church & receive the blessed Sacrament, with my precious husband next Sunday. The pastor says I can sit in the vestry in an easy chair during the common service, & come in for the communion service. Our benches are so wonderfully narrow & uncomfortable, I cannot possibly sit an hour & a half without moving. –

Koshkin is engaged to Sophie Klinkowström, since last night! He came early this

---

Presbyterians lost their appeal among the more conservative segment of the Tlingit population..." (Kan 1988, p. 518). See also Kan 1999 for a detailed account of the Tlingit and the Russian Orthodox Church before the sale of Alaska and the massive conversion to Orthodoxy in 1886-1895.

110 Anna's grandmother, Mary Frazer of Fairfield (1785-1843), went to India together with a sister who was married to an English officer. In India Mary Frazer of Fairfield married Alexander Campbell (1772-1821). Their daughters Ann and Mary were born in India, but went to school in England (Pipping 1972). Anna's aunt Mary returned to India, where she married Simon Frazer Hannay, who was an officer (Pipping 1967, p. 194).

morning to tell us, looking so happy & pleased. At 12. we went to congratulate the Braut [Ger. bride] & her parents – the latter are very pleased though the Mother sad at the thought of parting, & the young girl looked too sad & inclined to cry at the same thought. I have prayed God heartily & sincerely, that He may bless them, & that they will be happy. She is so young still, not quite 18! But a very good, sweet girl, & he is a good young man. I told her not to cry & look sad on her Verlobungs-tag [Ger. day of engagement], what would her fiancé think? & the parting is still so far off. But I could understand her too, & sympathize with her and the Mother. I remember well how it was with me – but that was only, when we were alone, before Hampus I did not look sad – his character is so modest & unostentatous, & his thoughts of himself so very, very small, it would have made him miserable to see me cry, & made him think I repented of the step I had taken, & could not love him. Besides which, was it wrong of me my Mother, or did it hurt or grieve you, I *did* feel joy in my heart, & such deep gratitude, I think it would have been wrong to mourn having once given my word. […]

Tuesday. Here I was interrupted by my Hampus, who had not been at home that evening. You must excuse bad & crooked writing & lines, as I sometimes write lying on the sopha, which is not so convenient. We are asked to the Maksutoffs tonight, Hampus will go alone, I do not wish or feel disposed to go any where now. The nurse came to see me yesterday & says the child is beginning to fall, so it is as I have calculated, there can only be 4. weeks remaining. I do not feel so well now, as I did with little Annie, & rather heavier. I shall indeed be truly thankful, when it is all over; of course I don't rejoice at the bodily pain in prospect, but still thank God I am not afraid. Perhaps this time 4. or 5. hours will finnish it all. God grant it may be so, & that I may nurse this Baby. I am preparing all the tiny, tiny things for the washing again – When I look at them, my whole heart fills with Joy, & I wonder how fast the time has gone! But a short time ago, our bonny Annie was wearing them, & now she is such a very big child. She has 4. large grinding teeth, & the eyeteeth are just coming, so she will have 14. But talking & walking she is backward in, tho' she understands all you say to her. Ida has taught her to show on the large map of the world which hangs in the diningroom, where Grandpapa, Grandmama, & little Annie lives – Just about the situation of Sitka, there happens to be a small hole in the map, so she never makes a mistake – but I am astonished to see how easily & fast she comprehends, or do all mothers think the same of their offspring? – […] We were reading about Geology last night, out of Chambers information for the people. A most useful, instructing work, touching on all subjects, both scientific and practical. It is wonderful how little I know; – when I read about geology for instance, it cannot help striking me, how many wonders are daily before our eyes, without our ever giving them a thought, or taking the slightest knowledge or notice of them. We take up a piece of stone, & find it interveined with some different substance, either softer or harder, or of a different colour, without ever thinking what it means, or what can have been the cause, but remain quite satisfied that it must always have been so, &

was originally from the foundation of the world, made so. I remember you began reading a german work on Geology to us aloud at Ilfracombe, but I did not care for it; now I grieve over my want of knowledge on so many, many things necessary for an educated person to be at home in; but, as it is never too late to learn, I hope I shall improve still, with Hampus help. Only fancy, gold[111] has been found in our colonies, without any means having been employed to find out its bed! this Hampus "kom underfund med" [Swed. learned] a few days ago, & of course the gentlemen upstairs have a new source for dissatisfaction.

Sunday 12/24. Today I was at church for the last time for many weeks; we went to the Sacrament together; it was so beautiful, & I feel so happy & thankful, & trust my sins are freely & fully forgiven me, & that the Holy Spirit will help & guide me to lead a better life here after. I sat all the time in the vestry where the good Pastor had put an easy chair & footstool for me, & was consequently able to enjoy the whole service comfortably, without growing faint or sick. When we came home, after prayers, I read a long chapter of the Saints everlasting rest, aloud to my Hampus, who enjoyed it as much as I did. I have from today stopped dining upstairs; there are only 3. weeks remaining now, & I prefer leading that time quietly & undisturbedly, preparing myself for the great Blessing God is promising us. It is also more convenient for me, for sitting strait & upright so long, fatigues me, & there is no knowing at what time, or how soon I may be taken ill. It might even be before the 3. weeks are out. The night before last I had 2 or 3. nightmares, one very bad one, but the others were slighter. I notice that I only have them when I am pregnant, & then usually if my bowels have not acted properly – as a young girl I never remember screaming in my dream. […] Annie now begins to understand the use of her feet, & is making her first tiny attempts at walking, being supported under the arms – I fancy she will make great progress in every way during the time I am ill and shall not see so much of her; may she only not be spoilt by Ida, who will see most of her, & for whom she is already "mycket svag" [Swed. very fond of], her own Baby instinct telling her I suppose, that Ida is very fond of children, & rather fond of giving them everything they ask for, which is not what I allow when I see it. I wonder if Florence will nurse her Baby long, and if it will agree well with her, which I hope & trust it may. The princesse here grew so dreadfully thin & had stitches in her shoulders, she was obliged to give up nursing at 6. months, & still has not recovered. In August she is again expecting to be confined, & has made up her mind not to nurse this time, as she is sure it would harm her. It is a great pity she should be so delicate. I saw her little Annie yesterday; she is a very fair child, not fat, but walks almost alone, tho' 6. weeks younger than our Annie; they will be such nice little playmates by & bye.

Monday March 4th/Feb[ruary] 20. Good morning my own beloved Mother. On this your youngest child's 25th Birthday, (O, how fast youth is going down hill! how! I don't like it at all) I must write to you, knowing for a certainty, that you

---

111 See the epilogue, p. 255.

are sometime of the day doing the same to me, & that you have prayed for me, & laid your precious hands on my head & sent me a true, deep & loving "God bless you, my child, & those whom the Lord has given you!" – I woke this morning by Hampus warm lips touching me, & his dear voice saying "God bless you my own darling Wife". He had prepared a surprise for me, notwithstanding his constant roguish assurance that he was so distressed at having nothing for me. When I came out from behind the curtains, I saw a pretty polished music stand beside the piano, with all my notes arranged on the shelves. I had often wished for one, and Hampus remembering it, had one made for me. It looks so nice, & gave me so much pleasure. On the breakfast table, on my place, covered with green twigs & leaves, lay a worked apron for little Annie, so nicely done, with a chain of blue silk loops worked all around it, by Constance. The Fürstin made one for her little Annie, & Constance on seeing me admire it, made one exactly the facimilar for me. My own bonny little darling came in all dressed in white, before I had left my room, to kiss & congratulate Mama. She gives such sweet little round kisses now, & is so amused at the sound. She is now wearing those pretty little red & black morocco shoes her darling Grand mama sent her; they are the first she is wearing; they fit so nicely, & give her great delight to look at & often pull off. The lilac ones, if you remember, are too small, as she began standing so late, but perhaps they will fit the next one! Annie begins to use her legs now, & calls it "tap, tap ta" but woefully crooked she moves her little legs, it cannot be called walking, but it amuses her to hear the sound of her feet. Poor Constance has been very ill since this day week; we have been quite separated, only seeing each other a minute or 2. during the day. On Thursday she had 5. fits in 9. hours, & bruised her poor face so – the whole afternoon she lay in an unconscious state, mostly sleeping, not touching a morsel of food. I did not recognize her the next morning, so she was changed – she has no remembrance of that day or notices anything around her since then, but seems like one in a dream; her articulation too is thick & confused. On Sunday she would insist it was friday & worked all the day. She has never been so ill here yet, & I grieve to say, she seems to be going back again. Today she has had no fit, & looks better & more like herself. On Saturday night quite late she came with her maid to ask for a soda powder – her heart was literally jumping, & her body shaking – poor, poor thing, it is the worst affliction I can think of. God has mercifully & wonderfully preserved me from seeing her fall. It is impossible the same medicin, which she has now been using nearly 4. years, can do any more good – It certainly strengthened her at first, but now her constitution is accustomed to it, & it cannot have the same effect more. We are curious to see what my father in law will write about her, as Hampus has proposed sending her home to live with poor solitary Esperance. A country life is what suits her best, & what she most likes.

This day week is my beloved's Birthday, & this day fortnight?!! – God knows *whose*! I am almost sure it will be on that day. Later than tomorrow fortnight it cannot. –

Wednesday March 15/27. Darling, precious Mother! A son! A little darling, blue eyed fat, bonny Boy! We have got him, the Boy you have all been expecting so impatiently! Are you not happy? I am so very, very happy. Our precious angel was born at ¼ to 1. on the morning of 4th/16 March, twelve days ago, & this is thank God the 3rd day I am on the sopha, & God be praised for His great mercy, am quite well, & all went well, though I suffered awfully this time.

On Thursday 3rd I felt very fatigued on going to bed. I had had a poor, unhappy lady with her child to dinner & spend the day with me, & in the afternoon Miss Klinkow-ström came. I was working & moving about as usual, but when they were gone I said to Puxti that I felt quite exhausted, & it would soon come on. That night Hampus slept in his own room, & we lighted a nightlamp, thinking it safest to be prepared. The room was quite in order since Wednesday, & every thing necessary was in its place. At a little before 6. on friday morning I awoke feeling a lazy kind of pain in the back & around the lower part of the stomach. I remained quiet for half an hour to see if they would continue, & as they did so went in to call & tell my Hampus. At 7. I sent for the midwife to ask her opinion, fancying a 2nd confinement would, or at least might progress so rapidly, it would be best not to delay too long. When she came and had made her examination, she said she could not say if I should be delivered that day or not, they were only false pains. However, she preferred remaining with me instead of coming up those awful stairs again. (she is 50 years old, has had 15. children & suffers much now.)[112] All day passed like that, wearisome & tiresome, the pains being very small. At 6. in the evening however they commenced to give real pain, & at 8. they were very severe, & I knew now real labour had come on, as violent shivering fits came over me, like the last time. I walked about, supported by Hampus mine, sitting also & lying alternately till 11. when I felt I must lie down. My own Puxti was very brave up till that time, & was constantly round me, and when I lay down for good, during the absence of pain he knelt down beside my bed & prayed with me! The pains were now very, very severe, more so than with Annie, but from 12. o'clock & especially the last half hour they were *so awful*, I thought I could not live through it. For one half hour I screamed without intermission, & would never have supposed it possible a woman could scream so. At last at ¼ to 1. my sufferings were at an end, & the strong crying of the child, filled my whole soul with deepest gratitude & infinite Joy. Hampus rushed into the room the same moment, & was indeed happy, for the last hour he had not been in the room. "A son"! were the nurses first words, & soon I held the little creature in my arms, wrapped up in its flanel shawl. How I wished to have you near me my own beloved Mother, & how I have longed for you all these days. *Friday 17/29.* This is the 14th day & I am getting stronger & stronger every day; in fact I think I might call myself quite well, were it not for one thing, which though much better than it was, still causes me pain. This is, sore nipples. O Mama! can I ever express my infinite joy & gratitude at having sufficient nourishment for my

---

112 Anna probably refers to her creole midwife E. Terent'eva.

child? – You know, how sadly disappointed I was not to be able to nurse my Annie, &
how I have prayed God to permit me this time to perform that sweetest of a Mothers
duties. Well, on the morning of 3rd day, the breasts were painfully hard & extended,
still there was little milk and the child cried & would not take the nipple. The nurse
thinking the nipple too small, (though Annie & a child of 4. months had taken it before
when I tried every means to induce the milk to come) applied an pulling out machine,
which pained me much, & immediately the nipples felt sore & tender. On [the] 4th
day there was milk & I suffered the first 4. days excrutiating pain, & could not help
crying, each time the child sucked. They were very hot & red & dry. I washed them
with "Benzen[?] Tincture" which Willebrand recommended, but after several days
trial and the nipples still being very painful, though no longer dry & hot, the nurse
persuaded me to try tallow, which she declared would cure them in 3 or 4. days. Well
I have been smearing them ever since with warm tallow, washing them before & after
suckling with milk & water, & certainly they are thank God much better, especially
the right breast, which is nearly healed, but the left breast has still got a big crack on
one side in the centre of the nipple, where I a little time ago discovered some matter;
Hampus made me again try the tincture, which he smeared into the crack, & I am now
only waiting for the child to wake to give him that breast, & then we shall see how it
feels. I am indeed happy to have got over the worst part as I trust, though it required
much courage & perseverance and I called in Ida to talk to me & einflössen mir Mut
[Ger. inspire me with courage] during nursing. My darling Hampus was immediately
for me giving up nursing when he saw how I suffered but that I would & could not
hear of. It is a great pity is it not – & I never thought my nipples would crack, as I
used Bulls lotions 2. months before both confinements, though I must confess this
last time not daily. So! now my little fellow is awake & crying for food. Goodbye so
long. – *Evening ¼ past 5.* Thank God the pain was not greater than it was yesterday,
& I trust in a few days the nipples will both be quite well. The first nights, or rather
all nights up to yesterday, Baby got the sucking bottle once or twice, in order to let
my sores heal faster; the first days I had not sufficient milk either, but now he has not
had the bottle at all, & I am thankful to say have enough to supply his wants. How
exquisitely sweet to feel your own child drawing its nourishment from yourself, and
to see how all tears & troubles cease as soon as it comes to its mothers breast. I know
you & darling Florence will rejoice with me to hear I can nurse this time. Now, my
own darling Mother I must tell you of a great, great joy I had on the 6th evening
after my confinement. "Nakimoff" came back from San Fr[ancisco] & brought me
such a delightful post. Ten thousands thanks precious Mother for y[ou]r sweet letter
No. 25. begun at Troizkoe & ended to my infinite surprize at Dresden; if you could
only picture to y[ou]rself my happiness on finding y[ou]r picture enclosed! I could
not satisfy myself looking at it, & shed tears of intense Joy. It is *so like you* though
you have grown very thin, & in y[ou]r whole face I read Sehnsucht [Ger. longing]
after y[ou]r absent children, though you do not look unhappy. Thank you over &
over again treasure Mother. O! I am so thankful to hear you are all well & calm &

happy & contented! Darling Mother! God will hear your children's warmest & ardent
prayer that your life henceforth may be full of peace, & joy hitherto unknown! &
O! He will permit us to meet again, & you to fold y[ou]r precious grandchildren to
y[ou]r heart, & rejoice in y[ou]r children's happiness. Though my Hampus forbid me
to read any of the letters he brought me, the temptation was too great, & I could not
sleep before I had slowly read yours, & my own Ponnies. All good news! thank God
for that. But my head is in a confusion about the Dresden visit; how came you to be
staying with the Miss Macleans? & then again with darling Mrs Hawthorne? *Tuesday
21/2nd April*. Again a few days have passed, and thank God we are both progressing
satisfactorily, though I cannot conceive why Baby's bowels will not get quite in order;
he passes rather curdled greenish, yellowish motions, & still I eat nothing improper,
not even venturing upon potatoes or any vegetables, only eating soups, meat & some
light puddings. Since yesterday I have begun nursing him at regular intervals of 3.
hours, & hope to stick to it, though it is a little bit difficult, when he sets up a dreadful screaming, as he did yesterday afternoon. The nurse would have me nurse him
continually, whenever he begins to cry, but that is nonsense, & must of course bring
on indigestion & deranged bowels. He slept exceedingly well all night, being nursed
at 9. ½ past 1. & again in the morning at 4. and did not cry at all.

Thank you, sweetest Mama, for the pleasant & unexpected surprize you gave
me. On the 8th day, in the afternoon, Hampus came to my bedside & asked me
what I would say to what he had to give me. He pulled out slowly 2. letters out of
his coatpocket, one from dearest Mrs H[awthorne] the other from Pauline, & said,
that was all – but I knew there would be something else – so out came first Mrs
H[awthorne] extra. A book with those lovely verses of yours & Mrs Duffins, which
I had so much wished to have, then the stamped embroidery frills, which are indeed
useful & the very thing I required, & lastly Dr v[on] Ammon's exellent little book
which I have nearly finished reading, & am delighted to have. It was indeed such
joy to get a present from you darling Mother, so perfectly unexpectedly, & to see
y[ou]r darling handwriting in the book – thank you over & over again my own
Mother. [...] Well are you not glad to hear of Prince Louis engagement to Princesse
Alice of England? I saw it in the newspaper, and was so pleased. I can fancy him very
much in love – he makes indeed a good match. I wonder where they will live. The
Bockelberg's palais would be too small I suppose, & the old palace, where the Balls
are given, is so dingy & dull. What preparations there will be at old D[armstadt] &
how nice to have an *english princesse*! I should like to see her, & am sure she will
be very popular & beloved. Some day I dare say the queen will be coming to visit
her daughter. To think that we knew Prince Louis so well, & have so often, often
danced with him; yes played & cooked pancakes too! – Can it be "Mr Point[?]" who
is announced as "Baron Westerweller" in his suit? Where will solus [Latin lonely,
single] Prince Heinrich find a Wife?[113] Perhaps he will be the Prince Emil of the fam-

---

113 Prince Heinrich later married morganatically in 1878 and in 1895.

ily – younger sons of small kingdoms are not to be envied. Do you think the Prince of Wales[114] will marry princesse Anna? Wilhelmine says, she is much liked, being perfectly free from ostentation or pride, but is very shy, & badly dressed at Balls. If there are engravings of the young betrothed I wish you could send them to me. –

And now darling Mother, how do you like England? och huru trifvas du der [Swed. how do you feel there]? if I only knew how you intend settling yourself & *where*? How is our dear old faithful Babette? give her my dear love, & einen schönen Gruss [Ger. best wishes] from my Hampus. You will both miss Ormelie much, but then it is well he is now settled in an english establishment, as english he is & England or India will be his Home. How charming to see him grown into a tall, fine youth! but God knows, when we shall meet again! for I suppose we must return thro' Siberia, though I should like going home the way we came, & then we would be the first to visit you in England! But I am afraid the Company would not give us enough, & with children, & consequently of necessity servants, it would be too expensive for us. […] Darling Mother! I suppose you will never receive the box with the real Colibris? the ship arrived at Cronstadt, just when you left S[ain]t P[eter]b[ur]g, and I fancy it would be very expensive to send it on to you. I am very sorry, & should not like the views of Sitka to be lost. Hampus had a letter from young Bergenheim from Honolulu, in which he thanks us so sincerely for all the pleasure our house had afforded him, & for the pleasure Mr Hackfeld's house had been thro' Hampus kind introduction. It is nice to see the young man's gratitude & good feeling. Mr Hackfeld congratulates Hampus on the high & honourable office he holds, & makes such a fine compliment about me, which he must have taken from the clouds. I wish fate would throw some of the english officers from the "Alert" in your way; it would be such a pleasure for you. I wonder if you met Capt[ain] Ridelle, & if he could tell you anything, for he is rather a lazy talker. I hope Henry did all I bid him, and that the russian Samovar arrived unbroken. He must be in England now, & my letter in your hands. O dear! how many of my letters to you are still unanswered. Well thank God! the effects of regular nursing are already apparent. A good & healthy motion has just been passed, so I am perfectly reconciled to let him cry when it is not time for him to be nursed. I am so very glad, for I already thought my milk might not be good. –

I had told the nurse to dress him in his english clothes from the beginning, but she insisted upon bandaging him up like a stick, with his poor little arms pinned to his side, saying he could not sleep with his arms free, but today I have thrown aside those horrible russian clothes, & dressed him in his nice english ones, which are warm lose & light. I am sure he would thank me if he only could. He looks about with his soft blue eyes, & even smiles with his eyes open, but I doubt that he recognizes any objects yet. Why can you not see & love my Babies? We ordered *"Dr Combe on*

---

114 Prince Edward of Wales, the future Edward VII (1841-1910), married Princess Alexandra of Denmark (1844-1925) in 1863.

infancy" from San Fr[ancisco]; it seems also to be a good & wholesome book, and doubtless by the author of the physiology of health. *Wednesday.* Today Hampus startled me by the intelligence that "Garitza" goes on Monday, & that he himself will go after one fortnight. I could not believe my ears. So soon! so soon he will be gone! O precious Mother, it is so very sad always to be separated, & not within reach of the post. I will write you a few lines again by Hampus, but this letter will afford you sufficient reading for one month at least. If we were fortunate enough to have a fine sumer, it would be a great recreation, for I could spend whole days with the children & my work in the garden, & even dine there. I must take regular walks too, & will ask the Pastor to accompany me. The princesse will not be able to take long walks in July & August, at the end of which month she expects her confinement. I like her very much, & am glad to say we agree & sympathize so well. The day before yesterday she came with her work & spent 4. hours with me. We came to speak about Gods beautiful & wonderful creations, about original sin, & how sad it was that for one man's sin's all the world to come should have fallen under the same doom, which she thought was difficult to understand or explain. But I said I did not think it more wonderful, than that one man should have died for all, & shed his precious blood to save *all mankind*, which is indeed past comprehension, for who can conceive such love, such a sacrifice? One thing led to the other, we compared our thoughts & views on a future state & involuntary I thought of our dearest Friend, Mrs Hawthorne, & spoke to her about her saintly life, & told her the story of her beloved ones, till she said "one cannot help feeling great interest in her, even though she is a complete stranger". – One day, I will read those lovely poems to her. Talking about friendship, & what a beautiful tie it is, & how God has favored us all our lives thro' in that respect, I said, that I also considered it a providential act, that we had been thrown together here, in this far remote out of the way place, & that I hoped we should always continue to be friends, seeing that any friendship founded on our circumstances, & many similarity in the story of our courtship & marriage, ought to be lasting & true. Her eyes filled with tears & she kissed me & said, she often thought with such regret of the time when we should leave Sitka & they be staying, & how much she would miss me. Now, the princesse is not a person of demonstrations, no more am I except to my *very own*, but I know that every word she says is true, and that she is an upright, sincere character. She said her father, to whom she had written to say we were on such good terms, had expressed his satisfaction at it & said, he hoped it would be a friendship, that neither *time* nor *distance* would change. Fancy how different it would be, if amongst all the ladies I meet here, & must often invite, there was not a single educated and refined mind, and one with whom you could find other, than merely trivial topics of conversation? besides it is true, as the princesse observed, though one is ever so happy with one's husband, a woman likes a female friend too. You will be glad to hear this.

Our little treasure Baby Boy, is thank God, thriving very well, his face is so round & fat & he was born with a double chin; my nipples are now healed I am happy to say, and I have more milk than he drinks, & am obliged to change hankerchiefs & towels continually, for when the breasts are overfull, the milk runs out in big drops, so that everything about me gets wet. Well darling Mother, how do you like the name "*Otto Edwin Furuhjelm*" as we have now decided upon calling him? I wanted one name to be Hampus, but my husband will not allow it on *any account*. Otto is after his Grandpapa, but he will be called Edwin, which I think is such a very pretty name. His Godparents will be: *Grandmama A[nn] & Grandpapa O[tto] Uncle Fabian & Marie L[angenskiöld], Mina Gripenberg & Harald F[uruhjelm], Henry Phillips & Dascha [von Schoultz], Eugénie Lille & Uncle Eduard [von] S[choultz], Constance & Esperance.*

My Puxti is a very lazy letter writer, though I must say he has abundance to write by each mail, & no very pleasant or agreeable letters, which makes him postpone private letters, always thinking he will have more time & leisure & less preoccupied thoughts next time. […]

Monday 27. The secretary has just asked me when my letters will be ready, & as he will call for them this afternoon, I must hasten to finnish. Thank God for His mercy in permitting me to conclude in good health, & the child too. My Hampus has written to you as you see – he is really overwhelmed with papers. I shall be truly glad when those gentlemen upstairs are gone, & our house will regain its usual quiet & peace. I do not think I have forgotten to tell you anything & feel really perfectly *outwritten* now – 9. letters is no small number – […] I fancy my last long letter with list of comissions has reached you now, & that you are beginning to buy for me. In a fortnight I will write a short letter with my own Darling. By the bye, have you ever had to pay for my letters? tell me please, for I never omit to put "paid" on them, & a letter of this thickness would I am afraid cost several shillings. Now Good bye & God bless & preserve you my own beloved Mother. Y[ou]r 2. precious God- & grandchildren send kisses, in which joins

Y[ou]r ever fondly loving Child

A[nna] Furuhjelm
April 8. 1861

No. 42   *Good friday*. April 21st/May 3 1861. Sitka.

My own precious Mother! Today I have been to church for the first time since my confinement, and cannot say how happy & thankful I am. Pastor Winter held german service & communion today – how much I wished to go to the Sacrament too, but without my beloved husband, who has now been gone a fortnight, I did not like to go, & have never been *alone* to the blessed Sacrament in all my life. Pastor W[inter] gave us a very good sermon – he preaches with true earnestness & conviction. He is a most worthy & excellent man, & I like him more and more. We have now become more acquainted with him, though you will be astonished to hear it has required nearly 2. years for that purpose. But he is so very shy & retiring, & seems always to be "generad" [Swed. (feel) awkward] with Hampus, tho' I cannot conceive *why*, as Hampus likes him very much and knows him many years.

Tuesday in Easter week. Such a lovely, warm day, the first fine one during the whole holy days. Not quite an hour ago, I came home from making my tours of visits; yesterday was my reception day, all the ladies came to congratulate, as is the custom here. I am glad it is over, & before New years day next year I shall not be obliged to receive them again. It has been a sad & dreary time for me, first because Hampus is not here, and secondly because I have had much to disturb me, and distress me in my household. I have before mentioned the little orphan Palasha, whom we had taken to bring up. I thought she would turn out a good child, seeing she was treated so well, & cared for like an own child – but unfortunately all pains are lost with her; I have really broken my head how to make her obey, & how to make her ashamed of always doing wrong. Good words & kindness, punishments small & great, forgiveness & forgetfulness over & over again, is all to the same purpose, she remains the same, & laughs at me behind my back, & is ten times worse. It has really grieved me to see her want of heart & appreciation of the goodness she has met with. *I* want no thanks, no! it is not for that I have tried to keep her these 2. years, but because she was a poor orphan, & has no one in the world to care for her – & it was pleasant to do good. But now I am after all obliged to send her to school, as I cannot manage her, & have daily, yes hourly "förargelse" [Swed. trouble] with her.

Sunday April 30. Precious Mother! Since I wrote these lines, I have had a very lovely surprise; my own Hampus returned last Thursday, looking so well & grown so sunburnt, after exactly three weeks absence. I am so happy to have him back again, you cannot think, and it was delightful to see him so much sooner than I expected. Now please God, I hope to keep him all this summer & all the year, tho' he sometimes frightens me by saying he will make another voyage this summer. All has thank God, gone well, & by next Thursday, we hope to be rid, & for ever, of our unpleasant winter guests. I have never yet met with, or come in contact with so thoroughly coarse & unprincipled man as the Statsrådet, he makes no secret of it either – I think the air we breathe will be purer when he is no more near us. Now I must tell you about myself & our children. Up to the day that Hampus went away, he had been sleeping in his own room, & our darling Baby & her nurse with me, but when he was gone, I moved Eddie & his nurse into Hampus room, in order that he might not be disturbed by my visitors or by Constance & myself. He had a bad cold in his nose & was even hoarse a few days, but now he is well again I am happy to say. However he gives me much anxiety in another way; his bowels are obstinately costive, & have been so all his little life. Two, 3. days pass without any motion, & I am again obliged to give him castor oil, or a lavement or Rhubarb & magnesia. I have tried rubbing his stomach with warm oil, but it has not the least effect on him, & *one* teaspoonful of castor oil does not either act, I must give him one & a half. I have taken doses of Epsom salt myself, but equally to no purpose, and I must say, that since I am nursing, my bowels are very, very sluggish and obstinate too. Today & yesterday the Darling has screamed dreadfully & slept very little, evidently some pain in his little stomach – I know not what to do, & I have asked our doctor too, who could give me no advise. Otherwise he is round & fat & plump & a very strong child, turning his head & looking all round about – he smiles & crows so sweetly, & is such a precious, precious Baby, with bright, bright eyes. Our Annie is growing cleverer each day; I mean she learns something new from day to day. You should see her now, running on her own little feet, so fast, so fast – She is only still afraid to go for any length of time quite alone, though she can walk alone, & calls it "tap, tap ta". She says: God dag! Adjö [Swed. hello, goodbye], good night, & is so droll and funny. Hampus is quite enchanted to come home to us all, & it is *such* joy to see his bright & happy face. –

I had such a "deménagement" [Fr. rearrangement of furniture] the evening my Darling came home, but during the one hour I had to do it in, all was got ready. Eddie was transported into the nursery, & brought back again the first night – but now conceive the discomfort of our house, as he disturbs his Papa at night, & it is unpleasant to have the nurse in the same room; he sleeps in the nursery, & I am obliged to get up at night & go there to nurse him, as it would never do to carry him once or twice during the night, over an "Vorplatz" [Ger. approximately landing] through the diningroom into our room. Is not this discomfort? but I cannot do it otherwise, without leaving my Hampus quite during the 9. months I hope to nurse, & sleeping in the nursery, which I would never do. My husband is my husband, & with him is my place, I would not agree to leave him. But this is not the only inconvenience, for of course a little Baby must cry, & then he disturbs poor little Annie. If Constance returns to Finland next year, we must take her room, which lies on the other side of the nursery, as a second nursery, & combine the two by a little passage which is easily done – It is a happiness to have *one* child, but it is nicer still to have two! O! what Blessings, what earthly bliss our Father grants & gives us! Can we ever sufficiently thank Him! – While Hampus was gone, my time past in attending to the children, in walking & working for Annie, who is so tall & so stout, she continually requires new clothes. Pastor Winter accompanied us daily to the Kolosch river through the wood. I like & esteem him much, he is an exellent man & truly serious Christian. I would be glad were he to remain here as long as we do, but it may be he returns next spring with Hjalmar. The Kolosches are afraid of Hampus, so I think we have nothing to fear of them – but still there are continual annoyances & disagreeables for Hampus, & I see daily more & more, that being Governor, is not exactly an enviable position, though it has its great advantages too – but the responsibility is great, & the demands made are great, & he has little peace during his reign. There is a great deal which ought to be better in our Colonies, but five years is not enough time to do any thing properly, & instead of every Governor continuing & finnishing what his predecessor has begun, each one begins over again with his new plans, & so, nothing "*helt*" [Swed. complete] can be accomplished.

Tuesday. The day after tomorrow the gentlemen will go, and our letters with them. I think I have not told you that our little Edwin was christened the Sunday before Hampus left home, & behaved so well all the time, he did not cry once, but kept his sweet blue eyes fixed on the Princesse all the time. He had the same long robe that Annie had worn, but the embroidered cap which I had bought in England but not used for her, as it was too large & unfortunately the lovely lace cap Mrs Hawthorne sent, was too small for him. He caught a severe cold in his head that day, which only has left him a short time ago. The Thursday after the christening his Papa went to Codiac, in most horrible weather & fair tho' strong wind. It was so sad to part, but still there was a solace in the thought of seeing him return after 5 weeks – what was then my Joy to receive him home on the very day 3. weeks. I had been walking every day since Good friday, & my Hampus found me looking well and strong, & thank God I feel quite well, & nursing does not fatigue me at all. The days & nights having become warmer, I have Edwin brought in to me to nurse at night, & find that a better arrangement. He is a prettier Baby than our darling Annie was, & smiles & crows so sweetly, but he cries much more, & sleeps rather less than she did during the day, tho' he sleeps very well at night. It is such infinite Joy to have these precious little Children! Annie gives us more pleasure each day, she runs about alone now, though at times she is a little afraid still, & screams aloud for Joy "Annie Annie tap tap". I taught her to say, "Papa Codiac" when she was asked where he was, and now she says *"Papa home"*. A conglomoration of languages is in her little head, she says *"ja! nein!"* [Ger. yes, no] *please, God dag! Adjö Golou! Golou!* (russian for pigeons) you see every thing mixed up together, and understands everything you ask her. The much longed for & eagerly expected Brigg from Hamburg with stores for our magazine has brought very little; prints & cottons which are so much wanted here have not been sent at all, but instead, 7 pieces of coloured silks!! – So now we must dress our children in silk frocks! & no one can scold us for being extravagant. I am curious to hear what they cost, they were sent up for me to look at today.

Wednesday. […] Write to darling Florence & tell her about us, & give our fondest love – tell me advise for little Babies stomachs – I have ordered Bull aperient lineament of soap & aloes to be made, as his bowels are *never* relieved without artificial help. Sitka is perfectly green already, & the air is mild, but our West wind is cold.

Hampus même [Fr. himself], is well & strong thank God, & in such good spirits – he sends his dearest love – May the peace of our Lord Jesus abide with you for ever, dearest, dearest Mother
prays Your own fondly loving Child

Annie Furuhjelm.

Love to dear Babette & Ormelie and all friends.

No. 43   Government House
                                                                 Sitka May 22. 1861.

This is the 3rd time this month that I am writing to you my own beloved Mother.
It seems almost wrong, were I to let any opportunity slip by, without sending you
some news of us, though it is not much or anything new I have to say. Two vessels
are expected from San Fr[ancisco] within a short time of each other. God grant I may
receive letters by each. I repeat my earnest request over and over again, precious
Mother, write regularly every month; for during the sumer months our vessels
often go to California, whereas during the winter we have no means of receiving
our letters. My long letter sent over Ajan on 20. May last year is still unanswered,
it was No. 35, consequently 7. letters are still unanswered. –

   If you still have my checked india muslin skirt, how I wish you had put it into
the parcel I am expecting next year, for *such* stuff I am so very much in need of;
more and more I mourn over the many things I left behind me, which would all
have been of use to me here. Our precious children are thank God quite well. Annie
walks quite alone & speaks many & mostly all, english words. "Bodder (brother)
Eddie" she says and is so very fond of him. Baby treasure crows & laughs so sweetly
and has a large appetite. He cries very little now, ever since I regulate his bowels
by giving him every morning a little oil; he is bathed in the evening at 6. & goes to
sleep generally at the breast about ½ past 6 from which time he sleeps till 3. or 4. in
the morning without budging, but this night to everybody's astonishment, he slept
his round 12. hours, a great deal for an infant of not yet 3. months. How you would
love our little pets, darling Mother. Eddie is a pretty baby; – his Pappa constantly
says: "really what a fine Boy he is" – I must still tell you one thing that surprised
and grieved me at first, but since I have seen that it does in no way affect my Baby, I
am quiet again. Four days ago my monthly periods returned, & I was afraid it would
much diminish & deteriorate my milk & make him restless. Thank God nothing of
the kind has happened and I feel *perfectly* well, stronger than I generally do at such
a time. Perhaps it will do Eddie good, as my milk is said to be too strong, & it may
become less so now. Please God, I hope each month Baby will thrive equally well. I
was quite astonished, as I never thought it would happen to me, but it may be that
I am too "vollblutig" [Ger. full of blood] –

   Darling Mother, I thought I had more time – but Hampus sends for my letter,
therefore forgive my abruptness, and write soon. With fondest love and kisses from
us all four and much love to Ponnie, Charlie & Mary, and all dear friends I bid you
Goodbye –
God bless you my own precious Mother, prays
   Y[ou]r own Child

                                                         Annie F[uruhjelm]

Otto Edwin Furuhjelm (1861-1918) as Imperial 'Kammerpage' (a young officer serving at court), probably 1880. By courtesy of Johan Furuhjelm.

No. 44   Sitka. May 14/26. 1861.

[...]

No. 45   Government House. Sitka. June 26/ July 7. 1861.

My own precious Mother,
[...] Our precious little Edwin is such a very bonny little boy, really pretty, & is
very gentle & good, as good as Annie was & cries still less than she did at his age.
He sleeps all night thro' sometimes being brought to me at 4. o'clock in the morning to be nursed for the first time since 6 or 7. But will you believe it, his bowels
are still at nearly 4. months as obstinate as they were when I last wrote. Nothing,
nothing but medicine every day or he has no motion. We have now tried everything
Bull recomends & are now giving him twice a day barley water with very little milk,
which Dr Combe recomends when the bowels are sluggish, but all the same; We are
now really quite at our wits end what to do, as nothing we try has any good effect &
are afraid if it goes on so, he will never be able to do without medicine. He is fat and
rosy, sleep well and is quiet, surely all signs that my milk is good – but why then is
his nature so costive? Oh that we had an experienced physician to call in for advise
what to do. The only consequence of the state of his bowels is Dandruff, which Bull
also mentions, & says it often comes from costiveness or ill management & general
want of cleanliness. The later is perfectly out of the question here, so I can only account for it in the other way, as Annie hadn't it. I have repeatedly washed Baby's
head with vinegar & smeared it with oil, but the little minute white scales grow so
very fast again. I was just now painfully interupted by poor Constance's 6th fit today.
Poor child! how deeply I pity her; I have now seen her fits, & of course instead of
runing away, have helped, having no reason to fear for myself; it is something awful
to see; the whole first night I could not forget it – the cramps are so powerful & the
distortion of the face so frightful to witness, it fills one with the deepest sympathy
– How merciful are Gods ways; even in the bitterest cup there is a Blessing, for what
excrutiating pain must it not be, when the cramps are sometimes so violent, that
persons have dislocated some or other joint, but as they are unconcious, they do not
feel it. The sight of her dreadful affliction, has filled my whole heart with repentance
for the feeling of annoyance & often impatience I have given way to, either created
by her great inquisitiveness and offence when we speak english before her, or her
wishing to interfere, when knowing how afflicted she is, one ought to carry her on
ones hands, & do everything to lighten her burden. I shall henceforth strive & pray
God for assistance to improve, that I may have more of the spirit of Charity the
apostle speaks of. I must now write a few words to Ponnie.
   Sunday 2/14 July. Yesterday and today have been 2. most anxious days for us
– poor, poor Constance is dreadfully ill; she had 11. attacks yesterday, & last night

11. and since that till now 6½ p.m. 14. or 15. She has been unconscious since yesterday, & has scarcely awoken from one fit, before falling into a second. O Mama!
it is beyond description painful to see – the poor figure prostrated so entirely, the
large, vacant eyes, no possibility of speech, the rushing in her throat, as I have
heard people have before they die, but the doctor says it is only the foaming from
the mouth which cannot all come out. We stand by her bedside with aching hearts,
& with the earnest prayer, that if it be Gods Holy Will, He would mercifully call
her home & make an end of her fearful suffering. She was already this morning so
weak, she could not turn alone in bed; nothing has crossed her lips but a few spoons
of cold water which I tried to put into her mouth. The doctor bled her at 2. o'clock,
and for a short time afterwards the determination of the blood to the head was less,
but now it is the same again. I do not think she can live through another night if
the fits continue in the same frequency, and O! who would mourn were she to go
Home? none, I hope, even her nearest would lament over that a mercifully Father
had called his child & freed her poor suffering body from such awful chains of woe.
There she will be safe in her Saviours bosom, & be joined to her Mother she loved so
much on earth. But, were she to recover, I fear her mind will never, never recover,
and that would be still worse than before. *Gods Will be done* Amen! O! that we had
our good Pastor Winter here to pray for her – but he is absent for the summer. We
have taken Wendla again to nurse her, & tonight we will have 3. watching.

Tuesday Ev[enin]g 4/16 July. She is gone! her spirit has fled, and is ever now
through her precious Saviours blood, joining in everlasting songs of praise and glory,
with all redeemed spirits in Gods own Kingdom above. It seems wonderful, sometimes
it even appears incredible that all should have gone so, so fast. But O darling Mother,
you can never picture to yourself, and I hope may never, never see such an awful,
awful strugle of Life and Death and who should have the victory. On Sunday night
when I wrote she was already evidently dying, though Hampus would not believe
it. She had been bled in the afternoon, but all the same the fits continued to return
every half hour. Hampus and I went to bed near 11. and gave orders to be awoken at
2. and earlier if any change should occur. As is so often the case before life ebbs out,
she had slept rather quietly between 11. and 2, and at that hour when Hampus went
to her room, the nurse found her a little better. At 4. I went again, but saw a great
change in her face. Though her eyes were closed, there was such a look of suffering
over them, her cheeks were burning hot, the perspiration runing, & her poor chest
heaving & heart beating so violently that you could see the bedclothes move. At 7.
o'clock her mouth was open and nostrils extended and that awful sound of suffoca-
tion in her throat worse. She had had 5. and 3. fits in one hour, now she could not
swallow anymore. O! may she soon, soon be called Home, was my fervent prayer. I
had so feared she would suddenly choke during a fit, and consequently her features
remained fearfully distorted, and really dreaded to be alone with her at that moment.
But God was merciful, and permitted at least the last 5. minutes to be perfect peace.
My Hampus was in despair to see her and could not remain in the room. He went

A contemporary sketch of the graves of Constance Furuhjelm and Princess A.I. Maksutova.

out at 8. and said he would be back very soon. I went into the sick chamber with Bible and Aunt Mathilda's pocket prayer book, out of which I was reading preparation for death, when the doctor entered. She fell into a fit, but the spasms were weak already and twice I thought she was dying with a scream. She kept her eyes open after the cramps had passed and did not fall asleep as usual; her colour did not quite return and her lips remained blue – "She is dying" I said to the doctor, "O! will she still suffer much" – "No – not more than she has already" he replied, and a second fit came on – he left the room and I now saw she would soon expire, sent immediately for my husband, and fell down on my knees beside her bed – With my one hand on her forehead, & the other on her breast, praying in agony and fervour, and really thanking the Lord that He was taking His precious Lamb to Himself, she expired! After the 2nd fit, the rushing in her throat ceased, the breathing grew fainter & fainter, her eyes were looking upwards and a serene Beauty rested on her face; she looked like an angel; over and over again I kissed her forehead and neck, both were quickly growing cold – I put my ear to her mouth and hand to her heart all was still! our patient angel was gone – was for ever and ever happy and could suffer no more. Those last five minutes were beautiful, and I shall never forget them. I remained on my knees till Hampus came home in despair at being too late; we prayed – and then I closed her eyes! – O Mama! her poor body was tortured and riven and torn to the very last half hour, though she felt and knew nothing. Still it was dreadful! and how merciful, O how good of our Father to let her die, & not live on without her mind. Now, her features have changed, already yesterday a few hours after her death, but still there is such peace over the eyes, and who would wish her back? She, who must now be so inexpressibly happy. After having witnessed Constance's last illness, I can wish for nothing better, than that poor, dear Emmy might be called too. Perhaps the Lord has already taken her. We miss her very much – her vacant place, & many, many things make the heart ache, but *she* is the gainer. Tomorrow evening we will follow her coffin to the church, where she will remain, till the Pastor returns, when she will be buried in the lutheraine churchyard. We have scarcely any flowers here; no possibility of making wreathes and decking her last earthly abode with flowers, a custom, which I like so much, especially for the young. All about her looks so peaceful and beautiful. Her hands folded on her breast, and her Bible lying above them. The few green leaves and buds we have around her head over the hankerchief, & 2. floor pots on either side of the cushion. We go in there to pray every evening. I feel as if I had some close and intimate communication with heaven, since she left us, & pray that her spirit might hover around us, and fill us with more of her own; for truly she was pure and good "an Israelite in whom was no guile" [St. John 1:47]. The last thing on earth she did before she became unconscious or at least absent, was reading her new testament – and that was her preparation for death. O! we can never, never doubt her salvation. –

Sunday 16th. Many days have now again passed, in which I have been so occupied cutting out dayshifts for my little Annie after a lovely pattern on the very same leaf of the "Bazar" you cut out nightcaps for Florence's "trouseau". I am making them of fine Åbo linen, Hampus gave me & the sleaves and lappets are embroidered. It takes a great deal of time working for children, who require so many clothes, as they must often be changed; it pleases me too to look at the childrens things & think I have made them & cut them out all myself. The Princesse helped me to fabricate a round hat for Annie as the one ordered from San Fr[ancisco] was too small for her. You have never asked about my music – and I am sorry to say I do not play every day, often very seldom, except at stated periods with the princesse; each time when I sit down to the piano and play over my favourites, it makes me quite sad that I do not do so oftener, & I again make a new resolution to practise regularly; but it is difficult for me here, having in everything to superintend the children, and consequently can seldom sit undisturbed at anything for a long time. I had given the domestic establishment the whole afternoon & evening for themselves today, and they went out sailing in the cooks boat, to a neighbouring island berry picking. Just now they returned, looking so happy & pleased, bringing a heaped fruit dish full of choice raspberries for us. They are very large and look beautiful, though in flavor have no resemblance to the european ones. This year they are particularly sweet and nice, owing to the unusually fine summer we have up till now had. While I think of it precious Mother, please send the Loyers[?] receipts for salt meat dishes, which were published in the Times, & we tried at Darmstadt. I have forgotten to ask for them each time, & Hampus would particularly like to try them for the men. I shall be so happy to receive the seeds you are sending me, & hope the little parcel will reach me safely. Thank you ten thousands times darling Mother for everything you are sending me. I was distressed to hear you have to pay for my letters, which are so heavy. I have always thought they would be prepaid at San Fr[ancisco] by our Consul, but as he seems not to have attended to it, Hampus will write and tell him to prepay them. [...]

The winter in England must have been very severe, and skating quite a common thing; but oh! how perfectly wretched I should have been at Nettleden; our rooms we keep at 15 R[éaumur] in winter, sometimes even 16 and so I like it. I fancy you sat in your fur tippet all day long. I am so sorry we cannot possibly send the fur you ask for this year, as your letter arrived after our ship had gone to Ajan. The fur is not to be had here; but as soon as possible we will send it. Of course it was *squirel*, & not black fox Hampus promised Henry, and ere this he ought to have had it. I give up all hope of ever hearing from him; he asked me to write & I have done so twice, but what is the use of answering Anna's stupid letters, "she who will never put the Thames on fire" as he said once of me. It is strange, that those people who are most negligent and off hand, seem to get the greater proportion of admirers; Hampus too is very fond of him. I wonder if he received the little box with a russian Samovar, & you the eider down. Did you meet Capt[ain] Ridell? Next spring Hjalmar & perhaps the Pastor return home via Panama; I would so like you to meet them, but am afraid it will not be possible. But soon darlingest Mother you will hear we are coming home; for time goes so fast, and this is already the 3rd year we are at Sitka. Our precious children will then please God be your joy, & will make up to you for all their Mama's faults. Annie is a very sweet, gentle child; she now says after me word for word "God bless Papa and Mama; God bless Annie; God bless Eddie; Amen". More she cannot say yet, or rather she cannot keep her attention longer. She is beginning to speak a great deal of russian lately, & consequently less english, still she understands quite well, and tries to say everything she hears. Her little feet are continually in motion, up and down the room she goes, carrying off whatever she can lay hold of; pens are her special delight; most likely because she knows she must not touch them; then she comes runing towards me saying: "Mama look! Mama look", and when I turn round, I see her round, bright little face looking smilingly up to mine. Baby is also a treasure. Thank God he is a strong & healthy child, though his bowels are obstinate; he is such a fine, handsome little fellow, & is already beginning to teeth; I have continually to take out his little fingers from his mouth. Babies are indeed "lovely blossoms"; nothing on earth can be sweeter than a Baby. O I feel as if I could quite, quite squeeze him when I have him in my arms, & look into his innocent, soft blue eyes. Children are the best Blessing from God, and even though they cause sorrow, much care and anxiety, & give pain to bring into the world, you would not wish to be without them for anything in the world. Precious Mother, I am sorry to see by a misunderstanding you have been over anxious about me. Thank God *that* is not what I suffered from (falling of the womb you meant?) but protrution of the bowel

(Entdarm), which is already much, much better. The former I thought would have been of very great consequence, & was astonished to see by dear Aunt Mathilda's letter, it would not be so. Many women here suffer from it, I suppose arising from over exertion & fatigue too soon after delivery. I hope I shall be permitted to nurse 9. months without another pregnancy occuring; thank God I am & look very well, & have more colour than ever before; I am now taking salt sea baths, which I enjoy much!

Monday. At 6. today my letters are to be finnished and I have still to write to Esperance & Ludmila, 2. painful letters which I have postponed writing till the last day. [...] Our good Constance has been dead one fortnight today; it still seems so wonderful not to see & hear her. I often fancy she must come in. My black dress already begins to look old, so bad is the stuff you buy here – half cotton, & still it costs 2/6 [..?] an archine. We have now got a new midwife; she is at the same time an exellent dressmaker. Did I tell you of the french Cashmere Hampus ordered for me from Hamburg? it costs about 160. [..?] Thaler, and is a very handsome and large one. Sturm says he bought it from an en gros magazine, with whose principle he was afriended, & therefore got it for the original price; turning it into £ it seems fabulously cheap. What would a french Cashmere cost in England? Now I must finnish darlingest Mother, hoping Kostromitinoff will not omit to prepay the letter this time. [...] My Hampus sends dear love, and darling Annie a kiss to "Grandmama" as she says, & precious Baby too. God ever bless and keep you prays

Y[ou]r own fondly, dearly loving dutiful child

Annie Furuhjelm

No. 46   *Government House. Sitka.*
                                                      September 13/25 1861.

My own precious, beloved Mother!
I had been speculating whether I should be so fortunate or not to receive an answer to my long epistle of 31st March, by this last mail, which arrived on Monday morning the 11th, when Hampus handed over to me your 2. last sweet letters, Nos. 30 and 31, the latter exactly being the one I was looking forward to with such delight. A thousand, thousand thanks my ownest Mother, for the joy they gave me; how can I sufficiently thank God for that *great and infinite mercy,* of mail after mail being permitted to get good intelligence of you & my own Ponnie! But this time your letters bore to me a very sad communication, which upset me for the whole day: First, how can I describe my painful astonishment at the news of our good Uncle Hannay's death! it fell like a thunderbolt upon me, & I could scarcely believe it to be true. So little can we accustom ourselves to Death! we live on as if we should never have to leave this world and all that is in it. [...]

Sunday 17. All these days I have been intensely engrossed reading Cuming's *"Great preparation"* which you must surely have read? How come you not to mention anything about this subject? for I guess England's shores from end to end must be talking about this great event. I must confess, that Dr Cumings beautiful lectures have won over my feeble conviction that the End is near, very near, even outside our doors, and that the year 1868 will see that glorious, thrice glorious day when the sun will rise to set no more, and the Lord's trumpet will sound, calling forth millions & myriads of redeemed & ransomed souls to put on their robes of incorruption & fall down before the Highest, in songs of thanksgiving & praise. O Mama! to think that that blessed millennial day should and *could* be so near? that *we* may be still alive then, if so be the Lord's will? The wars, the tribulations, the tempests & earthquakes, which are to be the precursor of all this, & which shall make "man's heart to fail" is indeed terrible; but he who steadfastly believes, & unwaveringly looks to Christ, & trusts & hopes in & through Him, shall surely, surely be safe & unhurt. If indeed Cuming, and all those other great divines who have essayed to explain prophecy, be true and why, on which ground can we doubt, that as every word which God has spoken, must most assuredly be fulfilled, He also at the right time, gives the aid of His Holy spirit to those & such of His servants, who have most studied their Bibles, in order that through them others too may be brought to believe & understand? then indeed we have no time to lose, to prepare ourselves for His coming. Happy England! to be the favoured & chosen country. But is there another land, where God is so much feared as in England? surely not. And nowhere is the Bible more read; though England too has her sins, her vices, & is also included under the curse, still she has ever, more than any other nation striven to follow Her maker, & adhere to His commandments.

Monday 18. This time I have again many letters to write, so I commence early, & make use of every leisure moment, in order to be ready when the time to send them off comes. Thank God my precious ones, big & small ones, are all well, & Edwin in possession of 2. teeth already since 3. or four weeks. He is fat, strong & healthy, & begins to crow so sweetly. Sometimes he says "Mama" quite distinctly; they are the joy of my heart these treasure children. Darling Annie has a bad cough just now; I called in the D[octo]r this morning to prescribe something for it; fancy his saying: "Was glauben Sie selbst, Sie sind der beste Doktor [Ger. What do you think, you are the best doctor]!" – so much for putting any hope in their knowledge. This is the trying time in our climate, for the air is damp & foggy, & colds & coughs are almost in every house. She has cut 2. of her last double teeth now, & they have often occassioned her fits of violent crying, & starting from sleep in the night, occuring so often, it made me anxious, I fancied her brain might suffer; again the doctor was mute & said "Es ist nichts" [Ger. It is nothing]. But else she is happy and merry and talking all day long; sometimes russian, sometimes english words or phrases. It made me laugh immoderately some time ago, when I heard her call her Papa *"Amptus"* with the accent on *"tus"*; the more I laughed, the oftener she repeated it, & laughing all the time herself; she made such a droll & bewitching little face, you could not resist her. To look strait into a childs eyes, how lovely is it not! That pure, angelic expression, that unalloyed joy & happiness! as you say, to study a child, is not only interesting and enticing for a Mother, but elevating "for of such is the Kingdom of heaven" [St. Matthew 19:14]; Gods own peculiar favorites. She is very tall for her age, plump and round too, but rather pale, which I attribute to the want of wet nursing from the beginning. Eddie has quite a different complexion. I am still nursing him, though now only twice a day; between times he gets cowsmilk, and now, at last, his bowels are in perfect order I am happy to say. [...]

I am quite disappointed darling Mama; only think the company writes, they are not sending any ships to the colonies this year, & so I shall miss my box, on which I had so much counted, unless you have been able in the Times advertisements, to find out some vessel going to San Francisco. And now I must let you into a little secret precious Mother, which is my *almost* full conviction, that this our "Hochlöblische" [Ger. Honourable/Glorious] Company, as Sturm calls it, is tottering fast, and will never rise again. The Grand Duke Constantin is quite embittered against it, & he has very great influence. Etholén, who must see what things are leading to, writes to Hampus that the company is in a very difficult & precarious position; still he says, we have every reason to believe the privileges will be renewed, but at the same time gives Hampus some advise which almost surely shows, *he* thinks too, the company will be given up. Next year will show what we have to expect, but with Hampus' permission, I thought it better to let you know how matters stand. To make Hampus quite comfortable, not enough with those horrible revisors, but now is coming an Ad[miral] Papoff, a favorite with the Grand Duke, who printed a downright false report about the colonies, and made use of Hampus name & put a lie into his mouth! – What do you say to that? Nothing but "obehagligheter" [Swed. trouble] has he on every side, & still how he tries, & how he prays God to help him to be a useful & good Governor. [...]

You say nothing about Prince Louis' engagement. I see the poor boy was attacked with meazles this spring; what an unpleasant thing for a *Bräutigam* [Ger. bride-groom]. I do not recognize you darling Mama, not writing politics, & still just look at that awful civil war in the United States.[115] England is said to be arming herself up to her teeth; what does she fear? An invation from France? I doubt it. Do you know already that the Emperor has graciously permitted Finland to have a Landtag[116] next summer & that Morbror [Swed. Uncle] Sebastian Gripenberg has been named Land Marshalk? what rejoicing for dear Moster Lisette. All this Etholén thinks, has

---

115 The Civil War 1861-1865 between the Northern and the Southern States of America.
116 The first Diet (Swed. Landtdag), after Finland became a part of the Russian empire in 1809, gathered already in 1809; the second in 1863. It included representatives of four classes: noblemen, priests, townsmen and peasants. The 'landtmarskalk' was the chairman of the nobility.

come about through Uncle Fabian's representation of Finland's real state & wants, to the Emperor. We have not yet got the swedish papers, but the princesse read the Emperors speech to Morbror Sebastian, in the russian papers. She was safely confined with a little girl on the 6th Aug[ust], who is to be christened "Helen" on Thursday next the 21st, when Mr Koshkin & I stand again proxy Godparents. His wedding will soon be, as his brides father goes to San Fr[ancisco] in place of Kostromitinoff who has been called home. *Sunday Sept[ember] 24/Oct[ober] 6.* Since I wrote these last lines, I have been made so supremely happy by a letter from my precious Florence, one from dearest Charlie, & a little box from her, containing such sweet little things, all her own making. Annie is today wearing a white pinafore with red braid, made by her own Auntie. The mail from Ajan came on friday evening, & we were up till 12. o'clock reading letters. You may judge of my delight at seeing so perfectly unexpectedly *your* handwriting on an enveloppe addressed in russian. It was the cover containing your Darmstadt letters; I dare say you have often wondered at my silence concerning them. It gave me much pleasure to peruse them. But how can I describe my supreme joy, at finding a coloured sketch of that precious child Mary in the box, which Florence has so cleverly made for me, & sent in a little frame. Of course it is without a face, but still so very, very dear to me; what a precious little being it must be, & how forward & strong for its age. God grant the second one may be equally healthy & strong. Florence promises to write soon again over Panama, so that I may expect to get a few letters again by next mail. Charlie wrote to both of us and sent Fänrik Stål's II h[ä]ft[e][117] which Aunt Albertina also sent me. Have you read it yet? Also Alexander Humboldts Biography, the same they were reading the first year of their marriage I suppose. But I am sorry we have no newspapers except "Papperslyktan" [Swed. The Chinese Lantern],[118] by which we know the theatre at Helsingfors is opened, & seems to be a very fine affair. [...]

My darlings are now both in bed, & the tea urn is waiting for its mistress, therefore Good night my beloved Mother! *Friday 29.* All these days I have been preparing my other letters, of which this mail again takes a considerable number from me. I have also written to congratulate my little Bridesmaid Emma, of whose engagement I was very happy to hear. It is a wonderful contrast, H[elsing]f[or]s and Darmstadt! in the northern town every letter can tell of some marriage, whereas in the southern one, the blood seems to be colder; four years seems to be the time, which must elapse between each wedding saison! I like the northerns in that respect better; a young man should always marry when his feelings are warm & ardent, & before he has had too many inmates of his heart, to make him blasé & indifferent. Of course you

---

117 *Fänrik Ståls Sägner* (Swed. The Tales of Ensign Stål), about Finnish heroes in the 1808-1809 war between Sweden and Russia, by J.L. Runeberg. The second part mentioned by Anna was published in 1860.

118 A weekly, published in Helsinki 1859-1862.

must have *enough* to support a family, but riches can come with years. Do you not also think so? [...]

Mina Gripenberg writes to me that "många förfärliga saker hafva stått om Onkel C[onstantin] i svenska tidningar; man tror deraf mångt och mycket" [Swed. many terrible things have been said about Uncle C. in Swedish newspapers; much of it is believed] – has he been accused of dishonesty? but Hampus says that of course he has taken his gain where ever he could, as everyone knows he could not live on his pay alone. That is what I utterly abhor & detest in russian appointments. Why not give a full allowance at once, & put an end to those secret sources of gaining more money than the world knows you receive. It is so degrading & miserable; but this system seems to prevail in high & low appointments through the all empire. In a certain way something of the same thing existed here; for instance the grain we receive for feeding fowls, & spoilt flour for feeding pigs, was entered in the books as used for the workmen, etc – etc – But my Hampus could not either bare the deception & wrote home to Etholén requesting him to let him know *what* things he *had a right* to take on the company's account; the Board of directors immediately sent an official paper to the counting house, entitling the *"Glavne Pravlitielne"* [incorrect Rus.: Governor] to this & this & that; and now it is as clear as daylight & entered under *our own name*, & not that of the men. –

You ask if those Kolosch women were put to death? I forget now which of the many slaves you mean. But of course not. Thank God not one has been sacrificed since Hampus is Governor; he has purchased them free on the C[ompany]'s account, & one slave woman we purchased by a general subscription for 700. R[oubles] B[anco] or 200 R[oubles] S[ilver] – A few months ago the indians had a great festival.[119] You must know that the conclusion of building new houses, or *Barabors* as they call them, is a great fête with them, to which they invite all their neighbors at a great distance. This summer on a similar occasion there were 400. guests invited, who remained here more than one month. They danced & capered in wild costumes on the beach, & sang & drank brandy all the night. One of the guests died of intoxication, for which our Indians had to pay. Before parting they give away everything they possess. Not only all their provisions, but blankets, in one word everything, so that they are quite, quite poor now. At the end of such a fête it is their custom to sacrifice slaves; but before these strangers arrived, Hampus called 7. or 8. of our *Teone* or chiefs, & forbade them to kill anyone. He promised to give them now & then some present, & to invite them each year to dinner, besides which positively told them, that the moment they attempted to kill one of their slaves, he would fire upon them & their

---

119 The 'festival' Anna describes, is probably a so-called potlatch. Varjola (1990, pp. 74-75) who gives a detailed description of the potlatch system, says "an Indian, having accumulated considerable wealth … invited guests on any convenient pretext … After the repast and dances which usually continued three or four days, he gave away to his guests all his wealth".

village. The consequence of this was, that they liberated 19. slaves & gave them as a present to the Company. I went with Hampus to see some of them, & expected to see their faces radiant with joy over their liberty. But you could not have guessed they had been doomed to die. To me it was something wonderful as I gazed at them; one was a pretty little girl of 9 – 11. years old, the others mostly old women, eaten up by disease. Perhaps I have told you all this in a former letter, but I do not now remember. How will the Company ever answer before God for their ignorance & heathenism? But true it is, the clergy are more in fault. It is a sad & deplorable thing altogether. Many & many a russian does not know *why* he prays to saints, why he believes in this or that thing, but only answers "the church teaches us so" – About our Saviour the Creoles know nothing; they go to the sacrament once a year *pro forma*, & then have great eating & drinking afterwards. Scott gave me a russian testament, & I have given it to the upper nurse maid, & told her to read & remember it. I hear her in the evenings reading aloud for an hour to the other 2. women; but as I cannot explain what she does not understand, I can only fervently pray God that He might teach them to understand, & that they may come to acknowledge & abhorrence of sin, & a true Love for God and our Saviour. –

How happy I am you received my letter announcing Eddies birth so soon. I am very anxious to read the lovely poem you speak about; I do not know it at all. But how? and when shall I receive my box. I wonder where you now are, precious Mother, & where you intend to live till we, please God, come home. Has Aunt Mary returned, or joy of joys, have you gone to Troitzkoi; these are questions I should like to have answered, but must wait Oh! so very long for still. You do not seem to like our little boys name? Ludmila writes to Hampus how astonished she is that he "som blifvande Caput för familjen, ha fått ett i slägten okänd namn" [Swed. as future Head of the family bears a name unknown in the family] – […] I don't remember having asked Carl & Florence as Godparents for our first Son, (tho' Carl certainly asked me for theirs) but sure enough, they are entered as Annies Godparents, & the certificates of their baptism has been sent to Riddarhuset [Swed. House of Nobles], after my father in law's desire. Our good Pastor has not returned yet, & our dear Constance still lies unburried; every day we are expecting him. Koshkins wedding will soon be, & he has asked us to be *père et mère asise*[120], as the russians must always have other parents besides their own for that occasion.

Tuesday 2/14 Oct[ober]. Yesterday Pastor Winter returned, looking very well tho' he had been dreadfully seasick. He was quite struck dumb at the news of Constance's

---

120 Père et mère assises [Fr. sitting father and mother] is a somewhat awkward translation
     from Russian referring to a Russian Orthodox custom that, instead of absent parents,
     a couple of relatives or friends – often in a higher position – give their blessing to the
     bride and to the bridegroom when they leave their houses for the church, and later oc-
     cupy the place of honour at the wedding feast and can give good advice and guidance in
     the marriage (Barsov 1898, pp. 657-58).

death & said such patients generally attain an old age. Soon the burial will be, & I shall be happy to know her body has been placed peacefully in its last earthly tenement.

The pastor brought me only a few lines from Hjalmar, & to Hampus a very disagreeable letter. I must tell you now, incase you might hear it through some indirect channel, and then probably in a false light, that there exists at this present moment a most painful & disagreeable breech between Hampus & Hjalmar. I cannot say how it grieves me, and how I regret it. The cause is this: *Private*: Last summer, just before we left Codiac, Hampus received the startling intelligence, that Hjalmar had settled a very large sum of money on an adopted & free purchased Kolosch girl, whom he intended to marry! The Bishop showed H[ampus] a letter from the priest who was to marry them, in which the date was even fixed; every thing seemed so clear & true – (of course all the particulars would be too long to relate) we could not for one moment doubt the truthfulness of the report. Now, as no one is permitted to marry here, without my husbands permission, he thought it was his duty to prevent such folly as much as lay in his power, feeling convinced, that when Hjalmar came to himself again, he would bitterly, bitterly repent the step he had taken. Hampus wrote to him, & at the same time recalled from Kinai, the family by whom the girl was adopted. – Would you not also have done the same? Could it not afterwards have been laid to Hampus doors, that he did not prevent such a foolish step? – &, who could ever have believed, such proofs of the truth of the story being offered, that it was all a black lie, made & spread out, by, I know not how many [..?] lips? – […] Hjalmar is returning Via Panama, next spring. In other circumstances I would have asked him to seek you up, but now, it is perhaps better not. The saying is, when Brothers quarrel, they never become friends again.[121] God grant it may not be so with them. –

And now let us turn to brighter subjects.

Last night I was with the princesse and spent a very pleasant evening. She read me many parts out of her fathers letter, which were exeedingly interesting. Sometimes I thought it was Addison, some times Dickens who was speaking. He is indeed a clever & an educated man, & seems to have an artists soul & comprehension & appreciation of what is high & beautiful. *Wednesday*. I wish I could show you a painting in oil made by a young Creole, who has been brought up on the Company's account in S[ain]t P[eters]b[ur]g. It shows decided talent I should say, & many a worse thing was at the H[elsing]f[or]s exhibition. But considering he is a *Creole* – has lived mostly here among uncivilized people, I am quite astonished. A great deal could be made of them by education; but morally perhaps, they stand still on the lowest step of civilization. It is quite an uncommon thing to meet with a Creole who is not a drunkard; or else they die of consumption in their youth, the sad consequence of every manner of excess & disipation. There is so very much which ought to be done, but unfortunately the means are wanting, the C[om]p[an]y cannot keep so many servants – the revenue

---

121 Fortunately, Hampus and Hjalmar Furuhjelm became friends again!

is decreasing, the most expensive skins only caught in very small quantities now, &
China open to all russian merchants, so the monopoly of our Company for tea is for
ever at an end. These are hard blows for her. In one of your former letters, you ask
us to give some detailed account of the country we are living in, etc – etc – questions
which Mr Cautley asks. Hampus would be able to do so very well, being so thoroughly
acquainted with the Colonies, but he has so much to think of, to read & write too (the
secretary has the great misfortune of being *stupid*) the spirit is wanting. He is sometimes quite tired of rewriting & changing Koshkins stupid official letters & reports,
& as recreation then rather takes up some interesting book, or the newspapers. But I
will tell you what I know; for instance our island Sitka is 75. miles long & 30. miles
broad, & is surrounded by an archeopelago of islands; the highest mountain, the
"Elias"[122] in the north parts of our Colonies is 16.900 f[eet] high. It must be splendid!
higher than Mont Blanc, which is the highest of those glories of Switzerland. About
Sitka, the highest mountain is 3000 feet.[123] In all, russians[124] & Indians included, our
Colonies are inhabited by 40.000 people, but the Koloshes of Sitka do not amount to
more than 3 or 400 souls. The most valuable animals for their skins, are the fur zeals
& sea utters, caught on the Aleutian islands; on the continent again, you find the
same animals as inhabit Siberia. An article which might perhaps bring in much, is the
Angora gout, the wool of which animal is beautifully fine & silvery. I have just now
had 13 lbs[?] sent me; if I only knew where to get it spun. I don't know if any one in
Finland would understand it well. I will enclose a little piece to show you. On further
consideration I think it wisest to await your reply; perhaps something might be made
of it in England. *Oct[ober] 16/28.* Today I must conclude this, darling Mama. I have
kept it open to be able to tell you about Mr Koschkins marriage, which we celebrated
by a Ball[125] last night. I was in church, in Mothers stead, & after the ceremony,
which pleased me much, hurried home in my sedan chair, it was dreadful weather, to
welcome the young couple, & bless them according to russian fashion. Before going
to church, the bridegroom came here with his marshalk, to receive our Blessing. He
must fall down on his knees, & first Hampus make the sign of the cross over his head
with the russian picture, and then with the loaf of bread and salt [traditional Russian
welcome]; the same thing must be repeated by me. When the ceremony is over, the
young couple both fall down on their knees, & we have to bless them again, after which

---

122 In July 1741, Bering had sighted Mount St. Elias from the sea. On July 20th, St. Elias'
    day, he sent some men ashore on an island and named the island (now Kayak) after
    St. Elias (Steller 1993, p. 63). Mount St. Elias was also named after this saint, perhaps
    by Bering himself. However, the highest mountain in Alaska (and in North America)
    is not Mount St. Elias (18,008 f.) on the U.S.-Canadian border, but Mount McKinley
    (20,320 f.).
123 Mount Edgecumbe, 3,200 feet.
124 There were never more than about 800 Russians in Alaska (Fedorova 1973, p. 151).
125 To which 80 persons were invited (from a letter to V. Gripenberg dated 10th October
    1861. Åbo Academy Library, Manuscript Division. Furuhjelm, Annie 15).

Sea otter.
Drawing by J. E.
Gray, 1865.

we shake hands, & kiss hands & foreheads. I prayed so earnestly for them, that God might bless them, & grant them happiness, & do so sincerely hope they may be so. She is so young, only 18; but it was sad to see how sad the bride looked – I have never seen so melancholly a bridal party. Why then have promised to become his wife? She seems not to be sure of her happiness. I will tell you more about them in my next letter. Tomorrow her father goes, & she has been crying her eyes out of her head. She kissed me over and over again, & "thanked for my great kindness & sympathy" – I like her much, & hope to be a friend to her when her Mother and sisters are gone. Our precious boy is now quite weaned. Just now he is sitting on his sisters bed, crowing & playing so sweetly. This is the first fine day for more than 2. weeks, so I must go out and take a walk, as I feel rather "katzenjammerich" [Ger. miserable]. When you are married & have children dancing & going out, gives you more trouble than pleasure. My precious husband kisses your hands, & begs you not be angry for not writing, but he has so much to worry & vex him! My Darlings send their own Grandmama a kiss – May God bless & preserve you prays your own loving, devoted child

Anna

No. 47   Government House.
                                          Sitka. Dec[ember] 17/29 1861

My own precious Mother!
Before sailing for San Francisco, I must begin a few lines to you, in order to give you the latest news from my dear and happy home, where I leave my greatest treasures alone. I am going on this long & most unpleasant voyage, in order to go to the dentists, my poor teeth having become so bad, it is only with great difficulty I can

eat. Annie darling goes with me; I could never go without any one of my 3. beloved ones, but O! it is so hard to part from my beloved Hampus, & darling angel Baby boy. Prince Maksutoff goes as the Captain, & his wife & child go too, their little 4. months old Baby, remaining with my Eddie, in good, trustworthy Ida's care. Were it not that the Princesse decided upon going, I could never, never have made up my mind to go to California, even though Hampus has been urging me to do so for a long time. You know how timorous I always have been, and how dependant upon others, so that this journey would never have come to any thing, had not circumstances turned out so favorable. In the Princesse I have a real friend, & a companion, & she will comfort me in my solitude. I was long undecided what to do; – no sooner had I settled upon going, than my courage again failed me, & the thought of leaving my husband alone to his anxious & melancholly thoughts, (for this year we have lost 2. ships) made me change my mind. But remembering how you my darling Mother, always used to do, I prayed God most earnestly to direct & lead me, & mercifully to show me what to do. After one whole weeks uneasiness & undecidedness, one morning after earnest praying, I felt as if it was all clear before me, I *should go*, & never wavered any more after that, but have felt quite calm & composed, except at the thought of parting! – God Almighty is every where near us, & so I commit my hearts treasures into His divine keeping, knowing & believing, that with Him they are safe, & pray, that if it be His Will, He will grant us soon a bright and happy reunion. *Amen.* How you would pray for me, if you knew of this journey. May my precious little girl remain well and strong! every thing on board has been made as warm & comfortable as possible, & for weeks past many fingers have been busy working warm clothes for Annie. All my things are on board already, but as the weather did not permit us to go out today, we remain till Tuesday, please God all is well. This is Sunday; tomorrow evening the Maksutoffs will in that case flit on board, & I will send my Annie and her nurse, remaining myself the last night with my Puxti, & going on board early in the morning. I think he will be so lonely and dreary! he has never been *at home* without me. I have asked our dear Pastor Winter to come & see him, & young Mrs Koshkin to look in at the Baby's some times. My Boy is such a fine child; every outline of his body shows health and strength; and he loves me so, and is so very sweet & friendly & good, I know not how I shall tare myself away from him. Goodnight my precious Mother! on board I hope some times to be able to write. God bless you, & us, & my own own husband & child.

On board "Kamtschatka". 1/13 January 1862.
San Francisco.

My own, most precious Mother! Here we are at last, praised be God, after a most speedy & prosperous voyage of 12. days. We left Sitka, my dear, dear Home, and my beloved husband and Baby, on Tuesday morning 19th Dec[ember] and had on the whole very good weather; indeed much better than could ever have been expected at this time of the year. Hampus does not yet think we are here; he reckoned 3. weeks would be quite necessary to accomplish our voyage, but thank God, who permitted us to arrive so much sooner. You will be glad to hear that I suffered *very* little from seasickness; indeed I was quite astonished, for I have never before been so well at sea. But O darling Mother! how sorely I repented having left my Puxti. I felt so wretched & miserable without him, so sad & lonely those dreary, long nights, when roling & pitching & howling & blowing, chased sleep quite away from my eyes. Then the thought that he was alone in that big house, perhaps uncomfortable, haunted me, & I made a vow never again, as well for his sake, as for my own, to undertake a sea voyage alone. But how merciful God has shown Himself towards us! We had all hoped to be here on friday 29th, & were as you may suppose, very disappointed when the wind changed, & circumstances became unfavorable. Had we *then* been 100. miles further on, than we were, we should have been exposed to a most furious storm, perhaps & most likely been in danger. We could not conceive why so near San Francisco there should be such a tremendous swell & high sea, which sent us rolling from one side to the other, without intermission. On arriving here on *New-years Eve* (old. sty[le]) we were told of the desperate gale it had been blowing, combined with awful rain, a kind of *Wolkenbruch* [Ger. cloudburst], which has caused great damages here, and all over the country. Was it not a merciful providence, which kept us out of that? But indeed when is man satisfied? always grumbling, always wishing, always thinking it could be better than it is. I cannot say with what a feeling of gratitude and joy, combined with sadness at being separated from my husband, I greeted the New year; grateful, because we had been brought safely through the perils of the sea, & through another year of goodness & mercy, health & happiness; and sorrowful you can guess why. I have never been so much out of spirits in my whole life, as during these 12. days; and oh! *how* I long to be back, to be at home with my hearts treasures! Our darling Annie, has thank God been perfectly well, excepting the first day & a half, & was so good all the time; without her I should have been *very* sad. The poor princesse was so ill, I hardly saw any thing of her, else her kindness & warm heart, would have been a great comfort to me. You take no notice of her; are you not glad to hear that I have found a friend in this distant country? We are still on board, as the town is overfull, & not a single room to be found in any of the hotels. Sacramento, a town not far from here, has been perfectly inundated by these late rains, that all the inhabitants have fled to San Francicso; I really don't know where we shall live. Every thing has become dreadfully dear; in fact San Fr[ancisco] has never seen such rain and such storms before. There are wonderful changes going on every where. Every thing seems to be changing too. But now my own precious Mother, let me thank you for your darling, O so precious letters, No. 32. and 33. which I found waiting for me. They filled my whole soul with joy & happiness. [...]

Saturday 18th n[ew] st[yle]. Own, precious Mother; here we have been six days, and I have not yet been able to write a single line to you. I don't know how the days pass; but I think the greatest reason *why* I have not yet written, is that I have been so much out of spirits, and missed my Puxti so very, very, very much. Last night we drove through dreadful roads to the Kostromitinoffs, and there I had great difficulty to keep from crying, it was so strange to be *there* without my husband. Every thing made me think of him, & the happy, happy time I spent there 3. years ago, then still almost a bride. How is he? What is he doing? O! I am *so* far away from him, my most precious, lovely Darling. I have not yet been to the dentist, as I am trying to recover my looks before going to the photographists, for Annies & my own picture, which will I know give you great joy. I hope it will succeed well; O! I do so hope it will! it makes me quite excited only to think of your joy at receiving a picture of your first grandchild; how I shall long for your answer. We have come to San Francisco at a most unfavorable time; it is most unfortunate the weather should be so bad. Generally there is frequent rain here, at this time of the year, but now, as you will most likely see in the papers, the whole country is under water. Such rain has *never yet* been known in California. It has been falling for 2. months & is still continuing to fall, sometimes very heavily. The streets are some of them impassable, large pieces being torn away, others represent a broad river, and if it is so at San Fr[ancisco] you can judge what it must be in those towns lying in the valley & near a river. The whole of the Sacramento inhabitants have fled from the floods, & have inundated this city, so that it was with the utmost difficulty we could get any lodgings. All hotels were cramed full, not a room to be had. At last we found 3. rooms, kitchen & dining room for *140 dollars* per month! Had we been one hour later, these too would have been hired, & we could have found no others. We stay 1. month, & I cannot say *how* extremely happy I shall be to go home again. First at fore most to see my precious Treasures, & next because this is an extravagant place to live in. What ever you put your hands to is expensive. We must pay 30. dol[lars] a month for a cook, & our food will not come to less than 100. dollars I am afraid, so that my portion for this séjour will be 160 dollars without extra expences. For myself I have bought a plain brown straw bonnet to replace the old one I had before & now was obliged to give to Annie's nurse. Several p[ai]rs of boots, gloves & a couple of woolen dresses is all I require; but I have presents to buy for all the servants at home & for some other poor people at Sitka and the children require some things too. For my husband I have bought such a nice flanel cashmere to make a dressing gown; it will be his Birthday present though he charged me to buy *nothing* for himself.

Sunday 19th. Another wet and rainy day, nevertheless we walked to church. I was so happy to go to our own english church again. The Rev[eren]d Inghim[?] B. Bishop of the Dyosis preached on the marriage at Cana, a very good and clear sermon. The singing was very fine; it quite warmed my heart to hear the beautiful Anthem sung. I had hoped to go again in the evening, but the rain will not cease, & there will be no service this evening in the church we were at in the morning. There were prayers for cessation of rain & war; this is a deplorable time for America, and who knows *when* & *how* the end of this civil war will be. I cannot conceive how you never mention politics in any form. But it is true that there is so much more of greater interest to me in your letters, I would grudge the room afforded to politics. How you are travelling! Scotland & England you have been in, & who knows how soon you will be in Russia again. [...] The company sends a ship after all, though it was at first said, none should come this year. I was in great distress about my box, & several other things I expected, but now I am pacified, & hope to be able to open the box packed by your darling darling fingers, soon after I get home. Did Uncle Hannay leave nothing at all to you? when, precious Mother, will you answer my repeated questions about your income. Annie just now is standing beside me saying: "Mama Grandmama writing". She says everything in english & russian. I am quite astonished at her progress in english, and delighted at the same time. She has decidedly improved in looks; how I wonder what you will think of her. My sweet little golden Baby boy at home, would make such a lovely picture, what would I not give to have it. At night when I go to bed I cannot keep from crying when I remember, *who* I have left at home. It is so lonely to be without my own Puxti; O! I cannot say *how* sad I am to be parted from him. Hampus wished me long ago to come to San Francisco alone; but no! I knew I could never bear it, & what should have become of me. Madame Maksutoff is such a nice, gentle person. I am very fond of her – I only wish she were not so delicate. She had a little *tiny* tiny Baby in August, & now 4. months afterwards, she is again I fear in the family way, & looks so very worn, pale thin & delicate. I am sure a good doctor would order separation for one year. But how is that to be managed at Sitka. They are so happy, I some times grieve to think her health, never very strong, is giving way.

Wednesday Ev[enin]g 29. Precious Mother! tomorrow my letter is to be posted, so I will not delay any longer, and rather send you another one before starting for Sitka, which will be soon I hope. I enclose our darling Firstborn's photograph, and hope it will tell you all the fond & true love of which it is meant to be the bearer. Annie could not be better; she is as like as she ever could be; I am so extremely happy, that it succeeded so well. She looks very serious, and she is a serious child. O Mama! is she not sweet & charming, and is she not every bit like her precious Father? Her eyes are in reality larger than they appear to be, and she is standing on a footstool which of course makes her look taller than she is. If I could only be near when you open the enveloppe! O, I would give a great deal to see you just then, and hear your exclamations. The Maksutoffs are delighted with my likeness, & you will see by it how stout I have grown. As one is never contented with one's own likeness, so I am not with mine, though it is exceedingly like me. I am not pleased that both hands are visible, but that is of no consequence, the most important thing, & the one I was most anxious for, is that our little angel should come out well, and so she has. If I had such a picture of my Eddie, my bonny treasure Boy, with his soft, dumpy body, and his pure blue eyes, with which he looks you strait in the face, I should be most supremely happy. I will send a copy to the dear Lambs, & several to Finland, and to the Charlie's, so do not send your copy to any of them to look at. They will go by the next mail. And now I must tell you a little about our life here. We go out shopping a great deal, even though it has been raining almost constantly, & the streets are extremely muddy. We have already made several acquaintances, & very nice & pleasant ones. Last week we were invited to make an excursion to an Island 30. miles from here, by the Capt[ain] and officers of H[is] I[mperial] M[ajesty's] corvet "*Kalevala*". The ship is built in Åbo, but is a russian man of war, & the Captain (Davidoff) the same officer we met here 3. years ago. There were many ladies & gentlemen invited, & according to the cordial & pleasant american & english custom, they had themselves introduced to us, & 2. called upon us immediately afterwards. The morning was extremely cold. We went on board at 9. o'clock, and were very miserable. In the Captains comfortable cabin there was a still more comfortable fire, & everything necessary for the comfort of the ladies. At 10. or a little before, we steamed off, and after having taken some warm refreshments we began to dance. We danced & danced & danced again till 6. o'clock in the evening, & I have never in my life been so tired before, nor have I danced *so much*, since I am married. The young officers are very nice young men, & have learnt the english language pretty tolerably during 3. months. Having met with such great hospitality & kindness here, they are quite in love with the place, & its many fair inhabitants. It is in truth wonderful to see so many pretty faces. The american ladies are decidedly handsome, & very gay and lively. The coast is very pretty, but unfortunately I saw very little of it, as I was constantly asked to dance. At 2. we arrived at "Mare Island". This place is the Dockyard for american ships. A most tremendous saloon built over the yard where the largest ship can be taken in, was decorated with flags & garlands all round & a place arranged for the musicians. The Commander of the place, a venerable faced old gentleman, with heavy epaulettes, received us at the entrance and conducted us upstairs. We danced quite like wilds, or rather the juvenile part of the company. They seemed as if they neither got tired nor out of breath, for if they were not dancing they were running & scampering all down the room like a parcel of schoolchildren. It was pleasant to see their enjoyment, without any stiffness or affectation. But how I missed, & *how* I longed for my husband! my own Hampus! It would have been interesting for him to see the place, & 10. times more interesting for me had he been there too.

We only stayed one hour, and then came on board again, where a most splendid collation of turkey & partridges, jellies & creams apples & pears, tarts & confitures was spread out, & done most ample justice to by every one present. Mr Davidoff came to me & drank "to my health & those who are absent" which pleased me much. One of the young officers "*Bernkoff*" knows Costi very well, & has been 3. years at Helsingfors. He also knows the Driesens, & Otto Furuhjelm. One of the ladies, a mexican by birth, & married to an irish gentleman, Doctor Nutall, charmed me exceedingly. She is so gentle & sweetmannered, & notwithstanding her great fortune, plain & unpretending in her dress. She was so kind, & called the next day, & offered her services in what ever way she could help us, & hopes to see us soon one evening, when the russian officers are to be invited. The "Kalevala" sails next week, & all on board seem to go very reluctantly. We returned the visit 2. days afterwards. They have a splendid house in the principal street here. Dr Nutall is such a warm & kind mannered man, who shakes hands, as only a true englishman can. He is tall & handsome, and his wife young & pretty, the mother of 3. children. The day before yesterday, whilst at Kostromitinoffs, Mrs. Johnson, the swedish Consuls wife, came in to pay a visit, & was also so kind & obliging to us, though perfect strangers, regretting that I was not living with her in her large & fine house. They are very wealthy people. She is a Virginian, & her husband a Norwegian.[126] The next day she too called upon us, & took us out for a long country drive in her carriage, driven by an old faithful negroe. She spoke to us about all her travels & indeed she seems to have been all over the world nearly, & hopes next year to visit Italy & Germany. But it was melancholly to see the state of the roads. Here is a huge ditch, the half of a street torn away, there again several houses are surrounded by water, & still the rain ceaseth not, though all churches are praying for it. It seems to me as if Gods wrath were over America. Floods & storms & other damages are heard of and read of in every paper you take up. The state of Sacramento is truly deplorable. How many families have been utterly ruined by this flood, & how many people have been drowned. San Fr[ancisco] is opening her generous arms to all the poor sufferers; they have done & are doing a great deal for them. Today at last I took courage & went to the dentist. I cannot be sufficiently thankful that he promised little or no pain from the operation. Tomorrow I am to go again, but just now I hear the rain pouring, & I think there will be no chance of getting out. *Thursday 30.* In a few days is our wedding day! I cannot believe I have been married 3. years already. What happy, happy, peaceful years they have been! O Mama! how good, how very good God has been towards your children. It is sad not to be at home, and to think that my Hampus is quite alone. I am so very, very impatient to get back to him and my Boy. The good Lord be with them & keep them in health and strength. Where should I be if I could not hope and trust in Him? I am so sorry that my Annie has become such a willful little thing since I brought her to San Francisco. At home she was so very good & obedient everyone was astonished at it, but unfortunately since she is in daily & hourly society with little Annie Maksutoff she has imitated all her capricious ways, & screams & cries very often. But I hope & trust she will become herself again when we come home. Annie Maksutoff can be so sweet and nice some times, but her character is very passionate, and she will not let any one touch her without screaming. Her Mama is quite sorry, & does not know how to stop it. It grieves my heart, several times already to have been obliged to give my Annie a few slaps on her little bottom. But how can I let her grow up so capricious, throwing herself down on the floor & screaming when she is to be dressed. Were it not for the pleasure it gives me to send you her picture, I should be sorry I brought her. You cannot think what compliments I get on my looks. Every one says Sitka air must

---

126 The Kingdom of Sweden and Norway formed a personal union 1814-1905.

have the power of improving peoples looks. I wonder, if you will think so too. –

It was pleasant to hear of your view of the Queen and all her family. I was grieved and shocked on reaching this place to hear of Prince Alberts sudden death. Sudden I suppose it was, as the papers of Nov[ember] mention him as well. I have not seen any later papers, and I am so anxious to know something more about it. I think you must have been so happy to be in Scotland once more and to visit all your friends there. [...]

Friday 31st. And now precious Mother, I must conclude. I am afraid this is a very poor, insipid letter, but it is rather difficult to keep your thoughts afloat with children playing & often crying in your ears, or the piano going & voices talking. I will write again before I go, & should I find the second set of visiting cards still more successful, I will send you another one. Give my fondest love to my own Ponnie & Charlie, & tell her my letter is already on stocks. To everybody give much love. [...] It is dreadfully cold here; a few nights ago the ice was thick on the streets, & the inhabitants say they have never had such a cold winter before. Last night we went to a Concert, but O – o – o! what stuff to call music. A young lady called Miss Anna Sonntag made her début & sang quite false but of course was applauded. Two irish girls *O'Kuffe*, sang much better. But music is no where understood or appreciated so much as in Germany. I see that more & more, *there* only a true & real taste for music is cultivated, & you are taught to understand & value, only what is truly good. In Russia music is but very superficially liked; operetic music is what is chiefly played & admired there. Once more Adieu own precious, best beloved treasure Mother. May the grace of our Lord be with thee, & us all Amen.

With my Annies love to Grandmama, and much from myself.

Ever and ever I am Your own loving Child

Anna Furuhjelm

How much I like my name.

No. 48   San Francisco Feb[ruary] 2nd 1862

On this day, own precious Mother, I again begin a letter to you. I know your prayers and thoughts have been & are surrounding us today. Charlie & Florence are thinking of us and no doubt all of you drinking our health. The only person, of whose *especial* thoughts on this blessed day, I am not quite sure of, is my own Hampus! As he generally does not heed dates, I am afraid he will not notice that the *21st Jan[uary] old sty[le]* makes 2nd *Feb[ruary]* n[ew] sty[le]. But should he really have forgotten it, I hope the Pastor will have reminded him of it, for he does not forget dates, having all our papers. I got up with a grateful & sad heart. The kind Princesse surprised me with a delicious german Kringel, and the table all decked in green leaves & flowers this morning. It was so nice and kind of her, & comforted me so much. Another great Joy & comfort to me on this day, separated as I am from Hampus, is that it is Sunday, and I have been to the Holy Sacrament. It is nearly 5. years since I have received it in an english church, and from english clergymen. How beautiful the Communion Service is; & it was so solemnly & worthily administered to us today, by the Bishop and a grey haired old priest with a kind face. The singing is beautiful in the churches here, & some of the Psalm & Hymn melodies most lovely.

You are perhaps writing to me my own Mother at this self same moment. O! if I could fly over to you for a moment; if I could fly home to Sitka! – One month hence, I hope with Gods help to be at home again, and unless we have very bad weather, we ought to be. The Prince expects & hopes to be ready for sailing on Tuesday 11th. Though I dread the horrible thought of going to sea again, it warms & encourages me to think our vessel is home ward bound. A few days ago, I despatched my long letter to you; the pictures it contained will have compensated for the insuficiency in other respects. Yesterday I sat again with Annie. It suceeded very well indeed. I am bringing our pictures on glass in a case for my Puxti. The little one he has of me is not at all good, but this one is exellent. *Sunday Ev[enin]g 9.* I had hoped darling Mother, to be off on Tuesday next, but now this hope is gone, & it seems we shall not be ready before Saturday. O! I *do* so ardently long for my treasures! O God! Keep them well and strong I pray thee! – The weather has changed, and it is so fine & pleasant now; it is a pity we had not such weather from the very beginning. Had I my Puxti & my darling Eddie here, I should be quite happy, & enjoyed my stay very much. I think I told you in my last letter about the excursion on the "Kalawala" and that we made several acquaintances there. We have been out to dinner & evening parties very often since then. One soirée was very pleasant indeed in consequence of the hostesse, a mexican lady by birth, & married to an Irishman, being the most charming, well bred & amiable person imaginable. She is pretty in appearance, & perfectly lovely in manners. To all her guests she shows civility, introduces them all to each other, is always making her tour, seeing that everyone is "at home and perfectly happy". – She has a very fine voice & sang several spanish airs most be-witchingly. There were as many gentlemen at this party as ladies (not like Ilfracombe) but such queer, vulgar looking people. A certain Baron, (the only one in the whole country) danced with me almost all the evening, I got quite tired of him. He danced so excrutiatingly badly, & had such unpleasant manners. I was not in good spirits that evening – home sickness was the cause of it. Mrs Maksutoff & I both played a little, & were loaded with praise. I had expected to see a very richly, if not elegantly & geschmackvoll [Ger. tastefully] dressed company, but dear me! how sadly I was disappointed. Fancy a lady coming in, arrayed in white pou de soie with 3. rows of *scarlet* silk puffs round the bottom of the shirt & the sleeves & berthe also scarlet covered with white brussels lace. In the hair nothing. When I saw her come in I thought she was dressed for a masquerade.

Other ladies were in high necks, but none were tastefully dressed. We came home after 2. o'clock. On Tuesday we are again going to a dancing party.

I go everywhere in black silk. My London black dress is still quite new, I had not worn it more than half a dozen times; some times I use it high, some times with black lace cape & sleeves. There is nothing in the world so useful as black silk. Last week we dined at the swedish Consuls. A very warm hearted, hospitable & kind man, but thoroughly vulgar & wealthy, making such a noise, & asking his guests if the soup is nice. His wife a Virginian lady, is a very quiet well informed person. She took us out for a drive once, & promised to come soon again. When you thank them for their kindness, they say "it is nothing at all – why have we got carriage & horses, but to take out our friends now and then". –

I have paid 30 dollars for my teeth. One new one like the one that dentist in Darmstadt put in, one plugged with gold, & three with a composition of silver & some thing else. Thank God I had very little pain, but a very nervous & highly unpleasant sensation. Fifteen dollars for photograph cards – 20 – for Hampus boots & cloggs. I don't know how the money flies. […] It is too true Mrs Maksutoff is again pregnant. She looks like a shadow some times; so pale & thin, it makes me quite sad. I hope she will get over her confinement well. The last was very easy, but still she was so exhausted, & the pains very weak. God help her through it well next September. Tomorrow we are going to see the mercantile library – and the day after we are going to the mint. Else there is nothing worth visiting.

Friday Ev[enin]g 14th. My own precious Mother! I must now finish this letter, & even though it will not be so long as I could have wished, you will forgive, considering how hurried I have been all the time. Since I last wrote, we have been out 2. evenings. On Tuesday we were at a dancing & musical party from which we returned at ½ past 4. in the morning. There is here a mexican gentleman, who plays most beautifully on the guitar. It is indeed a pity with all his talent & all his taste for music, he should have spent it on so ungrateful an instrument as the guitar. The mexican Consul, also a man of musical talent, with a very fine voice, accompanies him by ear. Their playing was almost lost at the first party I spoke of, for the rooms where too crowded for hearing. I was also asked to play, & somehow or other it was thought so nice, that to my utter surprise the mexican Consul, Mr Mugarietta, came up to me, offered his arm & said "Excuse the liberty, but please come" – upon which, not knowing what he intended doing, he led me into the dancing room, seated me beside the guitarist Mr Ferrer & said "pray accept what that gentleman is going to play for you" – I was quite astonished, & pleased. Last night we were asked to meet these 2. gentlemen at the house of that charming mexican lady I spoke of in my last. Of course we were able to enjoy the music much more; especially when later on, we went into the lofty dining room with a skylight, where the resonance was perfect, & the instruments sounded much better. We remained till 1. o'clock. I like very much what I have seen of the Spaniards. They are so chevalresque towards ladies, & so affable & kind mannered. There are a great many of them here. Today we have been paying farewell visits, & have now only to finish letters and packing. Our stay has been as pleasant as it could be. But my heart bounds at the idea of going home. May God of His infinite goodness grant us a speedy & safe passage. My Annie has grown so tall & rosy here; I cannot say how thankful I am. Today I had the unexpected joy of receiving a long letter from dearest Mrs Hawthorne. I had so hoped to hear from you too my beloved Mother, before closing, but all hopes are gone, and I shall have to wait patiently till next autumn. [...] Kiss dearest Ormelie from me, and be cheerful & happy darling, precious Mother, for with Gods help we are soon coming home. O! it makes me wild. The russian man of war, Kalewala, goes at the same time as we do on Sunday, & most likely we may expect a visit from her next summer. The young officers have enjoyed their stay exceedingly; And now Goodbye, goodnight and God bless you my own precious Mother. I must finish my other letters. I remembered you in my prayers, & my most especial love on *21st Sept[ember]* though I think I did not write, as we had no opportunity then. I shall not be at home on my birthday, nor on my darling Puxti's, unless miracles happen. Perhaps possibly on my Eddies birthday. How fat & funny he must have grown, the precious darling angel Boy! Give my love to kind, dear Charlotte Campbell & to Aunt C. at Culverden Castle. Write soon again most beloved Mother to your own, own loving Child

Annie Furuhjelm

No. 49   *Sitka. March 14/26 1862.*

From my own dear Home, I again take up my pen, dearly and best beloved of Mothers, to tell you of our safe passage & praised be God happy arrival. Before leaving San Francisco I despatched No. 48. with the second edition of myself and Annie, which I hope will soon reach you, & give you much pleasure. Opinions vary very much as to which likeness of myself is the best, though all agree that precious Annie is as like as can be on both pictures. I liked the *second* one of myself best; but Hampus & the Pastor & still others say, it has an expression foreign to me, & not at all like. – However now to tell you of my arrival. We had considering the time of the year, a very good passage up, reaching Sitka early on the morning of the 19th day, Saturday 24th Feb[ruary]/8 March. On Tuesday was my Birthday, and we had exellent wind & towards the evening only 80. miles remaining, so that my hopes were great to be at home on Wednesday evening. But when I awoke in the morning the wind changed, became contrary and very strong so that we stood almost still. On Thursday it became perfectly calm & continued so off & on till friday afternoon, when we had already some hours been in sight of Sitka land, & I for one was perfectly impatient, thinking we should never get home. A favorable breeze sprung up, & wafted us nearer & nearer home. We ought to have been recognized from Sitka, but the guards being new men just for that week, no one

Anna and Annie Furuhjelm in San Francisco 1862.

looked with the glass, so that no steamer came to our help. We fired 7. canons, the last being the first heard at Sitka, at ½ past 11 at night, when we were thank God already in our harbour, & half an hour afterwards cast anchor without the need of a pilot. You may fancy the hurry scurry our unexpected arrival in the middle of the night occassioned here. Hampus was awoken with the anouncement "Kamtschatka" is quite close for though no one could see us, every one knew that only one of our own ships & accustomed captains, would & could come in alone at night, past all these little rocks & islands. Now first the welcome light of the lighthouse shone out & marked where we were; soon a blue light appeared from the battery outside our nursery windows. I was so very, very happy & thankful, & prepared for going on shore immediately. Annie, who was soundly sleeping, I thought best to leave on board in Mrs Maksutoffs care, as I was afraid of exposing her to the cold night air. A little boat was seen coming towards us, & a man soon landed bringing "congratulations & greetings from the Governor, & he wishes to say that the children are quite well, & he is waiting on the bridge". – My heart was now at ease, the long & often asked question was answered & my whole soul felt *"thank God all's well"*. Hampus sent the big comfortable boat for me, & bidding goodbye to my floating home, I stepped in with the Prince, & in ten minutes was in my darling husbands arms. But here, before the eyes of strangers, was not the place for greeting; we hurried home, to my own, comfortable blessed Sitka home, where every room was lighted up, & every stove sparkling & cracking with bright fires, & it just looked like Heaven. My darling Puxti, was looking well, though grown thinner. O Mama! I was so exceedingly happy to see him again. Now I flew to the nursery, & there was my lovely Boy, sweetly & rosily sleeping in his cradle, grown such a large, fine, handsome child. I did not mean to wake him, but kissed his face, his hands, his feet over & over again, my heart quite running over for Joy. He opened his large blue eyes, looked at me steadily and smiled; gently, gently I took him out, thinking he would be frightened and cry, but he kept looking into my face, as if he was recalling my voice & looks, & then smiled so brightly. He evidently knew me again. I was quite wild with Joy, & could not tare myself away from him the darling, precious Boy. If you could but see him now, darling Mother! he is as fair as a lily, with red cheeks, & such a noble look. He walks a little, though not alone yet, but stands alone at a chair or what ever it may be, & jumps for Joy. Little Nelly Maksutoff too had grown, & become so fat, her parents did not know her. From having been the tinyest, thinest lightest Baby I ever saw, she is now so fat & heavy & also much more quiet than she was. My Hampus has taken such care of them, and Ida too, I cannot say how thankful I was, & most of all to our Heavenly Father, who granted us all this happy reunion again. – Hampus had been suffering much from severe nervous headache, on the top of the head, & had, *as I feel convinced*, increased the evil, by imoderate & injudicious use of ice. Five or 6. times a day during my absence, & when I first came home, he rubbed his poor bare head with ice till it was purple. This releived him for a time, but the pain & the pressure always returned, & tho' he had these headaches when I left, tho' not so strong, they grew worse & worse, during the 2. months of my absence. I beseeched him to leave it off; I was afraid he might seriously injure the brain, but to that degree is Hampus in love with all cold water, ice & snow applications, that it was several days before he would listen to my entreaty, at least to try. Thank God, he has decidedly been better this last week, & uses cold Sitzbäder [Ger. sitz-baths] morning and evening, & walks a great deal. The cause of his headaches, is plainly to be traced to all the "otur" [Swed. bad luck] and anxiety he has had during these 3. years. To have lost 2. ships & have 2. others seriously damaged, to have had revisors & now Admiral Papoff coming, is not very pleasant, & of course much will be laid to his charge. *Somebody* must always bear the blame, & tho' Hampus can no more help that these misfortunes have come, the Company may in all probability say "Why did you not do so? & why did you not send other Captains etc – etc." – He takes every thing in his service too much to heart, & is always fancying evil must come of everything. I shall be so very happy, when with Gods help we leave Sitka, mostly for the reason, that this weighing responsibility will be removed from my Hampus.

Palm Sunday 1/13 April. I think it is three weeks now, since I last wrote, but I am no ways in a hurry, as it will still last some time before this letter will be sent away. Before Easter, or any other great festival, there is always a great deal to be

done and got ready in a large household like ours, & I have also had my hands full
of work, for my little Boy, who requires a completely new wardrobe, of clothes
more suited to a boy, than his little sisters frocks were. I have made him several
frockblouses, which look so nice on him. Could I but show my sweetest, lovely Son
to you, beloved Mother, how happy I would be. He walks quite nicely now, though
not quite alone yet, but he can stand quite alone, & raises himself up holding fast
at a chair, or his bedposts, throws himself forwards on his hands & raises himself
on his toes, & is thank God so strong & full of health, crowing & chattering all day
long. He is so fond of me, and cries each time I leave him; his nurse is passionately
fond of him, indeed, who would not love such a good child? Darling Annie plays so
sweetly with him, I wish someone could paint the little pair for me, as she lies beside
him on the floor, with her arms encircling him. Hampus' eyes shine & sparkle with
happiness when he sits watching these 2. little Furuhjelm buds. Annie has become
so good now. Only fancy darling Mama, she has once tasted the rod! – I will tell
you why, we thought ourselves forced upon to punish her once properly so that
she might remember it, rather than several times slightly & ineffectually. She had
got into the habit of wetting herself, & doing still worse, each time she required.
If you tried to make her sit down of your own accord, she would cry violently &
say "Annie not wants" but do it in her trowsers immediately afterwards. You saw
that she quite well understood how naughty it was, but she did it on purpose, & I
had often slapped her little bottom, but without it doing her any good. At last we
were afraid it would become so regular a habit with her, that Hampus decided upon
punishing her, (I could not do it) & thank God, it has had a wonderful effect, tho'
it cost Hampus almost & me quite tears, & I hope it may have been the first & last
chastisement of that kind, it may ever be necessary to administer to her. She has
only wet herself 3. times since I think, & now always comes runing to you saying
"A a phui! Annie not do a a trowsers that not good; Papa give Annie *pou pou pou*"
(which means in her language every thing which hurts.) Tell me darling Mother,
how you did with us, & if you think we did right. Eddie says already now, when he
wants to be put on the little chair, tho' of course he often says it after it is done. She
never wets her bed at night, as she is taken out twice regularly. –

   This is the 7th week in the fasts, & the russian priests must be well high tired to
death. You know perhaps, that in the greek church, every russian *must*, it is a law,
go to the sacrament, if he be not detained by illness, before Easter. The whole week
he goes to church 3. times daily, & on friday he may not eat meat,[127] and must go
to the bath before the evening service. Then on Saturday he must fast altogether till
dinnertime, when he comes home from the holy Communion, to a table spread with
every thing that is good, & feasts the rest of the day.[128] The lower classes understands

---

127 The Russians not only fasted on Good Friday, but every Friday.
128 Actually, the fast did not end on Saturday, but on Easter morning after the long mid-
      night mass.

nothing about the importance & holiness of the act. To them it is a cold & formal duty that must be gone through, crowned by the trying to be dressed as richly & brightly as possible on Sacrament day, & then having the whole day for pleasure. I cannot say, how sad it makes me, how I long to be able to tell them, those *outward* ceremonies the Lord does not look to, nor find pleasure in, but it is the heart, the heart he searcheth & looks into, & the spirit He watches, & the love and knowledge we have of his blessed Son he requires of us. Do they know that in receiving the Sacrament, they eat & drink spiritually the flesh & blood of our crucified Lord, & that *His* blood alone cleanseth & redeems us? Alas no! this is not what they are taught; but to go to church only once or twice during the week they are preparing, or to omit the bath on friday, or the fasting on Saturday forenoon, would most surely endanger their souls. And Easter Day! – what a day of rioting, of noise, of eating & drinking too much it is – of pomp & show & vanity in church! of ringing & tingling of bells, rung any way, by who ever pleaseth. O! how I long for a quiet, peaceful Easter Day again, where that outward fuss & confusion can not disturb & distract your thoughts. Is it not a melancholly state of things. I feel so happy today, having been to the blessed Sacrament with my precious husband. I felt it so deeply today, & my heart was so warm. I cannot say how thankful I am to God for this mercy.

Good Friday 6/18. This is the first time we celebrate this Holy time, on the same day with you;[129] but still it is not the same thing. It shocks me so, I cannot even say how much, to see how Goodfriday means *nothing* with the russians. They work & wash on this day like any other common day, & tho' they dress finely enough, thus outwardly even showing reverence & respect, on any one of their multifarious Saints days, they do not even *that* today. We have had german service & communion today, & Pastor Winter preached again a most earnest sermon, beseeching those who go to the Lords supper, rightly to consider what it means, & how absolutely necessary it is to bring a humble & a contrite heart, & a full knowledge of the enormity of our sins, & a sincere longing after improvement & godliness. He exhorted those who wished & liked to mock at the christian religion, & true doctrin, to beware of what they were doing, & not to come to the Holy Communion, as they would only eat & drink their own damnation. There is a quite young german here, who seems to have got hold of Voltaires works, & tries as much as possible to talk & argue away, the little faith & knowledge some of the others have, with his rationalistic & atheistic ideas. The Pastor never ceases to preach against it, & to impress the truth of our Faith unfailingly upon the mind of his congregation. I saw him again in church today, & again go to the Sacrament table, & can only pray, his spirit may sooner or later be changed, and enlightened. – I have been quite sad today, by the non acknowledgement of this day, as the most holy & blessed day to all christians. For no blessed Easter morn would ever have shone, had there not been a good Friday before. –

---

129 The Russian Orthodox Church still uses the Julian calendar. Therefore the 'Russian Easter' and 'European Easter' seldom coincide.

My little Darlings have both got a bad cough, especially Eddie Boy; I cannot understand what makes him so often catch cold, I am often obliged to leave off his cold bath in the morning. He has cut 6. teeth since I came home, & had evidently a cough through teething, but as it is so strong now, I cannot attribute it wholly to this cause. At night it has latterly distressed him much, tho' otherwise he is quite merry & jolly. When I look at my Annie I am really amazed to think I have already so big a daughter; will it not be strange for you darling Mother, to see your Annie coming home with a little tribe of children? – –

I am not yet quite sure, but am almost assured another little offspring is since one month on the road. Before this letter goes, I shall be able to tell you for sure. I am very thankful there has been a proper space between them, & hope we may have no more than 3. children at Sitka, else it will be a difficult affair coming home through Siberia. You will most likely be astonished & perhaps feel grieved for me, when I tell you, Ida has asked to go to California next year, so I have lost her help. Considering her true & faithful services & attachment during these 3. years, & that she is no longer young, & had the offer of 50 dollars a month from a german merchant at San Francisco 3. years ago, which she refused having engaged herself to me for 5. years, & that she can never again have so good an opportunity of gaining & laying by some thing, we could not refuse her, though I cannot say, what a loss she will be to me, not only the last half year here, but also on the way home. Who I am to get in her stead, remains still to be ascertained, & I trust somebody will still turn up. – By this time I hope you have got both my Francisco letters. Kostromitinoff has been recalled, & Klinkoffström is denominated russian Consul, to whom our letters go as before. I cannot say how I am again longing for letters, and also to hear how darling Florence is, & if she is still nursing her little boy, & if Carl has found some other employment. I hope, should there be any difficulty, you will not hesitate to write to Count Berg, who might possibly say a good word again, as he was so very kind the first time. Hampus has read a great deal about the french railway company[130] in the russian papers, & is rather sanguine about Charlie. He thought first, the *company* was quite dissolved, but now he sees, it is only that Feodosia branch which they have refused to continue, so he may still be employed on another. Do you know darling Mother, O you precious Mother! – what pleasant castles in the air I often build, & hope one day to realize? that is, to go over to Sweden, we all & Charlie's all & you, & revisit Carlskrona[131] & especially the dear, dear Wredes. [...] Puxti has never been in Stockholm. I should like to go there with him, & also to Italy.

Wednesday after Easter 11/23. I think I told you darling Mother, about the anxiety which was beginning to prey up on my husband in consequence of the steamer "Constantins" non appearance. The Captain received orders from Hampus on no

---

130 Carl von Schoultz was employed by a French railway company that was building railways in Russia (Weissenberg 1946-1951, p. 54).

131 Karlskrona, the Swedish town in which Anna was born.

account to be home later than 1st April, & to arrange himself accordingly. Only last night, Hampus was really very miserable, thinking something must again have happened. You can understand that after the many misfortunes he has had he is easily disquieted, & is ever fancying new disasters are going to happen. Though I never could believe "Constantin" was not all right, I was more anxious on his[?] account than I wished to show, & often thought what would become of him, were such a frightful blow, as the loss of another ship, come over him. It has therefore for many days, been my constant occupation to look & gaze with my eyes, as far as possible, hoping to discover a ship. Twice I was deceived, but today I had the satisfaction of being the very first who noticed a black speck on the horizon. It was only 7. in the morning & Hampus was shaving, when I brought him the happy news, & you may think he was thankful. –

They have had a passage of 23. days from Codiac! – The winter there & at Kinaj has been so tremendously cold, & the snow is still lying deep – it has been the cause of much sickness, & here at Sitka several deaths. Hjalmar too has been a sufferer in that perfect desert of loneliness where he lives, & is now going home. [...]

At the end of this, or beginning of next week, "*Nikolaj*" may arrive, which will cause me no little joy you can be sure. A few weeks ago, it was found out, that several hundred calf skins had been stolen, & they were all found with 5. of the work men; one of them had formerly been accused of murder. You may think what an unpleasant & painful thing it was, especially as Hampus found himself obliged to have them chained & imprisoned. Another man, I saw him once in my husbands room (the guard was outside the door) is also accused of murder at the Michaelofsky redoutte,[132] & was sent here to be judged. His eyes, & his face speak against him, I cannot forget his dreadful look – it seems to be without a doubt that he has committed the horrible crime; he will together with the other 5. men be sent to the Amour, there to be judged by proper tribunals.[133] Excepting these extreme cases, there has thank God, been perfect peace here, & the indians are as quiet as possible. I think Hampus is the first Governor who has made any use of them,[134] the former ones, having been afraid to mix them with our own men, or to bring them inside our walls. Hampus employs daily about 22. men, & some of them have already become excellent carpenters. It is amusing to watch them, & to see their smeared faces peeping out behind some window frame. They go home at 11. f[ore]n[oon] to their

132 St. Michael Redoubt on the west coast of Alaska, Norton Bay.

133 They were sent to Nikolaevsk na Amure (this information was kindly provided by Mrs. T.S. Fedorova, the Russian State Naval Archive, St. Petersburg). Nikolaevsk na Amure was founded in 1850 and residence of the military governor of Russia's East Siberian Maritime Province.

134 Already by the late 1820s Tlingit men worked as sailors, longshoremen, woodcutters etc. for the RAC. H. Furuhjelm's predecessor, however, was opposed to the hiring of Tlingit workers (Kan 1999, pp. 76 and 139).

village for dinner, return at 12. & work till 6. Of course their interpreter is always at hand, but as yet no quarrels have arisen between them & the russian workmen. This is something very much to Hampus credit I think, & I hope the Company will acknowledge that he has understood how to gain their respect & fear, in fact how to manage these slippery indians.

Wednesday 18/30. Just now my Hampus said the letters must be ready at 5. o'clock this afternoon, so I prefer only sending this one letter off, & will finnish Florence's & begin one to Mrs Hawthorne, for the next mail which goes one month hence. I will write to you again precious Mother. I have been so anxious today about my little Edwin. It is the first day he has ever been ill. All night through he had strong fever, & just now again. I gave him twice castor oil without any effect, so I gave him 2. teaspoonfulls just now, & am bathing his head & hands with cold water. He is cutting his 14th tooth, a double one on the lower jaw, & that is what makes him ill. All the rest he cut without the slightest illness or difficulty. O! it makes mad & anxious to have a child ill. I called for the doctor, but as usual he knew not what to say, or what to do. God grant he may get relief after his doze of oil; just now he is sleeping a little. Thank God the childrens coughs are gone, and Annie treasure is runing about the room playing & chattering to herself all the time. She is such a good little darling child now, & looks so pretty. Hampus grows fonder & fonder of her, & likes to play with her. "Nikolaj" has not yet come. God grant all may be well. I hope to receive good news from you & my own Ponnie with "Alexanders" return from Codiac, one month hence. [...] Give me all the news you can of Finland, England & Germany, and keep up good courage darling Mother; soon your absent children are coming home, & then you shall have golden days please God. My Hampus sends his fondest love to you; he *would* write if he only had a peaceful moment, free from haressing thoughts, & asks you not to think ill or unkindly of him, but to love him dearly all the same. If he had not always such hosts of unpleasant letters to write, he would have more mind & head to write private ones. His head is thank God *much better.* He sees & confesses himself how injudicious & dangerous his ice cure was. I must now write a german letter to Mr Sturm for Hampus, & must send a few lines to Hjalmar. It rains unceasingly, but the *snow* melts in consequence. Hosts of wild geese have been flitting across the Sitka heaven, which is a sign that summer is near. Where will you spend it? I shall be alone without my own Hampus; I shall miss Constance, that good girl. – Love to all the Uncles in Finland & with dear fond kisses to yourself & many from Annie to dear Grandmama. I bid you goodbye & say God bless you my precious Mother. – [...]

   Your own loving, loving Child

                                                                        Annie Furuhjelm
P.S. If you & Florence would send y[ou]r letters to Sturm, addressed to me via Panama inside, & ask him to forward it immediately, it would save you the postage darling Mother.

No. 50   Government House.
                                              Sitka 28. April. 62-

How shall I ever thank you my own, best beloved, treasure Mother, for the happiness you gave me through the arrival of my box, with every thing so beautiful & nice. Who on earth, could ever have done it better than you my Mother. What fatigue & trouble the purchasing & collecting of the things must have given you, & how exquisitely all was packed, & how uncrumpled & well every thing arrived! Ten thousand times I thank and kiss you my own precious Mother, and for all the pretty & useful presents. Edwin is wearing the charming pink flanel frock today; it fits him charmingly, a little later it would have been too small. O darling Mother! you say, perhaps I will not be contented with your commissions. How could you ever for one moment suppose such a thing. What a wretch & ungrateful being would I not be, not to be delighted, charmed with what *you* the dearest, precioustest Mother on earth, have done for your child. I only marvel at the quantity & quality of things. How it was possible to buy so much & so very good. If you had seen my ecstasy yesterday, whilst unpacking what your darling hands had packed, & how I kissed the papers over and over again, you would have been repaid for all y[ou]r trouble. The little merino frock I must let out under the arm, the armhole is too small for Annie, else it fits perfectly. The hat is very pretty & fits too, so does Eddies, & the beautiful embroidered cape, is not at all too small. Please thank kind Aunt Mary much for everything. The little socks will do for No. 3. & one p[ai]r of shoes too. The rest Edwin will get, as they are all too tight for Annie, but for her I have from Hamb[u]rg & San Fr[ancisco]. The pink & blue merinos are indeed lovely, & I am only sorry there were not 12 y[a]rds instead of 8. of that fine purple delaine, for I would have used it for myself. The shawl is *exceedingly* pretty; quite according to my taste, it could not be better. I am so sorry you deprived yourself of the cap darling Mama, though it is doubly precious to me as you have worn it. The childrens books, & Bible pictures, are so very nice, & quite wonderfully cheap. The Fürstin is so much obliged to you for hers. Annie Gardiners picture is lovely. When I look at it long, I recognize her sweet, loveable smile. What joy is it not for me, to see my children wearing dearest Grandmamas presents & every thing chosen by her. Annie is delighted with her new dolls, one from Tante Margret, one from Ida's niece, which opens & shuts its eyes. She has got on just now on the yard, the white jane[?] hat, you sent, which far from laughing at, I find admirable, only it is rather small for her, & fits Eddie exactly. The red & white striped "Magnet" or how it is called, is very very nice, so is the lilac print, so is every, every thing, & I thank you over & over again my own, own darling Mother. O! if you knew, *how* I long to see you! – O Mother! it is a far, far way to be separated! –

I am now going to copy some of the patterns to send to my precious Florence. It is so nice the children wear things off the same piece. Ida was very pleased with her part. How dear & *just like you*, to forget no one. Hampus looked over all the bills and all your remarks, & could not cease wondering at the systematic, orderly way every thing was arranged. Yes! I told him, "there is no one on the whole earth like our Mother". – He has already been reading his book, & seems interested. First, on the top of the box, I found one of the dear Grandmamas old indian nightjackets. I kissed it reverently. *Saturday* 12/24 May. So many days have again passed, but I have been very busy indeed during them, and have already used so many of the things you sent darling Mother. The striped Magenta was enough for a frock for precious Annie, & blouse for Eddie, the lilac print too. For Edwin I made a pélise of the lilac musline de laine in one day! he was so much in need of it, that I was so industrious to finish it. For Florence I have made a pinafore pattern of the checked white muslin trimmed with the fine narrow edging you sent, & for Annie 6. draper[?] ones are in work. Then I send her a beautiful piqué pelise, Paris model, bought at San Francisco; it is striped white & pink, trimmed with braid & drop buttons; a white brilliantine blouse, with buff braid for little Freddy, and several other things not ready yet. It is so pleasant working for her little ones. Since I have heard that Dascha is really going to get married to Eugène, I am embroidering a pocket hankerchief for her, to show her, that I think of her. As I only begun it lately, it has disenabled me going on with my letters, as I want to send it in Florence's box. The pink piqué pattern pelise is too small for Annie, & even for Eddie without letting out the hem in front, he is such a large & tall boy. Mrs Krogius' little Lars, now 1. year and 9. months, is a little shorter than Edwin who is only 14. months old. I was so glad to see them again, they are such very nice people. I cannot say how much I like them. They have a 3rd child, two months old, born 6. weeks, or 2. months too soon, for whom I am Godmother; she was christened "Anna Gabriella" last Wednesday. God grant she may become strong, but she is so very, very tiny. Alice is a sweet child, & Annie often plays with her. I have never seen a so well brought up child. They are such a happy couple, it is a pleasure only to look at them. Lately we have been having very fine weather, & the children have been out all day long. This morning my long purposed breakfast picnic to the river took place. Mes dâmes [Fr. The ladies] Maksutoff, Krogius and Koshkin being the only guests, & the Pastor our knight, as my Hampus could not come. Both little Annies were present. But before we came home, the weather changed, & we had to battle with a very strong wind. We walked rather far, crossing the river over an old tree with a plank nailed over it, & then following a narrow winding path through the wood, at the foot of that high hill, which lies right behind the russian church, as you will have seen on the views I sent you. I was only vexed not to have my Puxti. It is a great pity we have no walks here, only this single one, which one gets rather tired of. –

You remember I told you of Miss Klinkowströms wedding Ball which was given by us. Hampus and I have always been so kind to the whole family & done much for them. I am sorry to be disappointed in the young lady, who though only 18. years old, is prone to give herself airs, and think too much of herself, so that she often wants in civility. But, as is generally the case with such people who have made a fortune & risen from nothing into something more, the Mother is a most proud & conceited woman, & leads her husband, as her daughter now leads her. The entire want of education makes itself still more visible than would be the case, were they not so *högmodig* [Swed. haughty]. Mrs Koshkin, had a miscarriage, but is now quite well again, & intends accompanying her husband this summer. I hope she will be more fortunate next time, for it is not only dangerous to have frequent miscarriages, but must be a sore, sore disappointment. The princesse cannot bear to think of our departure, & indeed I shall be sorry for her. For it is sad to have no lady friend at all. Of all people in Sitka, a Gouverneurskan [Swed. Governor's wife] is the most lonely, for nobody comes to her nor has she any she could associate with, & the Governor has really without exaggeration no quiet or peaceful moment. His head is always full of anxiety & trouble & responsibility. I always hope, as the Schneiders do not like Ajan, nor can get on well with Elfsberg, they will come to Sitka and that would be very nice for Mrs Maksutoff, who liked Ludmila very much. I cannot say *why* I have always as it were, felt shy & afraid of Ludmila, and I would rather she were not here, whilst we are. As she is so much older than I am, & seems to be *sorry* Hampus did not take a finish Wife, I fancy she might like to interfere. But all this is only *my* supposition, for those who know her praise her much. Last night I dreamt so vividly of you darling Mother. I thought we had met again. O! it was so beauti-ful. I am longing more than I can say to get home again; to see you once more, & to show you my happiness and the fruit of the same. Thank God! Hampus has lost his headache; he now acknowledges himself, that had he continued with that mad ice cure, he would have got mad, & just this feeling it was, which made him go on with it. But being of a nervous & anxious temperament, these harassing cares & continual mental fatigue, will never let him remain quite well as long as he is here. In a fortnight he again goes out on a tour to the north of the colonies. O Mother, these separations are so sad! and I shall be so, so alone. The only comfort is, that I pray God, and trust, a sea voyage will be good for his health. It is quite true, No. 3. is now already 2. months on the road. I am thank God quite well, though I suffer much from weakness in the back. I have not felt it so much with the other children, and ascribe it mostly to our awful staircase of nearly 70. steps, the coming up of which litterally exhausts me. As I have grown much stouter too, you may fancy how fatiguing it is. Annie kneels now, when she says her prayers; it makes me so happy to look at her. She speaks every thing now, and plays so nicely. Since she went with me to California, she has much improved in looks, having got good fresh colour in her cheeks, & she has become much stronger too. Just now, both children are eating their evening porridge before going to bed; they are so busy, you do not hear their little voices. Annie has come back now. I asked her "what shall Mama say to Grandmama", she answered: "Mama say Grandmama, Annie *paj*" – (good). Eddie has just found the "Minstrel" on my sofa, he took it up, opened it and began reading dadada. He is such a frolicsome little manikin.

I do not remember if I told you in my last letter that gold has been found in the Sticheen river.[135] This river runs partly through the Russian possessions, but according to a treaty made with England & Russia in the year 1825. though it is free for British vessels to pass through any of the rivers runing through russian territory, they may not "land at any place where there may be a russian establishment without the permission of the Governor" nor "may they form any establishment either upon the coast or upon the border of the continent comprised within the limits of the russian possessions". As we have been informed by american papers, large emigrations are taking place to the Sticheen river, & many large ships have already gone there. Hampus found it his bounden duty to send an expedition of investigation there, to let them see that we are alive and au fait, and to see whether our rights are not being infringed upon, and whether there may not also be gold in our part of the river, which seems to me to be most probable. Prince Maksutoff has gone there with the large steamer "Constantin" and the small one "Baranoff". On the latter he will go up the river. He has now been gone 10. days, and all are very curious to hear what he has to report. It is only 32. hours to the mouth of the river, and the weather has been very fine. What fine thing it would be for the Company, were gold enough to make it worth the while washing it, found there, as it would belong exclusively to them. *Sunday.* Mrs Maksutoff has just left me; this is the first separation of any duration from her husband, & she finds it so dull to be alone, we therefore asked her to dinner, and she has been with me the whole afternoon; she took her little girl home, but will come back to tea. I like her so very much. I know she will miss our house very much when we go; I wish Dr Schneider would come. Hampus has been so busy with his letters and papers since the "Nikolaj" arrived, that we were only able to read y[ou]r journal one evening, and as it interested him so much, and he wishes to hear it all, I have not gone on with it alone. How well it is written, indeed you describe scenery admirably. Hampus was exceedingly astonished not to find a single correction, or scratch, and said it might be printed as it stands. I admire your patience & perseverance in writing so detailed an account of all events of the day, at the close of it, when you must often have been tired enough. By the bye, what did you do with mine? – Has the fur cloak never come zum Vorschein [Ger. zum Vorschein kommen = turn up]? Give them our best love. I want to write to dearest Aunt Mathilda, but Hampus says, the letters must be ready tonight. Tomorrow "Kamtschatka" will take them over Codiac to San Fr[ancisco]. Captain Krogius is now the commander of that ship, & Nikolaj remains here. Last year we celebrated the same Xmas Eve. This year how will it be with me? May it please the Almighty to give us a healthy child, & may all go well with me. It makes ones heart sick to hear of such awful suffering as poor Henrietta had to go through. How kind Charlotte Campbell must be; I am quite thankful to her. Indeed it is dreadful to live & sleep in such cold rooms as you find in England. Though so far advanced in the season, we

---

135 See the epilogue, p. 255.

still have fires every day, & only 3. double windows are out. It looks as if summer were never coming. […]

10. at night. The wind is howling and I feel cold & sleepy, still I must finish this before I go to bed. I now send you a 3rd edition of myself, which Hampus likes best of all. It is very like me, the only pity is that I was not standing instead of sitting, which makes me look so short and dumpy.

It would seem Aunt Mary is not going to Nice. I am glad to think you will have dear old Babette. Give her our fond love, & receive ten thousand warm and fond kisses yourself from us all. May God bless you my own beloved Mother prays most fervently Y[ou]r own fond, fond Child

Anna Furuhjelm

No. 52   Government House Sitka. *September 9/21 1862.*

My own beloved darling Mother, This is your Birthday, and I can not let it pass without sending a few lines, or rather writing a few lines to you although it will be long before you read them. It is Sunday too, and I have been to church & prayed from the depth of my heart for you my precious Mother. May it have been a day of Peace & Joy to you, & may you have felt the spiritual presence of all your children. How happy would I not be, could I think you had spent the day with Charles, Florence & the sweet little children. O darling Mama! how I revel in the thought of soon seeing you again; our fondest love & attention will make you happy; it is one of my sweetest & happiest hopes, that our Love can still make up to you for all the sorrow & disappointment Life has given you. To see you surrounded by sons & daughters & a little tribe of Grandchildren fondling caressingly round your knees, will surely be Joy to all who love you. May it please the Almighty to hear our earnest prayers, & spare us all to realize this bright vision. You must never more be sad or sorrowful darling Mama when we come home, but we will all rejoice together & thank God for all His infinite Goodness & Mercy towards one & all of us. Have not *we all* reason to do so? O, who has ever received so much Goodness from His hands as we have? My own Puxti sends you a kiss, & says "God bless you dearest Mother" from his very heart, & the little ones kiss & embrace their own Grandmama over & over again. Thank God they are well now, though still pale. The Princesse was quickly & easily confined of a *Son* on Thursday morning, & is doing remarkably well thank God. She has been looking so ill & worn these last months, and had pains 2. nights & 2. days before the child was born. I was afraid she would have no strength for the real pains, but against all expectation it went very well at last, & with very little pain indeed. They are so happy to have a Son, & I am Godmother. He will be called Alexander.

Friday 5th/17 Oct[ober]. My own darling Mother, I see it is many days ago since I began this, almost one month. I have in the meantime had the very great pleasure of receiving a long & charming letter from darling Florence, which has thank God put my mind at ease regarding her health. [...] We received now also 2. letters from Uncle Charles, one written in June, the other in October *last year*! as the good people will persist in writing at the wrong time over Ajan, we cannot receive them till they are more than one year old. [...]

Darling Mother! I already count the days & weeks, & rejoice that very soon we can say "*next year* we are going home please God". Hampus & I talk daily about our journey through Siberia (for alas! I fear that is the route we must take) & how we had better arrange. It seems like a dream, the time has run out so fast, I can scarcely believe it to be so near. Next year we shall have our hands full of work, for in the autumn our boxes must go to Finland. Hampus often tells me, he foresees how cross and discontented I shall be on the journey. I hope I shall not be so, though I cannot deny that travelling through uncivilized Siberia must not be very charming or comfortable especially with small & several children, whose wants must constantly be attended to. Only fancy that you get *no beds* at the dirty holes called *Inns* in Siberia, but every night on arriving at one of these places you must pull out all your pillows & blankets & make up beds any way. Picture to yourself, Annie, Eddie & the still unnamed one, being tumbled out of the sledge at any hour of the night, fast asleep already, but of course as a natural consequence awakened by the deménagement [Fr. here 'moving of all things'], all beginning to cry & to whine & to be naughty at once, asking for milk & asking for bread & what not lie[?] besides, and then say if it will not be rather trying to be in the *sweetest mood* yourself? – But as other people have made the journey, & a lady of Hampus' acquaintance made it with ten children, why shall not we be able to do so with three. Going over Panama costs 500 dollars per head, & half for children and servants, so that we could not come home under 3000 dollars, besides the extra expences of outfit for self & children through the tropics. Going through Siberia Hampus gets about 4500 R[oubles] *Silver* travelling money which is more than 3000 dollars; but the difference is that we can save more than the half of it, which is a thing to be taken into consideration. Now, not only on my own account, but also very particularly on my darling husbands account do I not like the fatiguing journey by land, fearing it will add to, or help to increase, or bring on again these nervous headaches which have thanks be to God been much much better these last 3. weeks. I want to write to Tante Margret & pour out my heart to her and see if nothing can be done. I think the Company might be so generous as to compensate Hampus in some way for the trouble & annoyance they caused him through the revisors. [Here Anna Furuhjelm stops writing her letter, having received the news that her mother had unexpectedly passed away already in May.]

A telegram, dated 3/15 April 1865 St. Petersburg, from Hampus Furuhjelm to Anna Furuhjelm in Helsinki: "Just received official information about promotion to Admiral and appointment as Governor of the Amur region". By courtesy of Johan Furuhjelm.

Epilogue

Anna Furuhjelm started writing her last letter to her mother on September 9/21, 1862, on her mother's birthday, not knowing that Ann von Schoultz had passed away four months earlier on May 20, only 49 years old. The sad news reached Sitka on October 17 and brought Anna's day-to-day account of life in Russian America to an abrupt end. The remaining part of her five years in Alaska has left no comparable written record. As far as we know, only two of Anna's later letters from Sitka have survived. They are both in Swedish.[136]

The most interesting of them is dated January 5/17, 1863, and addressed to a more distant Finnish relative, Vilhelmina Gripenberg. Anna relates to Vilhelmina the major events from the months immediately following the unfinished letter. She is delighted to report that on December 22, 1862, she gave birth to her second son, Elis Campbell Nikolai. Still, the keynote of the letter is one of deep sorrow. Her mother's death had clearly left a void: "My only thought had been to see her again, to show her my happiness, to see her bless our children! Every day since we parted I had prayed that God in His mercy would allow this to happen. I looked forward to it as a child. More recently, hardly one day has gone by without Hampus and me talking about our home journey! Now we have only one year and a few months left, God willing, before we leave from here. Yet my joy is no longer the same. Ah, it is mixed with so much grief."

Shortly before New Year 1863, Anna's depression was deepened by the loss of her best friend at Sitka, Princess Maksutova who had died "from galloping consumption" some three months after having given birth to her third child, a boy. She was buried next to Constance Furuhjelm, Hampus's unmarried sister, in the small cemetery of Sitka, where her grave has been preserved to this day. Thus, the Princess did not live to see the day she had dreaded so much, when her friend Anna would leave Sitka. Instead, Anna was more than ever aching for that day. She confided to Vilhelmina that even her three-year-old daughter Annie was longing to "go home to Europe", and added: "How happy I shall be to present my three small Americans".

The departure of the Furuhjelms from Sitka has been described in a letter from Prince Dmitrii Maksutov to Ludmila Schneider, Hampus's other sister, who was married to a German doctor in Aian.[137] In early 1863, Maksutov was called to St.

---

136 Åbo Academy Library, Manuscript Division. Furuhjelm, Annie 15.
137 Furuhjelm 1932, p. 130.

Petersburg for consultations on company matters. Here he was officially appointed Furuhjelm's successor as governor. In early 1864, the widower remarried and departed once again for Alaska, bringing his eighteen-year-old second wife with him. They arrived in Sitka on May 26, 1864 on the Russian naval corvette "Bogatyr" from San Francisco. The Furuhjelm family was to make the first leg of their home voyage, to San Francisco, on that same ship. "On May 31, the day before the Furuhjelms were to depart, Maksutov gave them a farewell ball of the type for which Sitka was famous. It began at 8 o'clock in the evening and ended at 5 o'clock the following morning. During supper, Furuhjelm was presented with a magnificent silver bowl, filled with champagne. Made in St. Petersburg, the vessel was inscribed with a picture of the Governor's residence, land and sea animals of the colonies, and portraits of three chieftains typifying the most famous Indian tribes."[138] The ball ended with everybody accompanying Anna and Hampus in a splendid procession back to Government House for the last time. First came the musicians, then Maksutov with Anna, Hampus with the new Princess Maksutova, and after them the rest of the guests, couple by couple. On June 1, 1864, Anna, Hampus and their three children boarded the "Bogatyr" and returned to Helsinki via San Francisco and Panama.

A recurring theme in Anna's letters is Hampus's heavy workload. "Hampus sends his fondest love – he has very much to think of just now & cannot write", she told her mother at Easter 1860.[139]

Two years later we learn that Hampus resorted to "immoderate & injudicious use of ice" to get relief from his "severe nervous headache", the cause of which, in Anna's view, could be traced to the "bad luck and anxiety" he had experienced throughout his past three years of service in Russian America.[140]

Hampus' own official version of what he had accomplished as Governor of Alaska appeared in print in St. Petersburg at the end of 1864, shortly after his return to the Russian capital. It was an account of success and failure, of progress, setbacks and outstanding problems. Above all, it was a testimony to the Governor's untiring efforts "to implement the noble prospects and aspirations of the Board of Directors for the good of the region and the Company", as he stated in the conclusion.[141]

Furuhjelm had personally made four voyages to inspect different parts of the colonies. He had concluded a new and more favourable contract with the American firm in San Francisco that imported ice from Sitka and Kodiak. 17,448 tons of ice had been exported to San Francisco during the last five years, at a total price of 115,638 dollars. Export of salted fish had also been a paying proposition, though on a smaller scale: 2,977 barrels had brought the Company 15,449 dollars over five years. In order

---

138 Pierce 1986, p. 43. Unfortunately, a fire in 1972 destroyed the silver bowl (a gift from the RAC) together with many other valuable family objects.
139 Letter No. 33, p. 128.
140 Letter No. 49, p. 237.
141 Otchet 1864, p. 63.

to sustain the colonies' traditional fur trade, sea otters, otters, and several kinds of foxes had been put out on various locations. Thanks to earlier protection measures, the fur seal population had increased, allowing a raise of the annual sealing quota on the Pribilof Islands from 60,000 to 75,000 pelts in 1863. Many new buildings had been erected both in Novo-Arkhangel'sk and in other parts of the colonies, and the shipyard of Novo-Arkhangel'sk had launched a new paddle steamer, the "Baranov".[142]

The Governor's report showed the reverse of the medal as well. The Company had hoped to export coal to San Francisco. A coalmine had been opened on the Kenai Peninsula in 1856, under the management of Hampus's younger brother Enoch Hjalmar Furuhjelm, a mining engineer. However, the quality of the Kenai coal proved poor, and the export stopped as other coalmines developed on Vancouver Island and other places closer to the Californian market. Hjalmar Furuhjelm returned to Finland in 1862. The coal still extracted in the colonies was used only for the Company's own ships. The important Chinese fur market had collapsed, and in 1863 Furuhjelm had to prohibit the sale of colonial fur in exchange for tea at Shanghai, because of the fall of prices on fur there. The timber trade was also dwindling. The rise in colonial building activities had left little timber for export. Furuhjelm had to draw the discouraging conclusion that ice seemed to be the only colonial export article that could cover its own production costs. The recital of bad luck also included the loss of two ships from the colonial fleet. The sail ship "Kodiak" and the paddle steamer "Nikolai" suffered wreck in 1860 and 1861, respectively, but their crews and the steam engine were saved.[143]

Furuhjelm was responsible not only for the colonial business, but also for the welfare of the population, including all of its four basic groups: Russian employees of the Company, dependent natives, independent natives, and "colonial settlers" or creoles. A considerable part of his account is devoted to this aspect of his governorship. With regard to "the independent natives" (mainly the Koloshes or Tlingit) Furuhjelm reports with satisfaction that he always pursued a policy of rapprochement. "I have constantly endeavoured to show them confidence and not allow quarrels and violent clashes among them. I have given many Koloshes access to the port, where they have had every possibility to get acquainted with our way of life".[144] Furuhjelm's peacekeeping among the Koloshes probably refers to an incident in 1861, described in detail by the anthropologist Sergei Kan. Two rival clans were on the verge of bloodshed near the palisade of Novo-Arkhangel'sk. "Instead of standing back and watching the fighting, [Furuhjelm] ordered the cannon on the battery facing the Native village to be elevated and rockets prepared. He then informed the Tlingit, who had assembled near the palisade and were brandishing their weapons, that if they did

---

142 Otchet 1864, pp. 3-7, 13, 27-28, 44-56, 61-62.

143 Otchet 1864, pp. 13, 32, 62-63.

144 Otchet 1864, p. 21.

not immediately disperse to their homes and cease rioting, he would destroy their entire settlement. The Natives shouted that the Russians had no business interfering in their fighting but, realizing that [Furuhjelm] meant business (even though his threat was obviously an exaggeration), they returned to their homes."[145]

As for the "dependent natives", Furuhjelm believed that the Aleuts' dependence on the Company was so complete that they could not possibly sustain themselves if granted freedom. For the same reason he was opposed to any liberalization of the fur trade, arguing that the RAC monopoly was the natives' best guarantee for sustainable fur hunting and should not be given up.[146]

Supplying the colonies with foodstuffs, health services and education was also part of the Governor's obligations. During Furuhjelm's tenure, two secondary schools emerged in Novo-Arkhangel'sk. One of them, the Public School of the Russian American Colonies, was for boys. [147] It had an average of 20 students, who were trained according to a programme patterned after the Russian *uezd* (district) schools, but with the addition of two subjects "for colonial purposes": navigation and commerce. The other establishment was for "daughters of deserving parents" and had an average of 15 students. Their education was "in keeping with their social status" and included "sciences and needlework". Besides, there already existed two schools in Novo-Arkhangel'sk, one for male orphans and sons of workers and one for female creoles and orphans. Each had an average of 28 pupils. School subjects included reading, writing, scripture and arithmetic. Special attention was given to instilling good behaviour and a liking for hard work into the pupils. Yet Furuhjelm harboured no illusions about the quality of these two schools and recommended in his report that orphans from other parts of the colonies no longer be brought to Sitka as boarding school pupils at the Company's expense.[148]

A lasting result of Furuhjelm's governorship in Russian America, though one not mentioned in his report, is the 5 m long skeleton of a juvenile specimen of Steller's sea cow, then already extinct, which he arranged to ship back to Finland. It is now the gem of the Vertebrate Collection at the Finnish Museum of Natural History in Helsinki.

The main reason for Hampus's nervous headache and use of ice bags was undoubtedly the uncertainty about the future of Russian America and the Russian American Company. At the end of 1860, two officials arrived from St. Petersburg to inspect the colonies on behalf of the Russian government before a new issuance of privileges for the RAC. The third charter, issued in 1842, was to expire by New Year 1862.

---

145 Kan 1999, p. 148.
146 Otchet 1864, pp. 15, 20, 30.
147 For an English translation of the government decree from 1859 on the establishment of the Public School, cf. Dmytryshyn 1989, pp. 514-517.
148 Otchet 1864, pp. 57-59. Anna refers to the girls' school for creoles in several letters, e.g. Nos. 26 & 28, pp. 85, 101.

The inspectors, Sergei Kostlivtsev (representing the Ministry of Finance) and Pavel Golovin (representing the Naval Ministry), took up their quarters on the top floor of Government House, as described by Anna who clearly bore a grudge against them.[149] They returned to St. Petersburg in the autumn of 1861 and submitted separate reports, which were quite critical of the situation in the colonies, though not as critical as many had expected. Neither inspector questioned the *raison d'être* of the RAC. Kostlivtsev made the point that if the Company was deprived of all privileges, the government itself would have to assume responsibility for the administration and maintenance of the colonies, at its own expense.[150] Golovin suggested that the RAC should be limited "to the use of those localities where it presently has settlements or various kinds of enterprises", whereas Russians and creoles should be encouraged to establish new settlements and own land elsewhere on the vast Alaskan territory. The Aleuts and other dependent natives "should be relieved of any obligatory labor for the Company".[151] Back in St. Petersburg, the latter suggestion sounded like a colonial echo of a recent, but long awaited domestic reform: the emancipation of the Russian serfs in 1861.

Another historical event of that same year affected the immediate future of Russian America. The outbreak of the American Civil War in April 1861 ended for a while the Russian diplomatic exploration of the possibility of selling Alaska to the United States. Instead, the Russian government had to come to a decision on the future role of the RAC in Russian America after the expiry of the Company's charter. On May 29, 1861, the government prolonged the period of validity of the existing charter until the approval of a revised charter. A special committee on the organization of the Russo-American colonies was appointed to study the reports of Kostlivtsev, Golovin and others, and to propose reforms. The committee submitted its conclusions to the Ministry of Finance in the spring of 1863 for further consideration. During the following three years various authorities, including the RAC and several ministries, discussed the basic principles of a new charter, until, in the spring of 1866, the State Council (Russia's supreme legislative assembly) passed a final "Opinion" on the matter. Approved by Alexander II and signed by Grand Duke Konstantin, the Opinion recommended a slightly changed set of RAC privileges for another period of 20 years. The Company was to keep its old monopoly on fur trade and receive an annual state subsidy of 200,000 silver roubles, whereas the dependent natives were to be liberated from compulsory work for the Company. However, the new charter never came into force.[152]

By the time the Russian government reached its conclusion on the charter question, the American Civil War had ended. The Russian ambassador in Washington, Edouard

149 Letters Nos. 39-42, pp. 169, , 170, 178, 180, 184, 185, 189, 207.
150 Bolkhovitinov 1997-1999, 3, p. 403.
151 Golovin 1979, pp. 118, 108.
152 Bolkhovitinov 1997-1999, 3, pp. 407-413.

de Stoeckl, was due back in St. Petersburg in October 1866 for consultations, and the influential Grand Duke decided that this was a good time to re-launch his idea of ceding Alaska to the US. He and his sympathizers put forward three main arguments in favour of selling. The Russian American Company was in crisis and could only pull through thanks to artificial protection measures and state aid. The government had to concentrate its attention on the successful development of the Amur region, where Russia seemed to have a great future before her. Finally, friendly relations with the United States were most desirable for security reasons.[153] Paradoxically, even the news of gold strikes in the region, reported by Golovin and Furuhjelm, turned into an argument for ceding Alaska: both the government and the RAC feared an invasion of Russian America by hordes of foreign gold diggers.[154]

At a secret meeting held on December 16, with the participation of Emperor Alexander, his brother Konstantin, three ministers and Ambassador Stoeckl, the Russian government decided to offer Alaska for sale to the United States. Stoeckl left St. Petersburg in January 1867 and started negotiations in Washington with Secretary of State William H. Seward in early March. The Ministry of Finance had instructed Stoeckl to insist on a minimum price of five million dollars, and the Naval Ministry had proposed a future borderline between the two countries. The negotiations did not take long. Seward and Stoeckl signed the treaty ceding Alaska to the United States on March 30. Personally, Stoeckl was proud to get as much as 7.2 million dollars for the Russian overseas colonies. The transfer ceremony took place in Novo-Arkhangel'sk on October 6/18, 1867.[155]

The Furuhjelms spent almost a year in Finland after their return from Alaska. In April 1865, Hampus was promoted to the rank of Rear Admiral and appointed Military Governor of Russia's new Maritime Province in Eastern Siberia. He was now in command of the Siberian fleet and the troops in this region, and was commander-in-chief of the ports. Once again, Anna and Hampus had to set out on a long journey – some 10,000 kilometres – this time through Siberia with their three children. Fortunately, Ida Höerle, who had been Anna's maidservant in Sitka, came from Dresden to join them and stayed with the family for another five years. At the end of May 1865, they got on the train to Vladimir, where Anna's sister Florence (married to her second cousin Carl von Schoultz) lived. Carl built railways. He and Florence spent most of their lives in Russia, and both died from typhus in Ashabad in 1892. The Furuhjelms continued by boat on the Volga to Kazan'. Here Hampus bought three "tarantasses" (springless four wheeled carriages), one for Anna and himself, one for the three children and their German nanny and one for the servants. These sturdy vehicles took them all the way through Siberia to the river Amur. The

---

153 Bolkhovitinov 1997-1999, 3, pp. 426-428.
154 Bolkhovitinov 1997-1999, 3, pp. 441-442; Golovin 1979, p. 11; Otchet 1864, pp. 5-6.
155 Bolkhovitinov 1997-1999, 3, pp. 438-456, 476. For the English text of the treaty, cf. Dmytryshyn 1989, pp. 544-548.

last leg was by boat to Nikolaevsk na Amure, a small town founded only in 1850. They arrived here in September. [156]

As governor of the Maritime Province, Furuhjelm had to accommodate Russian settlers on the recently acquired territory and develop agriculture. The government hoped to transform the region into the larder of Eastern Siberia. He was also to promote the growth of new towns such as Vladivostok, which had 516 inhabitants by 1868. His own residence was located in the mainstreet of Nikolaevsk. It had a garden, a large ballroom with parquet flooring, and always a soldier on guard at the entrance. Annie, the eldest daughter, gives in her Swedish memoirs a lively description of her five years in Nikolaevsk.[157] On October 10, 1869, Anna Furuhjelm gave birth to a daughter, Mary Constance.

Hampus' tenure ended in 1870, but he had to wait for his successor who could only arrive in November 1871. Under the circumstances, Hampus and Anna decided that she should go back to Europe alone with the children. It was a difficult decision to make, but the children needed to go to school. Anna made the long and troublesome journey through Siberia in the spring of 1870 with four children, two nannies and two servants. She was, however, so fortunate as to have the company of a Russian colonel and his wife, who were also returning. Anna decided to settle in Dresden, until Hampus could join her. Here she enjoyed the company of her sister Florence who also spent a year with her four children in Dresden, while her husband was in Russia, looking for a new job.

In the spring of 1872, Anna was reunited with Hampus in St. Petersburg. He bought the big estate Hongola from some relatives, and the family could now settle down in Finland, although Hampus, still on active service in the Russian navy, had to spend much time in Saint Petersburg. The three eldest children continued their education at home, Annie with her German governess, Otto and Elis with their tutor. On March 24, 1873, Anna gave birth to her last child, a boy. He was baptized Johan Wladimir, but was always called Johnny.

In 1872, Furuhjelm was made Flag Officer of the Baltic Fleet. Two years later he was promoted to the rank of Vice Admiral and appointed town governor of Taganrog on the Sea of Azov, where he served for two years until 1876. Anna joined him in Taganrog for the winter 1874-1875 with the two youngest children. In 1878-1880, Hampus Furuhjelm served as commander of the naval port of Reval (now Tallinn). From 1880 until 1886, he was at the disposal of the commander of the port of St. Petersburg, though without occupying any specific post. In 1889, on the occasion of his jubilee as an officer in the Russian navy, he received a golden snuffbox, decorated with diamonds and the initials of the Emperor.

Anna died in 1894. Hampus lived on as a widower until 1909. As for the children, Johnny inherited his uncle Otto, who had no children of his own: Thus, at the age

---

156 Furuhjelm 1932, pp. 161-162.
157 Furuhjelm 1932.

of ten, he became a multimillionaire and bought Hongola in 1895. He died young from an operation in the stomach in 1904. Sitting by her writing case in Government House, Anna had committed to paper the following prophetical thought: "perhaps still in our Lifetime, [Russia's] sons will rise at a rush, & a dreadful revolution & cleansing will take place."[158] As it happened, her two sons, born in America, were both to lose their lives in the aftermath of the Russian revolution. Otto, an officer, and Elis, a lawyer, were shot in 1918 not far from Hongola, victims of the Finnish civil war. Mary married Nils Gustaf Ehrensvärd in 1898 and moved to Sweden, where she died from pneumonia in 1911. Annie survived her sister and brothers for many years. A journalist and writer, she also became an internationally renowned suffragette, and was elected a member of the Finnish Parliament several times. The great Swedish writer Selma Lagerlöf, herself a suffragette, was her friend. Never married, Annie died in 1937.

---

158 Letter No. 39, p. 175.

Bibliography

Al'perovich 1993

Альперович, М.С. (1993) *Россия и Новый Свет (последняя треть XVIII века)*, Москва: Наука.

Artem'ev 2001

Артемьев, А.Р. (ed.) (2001) *Русская Америка и Дальний Восток (конец XVIII в. – 1867 г.)*. К 200-Летию Образования Российско-Американской Компании Материалы Международной Научной Конференции (Владивосток, 11-13 октября 1999 г.), Владивосток: Российская Академия Наук Дальневосточное Отделение Институт Истории, Археологии и Этнографии Народов Дальнего Востока.

Barsov 1898

Барсов, Н.И. (1898) «Посаженые отец и мать». In *Энциклопедический Словарь*, том XXIV А, изд. Ф.А. Брокгауз и И.А. Эфрон, С.-Петербург: Типолитография И.А. Эфрона, pp. 657-58.

Bolgurtsev 1997

Болгурцев, Борис (1997) «По обе стороны океана», in: *Кают-Компания. Морской, исторический, литературно-художественный сборник* No. 1, С.-Петербург: Ольга, pp. 43-48.

Bolkhovitinov 1997-1999, 1-3

Болховитинов, Н.Н. (ed.) (1997-1999) *История Русской Америки 1732-1867* в трёх томах, Москва: Международные отношения.

Bolkhovitinov 1999

Болховитинов, Н.Н. (ed.) (1999) *Русская Америка 1799-1867* Материалы международной конференции «К 200-летию образования Российско-американской компании 1799-1999». Москва, 6-10 сентября 1999 г., Москва: Российская Академия Наук Институт Всеобщей Истории Центр Североамериканских Исследований.

Otchet 1864
Отчет по управлению Российско-Американскими Колониями с 1859 по 1864 год Капитана 1 ранга Фуругельма, С.-Петербург 1864.

Palamarchuk 1994-1995
Паламарчук, Б.Г. (1994-1995) *Сорок Сороков* в четырех томах, Москва: А.О. Книга и Бизнес и А.О. Кром.

Black 2004
Black, Lydia T. (2004) *Russians in Alaska 1732-1867*, Fairbanks: University of Alaska Press.

Carpelan 1954-1965
Carpelan, Tor (1954-1965) *Ättartavlor för de på Finlands Riddarhus inskrivna ätterna* 1-3, Helsingfors: Frenckellska Tryckeri Aktiebolagets Förlag.

Dmytryshyn 1989
Dmytryshyn, Basil, E.A.P. Crownhart-Vaughan & Thomas Vaughan (eds.) (1989) *The Russian American Colonies: A Documentary Record 1798-1867* (= To Siberia and Russian America, Volume 3), Portland, Oregon: Oregon Historical Society Press.

Fedorova 1973
Fedorova, Svetlana G. (1973) *The Russian Population in Alaska and California: Late 18th Century-1867*. Translated and Edited by Richard A. Pierce and Alton S. Donelly (= Materials for the Study of Alaska History, No. 4), Kingston, Ontario: The Limestone Press.

Furuhjelm 1932
Furuhjelm, Annie (1932) *Människor och Öden*, Helsingfors: Söderström & C:o Förlags-aktiebolag.

Furuhjelm 1912
Furuhjelm, Edvard (1912) *Anteckningar om Furuhjelmska Slägten och Hongola Gods* samlade af Edvard Furuhjelm 1910-1911, Helsingfors: J. Simelii Arfvingars Bok-tryckeriaktiebolag.

Gibson 1976
Gibson James R. (1976) *Imperial Russia in Frontier America: The Changing Geography of Supply of Russian America, 1784-1867*, New York: Oxford University Press.

Golovin 1979
The End of Russian America: Captain P. N. Golovin's last report 1862, Portland: Oregon
    Historical Society.

Haycox 1997
Haycox, Stephen, James Barnett & Caedmon Liburd (eds.) (1997) *Enlightenment and
    Exploration in the North Pacific, 1741-1805,* Seattle & London: The Cook Inlet His-
    torical Society.

Kan 1988
Kan, Sergei (1988) "The Russian Orthodox Church in Alaska", in: *Handbook of North
    American Indians.* Volume 4: *History of Indian-White Relations,* Washington, D.C.:
    Smithsonian Institution, pp. 506-521.

Kan 1999
Kan, Sergei (1999) *Memory Eternal: Tlingit Culture and Russian Orthodox Christianity
    through Two Centuries,* Seattle & London: University of Washington Press.

Pierce 1986
Pierce, Richard A. (1986) *Builders of Alaska: The Russian Governors 1818-1867,* Kingston,
    Ontario: The Limestone Press.

Pierce 1990
Pierce, Richard A. (1990) *Russian America*: A *Biographical Dictionary,* Kingston, Ontario:
    The Limestone Press.

Pipping 1967
Pipping, Ella (1967) *En Orons Legionär: Nils Gustaf von Schoultz 1807-1838,* Helsingfors:
    Schildts.

Pipping 1972
Pipping, Ella (1972) *Indien Bortom Haven,* Helsingfors: Schildts.

Steller 1993
Steller, Georg Wilhelm (1993) *Journal of a Voyage with Bering, 1741-1742.* Edited by
    O. W. Frost, Cambridge: Cambridge University Press.

Varjola 1990
Varjola, Pirjo (1990) *The Etholén Collection: The Ethnographic Alaskan Collection of
    Adolf Etholén and His Contemporaries in the National Museum of Finland,* Helsinki:
    National Board of Antiquities.

Unpublished materials

Полный послужной список Командира Ревельскаго порта Вице-Адмирала Ивана
Фуругельма – составлен к 12 Іюня 1880 г. Russian State Naval Archive (RGAVMF),
f. 406, op. 3, d. 834, l. 657a-667 ob.).

Weissenberg 1946-1951
Släkten von Schoultz i Finland. Släktkrönika: Krigare och fosterlandsvänner. Samman-
ställd av Axel von Weissenberg 1946-1951.

Åbo Academy Library, Manuscript Division. Furuhjelm, Annie 14 and 15. Finland.

Index of names

Russian names are given both in transcription from Russian and in the form, used by Anna.

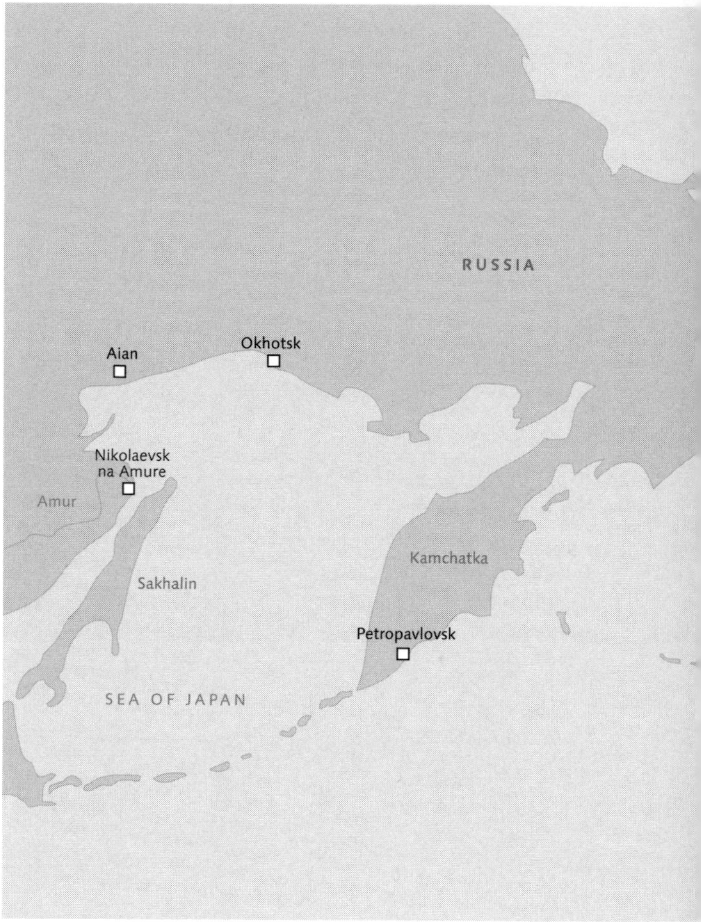
RUSSIA
Aian
Okhotsk
Nikolaevsk
na Amure
Amur
Sakhalin
Kamchatka
Petropavlovsk
SEA OF JAPAN

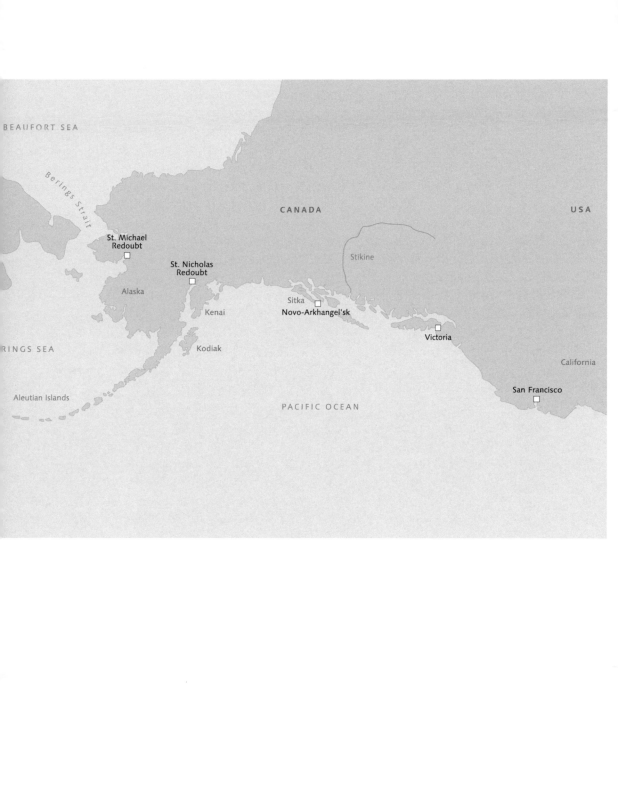